Planting
Growing
Churches
for the 21st Century

Other Books by Aubrey Malphurs

Planting
Growing
Churches
for the 21st Century

*A Comprehensive Guide
for New Churches and
Those Desiring Renewal*

Second Edition

Aubrey Malphurs

Baker Books

A Division of Baker Book House Co
Grand Rapids, Michigan 49516

Published by Baker Books
a division of Baker Book House Company
P.O. Box 6287, Grand Rapids, MI 49516-6287

Fifth printing, December 2001

Printed in the United States of America

Unless otherwise noted, Scripture quotations are from the Holy Bible, New International Version. Copyright 1973, 1978, 1984 by the International Bible Society. Used by permission.

Library of Congress Cataloging-in-Publication Data

Malphurs, Aubrey.
    Planting growing churches for the 21st century : a comprehensive guide for new churches and those desiring renewal / Aubrey Malphurs. — 2nd ed.
        p.   cm.
    Includes bibliographical references and index.
    ISBN 0-8010-9053-9 (pbk.)
    1. Church development, New. I. Title.
BV652.24.M35   1998
254′.1—dc21   98-24675

Figure 1 has been reprinted with permission of Jim Engel.

Figure 2 has been reprinted with permission of Willow Creek Community Church and Bill Hybels.

Figure 3 has been reprinted with permission of Rick Warren.

For information about academic books, resources for Christian leaders, and all new releases available from Baker Book House, visit our web site:
http://www.bakerbooks.com

To all of my students
who've caught the vision
and taken the risk

To Bob Logan who
has done so much to
promote church planting

Contents

     A Biblical, Culturally Relevant Evangelism
13   The Bigger We Get, The Smaller We Get   227
     A Robust Network of Small Groups

Part 4   The Process of Church Planting

14   We're Going to Have a Baby!   251
     The Conception Stage
15   Childbirth Classes   299
     The Development Stage
16   It's a Baby!   317
     The Birth Stage
17   Feed Them and They Grow!   341
     The Growth Stage
18   I'm No Longer a Kid!   362
     The Maturity Stage
19   Let's Have a Baby   377
     The Reproduction Stage

     Appendix A: Addresses for Resource Material   397
     Appendix B: A Sample New Church Feasibility Study   398
     Notes   407
     Index   419

List of Worksheets

Foreword

This book invades enemy territory and challenges the strongholds of the adversary. These strongholds don't exist "out there." They are the ideas and thoughts that are satanically designed to siphon life and vitality out of the living organism we call the church. These mind-sets inform decisions and determine directions that are often contrary to divine intent and strategy.

It is the nature of a living organism to grow. If it is not growing, something is wrong. The church, a living organism, is not growing in the United States. In fact, not a single country has experienced church growth in the past decade. Yet the Lord of the church declared that the gates of hell would not be able to withstand the attack of the church.

Something is wrong. Some thoughts have not been brought into captivity to Christ and his plan for the growth of his church.

Sometimes the roadblock is theological. More often the problem is cultural mind-sets that create invisible barriers to evangelism and church growth. By and large the old wineskins cannot contain the new wine of the Spirit. The letter kills, but the Spirit brings life.

According to Dr. Malphurs, the most effective and efficient way to reach the seeker is to plant new churches and, where possible, bring renewal to existing churches. Whatever route taken, growth is predicated on keeping that living organism healthy, biblically informed, and culturally relevant. Like a pediatrician, the author leads the reader through the church-planting process of conception, birth, growth, maturation, and reproduction.

Those with a heart for church planting will find no better treatment of the subject than *Planting Growing Churches for the Twenty-first Century*. We can be thankful for its breadth and depth, for its attention to detail and practicality. For those longing for church renewal the principles delineated in this book could be the key to the revitalization of the existing church. This book will aid church planters in tearing down the strongholds of doubt and misbelief and raising up vital churches prepared for the challenges of the twenty-first century.

Joe Aldrich
President of Multnomah School of the Bible

Introduction

I must have been daydreaming because I missed my exit off the freeway. It was Sunday morning, and I was on my way to fill a pulpit in a church located in a suburb of affluent north Dallas. The next exit was only a mile farther, so I was not greatly inconvenienced. It would cost me five minutes at the most. Yet that five minutes proved to be interesting and informative. Not far from the same exit, I drove past a family-oriented health club. I was amazed at all the cars and vans crowded into the parking lot. The attractive, well-kept facility was packed and it wasn't even 11:00 A.M.! A few minutes later I arrived at my destination. It was a small, rundown church with an unkempt lawn. As I pulled into the parking lot, I noted that there weren't many cars. I had my choice of parking places.

The last thirty years have proved increasingly difficult for the church in America, whether liberal or evangelical. Things have not progressed as planned. During the first half of the twentieth century, the future looked bright. The people who attended church were those born in the 1910–1930 era, people whom Lyle Schaller describes as "the most church-going generation in American history."[1] In general, America was a churched culture. On Sunday mornings, most people were found in their denominationally loyal churches; it was the thing to do. In fact, if people weren't in church on Sunday morning, chances were good that they had stayed home and slept in—behavior that was frowned upon. The 1940s and the 1950s were the "heyday" for the church. If this was any indication of things to come, then the future looked bright. Perhaps the church would win the world for Christ in the twentieth century.

The church situation in the latter half of the century (in particular the 1980s and 1990s) forms a stark contrast to the first half. Storm clouds have moved in and darkened the bright horizon of American Christianity. Rather than sending missionaries out from America and winning the world for Christ, America itself has become a mission field. In 1988, church growth expert Win Arn wrote that "Between 80% and 85% of all churches in America are either *plateaued* or are *declining*."[2] Then he added the following information:

America: 240 million population
            96 million (40%) have no religious affiliation
            73 million (31%) are Christians in "name only"
            169 million (71%) of total U.S. population[3]

At around the same period of time, George Gallup published *The Unchurched American—10 Years Later.* This was a sequel to a similar study that the organization had completed in 1977. In the latest work, he indicated that the number of unchurched Americans had increased. He noted:

> Trying to analyze the findings of *The Unchurched American—10 Years Later* is a little like trying to decide whether the glass is half-full or half-empty—there's evidence to support both views.
>
> For those who believe the glass is half-empty, the evidence is that the churches have not made any inroads into attracting the unchurched over the past decade: in 1978, 41 percent of all American adults (18 or older) were unchurched; in 1988, that figure rose to 44 percent. . . .
>
> The same evidence, however, also supports the contention that the glass is half-full. One might maintain that the churches have done well to keep slippage to a minimum in light of the continued high mobility among Americans during the last decade, the distractions of modern life and the apparent growing appeal of non-traditional religious movements.[4]

Regardless of whether the glass is viewed as half-empty or half-full, the future looks bleak in terms of reaching unchurched America. Gallup's research indicates that things are moving in the wrong direction. Many churches are plateaued or decreasing in numbers while the ranks of the unchurched are growing.

In *Effective Church Leadership,* Kennon Callahan summarizes what's taken place in the second half of the twentieth century:

> Yet, on all sides, it is self-evident that we are no longer in the churched culture that existed in the late 1940s and the 1950s.
>
> Statistical research, analyses of this culture, and long-range projections all clearly indicate that ours is no longer a churched culture. Study after study and the steady decline of many mainline denominations confirm this fact. We are clearly and decisively entering the mission field of the 1990s.[5]

All of this "doom and gloom" information raises an obvious question about the future of the church. Like the patient who's just been diagnosed with cancer, we want to know what our chances are for survival. Actually, we can be optimistic about the future of American Christianity. While there will be lots of church funerals and much grief, not only will the American church survive, but it will bounce back and thrive.

The reason we can have this optimism lies in the inerrant, absolute truth of the Scriptures. While on the one hand, we need to be aware of the severe problems facing the American church, on the other hand, we can claim the promise found in Matthew 16:18. Jesus says to Peter and to us, "And I tell you that you are Peter, and on this rock I will build my church, and the gates of Hades will not overcome it." Regardless of one's interpretation of this passage—and there are many—Jesus is saying that His church will survive. It has survived in the annals of church history. It has survived tremendous oppression in other countries in the nineteenth and twentieth centuries. And it will survive in America as we enter the twenty-first century.

But how can we reconcile Matthew 16:18 and the current state of the church in America? While the church will survive the twentieth century and thrive again in the twenty-first century, the present form of the church will change. The early twenty-first century church does not look the same as the typical, traditional church of the twentieth century. What has worked in the past will not work in the future.

This is not necessarily bad. There's a difference between what a church believes and what it practices. The church's faith must not change because it's based on the eternal, absolute truth of the Bible. The church's practices (how the church implements its faith), on the other hand, must change from generation to generation as well as from culture to culture if the church is to be relevant. If a church desires to reach its generation in its culture, it must adapt its practices (not its faith) to that culture. This is one of the important principles that the church of the twentieth century has missed. And this is one of the reasons why it has fared so poorly at the end of the century and beginning of the twenty-first century. If the culture rejects Christianity, it's important that this is because it has refused to hear the message of Christ rather than simply turning its back on the church's out-dated, culturally irrelevant methods (1 Cor. 1:23).

Another question that must be answered is where the churches that thrive in the twenty-first century will come from. A great number will be planted. In fact, at the end of the 1990s and into the twenty-first century, there has been an awakening of the church. Many are catching a vision for reaching lost, unchurched Americans through the planting of a number of dynamic, "cutting-edge" twenty-first century churches. As Peter Wagner says, *"The single most effective evangelistic methodology under heaven is planting new churches."*[6]

While some established churches will renew themselves and success-fully make the transition, this will be too painful and too difficult for the bulk of them, and they'll not survive. In fact, some predict that in just the next few years, 100,000 of the 350,000 churches in America will close their doors.[7] Consequently, church planting will be the future for the American church because it's far easier to plant a new church than to renew a dying one.

What will some of these twenty-first century thriving churches look like? That's not a hard question to answer. Actually, there are some positive signs that an awakening has started. God has already begun to sprinkle a number of these "cutting-edge" churches across America. There have been a number of pioneers in the recent past who have braved a lot of criticism[8] and taken the risk to start innovative, culturally relevant Great Commission churches that are reaching many unchurched lost. Today, there are a number of church planters who are catching the vision and spirit of these pioneers and are fanning out across America to reach the growing nonchurched population. What was a spark and is now a flame will become a roaring fire in the early twenty-first century.

The church needs to equip a generation of Christians with a deep passion to plant significant, biblically based Great Commission churches. These, in turn, will commit themselves to the task of sowing churches to reach various people groups at home and abroad. This is by no means a new vision; it is already present in the pages of the Book of Acts!

The purpose of this book is to encourage and equip individuals and churches to take a risk and become a vital part of this vision. Encouragement is essential because church planting isn't easy, and there are many within evangelical Christianity who are and will continue to cast stones. Yet we need to give God a chance! Take the risk! Ask the question, "What can God accomplish through *me?*"

It is essential to equip individuals and churches because not many have the vision to pursue, evangelize, and disciple lost, unchurched people. A significant number of those who have caught this vision are implementing it the wrong way and are experiencing failure and disillusionment. They're attempting to plant churches that are replicas of the pioneer churches that have been so successful at reaching the unchurched. Certainly, much can be learned from these churches and some of what they're doing is transferable. However, rather than imitate others, this book is committed to equipping church planters to design tailor-made, biblically based churches that are compatible with who they are (their unique identity), where they are (their unique location), and whom they're trying to reach (their unique community). The key is to ask the right questions, not to clone the ministry of others.

This book is divided into four parts. Part 1 concerns the preparation for church planting. Its purpose is to orient the prospective church planter to the topic. It consists of four chapters. The first chapter defines the topic. The second chapter presents some thought-provoking reasons for getting involved in church birthing. The third chapter addresses some of the means for planting churches and gives some practical tips on "how to" raise finances. The fourth chapter presents various assumptions that undergird this work such as the proper emphasis on numerical growth, the principles versus practice debate, the place of faith, and how to handle failure.

Part 2 examines the personnel for church planting. Its purpose is to help Christians identify their personal ministry visions and proper areas of ministry. In particular, it consists of two chapters that help individual answer the questions, "Am I a church planter?" and "Where do I fit into the process of starting churches?"

Part 3 looks at the principles for church planting. Its purpose is to help church planters answer the question "What kind of church should I plant?" It consists of seven chapters that present seven vital principles that should characterize the new work. The first is a Great Commission vision. Another is a strong servant-leadership. The third is a well-mobilized lay army. The fourth is a culturally relevant ministry. The fifth is an authentic, holistic worship. The sixth is a biblical, culturally relevant evangelism. And the seventh is robust network of small groups.

Part 4 examples the actual process of starting a church. It contains six chapters that are designed to help church planters understand the six stages that a new church passes through and what essentially takes place in each. These six stages—conception, development, birth, growth, maturity, and reproduction—are analogous to birthing a child.

This book is not only for church planters, but also for those who are already in a church but want to learn more about how growing churches function. I woke up to this reality when I noted that some students at Dallas Seminary were taking my church-planting course but desired to pastor an established church. When I questioned them about why they were in the course, they replied that much of the material was relevant to leading and pastoring in any church context.

Part 1

The Preparation for Church Planting

Last year my son planted his first garden: carrots, lettuce, tomatoes, green beans, potatoes, and onions. Unfortunately, it didn't do very well. Only the beans came up, and they left much to be desired. We had visions of fresh vegetables at each meal, so we were disappointed. Later we discovered that the problem was Mike had failed to prepare the soil before planting the seed!

Gardening has much in common with church planting. It's imperative that those involved prepare the soil by thinking through certain key issues before attempting to plant the seed. Once this is accomplished, the chances of a fruitful harvest are much more likely. Consequently, Part 1 covers four "seed" issues that are foundational. They include the definition, reasons for, means, and assumptions of church planting.

1

What Are We Talking About?

The Definition of Church Planting

How embarrassing! Yet it's happened to the best of us. You're intensely discussing a novel idea, a controversial issue, or a personal matter. Eventually, tempers flare. A heated discussion ensues, followed by a temporary "parting of the ways." Then, in subsequent discussions, you both discover to your amazement that you weren't even talking about the same thing! How much easier life would be if somehow we naturally trained ourselves to define and clarify our terms before engaging in potentially volatile discussions.

Consequently, in order to avoid the potential for misunderstanding and miscommunication, this book will begin with a definition of church planting. Church planting is an exhausting but exciting venture of faith that involves the planned process of beginning and growing new local churches as based on Jesus' promise and in obedience to His Great Commission.

Church Planting Exhausts

Church planting is not easy. It's hard, exhausting work! However, it's no different than any other ministry in that church planters "reap what they sow." If they work hard, the ministry grows; if they take it easy, the ministry plateaus. There are several reasons why church planting can be exhausting.

Church Planters Are Initiators

First, church planters are initiators, not maintainers. Far too many churches in America aren't aware that the churched culture of the 1940s and 1950s no longer exists and that America is now largely an unchurched culture. Whereas the thing to do in a churched culture was to attend church on Sunday, the thing to do in an unchurched culture is anything *but* attend church on Sunday. People spend time with their families, go to a shopping center, take in a movie, go to a ball game, watch their children play soccer, or go to the health club. Sunday may be their only day off. It's a day to relax and have fun. Consequently, why would anyone want to go to church?

In a churched culture, pastors could be maintainers because people sought them out for ministry. In an unchurched culture, pastors must be initiators or watch their churches die. Church planters also have to be initiators when it comes to reaching people and building churches. They cannot sit in their studies and wait for people to come to them because most people will not come. The days of maintenance ministry are over. Instead, leaders will have to develop strategies and lead their people in reaching the unchurched in their communities. Initiation takes far more mental, emotional, and physical effort than maintenance. The result is often exhaustion.

Church Planting Is Hard Work

A second reason church planting exhausts is because it's hard work. That's not to say that pastoring an established church isn't hard work. It is! But there's a difference. First, church planters spend less time in the study (at least initially) and more time in the field. This fieldwork consists of networking with core members and lost people. It involves countless hours of sharing a vision over coffee. It includes much time in the car driving to various appointments to meet with people who are interested in the new work or who are in places and positions to help it.

Second, church-planting pastors are criticized more than pastors of established churches. Because many established churches in America are still living and ministering with a 1940s or 1950s mentality, they're convinced that what has worked in the past will continue to work in the future. Consequently, there's a tendency among some to be critical of anything that's contemporary and innovative. The real tragedy is that they simply don't understand what it is they're criticizing. Regardless, the rocks they throw are big and they hurt: "It's of the devil!" "It's Christian hedonism!" "It's just secular entertainment!"

Criticism can be very hard and emotionally exhausting for those innovative pioneers who dare to "color outside the lines." They will have to pay a price to do what they believe is right, even with those who belong to the Christian community.

Church Planting Excites

While church planting may be exhausting, this is balanced by the fact that it is most exciting. I have attended or visited numerous established churches that, quite frankly, were rather boring. Not much is happening in these churches. Every Sunday there are the same old faces, the same old sermons, and the same old hymns played on the same old organ by the same old organist. Everything is predictable. In fact, eventually it is easy to predict which choir member will fall asleep first during the sermon and approximately when that will take place!

Boredom and routine are completely foreign to church planting. Starting a church is one of the most exciting spiritual ventures a group of Christians may ever undertake. There are several factors behind this intense excitement.

One is that church planting appeals to the pioneer spirit within most people. The idea of starting something new and different appeals to a spirit of entrepreneurship that lies deep within the souls of many of us. We relish the idea of being on the cutting edge of something new that God is doing!

Another factor is the sense of anticipation. As Christians we know that God is capable of doing extraordinary things in and through our lives such as building a great church. While we may never have experienced these things personally, we're aware that others have. But maybe it's our turn! Maybe God is about to do something extraordinary, and we're going to be part of it!

A third factor is expectation. Not only do we anticipate that God could do something special through the new church, but deep within our beings we expect Him to do so. We can feel it in our bones! We sense that the time is right, and that time is now! Life is too short, and we don't have many opportunities to be involved in something special for God. Consequently, let's step out in faith and be a part of a great new work for God. After all, how can we know what God intends to do until we've tried it?

Church Planting Requires Faith

Church planting is an exhausting but exciting venture of faith. Whenever people put on pioneer garb and ride off into the wilderness, they have entered the realm of faith. This means that they, like Abraham, will have to move outside their comfort zones of certainty and security and enter an unknown, somewhat frightening world. This involves taking risks, which is easier for some than for others. Yet faith and risk go hand in hand.

Anything of authentic spiritual significance is accomplished through faith. The writer of Hebrews affirms that "without faith it is impossible to please God" (Heb. 11:6a) Consequently, those who enlist in launching new churches must be men and women of strong, stretching faith in God. This involves both believing and obeying God.

People Who Believe God

We must be willing to believe God as Noah did when he built the ark in spite of the fact that there was no sign there was going to be a flood (Heb. 11:7). There are numerous commands in Scripture that require that Christians believe God can do the impossible. For example, in Matthew 6:25–34 the Savior says that if we seek first His kingdom and His righteousness that God will provide for the basic necessities of our lives, such as food, drink, and clothing. We either believe Him and act, or doubt and vacillate.

People Who Obey God

Second, we must be willing not only to believe but to obey God as Abraham did when he responded to God's call to leave Haran even though God didn't reveal where Abraham was going (Heb. 11:8). The command was simply, "Go!" Consequently, church planters must obey God and travel to locations that are new and foreign to them. It's important that they believe that God is sending them to a special place for a significant ministry and will provide for them along the way.

What kinds of things impress the Savior? In Matthew 8:5–13, a centurion had strong faith in Christ's ability to heal his servant. Jesus was astounded and said (v. 10), "I tell you the truth, I have not found anyone with such great faith in Israel." In Matthew 15:21–28, a Gentile woman trusted deeply in Jesus' ability to heal her daughter. The Savior healed her daughter and said, "Woman, you have great faith." God is impressed with men and women of faith who are willing to trust Him for the impossible.

Church planters are men and women of intense, authentic faith. They believe and obey God as demonstrated in their willingness to step out and boldly bring unchurched communities the saving message of Christ. They're people with whom the Savior is impressed; He acknowledges, "Your faith is great!"

Church Planting Involves a Process

Church planting is an exhausting but exciting venture of faith that involves a process. It's dynamic. It's not a once and for all kind of thing. This process is twofold.

Planting a Church Is a Process

The planting of the church, itself, is a process. In 1 Corinthians 12, Paul compares the church to the human body. In many ways, birthing a church is comparable to birthing a child. Consequently, the final section of this book, which concerns the process of church planting, will show church planters how to take the new work through the human lifecycle. This cycle consists of six stages of development: conception, development, birth, growth, maturity, and reproduction. Successful church planting involves taking the church through this entire process. To stop at any one stage in the process is to risk either plateauing or promoting the untimely death of the new church.

Planting Other Churches Is a Process

Once the church is started, the process doesn't end there. We must not sit back and be satisfied with maintaining what God has done! Christ's Great Commission is to disciple the world for Him, not simply to maintain new churches! Consequently, every planted church must not "forget its roots." Each church owes its existence to some person or church of vision. Each church has an obligation, in turn, to articulate the vision and start other churches. This is the final stage of the entire birth process of reproduction. It provides churches with the potential to evangelize unchurched communities all across America and throughout the world.

The idea is that planted churches reproduce themselves and make disciples by planting other churches. This is a process that will continue until the Savior returns. In fact, this is the true meaning of the Great Commission. If we desire to know how the early church understood Christ's commission, we can find the answer in the Book of Acts. Acts is a church-planting book because much of what takes place does so in the context of starting new churches. Therefore, it shouldn't surprise us when someone such as Peter Wagner says, "*The single most effective evangelistic methodology under heaven is planting new churches.*"[1]

Church Planting Requires a Plan

The Problem

The problem is that in the past many people with pure motives have attempted to start a new work but have no idea what they're doing. Often the result of this kind of approach is either a failed church or a small, struggling one.

This was my experience when I planted a church in Miami, Florida. I began with a group of motivated, excited people. The only problem was that none of us knew what we were doing! We simply started an evangelistic Bible study in my apartment that developed into a church. God blessed this effort and people came to faith in Christ, but we constantly found ourselves guessing about what we should do next. Consequently, after a mushrooming start we plateaued at under a hundred people due largely to our ignorance concerning how to start a church.

The Solution

Church planting that is intentional involves careful planning. Unlike the time when I planted the Miami church in the early 1970s, today there's much more information available. The field of church planting is becoming more sophisticated, and entrepreneurial church starters can get much help and direction so that they don't have to guess at what they're doing. In fact, this book is written to provide this very kind of help for the numerous people who'll be planting biblically based, "cutting-edge" churches in the twenty-first century.

Church Planting Involves Both Beginning and Growing Churches

Church planting is an exhausting but exciting venture of faith that involves the planned process of beginning and growing new local churches. There is more to planting churches than beginning churches. A major part of the process is to start a new church and do it correctly. This means that church planters must be familiar with biblical church growth principles, or they'll see their churches plateau and even begin to decline. It's this emphasis on church growth that is missing in most older works on church planting.

This book enumerates a number of biblical church growth principles, the bulk of which will be found in chapters 7–13 and in chapter 17, which covers the growth stage of church planting.

The Assumptions of Church Growth

A Numerical Balance

A number of smaller evangelical churches have a bias against large churches and church growth. Often this bias is expressed by such statements as, "We may not have quantity (lots of people), but we sure have quality (spiritual people) and that's what's really important to God."

While it's true that some churches overemphasize the importance of numbers, others often use this as an excuse to remain passive and not reach people. Quality churches with rare exceptions will become quantity churches because quality churches are actively involved in fulfilling Christ's Great Commission, which involves reaching and discipling lost people. This results in numerical growth.

A Biblical Focus

A second assumption is the idea that we must focus not only on what is pragmatic, that is, what works in growing churches, but on what is biblical. Our goal is to plant biblically based churches! The Church Growth Movement has had a positive effect on revitalizing and growing churches around the world. Indeed, the thinking of the pioneers in this field has had significant impact on some of the new, relevant churches that are reaching the Baby Boom and Gen X birth cohorts in America.

One of the accurate criticisms of this movement is that it has focused more on the pragmatic aspects of church growth than on the biblical or spiritual aspects. Peter Wagner, a church growth pioneer, has acknowledged this criticism as accurate and seeks to emphasize both the spiritual and pragmatic aspects of church planting.

The Principles of Church Growth

There are at least seven biblical principles that are critical to church growth and the planting of biblically based churches. The first is a Great Commission vision that involves pursuing, evangelizing, and discipling lost people (Matt. 28:19–20; the Gospel of Luke). The second is a strong servant-leadership (Acts; 1 Cor. 11:3); a plurality of lay leaders has proved insufficient to lead the church. The third is a well-equipped, mobilized lay army (1 Cor. 12–14; Eph. 4). The fourth is a culturally relevant ministry (1 Chron. 12:32; 1 Cor. 9). The fifth is a holistic, authentic worship (Rom. 12:1). The sixth is a biblical, culturally relevant evangelism that focuses on the various biblical styles of evangelism and emphasizes forms other than confrontational evangelism. The last is a robust network of small groups (Acts 2:46; 5:42; 20:20). (These principles will be treated in depth in part 3 on the principles of church planting.)

Church Planting Rests on Jesus' Promise

Church planting is an exhausting but exciting venture of faith that involves the planned process of beginning and growing local churches as based on Jesus' promise in Matthew 16:18: "And I tell you that you are Peter, and on this rock I will build my church, and the gates of Hades shall not overcome it." This promise concerns the fact that ultimately Jesus Christ is the builder of churches. He is the one who plants them, and He is the one who grows them.

The Problem

Currently, the church in America, evangelical as well as liberal, is in trouble.

The Culture Has Changed

According to one church growth expert, many of the churches in this country are either plateaued or in decline. At the same time, the number of unchurched Americans has grown to the point that the majority of people are unchurched. All of this has created a void that is being filled to some extent by a sudden growth in such major cults as Mormonism, the Jehovah's Witnesses, and some New Age groups.

As mentioned earlier in this chapter, the America of the 1990s and early twenty-first century is no longer the America of the 1940s and 1950s. Essentially, what was a churched culture has become an unchurched culture. People in our culture are not antichurch; they simply view the church as no longer relevant in their lives.

The Church Is Unprepared

These are dark and difficult days for the church, and a big part of the problem is the fact that many churches still aren't even aware that they're in trouble! They're like the proverbial ostrich with its head buried in the sand—completely oblivious to what is taking place all around, yet dangerously exposed.

A large number of these churches, even if they survive the 1990s, will die in the early twenty-first century. Haddon Robinson, the former president of Denver Seminary, views America as a post-Christian culture and indicates that Denver Seminary is now preparing their students, who desire to minister in America, as foreign missionaries in an alien world.

The Solution

We who make up the church must not throw up our hands in despair or assume a "gloom and doom" mentality. The Savior hasn't given up on His church.

An Old Promise

Although He made the promise in the first century, it still applies to the church today. Again, His promise is not to bury but to build the church. Consequently, not only will the church in America survive, but it has a wonderful, exciting future ahead. If Christ has promised to build His church, then it will not become extinct. This means that something will have to change drastically in the next ten to twenty years.

While some churches will change, undergo a transition period, and renew themselves, the future lies with church planting. As someone once said, "It is easier to have babies than to raise the dead!" The point is that God has already begun to challenge thousands to plant new, vibrant, cutting-edge churches for the twenty-first century as inspired by the ministries of Chuck Swindoll, Bill Hybels, Rick Warren, Chuck Smith, and many others. We are only at the very beginning of a groundswell that is about to sweep across America in the early twenty-first century.

A New Look

The churches of the twenty-first century will not look like the typical church of the twentieth century. A different culture calls for a different way in which we "do church." The biblical principles are eternal and will remain the same in the evangelical church. Yet our methods for implementing and manifesting these principles will have to change so the church will be more relevant to and able to reach the present Baby Boom and Baby Bust birth cohorts and the cultures that are yet on the horizon.

Church Planting Responds to Jesus' Great Commission

Finally, intentional church planting is an exhausting but exciting venture of faith that involves the process of beginning and growing new local churches as based on Jesus' promise in Matthew 16:18 and in obedience to His Great Commission. One of the critical problems in the typical church is that it's forgotten its mission. Somewhere in the process of "doing church" it has wandered away from its original intent.

The Problem

It's critical that any church pause and ask the important question, "Why are we doing what we're doing?" Essentially, "What is the mission of the church? What is it that Christ has left us here to do?" The answer to this question is found in the Great Commission, which involves pursuing, winning, and maturing lost people (in particular, unchurched lost people) for our Savior.

Apparently this isn't being accomplished by 80 percent to 85 percent of our churches. Indeed, George Barna writes, "In the past seven years, the proportion of adults who have accepted Jesus Christ as their personal Savior (34 percent) has not increased."[2] The problem is that far too many established American churches have missed their mission.

The Solution

At the same time, there's a new wind that's blowing across American soil. God is currently in the process of seeding America with new churches that are teaching the rest of us how to do evangelism and win our contemporary, unchurched culture to Christ in the local church. The ministries of such pastors as Bill Hybels, Rick Warren, Chuck Smith, and many others have seen countless numbers of unchurched lost people become "completely committed Christians."

Not only does this give us hope, but it creates vision and motivates the church of Jesus Christ to reaffirm its purpose and return to the Great Commission mandate. Indeed, the criterion of successful churches in the future is not how much Bible knowledge their people have, how strong their pastors are in the pulpit, or their abilities to manifest the sign gifts. While content and pulpit expertise aren't to be minimized, the biblical measure of success is whether they're making disciples.

2

Do We Need Another Church?

The Reasons for Church Planting

Bill Smith has just completed seminary, and his excitement and personal sense of destiny are much stronger than when he began. God in various ways had made it clear to Bill that he should pursue professional ministry, and pastoral ministry in particular, but first he needed some formal preparation. Now that seminary is behind him, he plans to start a church.

Initially, this was not part of the plan. In fact, both he and his wife, Betty, were just a little nervous about Bill quitting his job as an engineer, selling their house, and transporting themselves and their two children halfway across the country to live off their savings and odd jobs for the years that Bill pursued seminary training. During Bill's first year at seminary, both he and his wife had anticipated his taking an exciting, dynamic pastorate in an established church that had a first-class facility and a salary comparable to or better than what he had made as an engineer.

In Bill's second year, all that changed. The seminary required an elective in pastoral ministries, so he and a couple of friends decided to take a course in church planting. This proved to be the spark that ignited a flame that began to burn within his soul. The course, combined with an internship in a dynamic, recently planted church in the area, sealed his future ministry.

Of course, Betty was caught by surprise. In fact, at first, she was rather upset. This wasn't a part of their original plan! "Church planting—what's that!" she exclaimed. "Why would you want to go and do a thing like that?" But God worked in her heart in such a way that through her involvement in Bill's internship, she eventually caught the vision and became a vital part of the team.

Given some of the reasons for pastoring an established church, such as an existing congregation with existing facilities and in particular a salary, why would anyone in their right mind want to plant a church? Betty's question is a good one, and must be asked by all who desire to become involved in some way with starting a church. While there are numerous reasons, there are five important ones.

The Need

There is a tremendous need for more significant churches around the world in general and in America in particular.

The Decline of the American Church

The church in North America is not in good shape. A study of various sources reveals that a large number of churches have leveled out or are declining and many are dying.

Churches Are Plateaued and Declining

In *The Pastor's Manual for Effective Ministry,* Win Arn writes, "In the years following World War II thousands of new churches were established. Today, of the approximately 350,000 churches in America, four out of the five are either plateaued or declining."[1] He notes that "In the normal life cycle of churches, there is birth, and in time, death. Many churches begin a plateau and/or slow decline around their 15th–18th year." Then he offers a staggering statistic: "80–85% of the churches in America are on the down-side of this growth cycle."[2] Further, of the 15 percent that are growing, 14 percent are growing as the result of transfer rather than conversion growth.

Religious Bodies. This statistic is anticipated by an early study of Protestant, Roman Catholic, and Jewish membership trends in the United States from 1947 to 1973 by Carroll, Johnson, and Marty. It shows a general flattening out and a decline in these three groups in comparison to the general population in America from approximately 1965 to 1973. Regarding Protestant membership (which includes such bodies as Mormons and Jehovah's Witnesses), they write,

> Protestants grew more rapidly than the total population throughout the post World War II period, down to 1955. During the 1955 to 1965 decade, Protestant growth generally paralleled that of the population. From 1965 to 1970, Protestants continued to grow, but at a rate slightly less than the

total population; and from 1970 to 1973 the total number of Protestants showed a very slight loss (less than 1 percent).[3]

Mainline Churches. Arn's figure would include churches that are liberal as well as evangelical in their theology. For example, according to *The Yearbook of American and Canadian Churches,* in 1965 the United Methodist Church reported approximately 11 million members; in 1996 they reported 8.5 million. In 1965, the Presbyterian Church, U.S.A. reported 4 million members, but in 1996 reported a drop to 3 million people. The Disciples of Christ reported 2 million members in 1965; this figure dropped to 1 million in 1996. Finally, the Episcopal Church reported around 3.4 million members in 1965 and 2.5 million in 1996.[4]

Evangelical Churches. Many churches of an evangelical persuasion are struggling with statistical plateaus and decline as well. One example would be the Southern Baptist Convention. An article in *Missions USA,* a Southern Baptist publication, reported the following:

> The Southern Baptist statistical stall in 1987 is not a cause for alarm, but it should be fully discussed and explored, pollster George Gallup claimed. In the church year, ending September 30, 1987, some denominational programs reported small changes and had gains or totals smaller than have been seen in decades, according to statistics compiled by the Baptist Sunday School Board's research department. "Southern Baptist statistics appear to represent a leveling out rather than a reversal or sudden turnaround," Gallup said when asked to evaluate the denomination's most recent statistical results. Compared with other mainline denominations in the United States, Southern Baptists have defied national trends for years. The modest downward reports in the denomination's key program areas represent a flattening out of what had been moving up for years.[5]

The conservative Lutheran Church, Missouri Synod, showed significant growth up until about 1970. In that year, they reported 2,788,536 people. However, in 1980 they reported a drop to 2,625,650, and in 1996 they were around 2,596,927.[6]

A significant number of students from schools such as Moody Bible Institute, Multnomah School of the Bible, and Dallas Seminary graduate and take positions in churches that are part of the Bible Church Movement. These churches are popularly known primarily for their sound expository preaching of the Scriptures. Yet even this movement is plateaued and many churches have begun to experience a numerical decline.

In the early study cited above that compares Protestant, Catholic, and Jewish membership trends with general population growth, the authors noted that the conservative churches were growing in comparison to the liberal churches. However, it's important to note in their summary that conservative church growth in the groups they studied came as a result of what they call "a kind of circulation process, by which evangelicals move from one conservative church to another."[7] Then they added the following: "Bibby and Brinkerhoff conclude that conservative churches do a better job of retaining those already familiar with evangelical culture—both transfers and children of members—than moderate and liberal churches do in retaining their members."[8] This indicates that in the 1960s and 1970s most conservative churches were growing more as a result of what church growth experts call transfer growth and biological growth than through actual conversion growth.

My own studies indicate that at the present theologically conservative churches still tend to grow more numerically than theologically liberal churches. For example, the Assemblies of God, The Church of God (Cleveland), and the Christian Missionary and Alliance are experiencing growth.[9] The reason for their growth is the fact that they're planting churches. Wagner says, "Without exception, the growing denominations have been those that stress church planting."[10] Lyle Schaller notes that church planting "continues to be the most useful and productive component of any denominational church growth strategy."[11]

However, many, possibly the majority, of conservative churches are plateaued and in decline. This would seem to be contradicted by the statistics reported in the *Yearbook of American and Canadian Churches*. Helen Parmley alludes to this when she writes, "The news is the same. Many mainline Protestant denominations had small membership losses again in 1989, while the Roman Catholic Church and several conservative denominations recorded gains."[12]

But conservatives must not be too quick to rejoice. Some of these gains are due to transfer growth. In addition, it's up to each denomination to provide its own statistics for the yearbook, and different groups use different methods to gather those statistics. For example, Parmley writes:

> The yearbook, which probably has the most accurate statistics of American churches, is widely used and quoted. But before taking the figures to the bank, consider some of the methods denominations use to compile those statistics.
>
> According to the statistics in the yearbook, membership in the Southern Baptist Convention rose in 1989 from 14.8 million to 14.9 million, and membership in the Presbyterian Church (U.S.A.) fell from 2.9 million to 2.8 million.
>
> The Southern Baptists, however, record two membership lists. One is a "resident" membership, the other is a "total" membership. For example, in

1989, First Baptist Church of Dallas—the largest congregation in the denomination—recorded 13,271 "resident" members and 28,000 "total" members.

The church's sanctuary seats about 2,500 people and has three Sunday morning services.

The Presbyterian denomination, on the other hand, encourages its churches to keep membership rolls "clean" by assessing an annual per-capita tax. In 1989, for instance, the denominational tax per member was $3.70.

Some denominations accept baptized newborns as members, but other denominations don't. They wait until they are old enough to give their testimony or be confirmed.

Although the National Baptist Convention, U.S.A. Inc. is listed in the yearbook as the nation's fourth largest Protestant denomination, its latest membership count of 5.5 million was taken in 1958.[13]

Consequently, Win Arn's assertion that 80 percent to 85 percent of the churches in America are plateaued or in decline is an accurate assessment of the entire American church scene, evangelical as well as liberal.

Churches Are Dying

A large number of churches in America are dying. According to Arn, 3,500 to 4,000 churches die every year.[14] Lyle Schaller writes that "an estimated 30,000 congregations ceased to exist sometime during the 1980s."[15] This is remarkable because so many churches in the past have either grown to or declined at around 30 members and then plateaued at that figure for years. These are known as "family clan" churches, especially in rural areas, because many of them are made up of actual biological families or people who have developed a family-like closeness.

Another article points to the fact that there are approximately 350,000 churches in America. It predicts that in the next few years 100,000 of these will close their doors.[16] Consequently, at least a third or more of today's churches did not survive the 1990s!

The Growing Number of Unchurched People

While many liberal and conservative churches are plateaued or decreasing, at the same time the number of unchurched people in America is increasing. But how many unchurched people are there in America, and who are they?

How Many Are Unchurched?

In 1978 George Gallup conducted a poll in which he concluded that 41 percent of all American adults (18 years of age or older) were unchurched.[17] He defined the unchurched as "those who are not members of a church or have not attended services in the previous six months other than for special religious holidays, weddings, funerals or the like."[18] He conducted the poll again in 1988, and the figure had climbed to 44 percent. He concluded that "the churches have not made any inroads into attracting the unchurched over the past decade."[19]

How accurate are the polls? In commenting on one of his own polls, Louis Harris admits, "It should be noted that church attendance is notoriously overreported as a socially desirable activity, so true attendance figures are surely lower than those reported here."[20]

Peter Wagner indicates that at the beginning of the 1990s the number of nonchurched people was higher than Gallup's 41 percent. According to an interview in *Christianity Today*, "He points to the fact that in spite of church growth's advances in the eighties, the percentage of American adults attending church has remained almost the same (about 45 percent), while Protestant church membership has actually declined."[21] Therefore, he would set the figure at 55 percent.

In *The Frog in the Kettle*, George Barna predicted that around the year 2000 "Church attendance on Sunday mornings will decrease to about 35 percent of the population on any given weekend."[22] Consequently, he believed that the number of unchurched would continue to climb until it reached 65 percent of the population by the year 2000. He added that this figure would go even higher except for the fact that a number of churches will offer their worship services on Saturdays and Sunday afternoons as well as at the traditional Sunday morning time.[23]

In November 1993 *Christianity Today* presented a controversial new study to be published in the *American Sociological Review* that reported that 19.6 percent of Protestants and about 28 percent of Catholics attended church during the average week.[24]

Who Are the Unchurched?

For the most part the unchurched consist of the Baby Boom and Baby Bust or Generation X populations.

The Baby Boom Generation

The Baby Boom is the name that was given to the explosion of births following World War II from approximately 1946 to 1964. Those who were born during this time are commonly referred to as the Baby Boom Generation. Others refer to them as the Pepsi Generation and those born prior to them as the Harry Truman Generation. They number over 76 million and make up approximately one-third of America's population.

While these Baby Boomers are, in general, unchurched, Gallup's survey indicated a strong interest on their part in spiritual matters. For example, the survey showed that there's strong potential for these unchurched people to return to the church because they're more religious than a decade ago; a larger proportion are providing religious education for their children; 58 percent say that under certain conditions they would "definitely," "probably," or "possibly" return to church; 68 percent say they would even invite others to join them in their congregations.[25]

However, the Baby Boomers don't want the church, at least in its current traditional form. Jack Sims writes that the average Baby Boomer attends church only 6.2 times a year—"less than half as often as 'average' Americans over 40."[26] In discussing why Boomers don't go to church, Sims writes:

> Most of the babyboomers I have interviewed describe their experience with church and religious media as boring, irrelevant or high-pressured. They say things like: "I don't like the music. It sounds old-fashioned and strange." "It's too one-sided politically." "They are always asking for money."
>
> Some young believers I meet as I travel around the country are trying to hang on to a religion programmed to the tastes of the older generation. Others are hoping to find spiritual homes within parachurch organizations. But a growing number are deciding that the cultural pain of living inside traditional organizations is greater than the pain of pulling up their spiritual and emotional roots. Tom Stipe, the 33-year-old pastor of Colorado's second largest church says, "The church is the last standing barrier between our generation and Jesus."[27]

Sims has gone straight to the heart of the problem. It's not that the Boomers are uninterested in the *principles* of the faith; they simply aren't attracted to the *practices* of the faith, that is, how many churches "do church." This is most important because the way we "package" our faith is predominantly cultural and subject to change on the part of those who are willing to be flexible in order to reach unchurched lost people. What this means is that there's great hope for our predominantly unchurched generation!

The solution rests not only on their shoulders but on the shoulders of those of us who make up the church. If we value this lost, unchurched generation as Jesus valued the lost generation of His day (Luke 5:27–32; 15:1–10; 19:1–10), then it's imperative that we be willing to be flexible not only in regard to our principles but in terms of our practices and tastes.

This isn't a call to abandon certain biblical principles such as evangelism, worship, or teaching in our churches, but to reevaluate and abandon if necessary the ways we've practiced these principles in the past. In light of Matthew 28:19–20, Mark 16:15, and 1 Corinthians 9, not to do so is sin.

Generation X. Most of what's been said about the Baby Boom Generation can be said about the Baby Bust or Generation X as well. Presently America is experiencing a Baby Boomlet. Gary McIntosh writes,

> In 1989 births hit 4 million, the largest number of births since the post World War II baby boom ended in 1964. . . . Labeled Baby Busters due to the fact that they are a "bust" generation in comparison to that of their parents, this new generation is now between the ages of 8 and 25 years old.[28]

Many of these Xers are the children of Baby Boomers and are, therefore, second-generation unchurched people. Whereas a number of the Baby Boomers dropped out of church, the Baby Busters were never in church to begin with. Therefore, they know even less about church than their parents. For example, an article appeared in the *Dallas Morning News* in which a husband and wife who were Boomers had decided to return to church when they discovered the religious naivete of their son. The article, subtitled "Parents returning to religion to give children moral training," reported the following experience:

> John and Susan Jackson realized their firstborn son's spiritual development was lacking when he confused church with Church's.
> Blake, then 4, had slept overnight at his grandparents'. The next morning, the grandparents prepared for worship services. Mrs. Jackson said her son asked to stay longer, saying his grandparents were "going to Church's, and I want to stay for fried chicken."[29]

What is important to note is that the grandparents, who were of the Harry Truman Generation, still attended church. The parents, who were of the Pepsi Generation, had dropped out of church earlier in life but were still aware of its presence. However, their son, who was second-generation nonchurched, had virtually no awareness of the church. When he first heard the term from his grandparents, he didn't think of the white building in the community with a cross affixed to its steeple. He thought instead of a chain of fast food fried chicken stores called Church's Fried Chicken. And this incident took place in heavily churched Dallas, Texas!

What's so important about Generation X is that they have imbibed deeply of postmodernism. They have been taught what to think (that which is politically correct) but not how to think. They process truth and reality in an entirely different way. For example, many tend not to reason logically and don't follow the law of noncontradiction. Consequently, they can hold mutually contradictory positions without blinking an eye. Isaiah's plea, "'Come now, let us reason together,' says the LORD" (Isa. 1:18), may fall on logically deaf postmodern ears. Postmodernism undermines all possibility of knowing objective truth. It represents the death of truth as the Christian knows it, and it has infected many areas, including health care, literature, education, history, psychology, law, science, and religion.[30]

Generation X is a hurting generation (half of them come from divorced homes and one-third were aborted or abused) who desperately need the gospel. The point, again, is that we in the present American church need to reach out to this generation and be willing to change the way we "do church" so that we might begin to pursue the unchurched lost people of this generation and those of the Millennial Generation to follow.

The Growth of Cults and Nonevangelical Groups

Not only is the American church declining and the unchurched growing in numbers, but various cults and nonevangelical religions are filling the vacuum. *U.S. News and World Report* recorded the following:

> Today the Church of Jesus Christ of Latter-day Saints, better known as the Mormon Church, is one of the world's richest and fastest-growing religious movements. Since World War II, its ranks have quadrupled to more than 8.3 members worldwide. With 4.5 million U.S. members, Mormonism already outnumbers Presbyterians and Episcopalians combined. If current trends hold, by some estimates they will number 250 million worldwide by 2080 and surpass all but the Roman Catholic Church among Christian bodies.[31]

It's both significant and alarming that several major cults have doubled their size within recent years and that new religions are prospering. For example, according to the *Yearbook of American and Canadian Churches,* the Mormon Church practically tripled from 1,789,175 in 1965 to 4,613,000 in 1996. During the same period, the Jehovah's Witnesses grew from 330,358 to 945,990.[32]

We've also seen the rise of several new religious groups such as those connected with the New Age Movement. In light of this, Barna writes:

> On the other hand, groups outside evangelical and mainline Christianity will continue to expand rapidly. The Mormon church will reach 10 million members by 2000. . . . Eastern faiths, especially Buddhism and Islam, will more

than double. . . . The New Age religions will prosper, although many of the groups that will be prolific by 2000 are not yet in existence.[33]

All of this would seem to indicate strongly that not only do our churches need to make some critical changes in what they're doing, but they need to do so quickly. It's of utmost importance that our churches become aware of what's taking place across America so that they can deal intelligently with the problem and make critical adjustments before it's too late.

The Promise

The enemies of Christianity are aware of what's taking place on the American church scene, and they're rejoicing for they assume that America is entering a post-Christian era from which it will never recover. Indeed, the situation looks grim. Yet, the question needs to be asked, "How should Christians respond to all these events?" At first our response might understandably be that of discouragement and even a growing pessimism. However, there's a much better response that's based not so much on what's taking place presently in America but on an eternal biblical promise.

A Biblical Promise

In Matthew 16:18, the Savior says, "And I tell you that you are Peter, and on this rock I will build my church, and the gates of Hades will not overcome it." There are at least two promises in this passage. One is that Christ, not Christians, is ultimately the person who plants and grows churches. Second, Satan and all of his forces will not be able to prevail against the church.

The present situation would seem to contradict this second promise. However, there is in this passage much hope for the future of Christ's church. Since this passage was penned, the history of the church has been that of both numerical growth and decline. The point of the promise is that the church will continue to exist regardless of its size.

An Optimistic Future

Consequently, we can look to the twenty-first century with great hope and enthusiasm. Based on the current condition of the American church and the promises in Matthew 16:18, God has begun and will continue to plant a great number of high-impact, cutting-edge churches in the twenty-first century. In fact, there are already a number of individuals and organizations that are beginning to encourage church planting as a significant solution to the problem.

George Barna has observed an increasing emphasis among denominations on church planting. He writes, "Many denominations have targeted this decade as one for aggressive church planting. If existing plans are carried out, we can expect the number of Protestant churches in America to swell by another 75,000 congregations."[34]

Church growth analyst Lyle Schaller sees church planting as the key to reaching the next generation. While speaking at the annual meeting of the Southern Baptist New Work Fellowship in Atlanta, Schaller said, "If you are interested in reaching new people, by far the most effective way to do this is through church planting." Later in the same message he addressed the issue of making established churches relevant as opposed to planting new churches: "Some think we need to make all our existing congregations vital before starting new churches. What's wrong with that is nobody knows how to do that . . . and nobody's young enough to live long enough to do it."[35]

Various denominations have placed church planting among their top priorities. The Assemblies of God, which is one of the fastest-growing denominations in the United States, has a vision, which is "to plant 5,000 new churches, recruit 20,000 new ministers, win 5 million people to Christ, and enlist 1 million people to pray regularly for revival—all by the year 2000." In 1990, they planted 340 new churches—20 percent more than in 1989—and recorded just under 320,000 conversions.[36]

Southern Baptists have made church planting a major emphasis in their challenging and exciting program called Bold Mission Thrust. As part of its strategy, in 1976 the Southern Baptist Convention set a goal of reaching 50,000 churches by the year 2000! In the early 1990s, they were around 6,000 churches short of their goal. Consequently, in response the Home Mission Board decided to launch 1,500 churches a year for a total of 15,000 by the year 2000. They called this the 15,000 Campaign.[37]

Church growth expert Peter Wagner writes the following:

> We live in a time when general interest in church planting is higher than it has been since the 1950s. While some denominations continued to plant new churches and thereby have grown during the last 40 years, others have virtually eliminated that ministry with the exception of a new church here and there or a cluster of ethnic minority churches. They have been paying the price.
>
> Now the climate is changing. Denominational headquarters are adding church planting desks. Motivational material is appearing in denominational publications. Training programs for church planters are being developed.[38]

Later in the same work he writes, "I begin this book with a categorical statement that will seem bold and brash to some at first sight, even though it has been well substantiated by research over the past two or three decades: *The single most effective evangelistic methodology under heaven is planting new churches.*"[39]

The Great Commission

The Great Commission is found in Matthew 28:19–20, Mark 16:15, Luke 24:46–47, and Acts 1:8. A careful analysis of these passages reveals three components that make up the commission.

The first consists of the intentional pursuit of lost people. This is reflected in the word "go" found at the beginning of the commission as it is recorded in both Matthew 28:19 and Mark 16:15.

The Savior clarifies what He means by this word in such passages as Luke 5:27–32, 15:1–10, and 19:1–10, where He develops the concept of seeking lost people such as Levi the tax-gatherer and his friends, tax-gatherers and sinners in general, and Zacchaeus. Far too many churches at the end of the twentieth century are waiting for lost people to come to them. This tactic may have worked in the 1940s and 1950s when the culture was churched, but it doesn't work in the 1990s with a culture that's predominantly unchurched. The twenty-first-century church will have to take the initiative and pursue these lost people.

The second component of the Great Commission is evangelism. In Mark 16:15, Christ says, "Go into all the world and preach the good news to all creation." In Matthew 28:19–20, He says, "Therefore go and make disciples of all nations, baptizing them in the name of the Father and of the Son and of the Holy Spirit, and teaching them to obey everything I have commanded you. And surely I am with you always, to the very end of the age."

A Great Commission church is one that places a high priority on evangelism. The church in general and the people in particular aren't simply talking about evangelism, but they're actively seeking and reaching lost people. In fact, a church that isn't reaching lost people has lost its purpose!

The Final Component Is Edification

Once the church reaches lost people, it doesn't drop them but proceeds to enfold and disciple them. This is the process of edification, which involves bringing new believers to Christ-likeness (Eph. 4:11–16). This involves a personal commitment to Bible study (which transforms their worldview), fellowship, communion, and prayer (Acts 2:42). Consequently, the local church provides a place where a new believer is discipled and mobilized for service.

How Do We Implement the Great Commission?

Now that we know the three critical components of the Great Commission, a second vital question is, "How do we implement it?" Perhaps the best answer lies in a hermeneutic that examines how the early church implemented the commission. This information is found in the Book of Acts, where the early church sought to put into practice the commission command of our Lord. A careful reading of Acts reveals that the early church implemented the Great Commission mandate primarily by planting churches. A study of the missionary journeys recorded in Acts reveals that they, in fact, were church-planting forays into what was predominantly a pagan culture. As a result of these trips, Paul and others planted high-impact churches in key cities such as Derbe, Lystra, Iconium, Antioch, Philippi, Thessalonica, Berea, Corinth, and Ephesus.

Consequently, if the church is to obey its visionary Savior and implement His commission mandate, then it's imperative that it start significant churches that are led by visionary leaders. Indeed, if our churches are to reach the great cities of America and the world, they can't do so by themselves. Instead, they must multiply themselves by starting a network of significant, biblically based churches in their target area. Unfortunately, there aren't very many churches with this kind of vision. God is going to change this over the next several decades. It would be much more exciting and rewarding if churches could catch the vision now and not later!

The Advantages

New Churches Grow Faster Than Established Churches

The first advantage is the fact that new churches grow faster than older, established churches. Win Arn cites a study by the Southern Baptist Convention that demonstrates this advantage.[40] In this study, churches started between 1972 and 1981 were compared to those prior to 1971. These churches were examined according to their membership sizes, which included the categories of 1–50, 51–100, 101–200, 201–400, 401–600, 601–1000, and 1000+. The growth span on which the study was based was the percentage of growth of all these churches from 1981 to 1986. The result was that churches of all sizes that were started between 1972 and 1981 grew at a rate of 60 percent to 80 percent. Those started prior to 1971 grew at a rate of 20 percent to 60 percent, with the older and larger churches coming closer to the 20 percent figure. Certainly older churches shouldn't be overly discouraged by these figures. Instead, they should find in them a challenge to renewal and the planting of daughter churches.

Lyle Schaller reminds us that it's a mistake to attempt to revitalize existing congregations at the expense of church planting. The reasons are that nobody knows how to do it, and it takes too much time. Schaller also argues that new churches grow faster than long-established parishes.[41] The reason is the following:

> Perhaps the simplest explanation of this pattern is that new congregations are organized around evangelism and reaching people not actively involved in the life of any worshipping community. By contrast, powerful internal institutional pressures tend to encourage long-established churches to allocate most of their resources to the care of members.[42]

New Churches Evangelize Better Than Established Churches

The second advantage is that new churches evangelize better than older, established churches. In a study that appeared in *Christianity Today,* Bruce McNicol writes that among evangelical churches those under three years old will win ten people to Christ per year for every one hundred members. Those churches from three to fifteen years old will win five people per year for every one hundred church members. Finally, after a church reaches age fifteen, the figure drops to three people per year for every one hundred members.[43]

George Barna writes, "In the past seven years, the proportion of adults who have accepted Jesus Christ as their personal Savior (34%) has not increased."[44] Many in evangelical circles are tired of transfer growth and are calling for conversion growth.

Leaders Gain Credibility Faster in New Churches

The third advantage of church planting is that church planters gain credibility as leaders in planted churches faster than those who take pastorates in established churches.

Assuming the Leadership in Established Churches

Zunkel in *Growing the Small Church* writes that "Most pastorates proceed according to a pattern. They go from the minister as *chaplain to pastor to leader.*"[45] When new pastors take an established church, they proceed through these three stages on their way to becoming the leaders of their churches.

The chaplain stage. The first stage lasts from one to three years. During this time people often refer to church leaders as "pastors." They function much as chaplains, preaching and performing pastoral care but exercising little influence as leaders.

The pastor stage. The next stage may last from three to as few as five years at best, or it may last for the pastor's entire tenure at the church. The latter happens because some churches will not let their pastors become leaders. During this time people often refer to them as "our pastor." What has taken place and that which moves pastors through the stages is increased credibility and trust. As pastors build credibility and trust, people are more likely to let them lead.

The leader stage. The final stage is that of leader. This is that point in the pattern where pastors have come to a place where they can exercise great influence in their churches and are able to implement their visions. The only problem is that the process usually takes so long (if it happens at all) that most leave for greener pastures before reaching this point in their ministry. For example, the median tenure for Southern Baptist pastors in 1980 was 2.7 years, and 4.6 years in 1987.[46]

Assuming the Leadership in Planted Churches

Planting pastors often become leaders without having to go through the first two stages. While pastors taking established churches have to build credibility and trust, church planters are granted this up front, and they either maintain that trust or lose it in the process of exercising leadership.

Often this trust is granted because in established churches, pastors are "joining them," whereas, in planted churches the congregations are most likely "joining the pastors." The advantages of this phenomenon are obvious. In particular, the new church is able to go about accomplishing its vision from the very start as opposed to waiting several years or possibly never getting to that point.

People Are More Open to Change in New Churches

A fourth advantage is that those involved in church planting are more open to change than those in established, traditional churches. This relates to the difference between old and new wineskins.

The Problem of "Old Wineskins"

Over the years, established churches build up a number of traditions that become set in concrete. This is because they've proved valuable and helpful in the past. These are "excess baggage." Of course, the problem is that times change and so must those traditions. But this is never realized in far too many of these churches.

Some pastors, who are change agents, will accept the pastorate of one of these traditional churches with a view toward changing it. However, most aren't very patient and move rather quickly. In private, they say, "The twenty-first century is just around the corner; therefore, I want to bring this church into the twentieth century as soon as possible!" The result is one of two things. Either the pastor is asked to leave, which is usually what happens, or many of the people in the church leave. In both situations, there are lots of unhappy people.

This is the problem of "old wineskins." It's not anything unique to the twentieth century. In Matthew 9:16–17, the Savior says,

> No one sews a patch of unshrunk cloth on an old garment, for the patch will pull away from the garment, making the tear worse. Neither do men pour new wine into old wineskins. If they do, the skins will burst, the wine will run out and the wineskins will be ruined. No, they pour new wine into new wineskins, and both are preserved.

Jesus indicates that it's hard to change established traditions. He's not evaluating those traditions, or saying that one is better than the other. He's warning of the difficulties for those who attempt to bring change into situations where structures are already in place. We should rightly question the wisdom of attempting to bring significant change to older, established churches. Old skins don't stretch well! While it's imperative that some change take place if these churches are to survive, it's often gradual and over an extended period of time. There's simply not much stretch left! Otherwise, the tear is too great, and the old skin bursts.

The Solution of "New Wineskins"

The advantage of church planting is that the people who are attracted come into a new situation in which they're open to jettisoning much of their old "baggage." No one is attempting to sew a new patch onto an old wineskin; rather, new wine is being poured into new skins. The result is that not only are those involved extremely excited about the new church which, in turn, attracts other people, but they're open to change and are willing to try new and innovative ideas.

3

How Do You Make Ends Meet?

The Means for Church Planting

Bill Smith had completed seminary and was ready to move "full steam ahead" in birthing a church. His wife Betty had caught the vision as well, and now considers herself a part of the team although she spends much of her time at home with their children. But that doesn't mean she's not without her doubts and questions about the ministry and their future.

Perhaps the most frightening aspect of church planting for Betty is the finances. Generally speaking, there's more financial security in established churches than in new churches. In an established church, there's usually some kind of salary package for the pastor. Betty understands this and often lies awake at night thinking about it. Bill, on the other hand, has become so caught up in the vision of starting a new church that he's not put a lot of thought into the finances of church planting. Betty knows this, and at times it worries her. Consequently, her question for Bill is, "How are we going to make ends meet?"

The means of church planting are not the actual process one goes through in starting and growing a church, but the personal and ministry finances that are necessary for church planters and their ministries to survive.

Whether we like it or not, money is necessary for ministry, and intentional church planters such as Bill Smith must think about how to provide for his family's personal needs and those of the ministry. If certain finances aren't in place, then the planting process may not occur.

Financial Facts

Some people avoid the ministry of church planting because of the issue of finances. In order to address this important issue, we must briefly examine one of the great promises in Scripture that deals with God's provision for His disciples' personal needs. Also, we'll look at the condition and problems that surround this promise.

The Promise

The promise is found in Matthew 6:25–34. Jesus understands that while serving Him, the disciples at times worry about meeting their basic needs such as food, drink, and clothing. In verses 26–30, He tells them that in His kingdom worrying about these things accomplishes nothing. Instead, they must understand that just as God provides for the birds of the air and the lilies of the field, so He will provide for His disciples.

The Condition

However, there is one condition, which is found in verse 33. Christ's disciples must "seek first his kingdom and his righteousness." When this is the case, He promises, in return, to take care of His disciples' personal needs. The word "needs" is very important. The Savior is promising that He will provide for our "needs" but not necessarily for our "wants."

God is committed to supplying our needs. Whether or not He supplies our wants is optional and not part of the promise. When my children were small, they would come to me or my wife and say, "I need a bicycle!" or "I need a new doll!" To make sure they understood the difference between "needs" and "wants," we would ask, "Do you really need a doll or a bicycle, or do you just want one?" They understood the difference, but usually insisted that their "wants" were truly "needs." We did the very best we could to supply their "needs," but we would attempt to provide for their "wants" only if that was best for them.

The Problems

Meeting the condition of seeking first His kingdom and His righteousness are not without certain problems.

The Problem of Our Faith

In verse 30b, the Savior points to the real problem for most of His disciples: the problem of faith. Not to accept Jesus' teaching on His promised provision is a faith issue! The Savior has addressed the matter of our personal needs. As long as we put Him first, then He has promised to provide for us. We choose to either believe or disbelieve Him! Consequently, the first issue we must face in terms of our finances is the cold, hard fact of whether we believe the Savior when it comes to His provision for our basic needs.

The Problem of Our Feelings

The second problem area is our emotions and feelings. Most Americans in general and Christians as well have become used to a lifestyle that far surpasses that of the rest of the world, especially the third world, in terms of material things. While it isn't necessarily wrong to have material things, we take them for granted. This includes even basic material things such as housing and clothing. We tend to assume or feel that we have a right to these things; indeed, for many of us, being Americans means having and enjoying these things. In *The Spirit of the Disciplines*, Dallas Willard writes the following:

> Contemporary Westerners are nurtured on the faith that everyone has a *right* to do what they want when they want, to pursue happiness in all ways possible, to feel good, and to lead a "productive and successful life," understood largely in terms of self-contentment and material well-being. This vision of life has come, in the popular mind, to be identified with "the good life," and even with civilized existence. It is taught through the popular media, political rhetoric, and the educational system as the *natural* way for life to be.[1]

The obvious problem is that this mind-set can subtly prevent us from seeking God's kingdom and righteousness *first*. Our lifestyle begins to determine what we're willing to do in service for Christ. To suggest that Christians might be avoiding a particular ministry or place of ministry because it poses a change in lifestyle when they've subtly grown accustomed to that lifestyle is a very emotional matter. Most often they become both frightened and very angry.

Consequently, those who desire to pursue ministry, whether church planting or some other area, must take the time to think through the implications of Christ's teachings on this issue. In Matthew 6:25–34, He promises to provide for our needs, but not necessarily for our present lifestyles. However, this concept must be worked through not only cognitively, but emotionally as well. A hard, often guilt-producing question that must be asked is, "Are you pursuing a ministry or a lifestyle?" Not to do so is to enter ministry with certain expectations that may prevent Christians from putting Christ first.

This is true for anyone going into ministry. However, those coming out of a Bible college or seminary, such as Bill and Betty Smith, have an advantage over others. They've become somewhat accustomed to living on a limited income for three or four years. This is due to the amount of time they have to work and the nature of that work. Most work part-time because of the time spent in classes and studying. Seminarians are generally unable to secure higher paying, forty-hour-a-week jobs.[2] As a result, they are in a better position to live on less for the period of time it takes for a planted church to get on its "financial feet" and provide them with a regular income.

Financial Sources

While the Savior would have us trust Him to provide for our basic needs, He would also have us plan our finances (Luke 14:28–30). He uses a combination of both faith and planning in providing abundantly for our needs.[3] In planning for their finances, church planters should be aware of the various financial sources available to them.

A Mother Church

The best source is a sponsoring church, often referred to as the mother church. When a church catches a vision for starting a new work, church planters commonly refer to it as the "mother church" and the new church as the "daughter church."

The Advantages

The reason why this is the best method is because the sponsoring church already has a vision for church planting, or they wouldn't have initiated the process to begin with. Most often, this vision includes the desire to help the new church as much as possible.

Another advantage is that the sponsoring church can hold the new church accountable for those finances. In the 1990s and the twenty-first century, financial accountability will remain a priority for any ministry. The mother church has a responsibility to its people and the new church to serve in this capacity.

The Methods

There are various ways in which a "mother church" can assist a "daughter church" in providing it with finances. This could involve a one-time gift to help the new church get started. One church in the Dallas area encouraged the planting of several daughter churches and assisted them with a one-time gift of $10,000.

Another approach is to include church planting in the missions budget. Just as funds are regularly budgeted and set aside for missions, so the same can be done for new church starts. A third approach is to present the new church during a service or at a congregational meeting and encourage people to support it with their finances on an individual basis.

A Core Group

Another source of funding is the core group itself. Once a core group is established, the people involved must understand that they have a responsibility to support the new ministry as much as possible. Consequently, while the core group will provide some income for the church-planting team initially, within one to three years, they as a church should be able to assume much of the responsibility for all the team, depending on their personal finances and the church's rate of growth. Therefore, it's important that core groups discuss and commit to this before they begin the actual process of starting the church.

There are exceptions. There will be some core groups that will contribute to the ministry but may not be able to take over its full support. Some examples would be those that target special people groups such as the inner city or Muslim ministries.

Interested Friends and Acquaintances

A third source consists of interested friends and acquaintances. In general, these people know the prospective church planter and, therefore, may be predisposed to help financially in some way. In particular, this would include those who've been influenced by any prior ministry of the church planter.

These are people who already believe in the planter and often prove to be some of the best contributors. This is a very important source because an individual's ability to raise support from former constituents is often an indicator of that person's ability to plant churches.

A Denomination or Organization

A fourth source is a denomination or cooperating organization of churches. This source includes such groups as the Southern Baptists, the Nazarenes, the Assemblies of God, the Evangelical Free churches, the Christian Missionary and Alliance churches, and others.

Funding among these organizations varies from group to group. Often the Southern Baptists help with the purchase of land, the services of consultants, and the provision of demographic and psychographic services.

Others provide only limited funding or refer potential planters to member churches in their areas that might be able to lend support.

A word of caution needs to be offered at this point. First, it's unwise for any group to cover all the expenses of the new church because it's important that the church itself assume some of that responsibility. Otherwise it will remain forever tied to the sponsoring organization. Most organizations are aware of this and will help only for a limited period of time. Second, whenever an organization helps financially, there are usually "strings" attached—that's to be expected. Find out what those "strings" are, and determine if this will pose any problems.

Personal Employment

A fifth source is personal employment on the part of the church planter. Of all the options, this is the least preferable because it limits the time the planter can give to the new ministry. However, in a team context this may be unavoidable initially. This personal employment has several possibilities.

One is that of a "tentmaker." In this situation, church planters turn to a particular trade or profession only when there aren't enough funds available for their support. They may work one week and be off the next. The advantage is that they can determine when and how long they work. A good example of this would be Paul. He periodically used his talents as an actual tentmaker to provide for his personal needs. He was able to schedule work around his ministry. (This is how we got the term "tentmaker.")

Another kind of personal employment is the bivocational minister. In this situation, church planters find regular employment that occupies a certain portion of their time every week. The disadvantage of a bivocational ministry is that the ministry has to be scheduled around the particular job.

Another possibility is the employment of a spouse. A wife may work full-time to support her husband until the church can assume their support or they start a family.

It should be stressed that any outside employment on the part of the church-planting team must be viewed as temporary. Like most other ministries, church planting is a full-time responsibility. Anything less will hinder the work of this ministry.

The Sale of Existing Church Properties and Facilities

I noted in chapter 2 that a number of churches across North America are plateaued and many are in decline. One major reason for this is that they are located in older, gospel-resistant neighborhoods. A growing number of these churches have sold their property and facilities and used the funds to position themselves or others in a new, growing area as a church plant. Older, struggling churches who find themselves in this or a similar position should strongly consider this alternative.

Financial Principles

There are several important, practical financial principles that will help church planters in their efforts to raise funds. Three of them are negative and focus on what distracts or even alienates some potential contributors. The last two are positive and aid in knowing what attracts potential givers.

Givers Don't Like to Pay the Bills

Most contributors don't like to give funds to pay the bills. For example, they're not moved by appeals to contribute in order to pay for salaries, the electricity bill, or the mortgage. The problem they have with paying salaries is that they sense the potential for their funds to be used for "wants" and not "needs." Paying the electricity bill or the mortgage, though necessary, isn't very glamorous!

Contributors may be willing to help in other areas. For example, they like to give toward facilities where ministry takes place. Consequently, they'll give toward church buildings or libraries. They'll also contribute toward things that can be used to accomplish ministry such as Bibles, sound equipment, and lighting.

Givers Don't Respond Well to Guilt or Negativism

Potential givers don't respond well, if at all, to guilt and negativism. While they may give once or even twice, intelligent people resent this kind of approach and will not give long-term to ministries that use this tactic.

Actually, this is a wise, biblical response because Scripture warns against giving under these circumstances. In 2 Corinthians 9:7, Paul writes, "Each man should give what he has decided in his heart to give, not reluctantly or under compulsion, for God loves a cheerful giver." Appeals based on guilt or negativism often fall under compulsion and, consequently, are questionable at best.

Givers Don't Respond Well to Needs

Most contributors don't like to give to meet needs. This is because need motivates negatively. For many, the appeal to need is comparable to investing in businesses that are in the "red." As someone once said, "If need motivated giving, then everyone would be givers."

Regardless, many Christian organizations aren't aware of this principle and continue to appeal for funds primarily on the basis of their needs. Most people like to hear good news, not constant negative reports that conclude with a strong appeal based on present needs.

Givers Respond to Visions

The key to giving is a dynamic vision. Most contributors don't give regularly to meet needs; they give regularly to significant, dynamic visions that meet needs. In general, people enjoy spending money, and they're willing to spend it on something they feel is of significance. But what brings a sense of significance to a ministry? The answer is a well-cast vision.

Consequently, in the early stages of starting a church, visionary church planters must spend a significant amount of time cultivating and communicating a dynamic vision.[4] If the envisioning process is done well, then it catches people's attention more than the ministry needs no matter how dire. And, most often, the bigger the vision, the bigger the investment.

Givers Respond to Big Visions

The key to giving is a big, dynamic vision. The Savior cast a big vision in Matthew 28:19–20 when He commissioned His church to reach the entire world. In Ephesians 3:20, Paul gently admonishes the Ephesian church for not asking and thinking big enough.

For some reason, far too many Christians are low on vision. Perhaps some suffer from low self-esteem and feelings of insignificance. They feel that they're not worthy of anyone's support. They ask, "Why would anyone want to support me?" Others have a temperament that focuses more on present realities than future possibilities.

Church planters need to think big and cast big visions because they have a big God who wants to accomplish big things through them. Most knowledgeable givers understand this and want to give to ministries that desire to have a significant impact for the Savior.

Financial Provision

While fund-raising will not be necessary for all who go into church planting, it will affect many. Often the ability to raise funds for ministry is indicative of a past lifestyle of sacrificial ministry to people and is predictive of future success in church planting. People who've been ministered to by a servant of God are not quick to forget and usually are open to investing in their future ministries. Also, raising funds has the potential to free the church planter's time that might otherwise be occupied by full- or part-time employment in the secular world.

Presently, there isn't a lot of information available to help in terms of how to raise funds for personal and/or ministry support. There are two areas that must be discussed in covering the topic of fund-raising—whether for ministry in general or church planting in particular.

The Problems of Fund-raising

The Problem of Pride

Personal pride is a problem for most Americans for reasons that relate to the average American lifestyle and what we've come to expect as the way life should be.

A part of this is a sense of independence. There is great personal satisfaction in believing that we don't need anyone else because we can take care of ourselves. We're not used to asking others for help, especially in the area of finances. Actually, this attitude often is indicative of a sense of intense pride and a lack of dependence on God—which is sin! This problem area must be dealt with before commencing any work for Him.

The Problem of Fear

Another problem is fear. Some people aren't proud, but are too afraid to ask for support. Most don't like to be turned down for emotional reasons. They take this as personal rejection, which proves to be a very painful blow to self-worth.

This, too, is an area that needs to receive attention before starting a ministry because it may indicate a deeper emotional problem. We must realize that we can feel good about ourselves regardless of whether others accept us or are able to support us financially. Our self-worth has already been established through the grace of God in Jesus Christ. We have worth and are valuable because God has created us in His image and has totally and eternally accepted us through Jesus Christ (Rom. 5:10). Consequently, we must not be afraid to ask God's people for money to support God's work.

The Practice of Fund-raising

The Contacts

We don't know whom God will motivate to help us financially. Therefore, it's extremely important to have a large number of people to contact. This involves networking (John 1:40, 43–44). Many of us forget that over the years we have developed a large network of ministry friends and acquaintances. These people, in turn, also have a large number of Christian friends and acquaintances. Initially, all of these people can become our contacts for developing a support team.

The prospective church planter should begin to list all these names well in advance of starting the church and continue to add the names of new friends and acquaintances to that list. As the opportunity arises, planters should begin to cast their visions with these people, for God may use such vision casting to gain their initial attention and interest. When the time comes to raise support, there will already be a broad potential base of support available to harvest for advancing the kingdom.

The Conversation

Eventually, visionary church planters will begin to contact potential supporters. Initially, this will be done by telephone, especially if the network is large. It is necessary to develop a phone message that will communicate the essential information pleasantly and concisely.[5] The following procedure is recommended:

1. *Determine the goal in the initial phone conversation.* This could include three things. One is to inform the person of your vision and the fact that you are starting a church to implement this vision. Another is to explain that you're developing a financial support team to help initially in accomplishing this ministry. The last is to ask for an appointment to give more information about the ministry and its costs.

   A possible variation of this format would be to write a letter in which you explain your vision and ministry and the fact that you'll be following up the letter shortly with a phone call to answer any questions. When you call, you would answer questions and explain that you're developing a support team to help start the church. Then you could ask for an appointment to give more information about the ministry and its costs.

2. *In the initial phone conversation, communicate the essential information that people need to know regarding why you want to meet with them.* Save most of the conversation for the time when you're with them in person. Attempt to get as much personal time with them as possible. The better they know you, the greater the chance that they'll support you.

3. *Develop two phone conversations: one for people you know and another for people you don't know.* The following is a sample phone conversation designed by Dallas Seminary church planters for use with someone they don't know:

Hello, Mr./Mrs. _____. My name is _____. I'm a recent graduate of Dallas Seminary, and God has placed on my heart a significant vision to move to _____ and start a church for people who don't like church. Currently, I'm in the process of putting together a support team of people who might share this vision and desire to be a vital part of this ministry. _____ suggested that I call you because he/she thought you might be interested in what the Lord has put on my heart and learning more about a church designed to reach the nonchurched. I'm not asking you to make any kind of commitment now, only to get together with you at your convenience to explain the ministry to you. Would that be possible? What would be a good time for you?

A phone conversation with someone you already know should be more personal. You should talk about whatever is appropriate, depending on the nature of your relationship. Include a brief discussion of your vision and how you came to adopt it. You may want to address the area of financial support in more detail than you would with someone you don't know. It's helpful to provide additional details and allow your friend to interact and ask more questions over the phone. Even if you know someone well, it adds a personal touch when you follow up and meet with him or her personally.

4. *Prepare an attractive, well-designed brochure.* You may send it to the people who desire to meet with you and to those who don't but show some interest in the church. In this brochure, demonstrate through research and demographics why you're planting the church. Identify your target group and their need for the gospel. Present your core values, mission, vision, and strategy to accomplish the mission

and vision. (I cover these concepts in chapter 14.) Next, using mini-biographical statements, introduce your team and explain their qualifications and what part they'll play in accomplishing the vision. Finally, include a brief but clear budget that presents your plans and financial needs. Make sure the document is visually attractive. If necessary, invest some time and sufficient funds in working with a professional to develop the document. If you're not able to develop a quality piece of material, then it would be best not to use anything at all.

Should you send this brochure, include a personal handwritten note or letter explaining that you're forming a financial support team, and you'll visit them in a week or so to see if they have any questions and would like to become involved.

5. *When you meet with interested people, make sure they understand the vision.* Initially, after some introductory greetings and small talk, you may want to answer any questions they might have. However, you'll want to ask a few questions yourself that focus on the vision in order to determine if they understand it. Most likely, people who catch the vision will want to help in some way.

One advantage American church planters often have over cross-cultural missionaries is that they're raising support for a limited period of time, not for their lifetime. You should make this clear to those with whom you meet because it allows them to make a short-term commitment, which is much more appealing than a long-term or lifetime commitment. The idea is that the core group will grow and eventually take over each church planter's support.

In many cases, the core group should be able to take over the financial responsibility for the church planter anywhere from one to four or five years depending on the financial abilities of the people who make up the core group and the number of people on the church-planting team. I worked with one Baby Boom core group consisting of nine couples. After they had caught a vision for reaching their unchurched friends, they initially committed to provide $30,000 a year to get the church started.

6. *Finally, once you've established a support team, it's critical that you communicate with them regularly.* There are several ways to accom-

plish this. You could send your contacts a monthly letter to keep them informed as to the progress of the ministry. You could do the same with a more elaborate newsletter. If they live in the area, give them a phone call. Should you decide to use a mailer, then consider including a self-addressed envelope. Remind them periodically that by making their check payable to the new church, the Internal Revenue Service will allow this as a deduction at the end of the year.

Vision for CLPC

A Fund-raising Worksheet

1. Have you met the requirements of Matthew 6:33? Do you believe that God will take care of your needs? How might you demonstrate this belief? What would you be willing to give up in order to start a church?

2. Of the five sources for finances listed in this chapter, which are available to you? Do you have any other sources of funding that aren't listed among these five? Write them down.

3. Of the two problems in fund raising, which would characterize you?

   Pride
   Fear
   Both
   Neither

4. Make a list of any Christians you know or come in contact with who might be in a position financially to help whether you think they will or not. Include their addresses and phone numbers. Keep this list in an easily accessible place, and add names as they come to mind. This will be an important source for raising funds.

4

What You Don't Know Might Hurt You!

The Assumptions of Church Planting

At first, Bill Smith couldn't understand why one of his classmates from seminary reacted so negatively to his vision. Initially, this person had shown an interest in church planting and becoming a part of Bill's team. However, he quickly backed off when he heard Bill's vision for planting a large church. He didn't like big churches! Instead, he believed that the churches in the New Testament were small, and wasn't comfortable with the idea of planting what could be a large church. Also, he felt that Bill overemphasized the role of evangelism in church planting. He believed that there should be more emphasis on Bible knowledge. "What people need today is content!" he explained. Suddenly, Bill realized the nature of the problem. They both held different assumptions.

It's most important that those who make up a church-planting team examine their assumptions as they consider starting a church. Anyone who begins a ministry does so with certain prior practical and theological assumptions that are either consciously or subconsciously in place. These assumptions are important because they affect the initial planting of the new church and its survival. The following six assumptions will undergird all that is said about church planting in the rest of this book. These assumptions are basic and important to the planting of biblically based, Great Commission churches.

Evangelism Must Be Taken Seriously

The first assumption is that evangelicals are going to have to take evangelism seriously if they're going to plant growing churches. This seems to be a rather strange statement because evangelical churches and organizations are, after all, supposed to be evangelistic.

Churches and Schools Are Weak in Evangelism

Studies indicate that little evangelism is taking place in most American evangelical churches. George Barna states that "In the past seven years, the proportion of adults who have accepted Jesus Christ as their personal Savior (34%) has not increased."[1] Also, the fact that 80 percent to 85 percent of the churches are plateaued or declining signals a need for a greater emphasis on reaching lost people.

It's discouraging to examine the catalogs of some Christian colleges and evangelical seminaries for classes and field education work in the area of evangelism. Unfortunately, studies and fieldwork in this critical area are sadly lacking, especially in the seminaries.[2] The problem is that these institutions are training many of those who will assume key leadership positions in various church and parachurch ministries.

Those who teach in these institutions must constantly remind themselves that the three to five years that students spend in school are formative years during which they are developing the values that give shape to their future ministry. If an academic approach is valued over a practical approach during these formative years, the early ministry years will reflect this fact. The result is that pastors will spend much of their time in the study and little time with people. While schools are by nature academic institutions, they must strive to create more of a balance between the academic and the practical.

Several larger evangelistic churches have observed this tendency and have responded by discouraging prospective pastors from attending seminary. Instead, they bring the most promising people on staff and train them within the local church. While this has some advantages, it also has its disadvantages.[3]

Evangelism Accomplishes Church Growth

Church growth people indicate that there are three ways that a local church can grow numerically.

The first kind of growth is biological growth, which takes place when couples in the church have children who then become a part of their parents' church. These children grow up in the church and usually embrace Christ as their Savior as the result of the efforts of their parents and those in the church such as Sunday school teachers, vacation Bible school workers, and others. Although many drop out of their churches after high school, it's hoped that they'll continue to make the church an important part of their lives throughout the adult years.

The second kind of growth is transfer growth, which takes place as the result of people moving from one church to another. An article in *Christianity Today* indicates that in the early 1990s "more than 80 percent of all the growth taking place in growing churches comes through transfer, not conversion."[4]

Barna observes:

> Perhaps it is not surprising, then, to report that our studies of the Protestant churches that are growing the fastest are expanding primarily by incorporating people from other, declining churches. This is growth by transfer, rather than by conversion. Thus, while many churches across the nation receive attention for their explosive growth, relatively few of those churches are attracting adults who are newcomers to the faith. Most frequently, they are simply enlisting individuals who have left their existing church home to be part of the "happening" church. This is such a common behavior that an estimated 90 million adults in America have been "church shopping."[5]

The same appears to have been true in America in the 1960s and 1970s. For example, one study indicates that conservative church growth came as the result of what its authors call "a kind of circulation process, by which evangelicals move from one conservative church to another."[6]

Transfer growth can be either good or bad. In some cases, it's good. For example, some people transfer to a different church as the result of a geographical move from one part of the country to another. Others transfer when a new church locates in their neighborhood. This shortens their drive to church and allows more personal ministry to take place in their communities.

Transfer growth can be bad. There are people who transfer from one church to another because they're covering up personal sin in their lives, or they've been disciplined and asked to leave a particular church. Others habitually move from church to church each weekend, depending on their immediate personal needs or the whim of the moment. Barna notes that

> In the coming decade, however, increasing numbers of people will instead select between two and five local churches and consider those to be their

group of home churches. On any given weekend, they will determine which church to attend according to their own most keenly-felt needs, and the programs each of their favored churches has to offer. . . . Today, approximately 10 percent of adults follow this multiple home church pattern. By 2000, as much as one-quarter of all adults involved with the Christian church may be involved in this approach.[7]

The third way churches grow numerically is through conversion growth. This takes place when the church corporately or individually reaches lost people with the gospel of Christ. While most churches are generally aware of whether or not this is taking place, there's a way to determine this more accurately. A church can measure its conversion growth by determining how many of those joining the church have been won to Christ through the ministry of the church. Most believe that a conversion rate of 25 percent or higher is necessary if churches are going to make any impact in this world for the Savior.

Of the approximately 15 percent of evangelical churches that are experiencing growth today, much of it is biological or transfer growth. According to the figure cited above from *Christianity Today*, it's around 80 percent. While these may be legitimate forms of growth, the Savior had more than this in mind when in Matthew 28:19 He said, "Go and make disciples of all nations." This describes and demands conversion growth.

While a number of evangelical churches aren't very evangelistic, and some schools are weak in the area of evangelism, it's most refreshing to observe that God is sowing American soil with a number of new, biblically based evangelical churches with a Great Commission vision. Two excellent examples are Willow Creek Community Church in Barrington, Illinois, and Saddleback Valley Community Church in Mission Viejo, California. These churches have modeled for others the truth of the vision that this unchurched generation can be reached and discipled for Christ in large numbers.

Some denominations and organizations have also expressed a fresh interest in evangelism. A new criterion for success is evident in the Evangelical Free Church in America. Recently, they've announced that in the future, their success will be measured more along the lines of obedience to Christ's Great Commission. They desire to see their churches "Make disciples!"

Early in the twenty-first century, America will see the planting of a number of new, high-impact churches that will measure their success not so much by how well their people know the Scriptures (as important as that

is) or how many programs they have, but by whether or not they're making disciples. This is not to say that Bible knowledge and programs aren't
important, because they are. Bible knowledge is critical and programs are
essential in any church. But far too many of our evangelical churches have
majored in these areas to the exclusion of Christ's more comprehensive
Great Commission mandate.

Numerical Growth Is Important

The Forms of Biblical Growth

Three forms of growth are detailed in the Book of Acts. The first is spiritual growth. This takes place throughout the Book of Acts. It involves
such areas as evangelism, sound teaching, fellowship, the breaking of bread,
and prayer (Acts 2:41–42). The results can be observed in the practices
that are mentioned in verses 45–47 such as the common sharing of material possessions with the needy, meeting together for fellowship and meals,
and worship.

The second kind of growth is geographical. The key passage is Acts 1:8,
where shortly before His ascension the Savior announces, "But you will
receive power when the Holy Spirit comes on you; and you will be my witnesses in Jerusalem, and in all Judea and Samaria, and to the ends of the
earth."

Not only is this a Great Commission text, but it serves to outline the
spread of Christianity from the coming of the Holy Spirit on the day of
Pentecost to Paul's arrival in Rome. It provides a geographical outline of
the spread of Christianity as recorded in the Book of Acts. This growth
begins in Jerusalem (1:1–8:3), spreads throughout Judea and Samaria
(8:4–12:25), and then goes to the "ends of the earth," possibly Rome
(13:1–28:31).

The third kind of biblical growth is numerical growth. Luke is careful
to record the physical growth of various churches (1:13–15; 2:41; 4:4;
5:14–15; 6:1; 9:31; 11:21, 24; 14:1, 21; 16:5; 17:4, 12; 18:8, 10; 19:26;
21:20).

The first church, located in Jerusalem, was very large because about
three thousand people responded to Peter's sermon on Pentecost (Acts
2:41). Shortly thereafter, Acts 4:4 records that five thousand men
responded, not including women and children. In fact, a detailed study of
the passages listed above indicates that the churches in Acts were large
churches in terms of numbers, not small as many assume.

The Principles of Numerical Growth

All three kinds of growth were vital to the life of the first-century church and each influenced the other. Obviously, all three kinds of growth are still important to the twenty-first century church and continue to interact with one another. From this we can learn two important principles regarding numerical growth.

Don't Overemphasize or Denigrate Numerical Growth

It's wrong to either overemphasize or denigrate numerical growth. On the one hand, some larger churches place an undue emphasis on their size. They're very proud of their numbers and use them to bolster their self-esteem as well as their pride. In effect, they're playing the "numbers game" in an attempt to proclaim themselves as "spiritual king of the mountain."

On the other hand, some small churches clearly have a bias against large churches. They argue that the best churches are small churches, and tend to see themselves as some kind of spiritual remnant. They can often be overheard saying, "We may not have quantity (lots of people), but we have quality (spiritual people), and we'd prefer quality over quantity any day!" This leads to the next principle.

Quality Churches Become Quantity Churches

Quality churches don't stay small for very long. It's true that quality churches are spiritual churches. And because they're spiritual churches they're obedient to the Great Commission and are winning lost people for Christ. The result of this kind of obedience is quantity or numerical growth.

Many small churches don't have quantity because they don't have quality. They're weak in evangelism and will remain small. There are also some big churches that have quantity but are beginning to see some numerical decline because they're starting to lose their quality and aren't as active in winning lost people.

There are also some churches that are exceptions to the rule. They're small churches that serve a particular ministry niche such as the people in a small rural area or a spiritually resistant group like the Muslims in urban North America or a country like North Africa. However, the exceptions are rare, and many of our smaller churches need to re-examine their purpose for existence and initiate some kind of evangelistic thrust in their communities.

Functions Are More Important Than Forms

The third assumption is that the functions of the church (evangelism, worship, and others) are more important than its forms (how it accomplishes these ministries). This assumption is best understood by looking at an issue that is faced by every local church and the solution to that issue.

The Issue

The issue concerns whether today's evangelical churches should follow the forms as well as the functions of the New Testament church.

The Functions Plus the Forms

There are those in the church today who teach that the local church is bound to follow not only the biblical functions or principles of the early church but its forms (methods or patterns) as well. They argue that both the functions of the New Testament church and its forms related to those functions are obligatory and binding on local churches of all ages. Thus, the church is both instructed in what to do and how to do it. They believe that "apostolic precept is apostolic practice" or "God's work done in God's way will receive God's blessing."

An example would be when the church meets. They would argue that the local church should meet on Sunday because of the significance of the first day of the week and because it was the practice of some apostolic churches (possibly Troas—Acts 20:7) to meet on the first day of every week. Most would argue that other meetings such as Sunday school class or a singles' fellowship are permitted by Scripture as long as they don't interfere with the prescribed Sunday meeting of the church.

The Functions But Not the Forms

There are others who believe that the church is bound only to follow the scriptural mandates of the early church but not its practices or patterns for the latter are cultural and relative. For example, they would argue that when the church meets in terms of the day, time of day, or how long it meets isn't as important as the fact that it does meet and what happens when it does. They would also cite Romans 14:5–12.

The Solution

The latter view is the best solution to this issue. The key here is hermeneutics. The twenty-first-century church is bound to follow the prescriptive passages of the Bible (commands, prohibitions, and so forth), not the descriptive passages (such as those found in Acts 20:7 or 1 Cor. 16:2).[8] This affects the local church in terms of its liberty and relevance.

The Emphasis Is Liberty

The Scriptures appear to grant Christians a great deal of liberty in terms of *how* they do *what* they do and *when* they do it. While the patterns and practices of the apostolic church may be instructive and helpful, Scripture doesn't teach that some or all of these patterns are binding on the church throughout the ages.

Certainly, Sunday has significance for the Christian, but the early church met at various times throughout the week in different contexts for different reasons. We find in Acts 2:46 and 5:42 that the Jerusalem church held daily meetings in such places as the temple or various homes. The church at Corinth was instructed to set aside certain funds on the first day of the week (1 Cor. 16:1–2). However, this doesn't mean that they were bound to have the meeting of the church at this time. Romans 14:5–6 teaches that the church is free to choose when it meets. Consequently, we can see that it's very difficult even to determine the practices of the early church (such as when they met), much less to attempt to hold twenty-first-century churches to them.

The Result Is Relevance

God's intent was probably to instruct us in *what* we're to do, but He also gives us much liberty in *how* and *when* we're to do it. This allows the church to remain relevant to its particular culture, whether it's the first century or the twenty-first century, whether it's located in North America, South America, or the Middle East. Otherwise, it finds itself, much like the Amish, attempting to limit its practices to a particular time and culture such as the eighteenth century.

Scripture is delightfully refreshing when it comes to the forms (practices and patterns) of local churches. It gives each one the freedom to make itself relevant to its unique culture in terms of what it does. The reason is that it takes different kinds of churches to reach different kinds of people. Thus, our churches must constantly evaluate what they're doing in light of the culture and times in which they live. (They are to contextualize the culture, not accommodate or isolate themselves from the culture.) I believe that every pastor and church must develop a biblically based theology of culture that will direct their response to culture.

Whether we realize it or not, each church has its own unique culture. This isn't necessarily bad. Culture, in general, is neutral. (Adam and Eve lived in and with culture before the Fall. Also, see what Paul says about an item of culture–food—in Rom. 14:14–18.) Culture may be used for good or bad (James 3:9–10). Many older churches reflect the culture that surrounded them some thirty or forty years ago and clearly aren't in touch with the culture around them now. The result is that the unchurched lost in our present culture see this and reject the biblical beliefs of these churches because they sense that they're out of touch with reality and what's taking place in the world. They know a dinosaur when they see one!

We Must Pursue Excellence in Ministry

The fourth assumption that undergirds this book is that church planters must pursue excellence, not mediocrity, in ministry.

The Problem of Mediocrity

Far too many churches today don't pay enough attention to how well they do what they do. Consequently, they are maintaining ministry mediocrity.

Mediocrity Affects Ministry

This problem applies to various important areas of the church. One example would be the worship service. Characteristically, worship is poorly planned and poorly executed, especially in small churches.

I recall in one such church that a young lady stood up to sing a special song with her guitar. However, she had to stop in the middle of the song to tune her guitar because she had not done so prior to the service. So we all sat and watched and listened as she tuned the guitar. Once this was accomplished, she completed the rest of the song—only it was off key!

Another example would be the appearance of the church facilities where much ministry takes place. Many churches seem to forget that if they don't properly and regularly maintain their facilities, they'll deteriorate. It has to do with one of the laws of thermodynamics. As these facilities grow older, the problem becomes more acute. Consequently, leaks develop in the roof, the paint begins to peel, the sink in one of the bathrooms is hopelessly stopped up, and the nursery is not cleaned properly.

Mediocrity Affects People

Mediocrity affects two particular groups of people: the members and the visitors.

The members. Over a period of time, many church members grow accustomed to the above practices and conditions and don't really notice them anymore. As far as they're concerned, everything is fine. While they don't exactly prefer this situation, many have given in to the fact that "that's just the way it is around here." Others are more aware of the problem. While they've learned to live with the problems, they're constantly aware of them and are too embarrassed to invite any of their friends to church.

The visitors. The other group consists of those who visit the church, in particular, the unchurched lost. Many of these are people who live and work in a world that has come to expect nothing short of excellence. They work in facilities that are well maintained, and attend events that are well designed and programmed because the competition in the marketplace is so intense. These are people who are not impressed with and will not respond to mediocrity! Consequently, they attend church one time and never return because they've been convinced through ministry mediocrity that Christianity is second-class. If it's not worthy of the best efforts of those who profess it, then it's not worthy of further consideration by those who are curious.

If we're to ever reach these people for the Savior, we must begin to recognize the fact that the conditions of our facilities do, in fact, say something about those who worship there. We must also become aware that what we do sends a loud message about the hearts and attitudes of those who perform in such a manner. It's time for a change!

The Solution to Mediocrity

The solution to mediocrity is excellence. God desires that His church excel in its ministries in His behalf. Whatever we do for the Savior must be done well because we do it for Him and in His name. Mediocrity and Christianity must never be mentioned in the same breath. The two must never be associated.

The Biblical Documentation

But is this biblical? Scripture clearly teaches a theology of excellence. Its principles are found in both the Old and New Testaments.

A theology of excellence is found in the Old Testament. God wanted His people to give only their best when they worshiped Him. Thus, Moses instructed Israel to bring the best animals as a sacrifice to God (Lev. 22:20–22; Num. 18:29–30). It's important to note that when their hearts began to wander away from the Lord, it was reflected in their worship. Thus, in Malachi 1:8, the prophet warns, "When you bring blind animals for sacrifice, is that not wrong? When you sacrifice crippled or diseased animals, is that not wrong? Try offering them to your governor! Would he be pleased with you? Would he accept you? says the LORD Almighty."

We find the pursuit of excellence in the New Testament as well. In Ephesians 6:5–8 and Colossians 3:23–24, Paul tells us that God expects us to give our best in our work and to do it as if we're working for Him. We discover that even at the judgment seat of Christ we'll ultimately be judged according to the "quality" of our works (1 Cor. 3:13). The point is that our God gave His very best when he gave His Son for us. Consequently, He doesn't expect mediocrity in return.

The Need for Clarification

This doesn't mean that God expects Christians to be perfect and that there's no room for failure in any Christian endeavor. The key is to ask why we failed when we fail. If we tried our very best, but failed because of our less than perfect humanity, then this is understandable. For example, if a soloist practiced hard all week for a special song, yet fails to perform well on Sunday morning, then this is understandable. We all have bad days, no matter how hard we work! That's the nature of our humanity. However, it would not be acceptable if she didn't bother to practice at all during the week and then failed to sing well on Sunday morning. This is ministry mediocrity; this is offering up crippled and diseased animals to God!

The Importance of Evaluation

The key to the pursuit of excellence in ministry is constant evaluation. The most effective, relevant churches regularly and intensely evaluate how they "do church." The pastor's sermons are evaluated; the worship service is evaluated. This shows a healthy spiritual concern that Christ be honored in all the church does in His name before a lost but ruthlessly critical world.

God Wants People of Strong Faith

God desires to minister through men and women of strong faith who are willing to trust Him for big things.

The Importance of Faith

If we were to ask what kinds of things impressed the Savior when He walked the earth, we'd have to conclude that He was impressed by men and women of strong faith! Jesus constantly commended people for their faith (Matt. 8:10; 15:28), and even healed some according to their faith

(Matt. 9:2, 22, 29). His constant complaint regarding his disciples was their lack of faith. As we read of His ministry to them, the words "you of little faith" constantly ring in our ears (Matt. 6:30; 8:26; 14:31; 16:8; Mark 9:14–29).

The Examples of Faith

Hebrews 11 is instructive in terms of the importance of our faith. Repeatedly, the author encourages us with various cameo appearances of people of great faith. Initially he warns in verse 6 that "without faith it is impossible to please God." Then he illustrates this point using the lives of Noah and Abraham in verses 7–8.

Noah's great faith is seen in the fact that he believed God to the extent that he was willing to build a huge ark even though it hadn't even rained. We can only imagine what it must have been like trying to explain what he was doing to all of his neighbors! Abraham's faith is demonstrated in the fact that he was willing to believe God to the extent that he packed his bags and moved his family even though he had no idea where he was going. We can only imagine what it must have been like to attempt to explain his actions to his friends and family, including those who were believers in the Old Testament sense.

The Lesson of Faith

What church planters can learn from all this is that nothing of any spiritual significance is accomplished outside of faith. It's imperative that church planters be men and women of faith who are willing to trust God for big things in their lives and ministries. What Christ has commissioned His church to accomplish requires tremendous faith, for in Matthew 28:19–20 He's asked us to win the world!

The question we must ask is, "What can He accomplish through us?" Perhaps an even better question is, "What can't He accomplish through men and women of faith who are willing to trust Him to do big things?" We've already seen that Paul warns the Ephesian church against asking and thinking too small (Eph. 3:20). Asking and thinking too small is a sign of a small faith. As we, the church of Jesus Christ, minister in the twenty-first century, we need to realize that our esteem and significance are found not in our accomplishments or relationships but in the grace of God through Jesus Christ. And, therefore, we will begin to push ourselves beyond our protective comfort zones to attempt big things for our big God.

God Uses Courageous Christians

In ministry God uses courageous men and women who are willing to risk failure.

The Problem of Failure

We must be willing to fail in order to succeed. Yet far too many of our people who go into ministry are afraid of failure! They'll not attempt big things for God because they're afraid of what people will think if they fail. I'm convinced this was a part of Moses' problem in Exodus 3:11–14.

This is an alarming sign of a deep problem in the area of self-esteem and significance. However, as we understand better the grace of God in our lives through Jesus Christ we'll learn to value ourselves properly and discover our infinite value in Christ.[9] Consequently, we'll be able to develop a biblical understanding of failure.

The Solution to Failure

Quite simply, we must not be so afraid of failure. Of all God's prohibitions in the Bible, the Savior's words "fear not" seem to stand out the most.

The Response

The best response to failure is twofold. First, we must realize that risk and failure are inherent in any successful work for God. They go hand in hand. There is not a single successful church today that didn't take risks and experience failure along the way. Often people in ministry are afraid to take risks because they're afraid they may fail. However, not to take risks is to fail!

Second, it's important to realize that obeying God always involves an element of risk. In Acts 15:25–26, Luke notes that the Jerusalem Council sent out with Barnabas and Paul not just any men but "men who have risked their lives for the name of our Lord Jesus Christ." In the parable of the talents (Matt. 25:14–30), the Savior soundly condemns the one who is afraid to take risks and takes from him that which had been entrusted to him. Then He proceeds to honor and reward those who were willing to risk failure.

The Examples

Both the Scriptures and recent history provide numerous examples of people who took risks and endured failure to accomplish great things.

This was true of such biblical personalities as Abraham, Moses, David, and Peter. In Genesis 12, Abraham took a risk. Essentially, he obeyed God and stepped out in faith not knowing where he was going. Moses also took a risk when he defied the pharaoh and led Israel out of Egypt.

The same has been true of certain personalities in the twentieth century. For example, Babe Ruth is known in the baseball world for his record-setting number of home runs. The truth is that he struck out 1,330 times but hit 714 home runs in between. It has been reported that he once said, "Never let the fear of striking out keep you from taking a swing at the ball!" Thomas Edison experimented with numerous filaments before he found the right combination and invented the electric lightbulb. R. H. Macy failed in the retail business several times before he became a success.

The Lesson

We must not glamorize those who take foolish risks or habitually make the same mistakes throughout life. However, risk is not necessarily bad, as long as you know the risks and are willing to assume them. All good leaders, no matter what their profession, learn from their mistakes. The key is that leaders are always learning, and they learn from their mistakes as well as from their successes.

The problem is that just as there are people in ministry who are afraid to fail, so there are churches that don't tolerate failure. If ministers risk making a few mistakes, some established churches will begin to question their leadership credibility. This is another plus for planting churches. The key to starting a church is to create an environment where there's room for failure. According to Robert Metcalfe, chairperson of 3COM, innovation "'requires gambling and risk taking. We tell our folks to make at least ten mistakes a day. If they're not making ten mistakes a day, they're not trying hard enough.'"[10]

It's imperative that church planters prepare the soil before they sow the seed. Thus, we must know what it is we're doing and why we want to do it. We must also think through how we'll finance the venture and be aware of certain critical assumptions that will affect our ultimate success. Once this is accomplished, the next step is to make sure that God has designed us to start churches. This will involve us in the new and developing area of personal assessment, which the next section of this book discusses.

An Assumptions Worksheet

1. What are some of the key assumptions that you bring to the ministry of church planting?

2. Which of the six assumptions in this chapter do you agree with? Which do you disagree with? Why?

3. List some of the effects that your assumptions could have on the kind of church you would plant.

Part 2

The Personnel of Church Planting

Not only must farmers prepare the soil before they plant; they must also decide if they're farmers. Not everyone comes into this world with a "green thumb." Those who do, grow great gardens and enjoy it. Those who don't may grow great gardens but don't enjoy it. The latter need to discover the true color of their thumbs and involve themselves accordingly. Since his initial gardening experience in our backyard, my son has discovered that his thumb is of another color.

The same is true for church planters. The fact that you have an interest in starting new churches may or may not indicate you're a church planter. There are several ways to find out. The first is experimental. It involves making an attempt at planting a church. After a year or two, you'll know if you're a church planter. The question is whether the price you and others could pay is worth the experiment.

Another is to determine the nature of your divine design. This involves assessment, which is done before you attempt to start a church and can save you and others a lot of grief. The next few chapters will help you to determine how God has designed you and whether or not you should pursue church planting or some other area of ministry.

5

Understanding Who You Are

The Preparation for Assessment

One of the reasons Bill Smith responded so quickly and eagerly to the ministry of church planting was because the professor took his class through an assessment program. Bill knew within his spirit that God wanted him in the pastoral ministry. He had thought about teaching and possibly some form of parachurch ministry, but every time God had a way of turning Bill's thoughts back to the pastorate. Yet, when Bill dwelt on this, he always felt a sense of vagueness. He couldn't figure it out. Something was missing!

It was the assessment that brought to life the missing ingredient—especially the part where Bill examined his past experiences to see if there were any discernible patterns that could help him determine his future. It didn't take him long to recall his catalytic, entrepreneurial past. He was always starting things! In high school, he had started his own business. During the summer he and several friends operated a lawn care service. The business grew and did so well that Bill sold it when he went to college. At the university, he began a Bible study because there were no active ministries for students on or off campus. This ministry prospered and was eventually turned over to a national parachurch organization. Even at seminary, Bill began a neighborhood Bible study in his home that God used to attract a sizable number of unchurched lost people from the community.

There are several fundamental questions that anyone who desires to plant a church must ask. An obvious one that's often missed is, "Am I a church planter?" One of the best ways to answer the question is through assessment. In light of the fact that personal and ministry assessment is new to most Christians, whether laypersons or professionals, this chapter is intended to orient prospective church planters to this ministry. It will provide a window for them to look into their soul.[1] It will serve to prepare them for the next chapter, where we'll practice some assessment and attempt to answer the question, "Am I a church planter?" I have also written the book *Maximizing Your Effectiveness* (Baker Book House), which focuses totally on the divine design concept for those who wish to explore this concept and their own designs more fully.

The Value of Assessment

There are two ways that assessment can be of value to those who are either considering or are already involved in professional Christian ministry. One is personal and the other is organizational.

The Personal Value of Assessment

When prospective church planters go through a good assessment program, they benefit in several ways.

Knowing Who We Are

One benefit is *discovering* who we are, which naturally results in *knowing* who we are. Some people are initially afraid of personal assessment because in the past they've taken psychological tests that are designed to uncover any psychological abnormality or dysfunctional behavior. This can be a frightening and disconcerting experience. While there's an analytical side to assessment that is often associated with the field of psychological counseling, there's a positive side as well. Not only can we discover what's wrong with us, but we can discover what's right with us. The former concerns our depravity; the latter, our dignity. And it's the latter that represents the positive side of knowing who we are.

This positive side involves probing how God has designed us—our "divine design." Secularists often argue that we come into this world like pieces of clay in terms of who we are, and that our families and other forces in the environment act as potters to shape and mold our personalities. The problem with this view is that it strips us of personal responsibility. Consequently, when people habitually sin or even commit a heinous crime, it's not so much their fault as that of their parents or society in general.

At the time we're born, much of our divine design is already in place. Assessment helps us in knowing who we are by aiding in the discovery of this design. This is a very positive and exciting experience because we're probing God's sovereign and unique makeup of us as His special image bearers.

Liking Who We Are

A second personal benefit that is the result of *knowing* who we are is *liking* who we are. There are far too many Christians who struggle with poor self-esteem because when they look in a mirror they don't like what they see, or they continually evaluate themselves only in terms of the imprint of the flesh on their lives. The result is that they don't like themselves very much.

Yet Scripture speaks of loving ourselves in a positive light in such passages as Ephesians 5:28–29, 33. A vital key to loving ourselves biblically is liking ourselves, and liking ourselves is facilitated through assessment. Again, probing God's makeup of us reveals in a very positive way certain gifts, talents, and abilities we may not have been aware of. We begin to discover not what we're "bad at," but what we're "good at." We realize that there are some things that we enjoy doing because we were designed to do them well.

Being Who We Are

A third personal benefit is that *liking* who we are results in *being* who we are. People who don't like who they are often attempt to be someone else. They put on masks and play roles so that others will not discover their real identity. They fear that if people know them as they really are, they'll not like them and will reject them. And the pain from this would be unbearable and must be avoided at all costs.

However, when we discover who we are in Christ, and how God has individually designed us to contribute in a wonderful way to His kingdom work, we become authentic. We take off our masks and stop playing fictitious roles because we're no longer ashamed of what God has made. And this, in time, gets better because we discover a new freedom and liberty in Christ that we may never have experienced or even been aware of. In John 8:32, Christ says that truth has a freeing effect. The truth of knowing who Christ has made us to be frees us to be special persons.

The Organizational Value of Assessment

Assessment can be of immense value to ministry organizations and those in them. When a particular ministry organization understands the divine design of those who minister in it, the ministry as a whole will function more effectively. As we'll discover later, New Testament ministry is team ministry. But the object of a team is to minister well together. That's one of the reasons why the New Testament compares the body of Christ to the human body. A healthy human body is well coordinated, with each member performing its unique part for the benefit of the entire body (Eph. 4:16).

The problem is that when it comes to working with people, this analogy often breaks down. We've all experienced the ecstasy of working on a good team and the agony of working on a bad one. As in athletics, it's critical that we get the right players in the right positions if we expect to accomplish meaningful ministry. If in football, we place a potential quarterback at the offensive tackle position, the results will be disastrous for the team.

A good program of ministry assessment will result in effective teamwork. One aspect of this program is to determine what it is we want to accomplish in a ministry, and then to recruit someone who fits this position. Assessment helps locate the right person for the position. Another approach begins with the person rather than the position. First, the individual is assessed, and then the ministry is designed around the individual.

We attempt to do it both ways in church planting. We realize that we need certain positions in order to accomplish ministry. At the same time, it's fascinating to assess the people whom God has sent our way to discover the unique designs that He's sovereignly brought together. This, of course, is what contributes to the uniqueness of each church. It's imperative that we understand this and use it to further Christ's kingdom.

The Purpose of Assessment

Why would we want to implement an assessment program in a church or parachurch ministry such as a Christian college or seminary? Not only are there personal and organizational benefits, but there's a specific purpose for doing so.

To Discover Our Divine Design

Personal assessment enables us to discover our divine design. The general concept of divine design was discussed in the previous section. Here, two factors in particular will be the focus.

Everyone Has a Design from God

God is the author and source of our makeup long before we're born into this world (Job 10:8–9; Ps. 139:15–16; Isa. 49:1, 5; Jer. 1:5; Luke 1:15; 1 Cor. 12:18; Gal. 1:15).

Our divine design includes such things as our temperaments and our natural gifts, talents, and abilities. When we accept Christ, God adds to this other things as well, including our spiritual gifts. All of this constitutes our divine design or makeup, our special "wiring" or "chemistry."

Each Design Is Unique

While Christians may have similar designs, no two Christians have the same design. One way to view this concept is to think of the divine design as a "divine thumbprint." This emphasizes both its source and uniqueness. The source of the design is from the Creator-Designer. The uniqueness of the design can be compared to a human thumbprint. While each of us has a thumb print, and some prints are very close in appearance, none are exactly alike. And much the same is true of us as divine thumbprints. Realizing this can be very helpful when we're tempted to compare ourselves with other Christians and wish that we were like them.

To Develop a Personal Ministry Mission Statement

Personal assessment helps us develop a personal ministry mission statement or "ministry niche." Once we've discovered who we are (our design), the next step is to take that information and use it to determine what we can do or what God has designed us to do in terms of ministry.

Personal Ministry Mission and God's "Call"

Some accurately refer to this process as discovering God's will or "calling" for our lives. Often Christians agonize as they attempt to discover God's will in a particular situation or for the direction of their lives in general. Most often, God's will is found in His Word, the Scriptures. The same agonizing takes place in determining God's will for our lives in terms of future ministry.

Here, God's will or "calling" can be found both in His Word and in how He's designed us. In other words, God's call for our lives can to a great extent be detected by His design of our lives. If, for example, He's given us the gifts of leadership, faith, and evangelism coupled with an entrepreneurial spirit and a love for ministry in the local church, He may be directing or calling us to become church planters.

Personal Ministry Mission and Significance

All of us want to feel that what we're doing in life has significance, that our time in this life is going to count for the kingdom, and that when we die our lives will have made a difference. When we die, we want our epitaph to read like David's: "For when David had served God's purpose in his own generation, he fell asleep" (Acts 13:36). We want the joy of knowing that we've served God's purpose in our generation!

When these feelings are missing, people are affected deeply and adversely. Along with feelings of self-worth, a sense of significance is critical to our emotional health. Consequently, an important purpose of assessment is to help believers discover their ministry "fit" in terms of their personal ministry mission. This in turn enhances a sense of significance.

To Design a Personal Training Plan

Personal assessment helps us design a training plan. This involves a pattern and some possibilities.

The Pattern

Many people who decide to pursue professional ministry start at the end rather than at the beginning. For example, in the past, people attended seminary after making a decision to pursue professional ministry as a vocation. Today, more students are using seminary as a vehicle to determine if they should pursue ministry as a vocation.

This way of doing things puts the proverbial cart way out in front of the horse. The order is important. What is the proper pattern? It involves three steps: design, direction, and development. First, we discover who we are (our unique ministry design). Next, we determine what we can do in light of who we are (our ministry direction or mission). The last step is to design a training plan (ministry development) that will enable us to prepare for our ministry direction in light of our design.

The Possibilities

This tailor-made equipping plan includes several possibilities. Obviously, we can attend a school that will provide the academic preparation we need for ministry. This is one of the reasons God has raised up Bible colleges, Christian liberal arts colleges, and seminaries. The plan would dictate a specific major or ministry track and what electives are taken. In addition, this possibility should include formal and informal continuing education programs as well as seminars and conferences.

Another possibility is involvement in a church or parachurch organization that provides personal ministry experience. Those in academics attempt to accomplish this through Christian service assignments or internships. In general, there are those who believe this learning experience is superior to attending a school.

The Importance of Assessment

Assessment is important because it helps us know ourselves in terms of our strengths, limitations, and weaknesses.

Strengths

In the past, unfortunately, there's been too much emphasis on people's weaknesses. This was probably due to the early development of the fields of psychology and psychiatry. For example, my first exposure to the field of ministry assessment was as a faculty member with a group of students. An assessor asked all of us certain questions privately. I can remember how nervous I felt. I didn't understand; I was thinking pathologically not positively. This was because one graduate school that I'd attended used the *MMPI* (*Minnesota Multiphasic Personality Inventory*) as a tool in the admissions process to help in discerning dysfunctional applicants. I assumed this was going to be a similar process. I thought that the assessor was going to "tell all," and I'd be horribly embarrassed. This didn't take place. Not only was I not embarrassed, but when he finished, I wanted him to go on! I felt good about my "chemistry" and how God had "wired" me.

It's helpful and healthy to know what's good about us, to identify our gifts, passions, and temperaments. There's much strength in knowing our strengths as well as our weaknesses.

Limitations

A Clarification

Limitations are the gifts, talents, and abilities we *don't* have as a part of our makeup.[2] Since God in His sovereignty has decided not to give us these "tools," we are limited when we attempt to accomplish ministry that calls for them.

This doesn't mean it's wrong to use them or that we should attempt to avoid them entirely. What it means is that we're going to be somewhat limited when we attempt to use them in ministry. This also means that most likely we'll not derive as much satisfaction from their use. For example, we may not have the gift of evangelism. However, God desires that we share the gospel anyway. We'll not do it as effectively nor may we enjoy it as much as someone who has that gift, but we share our faith regardless.

The Advantages

Knowing our limitations can help us in our ministry in two ways.

Avoiding ministry burnout. First, we can avoid potential ministry burnout. If we should become involved in a ministry that primarily calls for a different mix of gifts or a different temperament, over a period of time we will most likely experience burnout. We should spend at least 60 percent or more of our time in the areas of our strengths. When we spend less than 60 percent, the chances of burnout increase proportionately. Obviously 100 percent involvement isn't possible because there's no perfect ministry, nor is it wise to attempt to do so.

Achieving maximum ministry effectiveness. Knowing our limitations helps us work toward maximum ministry effectiveness. By knowing what we don't do well, we can focus more on what we do well. This should also help us know when to say, "No." For example, if a ministry was seeking a staff evangelist, and someone approached you about the position, you could say "no" based on the fact that you're not gifted for the position. This doesn't mean you wouldn't continue to share your faith as much as possible. It does mean that your "no" response would allow you to pursue your area of giftedness to maximize your ministry efforts.

Weaknesses

A final reason why assessment is important is that it will uncover weaknesses. The term "limitations" refers to certain gifts, abilities, and temperaments that are outside our divine makeup. The term "weaknesses" refers primarily to negative character traits that are present in all of our lives to some extent. If not discovered and dealt with, these "emotional splinters" will work their way to the surface and cause us much pain in relating to others in both our public ministries and our private lives. Most in the field of assessment are of the opinion that we can't change our designs nor should we want to. However, we can change our negative character qualities and should attempt to do so with God's help. This is what Romans 6–8 is all about.

While the primary intent of assessment is not to uncover character flaws, nevertheless this should be done. In the process of discovering our dignity, we must deal with our depravity. As we begin to probe and learn about our dark side, which Scripture refers to as the "flesh," we'll learn to deal with that aspect of our person and grow in Christ-likeness as a result.

The Areas for Assessment

The Primary Areas

The primary areas of assessment help us determine our basic general design. They provide us with the "big picture." We give these areas priority in assessment because they reveal so much about us, and most of us can only spend a limited amount of time in the assessment process.

Spiritual Gifts

First, we should determine our spiritual gifts. A spiritual gift is a God-given ability for service.[3] The gifts are listed in 1 Corinthians 12–14, Romans 12, Ephesians 4, and possibly 1 Peter 4. (There are probably more gifts than those listed in the New Testament.) The spiritual gifts include teaching, helps, exhortation, giving, leading, administration, and pastoring. We should also include preaching as a gift in light of Paul's use of it in 2 Timothy 1:11. These spiritual gifts are important because our God-given gifts provide the special abilities or tools we need for ministry.

In addressing our spiritual gifts, we need to look for two areas. The first is our gift-mix.[4] This consists of the spiritual gifts that we commonly demonstrate in ministry. Most who are fairly experienced have three to five gifts. The first three are discernible while the fourth and fifth may not be as clear. The second area is our gift-cluster. This consists of our gift-mix, but one of the gifts is clearly dominant and is supported by the others.[5]

Passion

Next, we should seek to determine our passion. But what is passion, and why is it important?

The definition of passion. Passion is a God-given capacity to fervently attach ourselves to an object (people, a cause, an idea, and so on) over an extended period of time to meet a need. There are several elements that make up this definition.

First, passion involves fervency. It's an emotional concept. It's a feeling word; it's what we feel strongly about. It might be described as a "burning feeling deep in your soul" or as a "burning gut-feeling that a certain ministry is the most important place that God would have you." In essence, Paul has a passion for church planting (Rom. 15:20).

Second, passion has an object. We say that someone has a passion for or toward something. It often includes people such as the lost, the unchurched, the unborn, the poor and oppressed, or unreached people. It could include a cause or an issue such as abortion, civil rights, or the family. It could be a situation or condition such as poverty, oppression, abuse, or addiction. It might be a particular pursuit such as theology or communication. It might include a place such as an urban, suburban, or rural area or possibly a particular city, state, or country.

Third, passion stays with an individual for an extended period of time. We have to be careful not to confuse it with passing interests.

Fourth, passion often develops out of a strong sense of felt need. This need has a way of capturing our attention and pressing in on our heart. It may involve our own needs, the needs of others, or both. God used Chuck Colson's prison experience to impress upon him the need of those behind bars for Jesus Christ. As Jim Dobson has a passion for the family and Billy Graham has a passion for the lost in general, Chuck Colson has a passion for prisoners.

The importance of passion. Passion is particularly important in assessment for two reasons. First, it provides the necessary direction for ministry in general and spiritual gifts in particular. For example, two people may have the gift of evangelism. However, one may have a passion for poor and oppressed children, while the other may have a passion for college students or internationals. The other reason is that it provides the necessary motivation. Passion motivates or energizes; it pushes or compels us to take some definite action. It spurs us to activity, not inactivity.

Temperament

Once we have identified our spiritual gifts and passion, the next area is temperament. We can learn a great deal about ourselves and others when we explore the different personality types. Also, it is helpful to begin with normal or functional behavior rather than with abnormal or dysfunctional behavior.

In assessing temperament, we should begin with the traditional four-temperament model, which focuses on understanding normal, needs-based behavior. This model has been somewhat popularized by Tim LaHaye, who uses the terms *choleric, sanguine, phlegmatic,* and *melancholy* as based on the work of Hippocrates in the first century.

The personal profile. A useful tool for temperament assessment is the *Personal Profile System,* which was developed by John G. Geier and Dorothy E. Downey as based on the earlier work of William Marston who popularized the DiSC model. DiSC is an acronym for the four behavioral temperaments: Dominant, Influencing, Steadiness, and Compliance. This tool allows individuals to analyze their behavior in nine specific categories:

1. Emotional tendencies
2. Goals
3. The criteria used in judging others
4. The means used to influence others
5. The perceived value one has to an organization
6. The tendency one has to overuse certain traits
7. The typical reaction under pressure
8. Fears
9. What one needs to do to increase personal effectiveness[6]

This tool specifically helps determine who are the point or lead people in ministry and those who function best as support people.

The Myers-Briggs Type Indicator (MBTI). Another temperament tool is the *Myers-Briggs Type Indicator.* This tool takes a different approach to personality than the two profiles above in that it helps us discern how we handle key functional areas of our lives.

First, it seeks to determine preference for extraversion or introversion. This helps in knowing where we focus our attention (the inner or outer world) and what energizes us.

Second, it helps us discover how we perceive or take in information. We tend to prefer either sensing, which involves taking in information through the five senses, or intuition, which gathers information intuitively or beyond the senses. (Intuitive people are visionaries; sensing people are the practical realists.)

Third, it helps us discover how we use the information we take in or how we make decisions. This involves a preference for thinking or feeling. Those who prefer thinking make decisions based on logic and objective analysis. Those who prefer feeling make decisions based on personal values and judgments.

Finally, the *MBTI* helps in determining the lifestyle we adopt for dealing with the outer world. This involves a preference for judging or perceiving. Those who prefer judging are not judgmental people but those who take a very planned, organized approach. They like closure and are usually quick decision makers. Those who prefer perceiving are people who are adaptable and take a spontaneous, flexible approach to life. They don't like closure, preferring to wait until all the facts are in before making decisions.

Leadership

A fourth primary area of assessment is leadership. Two areas of leadership in particular should be assessed.

Leadership role. Assessment of leadership role involves determining if we're leaders, managers, or a combination of both. Most display a combination. We need to determine which is more dominant. Assessing one's leadership role involves looking for the gifts of leadership (Rom. 12:8) or administration (1 Cor. 12:28) and some interaction with temperament. This is a critical area in terms of leading teams for it helps to determine who should be the primary leader or "point person," and who shouldn't attempt to be the primary leader.

Leadership style. The second area of assessment is leadership style. In determining personal style, the *Personal Profile* is very helpful as a starting place. Ken Voges shows how the different styles correspond to the DiSC model. For example, the *D* prefers an autocratic style, the *I* a democratic style, the *S* a participatory style, and the *C* a more bureaucratic style.[7]

Ministry Lifecycle

The fifth primary area is determining where a person best fits in terms of the lifecycle of a ministry. All organizations and ministries have a lifecycle. They're born, grow, plateau, and die. The issue in assessment is where various individuals minister best. If they're good at bringing churches into this world, then they're church planters. If they're good at coming into dying churches and nursing them back to health, then they're "resurrection specialists."

The Secondary Areas

In addition to the primary areas of assessment such as spiritual gifts, passion, temperament, leadership, and lifecycle, there are secondary areas as well.

We must not conclude that what falls under the secondary areas isn't important. For example, one area is that of our natural gifts, talents, and abilities. Aren't these important? In many cases, they may prove to be critical. However, we can only assess so much in the time we have, and need to assign priority to the primary areas in terms of importance.

Assessing natural gifts, talents, and abilities can be most helpful. For example, some Christians have natural abilities in the area of leadership. They are born with a natural gift or predisposition for leadership. This is obvious from such natural leaders as Lee Iacocca, Ross Perot, Mary Kay Ash, and Steven Jobs. When a person who has this natural ability becomes a Christian, God may add to it the gift of leadership. All of this combined with some ministry experience and instruction adds up to the potential for excellence in leadership of a church or parachurch ministry. This combination is found in many if not most of those known for leadership excellence in the Christian world today. Other secondary areas are those that involve unique styles of thinking, learning, decision making, and evangelism. *Maximizing Your Effectiveness* will help you with these.

The Accuracy of Assessment

Several factors affect the accuracy of any program of assessment no matter how sophisticated the procedure may be.

One factor is self-knowledge. Some people know themselves quite well, while others don't know themselves at all. The former find assessment easier and often more confirming than illuminating. The latter are in for an amazing learning process.

The reason why knowledge of ourselves is so important is because we are the ones, ultimately, who determine the accuracy of any assessment program. We can use such highly valid and sophisticated tools as the *Personal Profile* or the *Myers-Briggs Type Indicator,* but they only reflect the information that we supply. If that information is based on who we want to be or who someone else thinks we are, and not on who we *really* are, then it tells us nothing. Next to our omniscient God, we're the ones who know ourselves best and are the final judges of any personal assessment. As we weigh the results of an assessment program in general or a tool in particular, it's our responsibility to determine its accuracy based on our self-knowledge.

Another factor that affects the accuracy of assessment is ministry experience. This is "seasoning." The more ministry experience people have, the more accurate will be their assessment of themselves. We know our leadership abilities best when we take advantage of opportunities to lead. The more we do this, the more "seasoned" we become and the better we're able to discern our strengths, limitations, and weaknesses. However, we face several problems in the area of ministry experience.

One obvious problem is that we're not able to gain experience in all the areas we desire. In fact, new believers may have very little ministry experience to turn to for help in assessment. A potential solution to the problem of a seeming lack of experience is to examine our pre-Christian lives for experiences that can parallel those of ministry. Again, we don't have to be Christians to exercise and experience leadership, teaching, counseling, and other abilities.

Another problem is a reluctance on the part of some to become involved in ministry areas in order to gain vital ministry experience. This seems to be a problem, particularly in the academic setting. Obviously, in an academic environment, people will value academic pursuits over practical pursuits. Students will prefer learning in the classroom over learning in a ministry situation. But the classroom or the library isn't the real world where most ministry takes place! That's why it's imperative that our Bible colleges and seminaries do a better job of encouraging the practical pursuits of ministry as well as the academic pursuits.

6

Are You a Church Planter?

The Practice of Assessment

It was more than Bill Smith's entrepreneurial past that led him to decide that starting churches was to be an important part of his future. He also discovered that his spiritual gifts, passion, temperament, and leadership abilities were ideally suited for the ministry of church planting. Like a surgeon's rubber glove pulled tightly over his extended hand, it was a natural fit.

But what exactly was the process that Bill went through and what specifically did he discover about himself? This chapter is intended to help those whom God has attracted to church planting determine if they are actually church-planter material.

The Spiritual Gifts

Knowing about spiritual gifts is important to the discovery of our "ministry niche." Spiritual gifts are discussed in the Scriptures (Rom. 12; 1 Cor. 12; Eph. 4). The Bible also reveals the exciting truth that God has sovereignly chosen to bestow some of these gifts on those of us who make up His family (1 Cor. 12:7, 11; Eph. 4:7). This knowledge alone should stimulate us to discover our unique gift-mix and gift-cluster, and how we may best use them for His glory.

The Explanation

A great deal of discussion has taken place in contemporary Christianity as to whether or not all the spiritual gifts are still operative and available today, especially the sign gifts of healings, miracles, tongues, and the interpretation of tongues. These and certain other gifts are not discussed in this chapter because of the divisive debate that surrounds them as well as the fact that we're not even sure what they were or how they were used.

In discovering our gift-mix and gift-cluster, we need to consider each of the following gifts and their explanations. As we seek to decide which gifts make up our divine design, we should consider in particular the gifts we feel attracted to or may have experienced in the past, our personal satisfaction with exercising them, and the response of others to our ministry with them.

Administration (1 Cor. 12:28)

Administration is the God-given ability to administer the affairs of the church. Administration involves such things as designing plans, setting goals, and establishing budgets. Administrators focus on the details, create organizational structures, and staff those structures. They monitor plans and solve problems as they arise. This gift is not to be confused with that of leadership (Rom. 12:8), as the two are clearly distinguished in Scripture.

Apostleship (1 Cor. 12:28; Eph. 4:11)

The gift of apostleship is included here not as the primary gift exercised by the twelve apostles who laid the foundation of the church and whose ministries were authenticated by certain sign gifts, but in a secondary sense as used by people such as Barnabas (Acts 14:3, 14), Silvanus and Timothy (1 Thess. 2:6), and Andronicus and Junias (Rom. 16:7). Essentially, this gift involves the capacity to adapt and minister cross-culturally (Eph. 4:11–12). It's important for those who decide to spend their lives planting churches and ministering in a cross-cultural context.

Evangelism (Eph. 4:11)

Those with the gift of evangelism are compassionate toward lost people and are attracted to and enjoy spending time with them. This gift is the ability to communicate clearly the gospel of Jesus Christ to unbelievers either individually or in a group context with the result that a number respond and come to faith in Christ. Evangelists may also enjoy training others to do evangelism (Eph. 4:11–12).

Exhortation (Rom. 12:8)

Those with the gift of exhortation usually feel a strong compassion for those who are hurting and discouraged. The gift involves exhorting, encouraging, consoling, and, when necessary, confronting and admonishing others so that they're benefited in the long run.

Faith (1 Cor. 12:9)

The gift of faith is the ability to envision what needs to be done and to trust God to accomplish it even though it seems impossible to most people. It may cluster with the gift of leadership and is often found in visionary Christians who dream big dreams and attempt big things for the Savior.

Giving (Rom. 12:8)

Those with the gift of giving have often been blessed with life's provisions. The gift concerns the ability to give eagerly, wisely, generously, and sacrificially of God's financial provisions to others, expecting little if anything in return.

Helps (1 Cor. 12:28)/Service (Rom. 12:7)

These two gifts appear to be the same gift and involve the capacity to recognize and provide assistance in meeting practical needs. This often concerns behind-the-scenes assistance and benefits others by freeing them up for other vital ministries.

Leading (Rom. 12:8)

Leaders are influencers. The gift of leading is found in people who have a clear, significant vision and are able to communicate it in such a way that they influence others to pursue that vision. It's not to be confused with the gift of administration.

Mercy (Rom. 12:8)

The gift of mercy is the capacity to feel and express unusual compassion and sympathy for those in difficult or crisis situations and to provide them with the necessary help and support to see them through these times.

Pastor (Eph. 4:11)

The term "pastor" literally means "shepherd." Consequently, the gift involves leading, nurturing, caring for, and protecting God's flock. While it's commonly associated with those who minister in a church on a professional basis, God bestows it on laypeople as well. In fact, much of the pastoral care in the church should be the ministry of the laypeople in the church. There are people who argue that this gift is to be associated with the gift of teaching according to its use in Ephesians 4:11. While it's possible that these gifts can cluster together, the original language doesn't demand it as some assert.[1]

Preaching (1 Tim. 2:7; 2 Tim. 1:11)

This gift isn't mentioned in the three common listings of gifts in the New Testament. However, it's associated with the gift of apostle in 1 Timothy 2:7 and the gifts of apostle and teacher in 2 Timothy 1:11. Preaching is the God-given ability to communicate God's Word with clarity and power in a culturally relevant way so that it applies to the specific situation of the hearers. Some associate this gift with that of prophecy.

Teaching (Rom. 12:7; 1 Cor. 12:28; Eph. 4:11)

The gift of teaching is the ability to understand and communicate the Scriptures clearly and with spiritual insight. Those with this gift spend much time studying their Bibles and delight in helping people to better understand the Scriptures.

We can read through all the gifts to discover if we have an affinity for certain ones. While this can be most productive, it's also very subjective. A more objective approach is to take one of the many spiritual gifts inventories that are available. They're often divided into those that test for all the gifts, including the sign gifts such as the *Wagner Modified Houts Questionnaire,* and those that don't such as the *Houts Inventory of Spiritual Gifts,* the *Spiritual Gifts Analysis,* and my Spiritual Gifts Inventory found in the Appendix (pages 199–207) of *Maximizing Your Effectiveness.*

The Application

The Lone Church Planter

The single or lone church planter attempts to start a church without the help of a team. (The best way to plant a church is with a team, but that's not always possible.)

Lone church planters should look in particular for such gifts as that of leadership, faith, evangelism, and preaching. If they plan to minister in a cross-cultural context, then the gift of apostleship would be most helpful. They should have at least one or more of these gifts. The more gifts they have, the greater will be their effectiveness.

The lone church planter will be the leader of the new church and would benefit greatly from the gift of leadership. It would be ideal if this gift was combined as well with either the gift of administration or abilities in the area of administration.

The gift of faith is important because it's related to vision. Vision is critical to leadership; consequently, this gift in combination with that of leadership would aid lone church planters immensely in projecting their visions for the future of their ministries.

The gift of evangelism would help new church planters to set a good example for their people regarding the importance of evangelism. Evangelism must be a priority in the new church, and the pastor's personal ministry of evangelism will directly influence it.

One of the critical areas in any church is the pastor's ability to communicate well from the pulpit. When the pastor stands up to preach, people expect a clear, relevant message from God. Unfortunately, people, especially unchurched lost people, gauge the effectiveness of a church on the pastor's abilities in the pulpit. Thus, the gift of preaching is important to church planting.

The Church-planting Team

The same gifts of leadership, faith, evangelism, preaching, and apostleship are necessary for a church-planting team, but may be spread out among the various members of the team. It will be to the team's advantage if its leader has the gift of leadership combined with evangelism and preaching. However, another member of the team could be strong in evangelism and gifted accordingly. A third could have the gifts of teaching and shepherding.

Passion

Passion is what you feel strongly about. It's important in assessment because it serves to both energize and provide the necessary direction for the exercise of the spiritual gifts. The biblical equivalent of this modern-day term is found in Paul's use of "ambition" in Romans 15:20.

An example of passion is found in the life of Paul. His passion was to preach the gospel to the Gentiles (the unchurched of the first century). Initially, his great passion was to preach the gospel (1 Cor. 9:16–23) to both Jews and Gentiles (Acts 9:15; Rom. 9:1–3; 10:1); however, because of the rejection of the Jews, he focused his full attention on the Gentiles (Acts 22:21; 26:17; Rom. 1:5; 11:13). In particular, he desired to preach the gospel to Gentiles in places where Christ was unknown (Rom. 15:20–21). This was what motivated Paul and gave direction to the use of his spiritual gifts.

There are several questions that will help us to discover our passion. Carefully think about each of the following questions:

1. Do you have a strong attraction toward a group of people, or a particular cause or pursuit?
2. Is this based on some kind of strongly felt need?
3. In light of your spiritual gifts, how or with whom do you desire to use these gifts?
4. If God would allow you to do just one thing for the rest of your life, what would you want most to do?

In evaluating passion, a helpful assessment tool is a "life map." Constructing a life map involves taking some time and reviewing life from the present as far back as one can remember. This should include as many events as possible, such as conversion, high and low points, significant people, jobs, hobbies, leisure activities, and so on.

These memories are then written down. Record them in a brief one- or two-page journal. Use a time-line, a spiral, a graph, a tree, or a puzzle. The life map is a helpful tool that can be used with the other primary areas as well, such as spiritual gifts, temperament, leadership roles and styles, and the ministry lifecycle.

Once we have identified our passion and have established the motivation and general direction of our spiritual gifts, how does this relate to church planting? Perhaps the answer lies in the example of Paul, who was a church planter par excellence.

In general, Paul's passion was for lost people. Throughout the Book of Acts and the epistles, he and the other disciples are pursuing, evangelizing, and discipling lost people. While the focus is on Jewish lost people initially, the Gentiles are brought into the picture as well according to the plan of God (Eph. 3:1–8).

Paul's passion is in accord with the vision of the early church—the Great Commission. In general, vision and passion don't have to be the same although this is often the case. Vision is a seeing word, whereas passion is a feeling word. It's important that those on a team have the same vision, but not necessarily the same passion.

In terms of lone church planters, there must be a close alignment between their passion and their vision. The vision of the church that they're starting is the Great Commission, which unfolds chronologically: (1) pursue the lost; (2) evangelize them; and (3) disciple them (Luke 19:10). Lone church planters will be spending a lot of time around lost people. Therefore, it's important that they, like Paul, have a passion for the lost, and the nonchurched lost in particular.

If they should have a passion for someone or something else, this would hamper the initial planting of the new church. For example, if a person has the gift of teaching and a passion for theology, then the chances are good that reaching lost people will not be of primary importance to this individual. This isn't to say that this person will not reach lost people, but a passion for the lost will not be a strong motivating factor. Consequently, this person might be better off teaching in a school where a passion for theology and for students is essential.

While it's critical that all members of a church-planting team have the same vision, there's more room for variation in passion. It's the vision of the team that unites it and gives it direction as a whole. Everyone on the team knows the direction of the entire team, which is the Great Commission mandate.

However, there's room for different passions within that mandate. For example, one member of the team may have a passion for helping people worship and value God apart from the sermon. Another person could be a Christian education specialist with a passion for ministering to children. As long as both of these team members have caught a vision for reaching the lost, their individual passions will contribute to, not distract from, the overarching vision of the entire team. The important thing is that someone on the team, preferably the team leader, has some kind of passion for reaching lost people.

Temperament

The assessment of temperament helps us deepen our understanding of ourselves and those with whom we come in contact. A knowledge of temperament allows us to see more clearly the strengths as well as the liabilities we and others bring to our ministry.

The Explanation

One method of temperament assessment uses a traditional four-temperament model, which is a variation of the *Personal Profile*. Generally speaking, an individual displays not just one style of temperament, but a combination of styles with one more dominant. Read the following descriptions and see if you can identify your temperament.

Doers

Doers attempt to control or overcome the environment to accomplish their vision. They're more task- than people-oriented. They're catalytic people who love a challenge and are not afraid to take risks. Doers make quick decisions and like immediate results. They love to challenge the status quo. In their environment, they need freedom from control and supervision and desire opportunity for individual accomplishments. They are "upfront" and "out-front" kinds of people. They are usually *D*s on the *Personal Profile*.

Influencers

Influencers attempt to persuade people to accomplish the vision. They are more people- than task-oriented. They're persuaders and promote their ideas in order to bring others into alliance with them. Influencers enjoy contact with people and desire to make a favorable impression. They are articulate and are very motivational and enthusiastic. They, too, will challenge the status quo. They need freedom from control and detail in order to minister at maximum effectiveness. They, like doers, are "upfront" and "out-front" people. They're usually *I*s on the *Personal Profile*.

Relators

Relators cooperate with others to accomplish their vision. They're more people- than task-oriented, and prefer the status quo unless given good reasons to change. They're very patient and loyal and are good listeners. They're very well-liked and pleasant to be around. They minister best in a secure and somewhat safe environment, where they receive credit for their accomplishments along with sincere appreciation. They prefer remaining "behind the scenes." They're *S*s on the *Personal Profile*.

Thinkers

Thinkers tend to be very diplomatic with people and comply with authority. They shape their environment by promoting high quality and accuracy in accomplishing the vision. Thinkers are more task- than people-oriented. They are critical thinkers who are analytical and focus on key details and accuracy. In their environment, they desire to work under known circumstances and prefer the status quo. They usually minister "behind the scenes." They're often *C*s on the *Personal Profile*.

It is important for the potential church planter to take the *Personal Profile* for two reasons. First, the above exercise is rather subjective in its approach. This profile provides a more objective approach to determining temperament. Second, the profile is a carefully refined, sophisticated instrument that will result in a far more accurate assessment of temperament.[2]

Also helpful are several books that are based on the four-temperament model. After taking one of the profiles, read *Understanding How Others Misunderstand You*,[3] *The Delicate Art of Dancing with Porcupines*,[4] and *Maximizing Your Effectiveness*. (The latter includes a temperament assessment.) These books supply additional insight and important information about temperament.

Another approach to temperament is that of the *Myers-Briggs Temperament Inventory (MBTI)*, which was developed by Isabel Myers and Katheryn Briggs. There's also a helpful book based on it by David Keirsey and Marilyn Bates entitled *Please Understand Me: Character and Temperament Types*. The theory behind both proposes that people approach four key areas of life in ways that are different but equally correct. These areas are called preferences because each person prefers one over the other much as we prefer to write with one of our hands, either right or left, over the other. Carefully read through the following descriptions and determine which most accurately describes your preferences.

Extroverts/Introverts

The first area of temperament assessment looks at where people like to focus their attention and interests and from where they derive their energy.

Extroverts like to work with the outer world of people and things. They are energized by contact with large numbers of people. When they're by themselves for long periods of time, they become fatigued and seek out people who stimulate and revitalize them. Consequently, they have many friends and acquaintances.

Introverts like the inner world of concepts and ideas. They prefer to spend time alone reading, studying, or meditating and are emotionally drained if around lots of people. When fatigued they're revitalized by "getting away from it all." Consequently, they have a limited number of acquaintances and only a few close friends.

Sensing/Intuition

The second area looks at how people find out about things, that is, how they take in and process information.

Sensing people prefer to take in information through their senses. They focus on facts and details that can be observed through the five senses—what they can see, hear, touch, taste, or smell. They are practical people who prefer to do things rather than study them. They love and follow systems and procedures. They dwell on present reality (the here and now), and for them "seeing is believing" (John 20:24–28).

Intuitive people take in information holistically, preferring the world of ideas, possibilities, and relationships. They're the big-picture types who shy away from meticulous facts and figures. They don't care for systems and procedures but would rather pursue change and new ideas. They're natural visionaries who focus on the possible future (what could be). For them "believing is seeing."

Thinking/Feeling

The third area affects what people do with the information they take in, or how they make decisions.

Thinking people make their decisions on the basis of logic and objective analysis. An example is Paul in Acts 15:36–41. They prefer to win people over by their logic. They take a more impersonal approach to decision making and can come across at times as insensitive. The truth is very important to them, and they're very task-oriented.

Feeling people make their decisions on the basis of personal values and motives. An example is Barnabas in Acts 15:36–41. They prefer to win people over through persuasion. They take a personal approach to decision making and communicate warmth and harmony. Human values are very important; consequently they're more people-oriented.

Judging/Perceiving

This area deals with how people orient to the outer world in terms of structure and the time it takes to make decisions.

Judging people prefer a more structured approach to life because they desire to control and regulate life. They're very organized and deal with the world in a planned and orderly way. Preferring to have things settled, they pursue closure. As a result, they tend to make decisions rather quickly.

Perceiving people take a less structured approach to life because they seek to understand life and adapt to it. They tend to be very adaptable, flexible, and spontaneous. They have little need for closure and prefer to make decisions only after all the facts are in.

In addition to identifying your preferences based on the above descriptions, you should take the *Myers-Briggs Temperament Inventory (MBTI)*.[5] If you have trouble obtaining this inventory, then order a copy of the book *Please Understand Me* by Keirsey and Bates from a local bookstore.[6] This book contains *The Keirsey Temperament Sorter,* which is shorter and similar to the *MBTI*. If the result of either of these inventories is different from that which you took based on the descriptions above, then you should opt for the inventory.

Once you've taken the *MBTI*, there are several books that might prove helpful. One is *Please Understand Me*, which will give you further insight into your temperament based on the *MBTI*. Another work that makes application of the *MBTI* material to ministry is *Personality Type and Religious Leadership* by Oswald and Kroeger.[7] Finally, *Maximizing Your Effectiveness* provides a shorter assessment similar to the *MBTI* with explanation.

The Application

Once you've discovered your temperament, as based on the descriptions above and/or taking one of the profiles and the *MBTI*, the next step is to apply the results to church planting.

The Lone Church Planter

The Personal Profile. Lone church planters need to be strong, visionary leaders. This proves most helpful in the early stages of starting churches when there is need for significant direction and numerical growth, and there's a potential for much discouragement. Those who score as High *D*s or *I*s or a combination of either on the *Personal Profile* or the description above *(DIRT)* are usually best suited for this position of leadership.

The Christian Churches/Churches of Christ performed a recent survey using the *Personal Profile* to correlate the personality types of sixty-six church planters with the growth of their churches. The survey revealed that the High *D* planters had an average attendance of 72 after the first year and 181 after an average of 5.2 years. The High *I*s had an average of 98 after the first year and an average of 174 after 3.6 years. The High *S*s had an average of 38 after the first year and 77 after 6.3 years, while the High *C*s had an average of 39 after one year and 71 after 4.3 years.[8]

The High *D* planter tends to be a strong, catalytic person who takes authority, makes quick decisions, and loves a challenge such as starting a church. The High *I* planter is a strong person who is exciting and enthusiastic and good at motivating people. Both the High *D* and the High *I* are best in the "point" position. The next best combination is either a primary High *D* or High *I* with a secondary *S* or *C* on the *Profile* (or *R* or *T* above).

The MBTI or equivalent. First, lone church planters function better as extroverts than as introverts. In *Personality Type and Religious Leadership*, Oswald and Kroeger conclude after a study of the functions of ministry normally expected of an ordained person "that the parish ministry is primarily an Extroverted profession."[9] The majority of the pastoral functions involve up-front work with large numbers of people. This certainly characterizes church planting. This energizes extroverts but exhausts introverts. Introverts function best in the team context of starting churches.

Second, in the "point" or primary leadership position, the intuitive-types are clearly stronger leaders in church planting than sensing-types. This is because church planters need to be strong, visionary leaders who are good at planning and prefer change and innovation that encourage growth. This describes well the intuitive-type person, especially in combination with thinking (*NTs*). Sensing-type people aren't that enthusiastic about vision, innovation, and change. They're very practical people who view ministry as doing; therefore, they make great workers.[10] They, like introverts, function best by working with a church-planting team rather than leading it.

Third, the thinking-types seem to have a slight advantage over the feeling-types in terms of leadership in church planting when combined with intuition *(NT)*. Oswald and Kroeger indicate that "Approximately 80% of what a pastor does on a day-to-day basis involves inter-personal relations," which favors feeling-type clergy.[11] They also point to the fact that many established churches predominantly consist of feeling-type cultures, which leaves thinking-type pastors at a disadvantage.[12] Therefore, feeling-types can make good church planters.

Idealistically speaking, however, thinking-types plus intuition (*NTs*) have the edge for several reasons. First, the feeling-types eventually stop exercising consistent strong leadership, which could plateau a church in terms of numerical growth. This isn't true of *NT* clergy.[13] Next, *NT* clergy are strong leaders who are visionary and prefer change.[14] Third, *NT* clergy press toward excellence, which is very important in church planting.[15] Fourth, the fact that *NTs* are not as strong at interpersonal skills is a disadvantage that can be overcome by recognizing the problem and involving others in the core group to help offset this.

Fourth, the perceiving-types also have a slight advantage in church planting over the judging-types. The judging-types have the ability to make hard decisions, take a strong stand, and commit themselves to a clear course of action.[16] However, when combined with the sensing-type (*SJs*), they can become very rigid and inflexible, preferring the status quo—a preference that spells "death" for Great Commission churches.[17] They're the originators of the famous seven last words of the church: "We've never done it that way before!" The perceiving types have an advantage in their openness to change, which brings both new options and a freshness to their ministries. They're also masters at handling the unplanned and unexpected, which constantly characterize church planting.[18]

The Church-planting Team

Certain temperament styles or types are preferable for those who are the primary leaders and catalysts in planting churches. However, there's a unique place for all temperaments in the context of team ministry in church planting. It's the other temperament types or styles that fill in all the important and necessary leadership and ministry gaps. Pastoral ministry by nature and probably by design demands a broad range of ministry capabilities and functions. First Corinthians 12:4–12 makes it very clear that no one individual can provide all of these in the church setting. Instead, each individual makes a significant contribution to the working of the whole. What's important is that the right style or type be matched with the right position according to leadership capability and the individual ministry function. Then the strengths of the various temperaments under the Spirit's control function effectively and offset the weakness of one another.

Leadership

The Explanation

It goes without saying that leadership is critical to the success of any venture, and especially church planting. As the leadership goes, so goes the church!

The Leadership Role

Leadership is fundamentally different from management or administration. Scripture acknowledges this difference when it distinguishes between the gifts of leadership (Rom. 12:8) and administration (1 Cor. 12:28). Others who are students of leadership make this same distinction. For example, in the *Harvard Business Review,* John Kotter notes that "Leadership is different from management, but not for the reasons most people think."[19] He goes on to explain that "leadership and management are two distinctive and complementary systems of action. Each has its own function and characteristic activities."[20]

Leaders. Currently, tremendous change is sweeping across North America and the world. This is no problem for leaders because they're able to cope with the change that comes from outside the organization and create change within the ministry organization. Indeed, a key function of leadership is coping with change.[21] The result is that the ministries of leaders stay in touch with and relate relevantly and meaningfully to contemporary culture.

The way leaders cope with and accomplish this change is through influence. Leadership involves influencing people to change in the direction of maximum Christ-likeness and ministry effectiveness.

But how do leaders influence people? The answer lies in the definition of a Christian leader. Christian leaders are godly people (character) who know where they're going (vision) and have followers (influence). The key to the third characteristic, influence, is character and vision. Leaders who constantly walk with God and have a clear, significant vision attract followers.

In addition, leaders are adept at developing visions and strategies and motivating people to accomplish their visions through those strategies. They tend to think inductively more than deductively, and are visionaries. They're also more proactive than reactive, and many have the gift of leadership (Rom. 12:8).

Managers. Managers complement and work best under leaders by coping with this complexity. In fact, a major distinction between leaders and managers is that while the former cope with change, the latter deal with the complexity brought about by the change.[22] Managers attempt to bring order and consistency to this complexity. The way they accomplish this is through planning, budgeting, and organizing. In fact, managers are godly persons (character) who help us get where we're going (plan) and maximize our resources to get there (budgeting, organizing, staffing, controlling). Managers tend to think deductively more than inductively. They're also more reactive than proactive, and may have the gift of administration (1 Cor. 12:28).

Leadership Styles

There are four leadership styles that correspond to the four DiSC profiles. In *Understanding How Others Misunderstand You,* Voges and Braund have done an excellent job of succinctly identifying and summarizing these styles.

The autocratic style. This style is characteristic of High *D* leaders. These leaders are self-starters who love a challenge and want immediate results. They're decision makers who are quick to take authority and are good at managing trouble and solving problems.[23] Of these leaders, Voges and Braund note that "An hierarchy of leadership is usually installed so that there is a direct line of authority."[24]

The democratic style. This style is characteristic of High *I* leaders. They're enthusiastic people who enjoy being around and motivating people. They make favorable impressions and are usually very articulate. They enjoy helping others and prefer to minister in teams.[25] "The Influencing leader usually prefers to have the authority to make the final decision after representative views are expressed."[26]

The participatory style. This style is characteristic of leaders with a High *S.* They're very patient people who are good at listening and calming excited people. They're also loyal and are focused and cooperative.[27] Voges and Braund note that "Most of the daily decisions are delegated to others while the High S leader offers support by listening to others and allowing everyone in the organization the opportunity to follow through on individual assignments. This facilitating leader strives for peace and smooth operation in the company."[28]

The bureaucratic style. This is the leadership style of the High *C* personality. They're very analytical people who pay attention to key directives and standards and focus on key details. They're critical thinkers who check for accuracy and comply with authority.[29] Voges and Braund observe that "As long as there is compliance to policies, people in the organization can have their own responsibilities and make their own decisions. The organizational system and not personality style tends to be in charge."[30]

The Application

How does this information on role and styles affect leadership in church planting? Again, it's important to look at it in two contexts.

The Lone Church Planter

In terms of the roles of leadership and management, Kotter writes that "Both are necessary for success in an increasingly complex and volatile business environment."[31] Consequently, he recommends that both roles be combined as much as possible in the one person who heads the organization. He calls such a leader a "leader-manager."[32]

The ideal for church planting would be the leader who has struck a balance between both roles. This would involve the dual gifts of leadership and administration and strong natural abilities in both areas. The next best combination would be the person who is strong in leadership (possibly with the gift of leadership) along with some natural abilities in management.

In terms of the leadership styles, nothing has changed significantly from what was said about sole leaders and the DiSC profile in the section above on temperament. The High *D* and *I* temperaments or a combination of both provide the best leadership styles for those in the primary positions of leadership. The next best styles would be those with a High *D* or *I* combined with the High *S* or *C* on the *Profile* (or *R* or *T* above). The High *S* or *C* functions best in the team context under the leadership of a *D* or *I*.

The Church-planting Team

All that has been said above regarding the sole leader would be true here as well. However, there's an additional advantage to team ministry: a person who is a pure leader with little or no management abilities could function well by teaming up with another who has strong gifts and natural abilities in the area of management or administration. United under the same vision, chances are good that they'd make a great team.

Church planting in a team context would be greatly enhanced by having more than one or a blend of two leadership styles present. The leader of the team would need the High *D* or *I* style or a combination. The others on the team could supply the other styles such as the High *S* and *C* (or *R* or *T*), which would add strength to the overall leadership of the entire team.

Ministry Role

The Explanation

All ministries have a lifecycle. They are born, grow, and eventually die unless revived. The issue for assessment is the question, "Where along the lifecycle of a ministry or organization does one function best?"[33]

Visionaries/Implementers

Visionaries/implementers are able to take fresh, innovative ideas and implement them in practical ways. They approach problems first by getting the big picture in order to see how everything fits together. They view change as an opportunity to try fresh ideas to see if they're practical and are willing to take risks if they produce results. Visionaries/implementers prefer a variety of ministry tasks as long as they produce practical results. They opt for a variety of ministry tasks in various stages of development at the same time. They like to take just enough time to implement an idea or vision to see if it's practical and then move on to a new challenge, usually in another ministry setting. If a ministry develops very slowly so that the challenge fades, they become frustrated and begin to look for "greener pastures."

Implementers

Implementers are very good at taking another's ideas or vision and implementing it for the first time. They love a challenge and view problems as challenges. Implementers are motivated by taking risks and like change because it enables them to make things happen. They choose to spend their time implementing ideas but not working out all the details. They'll usually initiate one significant task or ministry and then move on to another new challenge within the same ministry setting.

Developers

Developers are very good at taking another's idea, vision, or strategy and developing it to its greatest potential. They work best by developing the programs or systems necessary to accomplish another's ministry vision. They view problems not as challenges but as obstacles that need to be removed if there's to be any progress. They believe that risks should be avoided by careful planning, but know that change is inevitable and, given enough time and good reasons, will pursue change. They prefer to develop to a maximum one program or system at a time and become frustrated if not given enough time to accomplish this goal.

Maximizers

Maximizers are practical, efficient, well-organized people who take a ministry that has already been established and is doing reasonably well and attempt to control and maintain it as efficiently as possible. Their approach to problem solving is to spend a lot of time trying to get problems under control so that the ministry can continue to function efficiently. Maximizers work hard at keeping things under control and running smoothly so as to eliminate the need for taking risks and making any major changes. They're focused, detail-oriented people who work best within a structured environment. They prefer to approach one task at a time and can become easily frustrated when things become disorganized and inefficient.

Rescuers

Rescuers have the uncanny ability to see great potential in ministries that are not doing well and are good at renewing and turning them around. They view problems from a different angle and take a creative approach to their solutions. Rescuers are enthusiastic hope-builders and risk-takers who believe that change is critical for struggling ministries. They do expect to see some changes eventually and can become discouraged when people don't give their new ideas and vision a chance. They usually pursue a few ministry tasks in various stages of development at the same time.

The Application

The Lone Church Planter

The best role for a lone church planter would be either the visionary/implementer or the implementer. These two roles are found at the beginning of the lifecycle of any ministry in general and the local church in particular. Consequently, they are the roles most comparable to that of church planters.

The visionary/implementer and the implementer are entrepreneurs who are designed to start new ministries within any context. When these people look back on their past (life map), they discover that they have a history of starting new projects.

Usually, visionaries/implementers start a new church but eventually leave it or turn it over to another person to continue the ministry. They are "wired" in such a way that they love a challenge but usually find it in a new and different environment. Consequently, they'll start a number of new churches in their lifetimes. Paul was this kind of church planter.

Implementers will start a new church and, most often, will stay with it for a long period of time, possibly until they or the church dies. They're "put together" in such a way that they, too, love a challenge but manage to find new challenges in the same church. An excellent example is Pastor Rick Warren, who planted Saddleback Valley Community Church in Mission Viejo, California. He states that from the very beginning his prayer to God was that he be allowed to start a church where he could minister for the rest of his life. God has granted him this prayer, at least to this point in the ministry. Warren is a very creative person who loves a challenge. He's used this aspect of his design to stay and grow Saddleback Church to one of the largest in North America.

The Church-planting Team

Starting a church with a team has more advantages because it involves people on the team with other roles that serve to complement the visionary/implementer or the implementer. For example, either the visionary/implementer or the implementer needs the developer and/or the maximizer if the ministry is going to grow. The former are designed to catalyze and grow churches. The latter, however, design systems that develop the church and refine it so that it functions at its optimum while expanding. We can compare it to the life of a tree. A tree requires a good root system to nourish it and keep it from falling over or being uprooted in a storm. Visionaries/implementers plant and grow good trees but need developers and maximizers to develop and maximize the root system so that the tree has proper nourishment and doesn't fall over.

The Family

The Importance of the Family

An important, essential ingredient to any ministry is the family. This of course applies to church planters who are married or married with children. If church planters don't have the backing of their families, especially their wives, their ministries will suffer. Without the support of their families, church planters are doomed to failure. While the family may not necessarily be directly involved in the ministry, it must at least be supportive of the ministry. In fact, the church planter's family must come before the ministry. If the family isn't behind the vision, then God is telling prospective church planters that the time isn't right.

The Qualifications for the Family

Some of the qualifications for church planters such as motives and character will be covered in chapter 8, which concerns leadership. The focus there will be on 1 Thessalonians 2. But there are also family qualifications for men, their wives, and their children.

Men

The qualifications found in 1 Timothy 3:1–7 and Titus 1:5–9 deal primarily with character. These are qualifications for elders but are also essential for church planters.

One important qualification in terms of the family is found in 1 Timothy 3:4–5: "He must manage his own family well and see that his children obey him with proper respect. (If anyone does not know how to manage his own family, how can he take care of God's church?)." Those who go into ministry must be good managers of their families and have the obedience and respect of their children. If this isn't the case, then the prospective church planter is disqualified.

Wives

Wives, like their husbands, must be pursuing Christ-likeness. This doesn't mean they've arrived, but they're in active pursuit.

Wives of church planters shouldn't be in opposition to the ministry. They either need to be for it or at least open to it. If the wife is opposed to it, then the potential church planter should not pursue this ministry until or unless she changes her mind.

There are no qualifications listed for elders' wives in 1 Timothy 3. There are some qualifications for women in 1 Timothy 3:11: "In the same way their wives are to be women worthy of respect, not malicious talkers but temperate and trustworthy in everything." The question is, to whom is this passage referring? Some commentators feel that it's a reference to deacons' wives; others feel that it refers to a group of women who served in the church as deaconesses.

Wives of church planters must be worthy of respect, not malicious talkers but temperate and trustworthy people.

Children

There is a qualification for children of those in ministry. First Timothy 3:4 says that they should obey and respect their fathers. If this isn't the case, then there is question if the father is qualified for any professional ministry.

The Expectations of the Family

Churches have certain expectations of pastors' wives and children. Congregation members may expect wives to be involved in such ministries as teaching children, leading women's Bible studies, entertaining people in their homes, playing the piano or organ in a traditional church, or singing.

These expectations may be either obvious or subtle. Some churches will demand these things up front. Others may not voice them. In some churches, the board may not have expectations but the people in the church do.

Scripture places no expectations on pastors' wives in terms of ministry in the church. It does place certain family responsibilities upon them as wives and mothers. These are found in Titus 2:4–5 and include such things as loving their husbands and children and being busy at home. Consequently, the church should expect nothing more from the church planter's wife than being a good wife and mother. If she has the time and desires to become more involved in ministry in the church, that's her decision. But this must not be a requirement or expectation for the position.

Another issue is the career-oriented wife. Should she pursue a professional career while her husband pastors the church? If there are no children, there is no problem with this as long as she's able to love her husband, maintain the household, and encourage and support him in the ministry. In fact, in a planted church that targets Boomers or Gen Xers, most of the wives in the church will be employed. However, once they begin a family, the wife should be at home rearing the family.

Churches generally don't have ministry expectations of children, especially if they're young. They do, however, expect them to be examples in terms of their behavior. This is one of the reasons why some pastors' families feel that they live in a "fishbowl."

The church should understand that it's not realistic to expect the pastors' children to set the example for all the other children in terms of their behavior. They aren't and cannot be perfect! This puts unfair pressure on them and added pressure on their parents.

The Advantages and Disadvantages for the Family

The Disadvantages

There are several disadvantages for families in church planting. First, church planters may not have a lot of time for their families. While their schedules are rather flexible, church planting is hard work, and there's always something that needs to be done. If church planters don't know how to handle their time, or if they're obsessive, they might fail to spend adequate time with their wives and children.

Second, a church-planting ministry can create special problems for a wife. For example, if meetings are constantly held in her house or apartment, she may find herself functioning as a permanent hostess. In addition, if she's a "neatnik," she may feel a lot of pressure to keep the house immaculate to set a good example. With lots of traffic this will not be possible and will prove to be most frustrating.

Third, there's a lot of risk involved in church planting. This is difficult for some wives to handle. They may prefer a more secure position in an established church or another form of ministry.

The Advantages

First, a church-planting ministry can involve the entire family in a positive way. In an interview in *Leadership,* church planter Victor Fry says, "We started our second mission congregation when our children were in sixth grade, second grade, and kindergarten. They were involved delivering fliers and even got the neighborhood kids to help, too. They were caught up in the excitement of starting a new church."[34] In the same interview, another church planter, Kaye Pattison, says, "It's been very positive for us. All of my daughters ended up teaching Sunday school and doing other things they couldn't have done in a large established church."[35] He indicates that this has resulted in their continued activity in ministry later in life after marriage and children.

Second, a church-planting ministry often makes life easier on the pastor's wife. The expectations of the pastor's wife are minimal if any at all. Regarding this, Kaye Pattison says, "I've even found being a church planter is easier on one's spouse. It eliminates many of the rigors of being a 'pastor's wife.' If your spouse fears the limelight and always has to have every hair in place, church planting is a more relaxed alternative."[36]

Third, church planters often have more time for their families. They're responsible for their own schedules. Thus, if they aren't workaholics, they can be sure that they have sufficient time for their families. Again, Kaye Pattison says, "Church planters also have more time for family. If you're in a church of five hundred, someone's always calling, and the kids think Daddy loves the congregation more than them. That's not a problem in the early stages of a church."[37]

Your Divine Design

1. What are your spiritual gifts? Is one a primary gift about which the others cluster? If so, then list it first.

   a.

   b.

   c.

   d.

   e.

2. What is your passion?

3. What is your temperament?

a.	*DIRT*	Primary:	DIRT
b.		Secondary:	DIRT
b.	*PPS/BPP*	Primary:	DiSC
		Secondary:	DiSC
c.	*MBTI*	E	I
		S	N
		T	F
		J	P

4. What is your role? Are you a leader or a manager or both? If both, which is stronger?

   a. Leader

   b. Manager

   c. Leader-manager

   d. Manager-leader

5. What is your leadership style? Are you a combination of two of them? If so, which is dominant?

   a. Autocratic

   b. Democratic

   c. Participatory

   d. Bureaucratic

6. What is your ministry role? Are you a combination of two of them? If so, which is dominant?

   a. Visionary/Implementer

   b. Implementer

   c. Developer

   d. Maximizer

   e. Rescuer

7. How do your spouse and family feel about being involved in a church-planting situation? Do they meet the qualifications for the family? Is your spouse excited about or at least open to church planting?

8. Based on your personal divine design and your family situation, what is your answer to the question, "Am I a church planter?"

Part 3

The Principles
of Church Planting

So far we've discovered that before planting any crop, farmers must prepare the soil first. They also need to discover whether or not they're cut out to be farmers. However, satisfying the first two requirements isn't enough. There's a third: they must decide what kind of crops they're going to plant. To spread out just any seed randomly across any kind of soil in most cases would spell disaster! Some soils and climates won't normally tolerate certain crops. For example, you don't plant oranges outdoors in Alaska. Other climates support a wide variety of crops.

The same is true of church planting. Someone has said that it takes all kinds of churches to reach all kinds of people. Consequently, church planters need to determine what kinds of churches they're going to plant. However, there are at least seven biblical vital signs that should characterize all churches. In the next several chapters, we'll examine each of these seven vital signs, which make up seven key principles for planting significant, biblically based twenty-first-century churches.

7

Building a Fire in the Furnace

A Great Commission Vision

Seven foundational principles are crucial to church planting. You may apply these timeless church growth principles cross-culturally to either a new church or to an established church. They describe what kind of church you will plant and what it will look like. Church planters must think through these principles carefully because they will make up their core values. The first principle, which is the subject of this chapter, focuses on a Great Commission vision.

A Single, Clear Vision

It's critical to the ultimate success of the new church that it have a single, clear vision. The church must know where it's going! Without a vision, the church will quickly plateau and simply begin to maintain itself. Maintenance will be followed by a downward spiral that will eventuate in its ultimate, untimely demise.

Unfortunately, the majority of churches have little or no vision. If you were to visit one of these churches on Sunday morning and ask laypeople what they see when they envision the church five or ten years in the future, most would respond with a blank stare. More than likely, they would direct you to a deacon or an elder, who, in turn, would probably tell you to talk to the pastor. The chances are good that the pastor would send you back to someone on the board. This reflects an ecclesiastical "hot potato" routine. After a while you begin to wonder if you're playing football; everyone keeps punting the vision question to someone else.

The truth is that many of these churches aren't going anywhere. They tend to be passive churches often pastored by either passive or frustrated pastors. They are maintenance-minded, fearful of change, and desperately clinging to the status quo. A museum mentality prevails throughout these ministries; the programs and methods are all reminders of the distant past. These churches serve as relics of the 1940s and 1950s when America was primarily a churched culture..

Some churches have several visions. I had an opportunity to preach at one of these churches. It was a denominational church located in the South. I flew into the city early, and visited with several of its lay board leaders. What I discovered was that each had a different vision for the future of the church. One leader envisioned a Christian school. Another envisioned reaching a nearby community.

While some might think that multiple visions are better than no vision, this isn't the case. Where there are multiple visions, there will be multiple struggles and much unhappiness. In reality, many of these churches are "splits waiting to happen." In fact, they're already down on the calendar; it's just a matter of time! The reason is because each leader tends to push for a particular vision, which often results in a "July 4 mentality"—lots of fireworks in the board meetings!

Some churches have a single, clear vision. The only problem is that it's the *wrong* vision! Specialist churches in larger urban areas tend to focus on a specific area of ministry such as counseling, family, preaching, or teaching. Should people have a need in one of these areas, they go to one of the churches in the city that specializes in that area. For example, if you or someone in your family is struggling emotionally, then you attend one of the churches in the area that's acquired an excellent reputation for its primary focus on the counseling ministry. However, if you need a church for the family with an excellent children's program, then you may want to select another church in the same area that's known for its family ministries. If it's good preaching or good Bible teaching, then there's usually a church in the city that's known for its expertise in one of these areas.

Unfortunately, specialist churches contribute to a consumer mind-set that, in turn, produces a consumer Christianity. Christians in these situations develop a "shop-around" mentality. If the church they are in now stops meeting their needs, they simply shop around until they find another church that does. Such believers are constantly transferring from one church to another without really ever putting down any roots. In many cases, smaller churches limited by finances and facilities will lose their people to the larger churches that have both, thus creating a "D&R situation." The D stands for depopulation and the R for repopulation. The smaller churches are being depopulated and die while the larger churches are repopulated and grow (transfer growth).

Concerning this present phenomenon, George Barna indicates that in the future many Christians will have multiple "church homes." It appears that the concept of a church home is presently undergoing a redefinition. In *The Frog in the Kettle,* he writes,

> In the coming decade, however, increasing numbers of people will instead select between two and five local churches and consider those to be their *group* of home churches. On any given weekend, they will determine which church to attend according to their own most keenly-felt needs, and the programs each of their favored churches has to offer. Their financial support will be splintered among each of those churches, and the aggregate amounts given are likely to be less than average since they will have decreased loyalty and a softer commitment to any single church.[1]

A Great Commission Vision

It's important that church planters periodically ask themselves the basic questions, "What's Christ's church supposed to be doing, and who are we trying to reach?" Asking these questions forces us to return to the basics. The answers to the questions undoubtedly are the Great Commission and lost people. Yet, there's a temptation in every ministry to start with the basics and then stray from them over a period of time. Church planters become involved in a ministry and discover that they are very good at teaching, preaching, or counseling. Then they begin subtly to focus on that area to the exclusion of other important areas. This is what has happened in many churches.

This raises another equally important question: "What specifically is the Great Commission?" The Great Commission mandate consists of three components that unfold chronologically.

The Pursuit of Lost People

The first component of the Great Commission is the intentional pursuit of lost people. This is reflected in the word "go" found at the beginning of the commission in Matthew 28:19: "Therefore go and make disciples of all nations, baptizing them in the name of the Father, and of the Son and of the Holy Spirit." It's also found in Mark 16:15: "He said to them, 'Go into all the world and preach the good news to all creation.'" Jesus is exhorting His people, the church, to pursue or seek lost people, which involves an "invasion" mentality. This was true in the first century, and it's true today.

Pursuing the Lost in the First Century

The pursuit of the lost is a common theme in the Gospels. This is strongly reflected in several key passages in the Gospel of Luke.

Luke 19:1–10. In verse 10, the Savior summarizes verses 1–9 and states, "For the Son of Man came to seek and save what was lost." In this passage we discover the Savior's heartbeat. If we could take His pulse, this is what we would feel. Walter Liefeld states that "Verse 10 could well be considered the 'key verse' of Luke. . . . The verse itself expresses the heart of Jesus' ministry as presented by Luke, both his work of salvation and his quest for the lost."[2] If we grasp this passage, then we grasp the Savior's mission according to the Gospel of Luke.

It's important to note that the infinitive "to save" is preceded by the infinitive "to seek." These two infinitives alert us to the structure of this section. Verses 1–9 are divided into two parts: a seeking part (vv. 1–7) followed by a saving part (vv. 8–9). Verse 10 summarizes the entire section. The Savior's mission was first to seek out or pursue lost people and then to save them. While Zacchaeus is a "seeker" in the sense that he's seeking the Savior (v. 3a), what's most important to observe in verses 1–7 is that Jesus is intentionally seeking Zacchaeus. Jesus walks up to the sycamore, looks up at Zacchaeus, and tells him that He will be his guest that day.

Luke 15:1–10. In verses 1–2, the Pharisees and the teachers of the law are complaining because the Savior shared a meal with tax collectors and "sinners." Eating with these people was something that no self-respecting, religious Jew would have done, especially a rabbi. Liefeld writes, "In OT times it was taken for granted that God's people did not consort with sinners (cf. Ps 1), but the Pharisees extended this beyond the biblical intent. To go so far as to "welcome" them especially to "eat" with them, implying table fellowship, was unthinkable to the Pharisees."[3]

Jesus explains His behavior by telling a parable about a man who pursued a lost sheep and a woman who sought a lost coin. The man is the Savior and the lost sheep represents the tax collectors and "sinners." The man doesn't wait for the lost sheep to return but pursues it. Not only does he pursue it, but he pursues it until he finds it! In commenting on this first parable, Liefeld writes that "in the obvious analogy to the search for the sheep, Jesus takes the initiative in seeking out lost people—a major theme in Luke (cf. 19:10)."[4] The analogies are the same with the woman and the lost silver coin. The woman loses only one coin but searches for it until she finds it. Just as both a sheep and a coin have value, the Savior is teaching that sinners have value to God and are worth His intense pursuit.

Luke 5:27–32. The Savior has won the heart of Levi, who was a tax-gatherer. Instantly, Levi becomes a disciple and invites all his lost friends to a reception to meet Jesus. The Pharisees and scribes note that the Savior is paying undue attention to lost "sinners" and strongly criticize Him for His efforts. Again, we see here that Jesus spent time with lost people; they mattered to Him. He didn't accept their sin, but He accepted and pursued them. He knew who would be at the party, and He didn't have to go. But He chose to do so. The religious crowd (Pharisees and scribes) threw the proverbial baby out with the bathwater. They didn't accept the sinners as well as their sin.

In each of these passages of Scripture Christ is intentionally targeting and seeking the nonreligious crowd, those who were the "unchurched people" of the first century. Here He clearly displays a "penetration" mentality.

Pursuing the Unchurched Lost in the Twenty-first Century

The pursuit of the unchurched lost will continue to be the responsibility of the church in the twenty-first century.

North America is an unchurched culture. As we saw in the second chapter, within the past thirty to forty years, America has experienced a shift from what was in the 1940s and 1950s primarily a churched culture to what at the beginning of the twenty-first century has largely become an unchurched culture. Kennon Callahan comments on this shift:

> Statistical research, analysis of this culture, and long-range projections all clearly indicate that ours is no longer a churched culture. Study after study and the steady decline of many mainline denominations confirm this fact.[5]

The church must pursue this culture. Before the culture shifted in its attitude toward the church, much evangelism took place within the walls of the facility on Sunday mornings. The custom was for most people, whether lost or saved, to go to church on Sunday. Callahan notes that

> Within the broad-based culture after World War II, people held the value that church was important. There was a commonly held belief that participation in church helped one to live a good life. Newcomers, when they moved into a community, were asked, "What church do you belong to? We want

to invite you to visit our church." People sought the church out and self-initiated their own participation. It was "the thing to do" to go to church.[6]

Today that custom has changed, and the evangelical church will not survive unless it aggressively pursues unchurched lost people outside its "four walls." It must adopt an "invasion" or "penetration" mentality. The days have long passed when the church could sit back and wait for lost people to come to it. It's not that lost people are angry with the typical church or express an antichurch sentiment. They're more interested in doing other things on Sunday morning. Again, Callahan observes, "In an unchurched culture, people do not necessarily view the church as harmful or hurtful. Rather, people simply view the church as not particularly relevant or helpful."[7]

It's true that on occasion some unchurched will come back for a visit, especially when they marry or have children. Gallup refers to this as the "lifecycle effect." Young people often leave the church either in their late teens or early twenties but may return in their late twenties.[8] After high school a number of churched children drop out of church. They pursue other things such as college and career, but not the church. They eventually come to a point in their lives, however, where God gets their attention—often as the result of some stressful event such as a marriage, a child, a sickness, or the untimely death of a friend or loved one. It's critical that they find a church that holds to orthodox Christianity while maintaining a culturally relevant methodology.

Regardless of whether these people come back or not, the mission of the church is now and always has been to pursue them wherever they are. Just as the Savior spent a lot of time with lost people in the first century, so His church will need to spend a lot of time with lost, unchurched people in the twenty-first century.

The church will have to change. This means that a lot of changes will have to take place in our churches. The prospect of change can be frightening and threatening to churched people. But we have no choice if we take the Savior's mandate seriously. We must not live in the past, but we must learn from the past in order to reach the world of the future (Phil. 3:13). Callahan believes that

> The loss and the decline should be teaching us something. The ways in which we have been doing leadership are no longer working on this mission field on which we now find ourselves. In a clear sense, I think this is God's way of teaching us that what we have been doing no longer works. Ultimately, we will continue to lose members until we finally figure that out.[9]

The application to church planting. It's the responsibility of those who will be planting churches in the twenty-first century to start congregations that pursue these unchurched lost people in culturally relevant ways. We must study our culture and show lost people that Scripture is relevant to their lives today. We would be wise to take time to study the programs and methods of churches that are effective in reaching this lost, unchurched generation. As long as these methods aren't in violation of Scripture, then we should determine which of them might be effective for reaching the people in our area of the country.

The Evangelism of Lost People

The second component of the Great Commission is evangelism. In Mark 16:15, Christ says, "Go into all the world and preach the good news to all creation." A Great Commission church makes evangelism a high priority. The church in general and the people in particular aren't just actively *seeking* lost people; they're *reaching* lost people. And this is evident in the fact that these churches are growing numerically. How do they do it? There are several characteristics that distinguish Great Commission churches from most typical churches in the area of evangelism.

Style

The evangelistic style of most typical churches is confrontational. While not many people are sharing their faith in today's churches, those who are do so by confronting lost people. This is more the old hard-sell approach that worked reasonably well in the 1940s and 1950s, when many lost people attended a church.

The evangelistic style of today's Great Commission churches is both relational and confrontational. Because so many lost people are unchurched, these churches encourage their people to build a relationship with lost people before presenting the gospel to them. This is a soft-sell approach. The idea is that it's more productive to witness to a friend than a stranger. However, they may also use confrontation if it fits the situation.

Motive

The motive for evangelism in many typical churches is guilt. When people in these congregations share the gospel it's because they feel they have to. The use of guilt to stimulate evangelistic effort is a self-defeating strategy. No wonder so many people in these churches avoid witnessing— it's usually associated in some way with guilt.

The motive in Great Commission churches is gratitude. When people in these churches witness, it's because they want to. Many of them are in their twenties to forties and have only recently come to faith. They're very grateful for what Christ has done, and are so excited about it that they want to tell all their lost, unchurched friends.

Methods

The methods for evangelism in many of today's churches are limited. Most rely on an evangelistic presentation in a sermon followed by an altar call. Others rely on some form of evangelism for children such as Good News Clubs or vacation Bible school but have no programs for adults. Some have tried knocking on doors in the community, but have experienced little success and a low turnout of volunteers.

The methods of evangelism in Great Commission churches are numerous. A number of them provide opportunities for lost people to be exposed to the church and the people of the church. For example, Lakepointe Baptist Church in Rowlett, Texas, a suburb of Dallas, has sponsored a health fair, a 10K run, and a power lift contest for weight lifters. Some of the people who attended these events would have never intentionally set foot inside a church prior to this.

Missions

The missions program in many traditional evangelical churches focuses on information and giving. In most cases, the people support missions. Missionaries come to the church and tell about their ministries, which are usually overseas. The expected response is prayer and financial support.

The missions program in Great Commission churches focuses on going. In many cases, the people themselves do missions. Missionaries may come to the church, but many are also sent out by the church. They not only go overseas, but many go next door. Others are targeting unchurched, unreached peoples in America. The expected response is not only prayer but personal involvement, which may include short-term missions and one- or two-week missions trips for exposure.

Expectations

Typical churches are often unrealistic in their expectations of the lost. If lost people come to their meetings, they do so only on the church's terms.

Great Commission churches realize that lost people are lost people! They don't expect lost people to behave like saved people *until they're saved people*. They design church meetings for them. The meeting could be a "seeker-friendly" Bible study or some kind of "seekers' service" on Sunday. In these meetings, the dress may be casual, there's no "Christianeze" (church talk), and no pressure is put on people to sing, sign, or say anything.

Finances

The churches that aren't reaching lost people don't budget for evangelism. If there's any money set aside at all for evangelism, it's very little. In fact, George Barna notes,

> Some question the way in which we spend our money. One study showed that while most churches believe they are in business to spread the gospel, they actually spend very little money on such activities. The average church in America allocates about 5 percent of its budget for evangelism, but approximately 30 percent of its budget for buildings and maintenance.[10]

The litmus test of a church's values is where it spends its money! Congregations spend money on the things they feel are important. If little or no money is set aside for evangelism, then, regardless of what excuse it may offer, the church doesn't value evangelism.

Great Commission churches value evangelism and this is reflected in their budgets. They may designate from one-third to one-half of the budget for evangelism. This is because one-third to one-half of their programs involves some form of evangelism. Consequently, they don't just talk about evangelism; they "put their money where their mouth is."

The Edification of Saved People

The third component of the Great Commission is edification. When the church reaches lost people, it doesn't drop them there but enfolds and disciples them. The goal is to equip them to reproduce themselves. This is the process of edification, which involves bringing new believers to Christ-likeness (Eph. 4:11–16). There are several characteristics that distinguish Great Commission churches from other typical churches in the area of edification.

Knowledge

The emphasis in many typical churches is on knowledge. Edification involves the communication of biblical content. The general idea is that the more of the Bible you know, the more spiritual you are. The road that leads to maturity is Bible knowledge. The result is that most of the church's programs focus on communicating the Scriptures. Consequently, people feel like they've served God because they've come to church, put some money in the offering, and taken lots of notes (some can even show you their notebooks to prove it).

In Great Commission churches, the emphasis is on knowing, being, and doing. They take seriously James' admonition to be doers of the word as well as hearers (1:22). Hearing the word is important, but the church also puts a lot of effort into doing the word. The road that leads to maturity is applied Bible knowledge. Thus, people feel like they've not served Christ if they're not applying the Scriptures to their lives (Heb. 5:14).

Christian Education

In many of today's typical churches, the primary vehicle for edification is the Sunday school. While education takes place in the service, the focus there is primarily on adults. The Sunday school program attempts to reach people of all ages. Most are grouped according to age and some by sex. The curriculum is determined by the Christian education board and is often standardized so that everyone studies the same thing at the same time.

Great Commission churches have turned to small groups as their primary vehicle of edification. Some may include a Sunday school, but it's only one of many options. These groups are set up for everyone in the church, including the children. Rather than grouping people together based on age or sex, they come together based on affinity for one another. The curriculum consists of multiple options depending on people's felt needs and styles of learning. Thus, the people determine the curriculum, not a Christian education board.

The Goal

The end of what many traditional evangelical churches are attempting to accomplish is maturity. This is because Scripture places such emphasis on moving new believers from infancy to adulthood (1 Cor. 3:1–2; Heb. 5:11–14). The measure of this maturity is usually Bible knowledge. Mature Christians are those who know a lot about the Bible.

Great Commission churches are also seeking to bring their people to maturity. They would agree with most evangelical traditional churches that this is the goal for their people. However, they would disagree strongly with the way these churches measure that maturity. They believe that what a person knows about the Scriptures is very important because the Bible communicates absolute, eternal truth from God. Yet they believe that maturity is for ministry. People must not only study Scripture, but must be involved in some form of ministry. Knowledge of the Bible must be balanced with service. Consequently, true maturity results in ministry.

Doctrinal Statements

Most typical churches have a doctrinal statement that explains what they believe. It often attempts to communicate the contents of their faith in great detail. This ranges from the deity of Christ to eschatological issues such as premillennialism, amillennialism, or postmillennialism and where one stands on the issue of the time of the rapture of the church in relation to the tribulation. Thus, it includes what it feels are the essentials of the faith. Those who desire to join these churches must read and agree with their doctrinal statement.

Great Commission churches also have a doctrinal statement that explains what they believe. However, many may not include what they believe about certain issues such as eschatology. Rightly or wrongly they would classify these issues as nonessentials. They argue that membership in the church shouldn't be dependent on where people stand on doctrinal issues. They believe that many people aren't even aware of these issues and haven't formed an opinion on them, especially if they are recent converts. They also believe that even if people disagree with the church on one of these issues that this shouldn't exclude them from membership. Some would ask that their teachers agree in the areas of nonessentials, especially those teaching adults.

Meetings

A large number of typical traditional churches still have most of their meetings on Sunday and Wednesday. Usually, there are two preaching services on Sunday, one in the morning and one in the evening. There's also a meeting on Wednesday night for the purpose of prayer. Faithful members are expected to show up at all three meetings each week, especially at the Wednesday night prayer meeting.

Great Commission churches are characterized by meetings all throughout the week. One or two of these may be services; however, the bulk of them are small group meetings. People aren't expected to be at all the meetings, but they are expected to come to at least one worship service and to be involved in a small group. Indeed, these small groups are key to edification because much of the ministry takes place in small group communities. These are places where people teach and are taught, they love and are loved, pray and are prayed for, encourage and are encouraged, confront and are confronted, hold accountable and are held accountable. It's possible that in many churches this is where people come to faith in Christ.

A Vision Exercise

1. As you are considering planting a church, do you have a single, clear vision? If so, what is it?

2. If you do have a vision, then it's very important for the purpose of communication that you be able to articulate that vision both verbally and in writing. In the space below, write your vision.

3. Is your vision ultimately the Great Commission? Does it involve pursuing, evangelizing, and discipling lost people? Why or why not?

8

Leading with Sustained Excellence

A Strong Servant-Leadership

The fact that 80 percent to 85 percent of the churches in North America are plateaued or in decline shows that we're facing a serious crisis in the area of leadership. Actually, the problem is because of a leadership vacuum in the church. In the foreword of Robert Clinton's *The Making of a Leader*, Leighton Ford writes the following:

> "Leadership" is a topic high on many agendas today, whether in politics, business, or the church.
>
> In part, this is because of a perceived leadership vacuum. In his leadership essays, John Gardner pointed out that at the time the United States was formed, the population stood at 3 million. That 3 million produced at least six leaders of world class—Washington, Adams, Jefferson, Franklin, Madison, and Hamilton. Today's American population of 240 million might be expected to produce eighty times as many world class leaders. But, asks Gardner, "Where are they?"
>
> At a recent convention of the National Association of Evangelicals, college president George Brushaber spoke of "a missing generation" of younger leaders ready to take the places of the senior post–World War II group of evangelical pioneers.
>
> My own travels and observations have led me to believe this is a worldwide phenomenon. Yet I am encouraged to believe there is a new group of younger men and women, roughly forty and under, emerging into leadership around the world.
>
> In response to both the lack of and the new wave of leaders, there is an urgent need for the cultivation of godly and spiritual leadership.[1]

A Great Commission vision is vital to any planted church. From the outset it provides a sense of direction for the church. Everyone knows where the church is going. But it takes leadership excellence to implement this vision. Ford is correct when he says that "there is a new group of younger men and women, roughly forty and under, emerging into leadership around the world." It is easy to get excited about what God has in store for the twenty-first century. The challenge, however, is to prepare this new generation to lead with sustained excellence.

What's vital for today's church in general and church planting in particular is a strong servant-leader. Consequently, the second church planting principle concerns strong servant-leadership. But exactly what is a strong servant-leader? How would we know one if we saw one?

A Leader

Christian leaders are godly persons (character) who know where they are going (vision) and have followers (influence).

Character

Godly character is the foundation of any leadership. It's the essential element that qualifies Christians to lead others. It earns people's respect and produces trust—the most essential factor in all relationships. A leader must be trusted to be followed. Since character forms the very foundation for ministry, if something goes wrong here, then the entire ministry will suffer the consequences. But what is godly character, and how do we develop it?

In examining the area of character, we must focus first on motives.

The Church Planter's Motives. Paul, a first-century church planter par excellence, gives us his motives for planting churches in 1 Thessalonians 2:2–6.

The first motive is to spread the gospel (v. 2). Paul had dared to proclaim the gospel to the Thessalonians in spite of much opposition. However, everywhere Paul went it was his goal to spread the gospel. In 1 Corinthians 9:16, he confesses, "Woe to me if I do not preach the gospel!" Church planters must have a strong desire to see lost people come to faith in the Savior as the result of their ministry.

The second motive is to please God (v. 4). It's God, not people, to whom we're ultimately accountable. We should minister in such a way that we look forward someday to hearing the words, "Well done, good and faithful servant!"

The third motive is to tell people what they need to hear (v. 5). Paul was careful to avoid telling people what they wanted to hear. Instead, he told them what they needed to hear. Prospective church planters must expect criticism when they tell people what they need to hear and be prepared for it when it comes.

The fourth motive for church planting is to serve God (v. 5). Church planting is not to be done for personal gain. At some point in ministry, church planters are tempted to ask Peter's question (Matt. 19:27b): "What then will there be for us?" (my translation: What's in it for us?) The Savior's answer in the rest of chapter 19 and chapter 20 is that the Father is most pleased when we serve Him without regard for personal reward. When this is the case, He blesses us beyond all expectation.

The last motive is the grace of God in Jesus Christ and what He has done on the cross (v. 6). Church planting is not done for personal praise. Praise feeds our self-esteem and gives us a feeling of significance. If we minister because we want to earn the praise of others, we're headed for a fall because our worth and significance rest on the grace of God, not what we've done in planting churches.

The Church Planter's Character. Not only does Paul list the church planter's motives, but he lists certain character qualities in 1 Thessalonians 2:2–8.

In verse 2, Paul says that church planting takes courage. Church planting isn't easy even though it's very exciting. There will be times when church planters may be attacked and even insulted. It takes men and women of courage who are not afraid to take risks and step out in faith in obedience to the Savior. It is spiritually refreshing to read Hebrews 11, which contains various faith cameos of courageous people who trusted God in difficult times.

Another quality Paul puts forward in verse 2 is endurance. Paul wasn't "quick to quit." With all the persecution and the criticism, there were times when he experienced devastating discouragement. It would have been so much easier to quit! Yet, he was determined to "hang tough," knowing that his circumstances would change in time and that he would benefit spiritually by enduring them.

In verse 3, Paul lists three character qualities of a person who has integrity: truthfulness (freedom from error), purity of motive, and honesty. Paul was a man of integrity and authenticity. His character was like that of Jesus Christ. He realized that if there was a problem in any of these areas that the entire cause of Christ would suffer. Just as in the first century, so today we must be men and women who speak and live what we know to be the truth out of a spirit of purity and honesty. Christian ministry in the 1980s and 1990s was adversely affected by those who professed the Savior publicly but lacked personal truthfulness, purity of motive, and honesty.

The last two character qualities are gentleness and affection. In verse 7, Paul compares himself to a caring mother. This is important because he was able to balance his High *D* temperament, which tends to be more task-oriented than people-oriented, with a sensitivity to people. In verse 8, he tells his people of his love for them. Though he was a strong leader who got things done, he was a caring, loving leader who was careful to let his people know how much he cared for them. It's amazing what people will accomplish when they know you love them!

How do we develop godly character? With all the problems Christian leaders have experienced in terms of their character, if church planters are not serious about developing their character, then it would be best for them not to consider professional Christian ministry. There are several sources that may serve to help us in the development of our character.

In his book, *Too Busy Not to Pray,*[2] Bill Hybels tells of his spiritual struggles and how God has helped him grow and mature as a Christian leader. He discusses several areas of quiet time (adoration, confession, thanksgiving, and supplication). Since we're all unique individuals, you may want to vary this with that which is particularly helpful to you. For example, I've placed commitment between thanksgiving and supplication. I've found in my worship of God that after realizing all that I have to be thankful for, I'm often moved to commit my life afresh to Him in terms of His service.

Another helpful source in developing character is Dallas Willard's *Spirit of the Disciplines.*[3] In light of Paul's challenge in 1 Timothy 4:7, this book is helpful in showing leaders how to discipline themselves for godliness in character. Willard is particularly helpful in two specific areas: abstinence (solitude, silence, and sacrifice) and engagement (confession, celebration, study, and submission).

Willard has done us a real service in that he's restored the disciplines to their proper place in our spiritual formation. In general, evangelical Christianity has overreacted to early monasticism and its excesses with the result that it has tossed out the proverbial baby with the bath water. We read in church history of believers who abused themselves in all kinds of ways such as living on top of a pillar for as much as twenty or thirty years in an attempt to be closer to God. Who wouldn't walk away from this kind of excess! Yet, when we look closer, we discover that the monastic movement in general has much to offer us in terms of our spiritual development. Willard has done much to help us recover this critical aspect of the movement.

Vision

The clear casting of leaders' visions tells where they're going and at the same time supplies the motivation they need to get there.

Personal Ministry Vision

A personal vision is a clear and challenging vision of a leader's future personal ministry. A leader's recognition of unique design leads to determining the future direction of ministry within the body of Christ. The process is threefold: (1) assessment to discover design; (2) development of a ministry vision; and (3) designing a program to accomplish the ministry vision.

Organizational Ministry Vision

Organizational or institutional vision relates directly to the ministry of a particular organization. An institutional vision is a clear and challenging picture of the future of the ministry organization as it can and must be. Once leaders have determined their personal ministry vision, it's extremely important that they identify with a ministry organization that has a significant organizational vision that is closely related to their personal vision. The alignment of the two will directly influence the long-term effectiveness of the leader in the ministry.

Influence

A third characteristic of leadership is influence. Not only is it important, but it's affected by character and vision.

The Importance of Influence

Most definitions of leadership, both secular and Christian, include the concept of influence. An example from the Christian sector is the definition of Chuck Swindoll, who writes, "At the risk of oversimplifying, I'm going to resist a long, drawn-out definition and settle on one word. It's the word *influence*. If you will allow me two words—*inspiring influence*."[4] Then he explains further: "Those who do the best job of management—those most successful as leaders—use their influence to inspire others to follow, to work harder, to sacrifice, if necessary."[5] While there's some confusion of management with leadership, Swindoll accurately underscores the importance of influence in leadership.

Good leaders exert a powerful influence on people. They are like magnets in that they attract people. When they turn around and look behind them, they see people. Those who insist that they're leaders, but have no one following them, are not leaders at all.

The Key to Influence

The key to influence is character and a significant vision (both personal and institutional). <u>Godliness has a great attraction</u>. Take, for example, the early ministry of the Savior. In John 1, the disciples appear to have been especially attracted to Him. For example, in verse 37, John the Baptist introduces Jesus to Peter and another disciple and the result is they follow Him. In verse 38, Jesus turns around to look and finds them standing there, probably in awe. Then in verse 43, He simply instructs Philip, "Follow me," and Philip responds without question.

People who are able to communicate a clear, significant vision for both themselves and their ministries will also draw people. There's something attractive about leaders who know where they're going. They seem to have grasped a purpose in life that often intrigues and draws those who aren't sure about their own direction.

When godliness and vision are combined in the same person, that individual is able to exert a great influence over people. This is what Swindoll refers to as inspiring influence. Should this be combined with other qualities, such as natural leadership abilities or the ability to communicate with articulateness, the result is powerful, inspiring leadership.

A Strong Leader

Not only must church planters be leaders, but they must also be strong leaders. One of the reasons so many American churches are struggling today is because pastors are not exercising strong leadership.

The Problem of Co-Leadership

A primary leadership problem facing many pastors is the struggle they're facing with their lay boards over who will lead the church. In most cases, the boards have won the battle, and the church is led by a consensus of the board members. The result is that in a large number of churches the pastor is regarded as just one more leader in the church, or worse, as an employee of the board who follows orders that have "come down from on high." This is a constant complaint on the part of many pastors.[6] But how did this situation develop and what has been the result?

The Historical Development

There are at least three factors that have influenced strong lay leadership of church boards.

The first is a reaction on the part of most Americans to the various totalitarian regimes that have suppressed and brutalized people from World War II up to the present. Some obvious examples would be Adolph Hitler in Nazi Germany, Idi Amin in Uganda, and the Ayatollah Khomeni in Iran. A combination of these factors along with the financial and sexual indulgences of leaders such as Jim Bakker and Jimmy Swaggert has created a somewhat popular anti-authoritarian mood across America, especially toward pastors. Consequently, the idea of following a single, primary leader in the church frightens many.

The enabler model is another factor. Peter Wagner notes that this model arose and became popular in a number of seminaries because it emphasized the servant role of pastors and their need to train laypeople for ministry.[7] This sounds very biblical. Yet there was another side to this model that proved disastrous. Lyle Schaller, impersonating a dissatisfied church layperson, writes, "We called a self-identified enabler type minister and we got burned. We found the word enabler was a synonym for not being an initiator, not calling, not being aggressive, and not taking leadership responsibilities."[8] The problem is that this view continues to be taught in seminaries today.

A third factor is the Church Renewal Movement of the 1960s and 1970s, which emphasized lay involvement in the leadership, ministries, and worship of the local church. And again, who could argue with this in light of such clear passages as 1 Corinthians 12 and Ephesians 4:11–12? However, there emerged from this the idea that laypeople were to lead the church. Consequently, many pastors turned their leadership authority over to various lay elder or deacon boards and assumed positions alongside of or under them.

The Result

Someone has said, "The proof of the pudding is in the tasting." This certainly has proved to be the case in terms of lay control of church boards. Essentially, lay control of the church's leadership at the board level has resulted in "power blocks" that stifle good pastoral leadership.

The argument of the Church Renewal Movement that lay board leadership is critical to church renewal has proved incorrect. The majority of these churches are in decline with poor lay participation in ministries, the one exception being that of lay participation and control on elder or deacon boards.

Why is this the case? The reason is because pastors are the best qualified to lead in most situations. This isn't because they're necessarily more spiritual or more intelligent than the laypeople on their boards. It's because they have two critical factors in their favor. In *The Unity Factor,* Larry Osborne identifies these as time and training.

Essentially, pastors immerse themselves in the church's ministry on a full-time basis. A typical week consumes anywhere from fifty to sixty hours or more. What difference does this make?

> As a full-time pastor, I'm immersed in the day-to-day ministry of the church. Unlike any of my board members, I'm thinking about our problems and opportunities full-time. I have the time to plan, pray, consult, and solve problems.
>
> To lead, a person needs to know the organization inside out—how the parts fit together and how each will be affected by proposed changes. And that takes time, lots of it. In all but the smallest churches, it can't be done on a spare-time basis. In a church with multiple staff, Lyle Schaller claims, it takes between fifty and sixty hours a week.
>
> Not that our board members are incapable of leading an organization. That's what a number do for a living. But they do it on a full-time basis. None would think of trying to do it in his or her spare time. Yet that is exactly what happens in a church where the board or a powerful lay leader tries to take on the primary leadership role.[9]

Not only do pastors spend much of their time in ministry, but many have been specifically trained for what they do. This may range anywhere from basic on-the-job experience to advanced studies in seminary. Osborne explains the advantages of this:

> I also have a decided advantage when it comes to training. Like most pastors, my formal education and ongoing studies have equipped me specifically to lead a church. Add to that a network of fellow pastors and church leaders, and I have a wealth of information from which to draw. When a church faces a tough situation or golden opportunity, the pastor is the one most likely to have been exposed to a similar situation. If not, he'll usually know where to find out what the experts recommend.
>
> By contrast, most board members are limited in their exposure to other ministries. They don't have the time to read the literature. And their network of experts is usually limited to a previous pastor or two. Because the church is spiritually centered, volunteer run, and educationally focused, it's different from any other organization, and as a rule, the pastor has more

training in how to lead it than anyone else. Are there exceptions? Certainly, but that's the point: they're *exceptions*. A friend tried to model his church after one with an incredibly strong and competent group of lay elders. In his model church, the pastor simply prayed, taught, and counseled, while the elders took care of everything else. There was no need for strong pastoral leadership, he told me, if you picked the right people and discipled them properly. But he failed to notice that the key elders in his model church were self-employed and independently wealthy. They had all the time in the world, and they attended seminars and seminary classes and read in their spare time.

His elders, on the other hand, all had jobs that called for fifty to sixty hours a week. They had neither the time nor the training to take a strong leadership role. As long as my friend waited for the elders to take charge, the church floundered.[10]

The Arguments for Primary Pastoral Leadership

Passive pastors need to step out and take the lead in churches. This doesn't mean that others aren't involved in leadership. What it means is that the pastor becomes the leader of leaders, the point person on the ministry team. There are three strong arguments for this view.

The Theological Argument

Where two or more people relate together functionally for any period of time, such as in a ministry or even a family context, one person must take the position as the leader or head of the team. Scripture provides us with several examples, especially in 1 Corinthians 11:3.

One obvious example is the relationship between Christ and man. In 1 Corinthians 11:3, Paul writes that "the head of every man is Christ." The point is that in the leadership and ministry of the local church, Christ assumes the position of head.

A second example is the relationship between the man and the woman. Again, in 1 Corinthians 11:3, Paul writes "and the head of the woman is man." The debate over this passage concerns the identity of the man and the woman. Are they husband and wife, or are they representative of the male–female relationship in the church? The context indicates that this passage is concerned with the practices of the church in the worship services. Paul addresses the subordination of the wife to the husband in other places such as Ephesians 5:22–24. It's generally accepted that this functional subordination concerns their relationship in all areas of life, including the church. Thus, there would be no need to relate this to the church in particular. Consequently, Paul is teaching that in the local church context, where men are worshiping and ministering with women, that the men are to take the lead.

A third example is the relationship of the Godhead. Paul writes in 1 Corinthians 11:3 that "the head of Christ is God." This passage is talking about the relationship among the various members of the Trinity. Scripture teaches that in terms of their essence, the Father, Son, and Holy Spirit are all one and equally divine. Therefore, this passage must be discussing the functional relationship of the Godhead.

While all three are equal in essence, one is the head in terms of function. Robert Gromacki describes it this way: "Thus, even though there was an equality of persons within the divine oneness, there was an order (a headship) to execute the divine counsel."[11] And in this functional relationship, one Person, the Father, was the head.

This should be most instructive theologically for the functioning of pastor–lay board relationships. If the most perfect relationship that exists (the Godhead) functions with a single head (the Father), what about our less than perfect lay elder and deacon boards in the churches? Who should that leader be? In light of Osborne's two points concerning time and training, the obvious answer is the pastor.

The Biblical Argument

The Bible presents a number of examples where individuals exercised primary leadership in ministry contexts. The classic example would be the ministry relationship of Christ and His disciples. There's little question that He was the primary leader of this band of men.

Another example is Peter. F. F. Bruce notes that in the lists of the apostles in the Gospels, Peter is always mentioned first.[12] Peter's name appears in the Book of Acts no less than fifty-seven times in chapters 1–5, 8–12, and 15, while the other apostles are mentioned only twenty-five times. He's the chief spokesman and preacher in the Book of Acts (1:16–22; 2:14–36; 3:12–26; 4:8–12; 10:34–43; 11:4–17; 15:7–11). Finally, Peter is singled out and placed in juxtaposition to the other apostles in such places as Acts 2:37 and 5:29. Thus, it would appear that among the apostles Peter was the leader of leaders.

A third example is James and his position in the Jerusalem church. In Acts 12:17, it's interesting to note that Peter instructs a small group that had been praying for his freedom to go and tell "James and the brothers" about his miraculous deliverance. Why does Peter specifically mention James and not the others? In Acts 15, the Jerusalem church had gathered with the elders and apostles to determine the relationship of the law to the gospel, James is the one who issues a summary directive. Finally, in Acts 21:18, James is mentioned first and in juxtaposition to the elders of the church. It would seem evident from all this that he was the primary leader in the church. In fact, F. F. Bruce refers to the elders as "a sort of Sanhedrin, with James as their president."[13]

If it's God's will that local churches be led by a group of men (co-leadership) without a single leader or leader of leaders, then how do we explain these biblical examples? They would certainly be setting a poor example if there's to be no leader of leaders. One could argue that the example of Christ and the disciples is an exception because He's God. But then how do we explain Peter's obvious position of prominence? Again, one might want to argue that he was an exception because he was an apostle. But it is more difficult to explain James' position in the Jerusalem church; he wasn't an apostle but was the Lord's half brother.

The Practical Argument

All people aren't created equal in terms of their leadership abilities, knowledge, experience, reputation, training, and commitment. Some have the spiritual gift of leadership (Rom. 12:8) while others don't. Some are gifted naturally with leadership skills and abilities while others aren't.

To put a group of people together on a board and not recognize and give primary leadership to the one with the greater leadership gifts, abilities, and training doesn't make sense. This, in essence, is what true co-leadership attempts to do! Consequently, true co-leadership most often results in no leadership. The fact of the matter is that a group can't lead a church.

Of course, this assumes that the full-time pastor is fully qualified as a leader. This breaks down when a church selects a pastor who is not a leader. Some churches are looking primarily for a pastor who is a teacher or an evangelist to lead them. When this happens, there may very well be laypeople on the board who are better at leading than the pastor. It makes better sense to look for a leader who has the other qualities and gifts as well, especially if this person is going to lead the church.

The Arguments for Strong Pastoral Leadership

It's a basic fact of life that in every organization there have to be leaders who have the power and the necessary authority to exercise that power. Without these strong leaders, no organization could function properly. This is true in the church as well as the marketplace. However, the issue for the church concerns who has this power and authority to lead.

Scripture teaches that this power and the authority to exercise it rest in the elders of the church. Of course, Christ is the ultimate head of His church. Just as the Father is the head of the Trinity (1 Cor. 11:3), so the Son is the head of the church (Eph. 5:23). Consequently, He has all power and the authority to exercise that headship.

Yet it would appear from the Scriptures that He has passed some power and authority on through the apostles to the elders of the church. Thus, while the apostles are no longer on the scene, the elders remain and are the leaders in the churches. Apparently, each church had a plurality of elders (Acts 11:30; 16:4; 20:17; 21:18). Passages such as 1 Timothy 5:17, 1 Thessalonians 5:12, and Hebrews 13:7, 17 indicate that these people had the power and authority to lead and direct the affairs of each local church.

The issue at hand concerns whether these elders were part-time laypeople as found in many evangelical churches or full-time professionals. There are three biblical arguments that indicate the latter.

The Size of the New Testament Churches

Many, if not all, of the churches in the Book of Acts were large churches requiring the leadership of a substantial number of full-time elders. There are a number of passages that indicate that the churches in Acts, unlike the majority of churches in America today,[14] were large (1:13; 2:41, 44, 47; 4:4; 5:14; 6:1, 7; 9:31, 35, 42; 11:21, 24, 26; 14:1, 21; 16:5; 17:4, 12; 18:8, 10; 19:26; 21:10).

The Jerusalem Church. The first example is the church at Jerusalem. It began with 120 people (Acts 1:13), but as the result of Peter's two sermons gained 3,000 people (Acts 2:41), and then an additional 5,000 men not including women and children (Acts 4:4).[15] This growth continued, for Luke writes in Acts 5:14, "Nevertheless, more and more men and women believed in the Lord and were added to their number." Then in Acts 6:1 he writes, "In those days when the number of disciples were increasing." And again in Acts 6:7: "The number of disciples in Jerusalem increased rapidly, and a large number of priests became obedient to the faith." Luke's use of numbers in describing the Jerusalem church is important hermeneutically because it helps us gain an understanding of what he means in terms of size later in Acts when he uses such qualifiers as "many" or "great" instead of exact numbers.

The Church in Judea, Galilee, and Samaria. In Acts 9, Luke directs the reader's attention to the church in Judea, Galilee, and Samaria. Like the Jerusalem church, "it grew in numbers" (Acts 9:31). In verse 35, he comments on Lydda and Sharon: "All those who lived in Lydda and Sharon saw him and turned to the Lord." In verse 42 Luke notes that "This became known all over to Joppa, and many believed in the Lord."

The Antioch Church. Luke gives evidence in Acts 11 that the church at Antioch was very large. In verse 21, he writes that "a great number of people believed and turned to the Lord." In verse 24 he adds that "a great number of people were brought to the Lord." Finally, in verse 26, he says that they "taught great numbers of people."

The churches of the first missionary journey. Paul's three missionary church-planting journeys also resulted in large planted churches. The first missionary journey produced a number of growing churches. For example, in Iconium "a great number of Jews and Gentiles believed" (Acts 14:1). At Derbe, they "won a large number of disciples" (Acts 14:21). Then, in a final summary comment at the end of the first journey, Luke writes, "So the churches were strengthened in the faith and grew daily in numbers" (Acts 16:5).

The churches of the second missionary journey. The results of the second church-planting journey were much the same. The Corinthian church consisted of "a large number of God-fearing Greeks and not a few prominent women" (Acts 17:4). In reference to the church at Berea, Luke writes in verse 12, "Many of the Jews believed, as did also a number of prominent Greek women and many Greek men." He returns to the Corinthian church in Acts 18:8 and writes "many of the Corinthians who heard him believed and were baptized." In verse 10, he concludes that "I have many people in this city."

The churches of the third missionary journey. The third church-planting journey also resulted in the starting of a number of large churches. For example, in Acts 19:26, an enemy of the faith, Demetrius, says, "And you see and hear how this fellow Paul has convinced and led astray large numbers of people here in Ephesus and in practically the whole province of Asia."

The evidence indicates that many if not most of the New Testament churches were large. A very conservative estimate of the size of the Jerusalem church using only Acts 2:41 and not counting the women and children in Acts 4:4 is 8,000 people. In his commentary on Acts, Lenski remarks, "It has been conservatively estimated that at this time the total number of disciples was between twenty and twenty-five thousand."[16]

The sheer size of these first-century megachurches would necessitate a significant number of full-time elders. If the early churches were led by part-time elders, how many would it require to shepherd these large churches? Consider for a moment the Jerusalem church. If it only had 8,000 people, and a part-time lay elder could adequately shepherd five families, then this church would have had as many as 1,600 elders! It would not seem likely that these elders were part-time laypeople as so many assume who advocate lay co-leadership today.

What we must understand is that the apostolic church functioned at two levels. One was the large city-church meeting described above. When Paul wrote to the churches at Rome, Corinth, and so on, he was writing to the city-church. The other level was the house-church meeting that gathered more frequently. That is where much of the ministry took place. Scripture refers to these in Acts 2:46, 12:12–17; Rom. 16:3–5, 14–15; 1 Cor. 16:19, and so on. Paul's letters to the city-churches were circulated through these (Col. 4:16). My point is that today's local congregation is a slightly larger version of a first century house-church that was pastored by a first-century elder. The city-churches had a plurality of elders, each of whom pastored house-churches.

The Ministry of the Elders

A second argument that the elders in the early church were full-time is based on their ministry in the church.

The function of their ministry. Essentially, the elders were expected to oversee and minister by shepherding the flock. For example, in Acts 20:28 Paul instructs, "Keep watch over yourselves and all the flock of which the Holy Spirit has made you overseers. Be shepherds of the church of God, which he bought with his own blood." In 1 Peter 5:2a, Peter writes, "Be shepherds of God's flock that is under your care." In light of what real shepherds did with a flock of sheep on a Palestinian hillside, this would probably involve leading, caring for, guiding, instructing, and protecting people in the church.

The time for their ministry. This ministry in itself would require a large amount of time on the part of the elders. Good shepherding necessitates both a reasonable amount of preparation time (as in a teaching ministry) as well as actual ministry time.

But does the part-time person have adequate time to devote to a shepherding ministry? The majority of those who are elders are married and have children. They also work a lot of hours. For instance, a survey in *Leadership* revealed that "77% of all middle-level executives spend 50 or more hours per week on their jobs." And "26% of executives spend more than 60 hours per week."[17] It would seem doubtful that an elder with a family and full-time employment would have enough time available to shepherd a flock. Indeed, in addition to employment, simply ministering to and rearing a family is a full-time job.

Another consideration is whether it's fair to expect a layperson to set aside the time necessary to shepherd a flock. If that person was single or married without children, it might be possible. But not for a married person who has children. Such demands on a person's time seem unfair and could result in feelings of strong guilt and inadequacy when that person isn't able to deliver. In fact, in many churches with lay elder boards very little if any shepherding takes place. This is because in most cases, it's not possible for them to deliver. Instead, most meet approximately once a month and make important decisions regarding matters they know little about. In effect, most function in a decision-making rather than a shepherding capacity.

The Remuneration of the Elders

A third argument that the elders in the early churches were full-time is the fact that many, if not all, were remunerated. There's no specific mention as to whether the elders in the earlier churches in the Book of Acts were remunerated. They were probably among those who were helped through a mutual sharing of goods (Acts 2:44–45; 4:32, 34–35).

The strong evidence is found in the later churches according to 1 Timothy 5:17–18 and 1 Peter 5:2. In 1 Timothy 5:17–18, Paul tells Timothy, "The elders who direct the affairs of the church well are worthy of double honor, especially those whose work is preaching and teaching. For the Scripture says, 'Do not muzzle the ox while it is treading out the grain,' and 'The worker deserves his wages.'" It's obvious from verse 18 that "honor" is a reference to some kind of remuneration such as "wages."

In 1 Peter 5:2, Peter addresses the motives of those who would be elders. In particular, he warns elders against shepherding the flock out of greediness for money. This would obviously imply that elders were remunerated for their ministry.

The Conclusion

The conclusion of all this is that the elders who were given power and the authority to exercise that power in the local churches were not part-time but full-time people. Consequently, the present system of lay co-leadership that is practiced in so many churches across the land isn't based on Scripture as so many have been led to think.

Application. But how does all this apply to churches today? New or established churches should be led by professional staff pastors who are equivalent to the first-century elders. These leaders are given the power and authority to lead and direct the ministries of the churches. They have the time and the training to do the job most effectively, as opposed to a group of part-time lay co-leaders. This would enable them to exert the strong pastoral leadership that is needed in so many of our floundering churches at the end of the twentieth century. This is also critical to planting churches, especially in the early stages where strong leadership is key to the growth and survival of the new church.

Accountability. One important issue that must naturally be raised is that of accountability.

First, it's imperative that churches do a better job in selecting pastors in the first place. Paul in 1 Timothy 5:22 warns believers about selecting these individuals too quickly. When a pastor leaves a church the congregation may not be in any real hurry to find a new pastor, so they move too slowly. When they finally realize that the church is starting to lose a lot of people, they take the first person who comes along.

When a pastor leaves, the church should begin to search for a new pastor immediately. The search process should focus on character (1 Tim. 3:1–7; Titus 1:5–9) and servanthood (Mark 10:42–45). References should be contacted. A key request would be, "Tell me three positive character traits and two negative character traits about this person." This gives the references permission to tell the whole story. The problem is that far too many churches don't properly check out a potential candidate's character before they call that individual.

Second, primary leaders should be accountable not only to some lay board of co-leaders, but to the entire church. The biblical teaching on accountability is that all of us are to be involved (Matt. 5:23–24; 18:15–20; Gal. 6:1). Thus, the entire church is responsible to hold the pastor as well as one another accountable for character and conduct. This is to be done according to the guidelines found in 1 Timothy 5:19–20.

Those who are on the professional leadership team are especially responsible to hold one another accountable. A good example of this would be Peter and Paul in Galatians 2:11–14. Wise leaders make themselves accountable to a group or to single individuals.

One final word is necessary. This doesn't mean that part-time laypeople aren't involved in leadership and ministry in the local church. Actually, their involvement is necessary to the health and stability of the entire church according to 1 Corinthians 12 and other passages. The difference is that they lead in terms of directing and ministering in small groups, evangelism teams, and target group ministries according to their time schedules. This is to be preferred over meeting once or twice a month and sitting on a church board.

A Strong Servant-Leader

Not only must church planters be strong leaders, but it's also imperative that they be strong servant-leaders. In understanding this, it's helpful to view the different approaches to leadership in terms of a continuum.

At one end of the leadership continuum is absolute leadership. This is typical of professional despots or tyrants. These are people who rule with an "iron fist" and are accountable to no one. They're so authoritarian that whatever they want gets done and nothing takes place in their churches without their approval. In Mark 10:42, Christ called the disciples together and said, "You know that those who are regarded as rulers of the Gentiles lord it over them, and their high officials exercise authority over them." This is the Savior's evaluation of absolute leadership. He describes it as a characteristic of pagan not Christian leaders.

This is the kind of authoritarian leader that Christians living at the end of the twentieth century fear. This is the very picture that comes to mind whenever they hear or think of strong leadership. Consequently, they react most negatively: "We're Americans and we're free, nobody's going to tell us what to do!"

At the other end of the continuum from absolute leadership is co-leadership. Co-leadership is characteristic of church boards that are controlled and run by part-time laypeople. Leadership is by compromise. The full-time professionals are primarily involved in ministry, not leadership. This is the form that seems most prevalent in many of our churches today. In essence, it's an overreaction to absolute leadership. Having rejected the one extreme, many have simply moved to the other extreme. Co-leadership isn't characteristic of biblical leadership and most commonly results in no leadership.

Peter Wagner makes several important observations about the issue of co-leadership. The first is that "the plurality-of-elders structure is good for small churches and nongrowing churches. But as a church gains growth momentum and becomes larger, the system becomes more dysfunctional."[18] Co-leadership is probably the reason why these churches are small and aren't growing.

The second observation concerns who is actually leading in the larger plurality-of-elder churches. Wagner notes that "in almost all of the plurality-of-elder churches which are growing, a top leader has emerged even though one was not supposed to. Some of the strongest leaders I know say 'I don't lead' and go ahead and do it."[19] Those churches that grow do so not because of lay leadership but because of the leadership of the pastor.

Many are starting to admit this. For example, in an interview in *Leadership,* Gene Getz was asked, "How has your leadership style changed since your early days in the first Fellowship Bible Church?" He responded with the following:

> I think I've gained more self-awareness—more self-honesty, if I may coin the word. If you had asked me ten years ago, "What makes this church work?" I would have said, "Humanly speaking, it's our multiple leadership, primarily the elders."
>
> Today I'd answer that question by saying, "Our elders are key, but I'm the key to helping the elders function."
>
> In the early days I overreacted to authoritarian leadership styles—which I still think are unfortunate—but I've always led. Now I feel I'm more honest with myself and others about the importance of a strong leader, particularly in a growing church, and yet developing a strong multiple leadership that *does* lead as a team.[20]

In the middle of the leadership continuum is the biblical form of servant-leadership. In Mark 10:45, the Savior says, "For even the Son of Man did not come to be served but to serve, and to give his life as a ransom for many." But what does this mean?

The greatest example of a servant-leader is the Savior. He proved to be both a strong leader and a servant-leader. For example, no one would question the fact that He was in charge. His entire ministry was characterized by a personal, spiritual strength.

Yet the Savior also displayed a servant's heart. This is clear from such passages as Mark 10:45 and Matthew 20:28 and is illustrated in John 13, where He assumes the posture of a servant and washes the disciples' feet. Not only did He lead the disciples strongly, but He loved them passionately, and ultimately gave His life for them.

Strong servant-leaders are the kinds of people who lead with sustained excellence. We desperately need these kinds of leaders to take the church of Jesus Christ into the twenty-first century. Just as important, we need strong servant-leaders to plant Great Commission churches that will win for Christ the unchurched lost people of the twenty-first century.

A Leadership Exercise

1. What is your definition of leadership? What is your definition of Christian leadership? Does it agree with the one in this book or does it differ? Why?

2. What are your motives for wanting to plant a church? Are they the same as those found in 1 Thessalonians 2:2–6?

3. How would you describe your character? Does your character match up to that of Paul in 1 Thessalonians 2:2–8?

4. What are you doing to develop your character?

5. Do you have a vision? Do you believe that a vision is important to leadership? Why?

6. Do people naturally follow you? If they do, then why are they following you? Conversely, if they don't, then why aren't they following you? If you're not sure about any of these questions, ask someone you can trust to tell you the truth.

9

Every Member a Minister

A Well-Mobilized Lay Army

In his book *Honest to God?* Bill Hybels describes the following scene:

It's August. Throughout the country, the late summer ritual begins. And it's not a pretty sight.

Pastor Bob has just received his annual flood of resignation notes. Sunday school teachers, ushers, Bible study leaders, youth leaders, and assorted other "servers" have called it quits. He's not surprised. It happens every year. Some people offer lengthy explanations. Others say simply, "I've done my part."

Now Pastor Bob knows that the ministries of the church can't continue unless someone fills all these empty positions. So, with unprecedented determination, he begins psyching up for the annual "August Recruitment Campaign."

Pastor Bob isn't the first to fight this battle. His predecessor fought it, too. In fact, it's become somewhat of a tradition—one that even his most tradition-bound congregants would like to do without. So while Pastor Bob is psyching himself up, his two hundred members are doing the same. They know they'll have to be tough to resist this year's recruitment campaign. It's going to be war!

A man named Jim says to himself, "He's not going to get me this year. So help me, I don't care what he preaches on, or how often he threatens God's judgment. I'm not going to cave in—even if he starts to cry! Three years ago he cried and I ended up as a center aisle usher—and I don't even like people. This year I'll resist to the end."

Pastor Bob does know how much resistance has surfaced in his congregation. So this year he's bringing out the heavy artillery. He's planning a four-sided series called "Serve or Burn." Every week he'll use a dramatic illustration from *Foxe's Book of Martyrs*. There's nothing like true-to-life stories of people who gave up their lives for serving Christ.

He's already decided to wear a lapel microphone. Then he can walk the length of the stage, raise his voice, perspire a little bit, and wave his Bible in the air.

On the fourth week, he'll bring out his secret weapon. Seven-year-old Suzi Miller. He'll cradle the little darling on his lap and ask her what it will be like to spend a whole year in second grade Sunday school with no teacher. He hopes against hope that she'll cry. If she does, he'll win the war hands down. Sure as shootin' he'll win the war.

So the stage is set. It's going to be an interesting August.[1]

Unfortunately, all too often the above scenario describes the typical solution to a problem that every church across America faces: the unemployment problem. Not that people in the church are looking for things to do. In fact, there's lots to be done, but no one's particularly excited about doing it—even those who are presently involved. Consequently, the church has no alternative but to hang a "Help Wanted" sign out front.

A vital principle for church planting is lay mobilization. Peter Drucker writes, "People determine the performance capacity of an organization. No organization can do better than the people it has."[2] Lay mobilization is the solution to the unemployment problem and involves the process of recruiting and equipping a well-mobilized lay army to accomplish the various ministries of the church. The object in church planting is not to pursue a corrective approach in order to take down the "Help Wanted" signs, but to pursue a preventative one to see that none go up in the first place.

In 1 Corinthians 12, Paul compares the church to a vibrant, healthy human body. Just as it's critical that all the parts of the human body be present and functioning in their proper places, so it is in the life of the church. This is the task of lay mobilization. This principle is placing the right people in the right places for the right reasons with the result that every member becomes a minister.

The Plan for Lay Mobilization

An important part of the Father's plan for blessing is our involvement in fruitful service for Him in the church. This is evident from His divine accomplishments in our lives. First, He's created each of us with a unique design (Job 10:8–9; Ps. 139:15–16; Jer. 1:5; Luke 1:15; Gal. 1:15). As we've already seen, this includes our temperament, natural skills, talents, and abilities.

Second, all of us who are Christians have the Holy Spirit within us. At the point of conversion, God, the Holy Spirit, indwells each of us. He, in turn, supplies us with all the power we need to accomplish His ministry in this world (Eph. 3:16, 20). Consequently, it's the Holy Spirit, not us, who provides the divine power and accomplishes Christ's work through us.

Third, the Savior has placed us in His body, the church, and given us spiritual gifts (Eph. 4:7–11). These are special God-given abilities for service and are listed in 1 Corinthians 12–14, Romans 12, and Ephesians 4. All Christians have at least one gift and probably more.

Fourth, all Christians are believer-priests (1 Peter 2:5–9; Rev. 1:6). This priesthood involves such services as sacrifice, worship, and prayer. Sacrificial service includes the commitment of ourselves to God along with our praise and giving. Worship concerns the acts of adoration, confession, and thanksgiving. Finally, prayer involves intercession for God's people as they attempt to carry out His work.

Fifth, the Father has placed us in various difficult circumstances in life for more effective service. This is the point of 2 Corinthians 1:3–7. No one Christian, including a pastor, can or ever will experience all the difficulties of life. However, God allows different individuals to experience various trials and tragedies so that they can minister effectively as others go through similar trying circumstances.

God has accomplished all of this for us and much more. Does He desire that His people merely show up on Sunday morning and occupy space? Is there more to Christianity and local church involvement than "sitting and soaking" in some pew?

God's divine accomplishments are for the purpose of enabling us to be instruments of His grace in the lives of both believers and unbelievers alike in this world. The New Testament shows little patience for noninvolvement in the body of Christ.

The Problem of Lay Mobilization

The Problem

The great tragedy is that far too many Christians are either not involved or not properly involved in any service for Christ or His church. The Lay Renewal Movement of the 1950s and 1960s was a great idea and did result in more lay involvement in church ministries. However, this movement didn't survive well in the 1980s and 1990s.

There is ample evidence of this lack of lay involvement. John Maxwell, the pastor of Skyline Wesleyan Church in San Diego, California, has observed the 20–80 principle. Essentially, this is the time-tested principle that 20 percent of the people in the church are doing 80 percent of the work of the church. This means that 80 percent of the people in the majority of our churches aren't using their gifts and talents for the Savior. As far as the church is concerned, they're unemployed! Their names are on both the membership rolls and the unemployment rolls of the church at the same time. Consequently, there's a small faithful, but exhausted group in every church who are doing much of the work of the church.

According to a survey by George Gallup, Maxwell is too optimistic. Gallup indicates that only 10 percent of the people in the church are doing 90 percent of the ministry of the church. Thus, 90 percent of the people are typically unemployed "sitters and soakers." Of the 90 percent, approximately 50 percent say they'll not become involved for whatever reason. The remaining 40 percent say they'd like to become involved, but they've not been asked or trained.

The church in America doesn't simply have an unemployment problem; it has a massive unemployment problem!

In his book, *Say It With Love,* Howard Hendricks laments the unemployment problem. He refers to an analogy between it and the game of football:

> Make no mistake: the greatest curse on the Church today is that we are expecting a small corps of professionals to get God's work done. No way!
>
> Bud Wilkinson, former football coach at the University of Oklahoma, was in Dallas for a series of lectures on physical fitness. A TV reporter interviewed him about the President's physical fitness program and asked: "Mr. Wilkinson, what would you say is the contribution of modern football to physical fitness?" The reporter expected a lengthy speech.
>
> As if he had been waiting 30 years for this question, he said, "Absolutely nothing."
>
> The young reporter stared and squirmed and finally stuttered, "Would you care to elaborate on that?"
>
> Wilkinson said, "Certainly. I define football as 22 men on the field who desperately need rest and 50,000 people in the stands who desperately need exercise."
>
> I thought to myself: What a definition of a church! A few compulsively active people run around the field while the mass of the people rest in the stands. But not according to the Word of God![3]

"Larry Richards and his colleagues asked 5,000 pastors what the greatest needs are for strengthening the church. On a scale of five from a twenty-five-item list, nearly 100 percent gave a first or second priority to 'Getting my lay people involved as ministering men and women.'"[4]

The state of lay involvement in the church today raises the obvious question, "Why is it that so many people are so uninvolved in the ministries of their churches?" There are several reasons.

One is a faulty recruitment process—one that is based on emotion and coercion. A good example is Pastor Bob, who began his August recruitment campaign using such coercive techniques as *Foxe's Book of Martyrs* and his four-sided series of sermons called "Serve or Burn." If that tactic didn't work, then he would abandon it for an emotional technique. His plan was to bring out his secret weapon, little seven-year-old Suzi Miller. If Pastor Bob prays hard enough or accidentally pinches the precious little girl, maybe she'll cry. And if she does, he's won the day. Even the most calloused, task-oriented person would have difficulty resisting the tears of Suzi Miller. Many laugh at all this on the outside, but cringe on the inside.

People in the church grow weary of hearing tired and disgruntled church people telling all sorts of "tear-filled" or "arm-twisting" recruitment stories. For example, "When the pastor began to cry, I broke down and gave in. I can't stand to see grown men cry!" "The pastor kept bugging me. He called me at home and at work, regardless of the hour. It was either give in or get out, and we weren't ready to look for another church." And finally, "He thinks so highly of me! He'd be so disappointed if I said 'No.'"

Another reason why laypeople end up on the "unemployment" rolls is because of a lack of knowledge and expertise on the part of those who would attempt to mobilize them. Seminaries, Bible colleges, and various Christian schools offer little or nothing on lay mobilization.

In churches, evangelical pastors teach their people about spiritual gifts. But that's all they know to do. They expect people to respond based on information alone. Most pastors don't know how to devise a system to help the "unemployed" discover their gifts and implement them in ministry. They have a good biblical theology of the gifts, but lack a practical theology.

A third reason why some laypeople aren't responding is because they're waiting for a personal invitation. Many people will not respond to a public invitation to service but will respond to a personal, private invitation. They want to serve in some capacity, but they want to be asked personally. Perhaps the public invitation is too informal, or they feel special if someone approaches them individually. Regardless, the church will have to take a more aggressive, personal approach to lay recruitment in the future.

A fourth reason for lay uninvolvement is a failure on the part of some pastors to appreciate and value the layperson's abilities to minister in the church. In some cases, pastors assume that ministry is their responsibility. They're the ones who've been specifically trained for ministry. A significant number have attended seminary or some equivalent. Why involve inexperienced laypeople who wouldn't know what to do and wouldn't have the time even if they did?

In other cases, this attitude may be due to problems of co-dependency on the part of the pastor. A church consultant once asked a non-Christian psychiatrist his opinion of church pastors in general. The surprising response was that a number of them are co-dependent. They derive a sense of significance from feeling needed. When someone requests help, they respond partly because if feels so good to be needed.

The fifth reason why many laypeople are "unemployed" is because they're convinced that ministry is the pastor's job. They sincerely believe that pastors are the ones who are supposed to do the work of the ministry. After all, they're ordained and have been trained for ministry. They know what to do. In fact, that's what we pay them for.

Many feel that laypeople aren't qualified or as able to minister to other people. Their job is to be faithful and to be there on Sunday mornings and to support the church financially. They sincerely appreciate it when other laypeople in the church visit with them whether at home or in the hospital, but that isn't the same as when the pastor visits. This is a common view held by many who are of the generation of Americans preceding the Baby Boom. We call them Pre-Boomers or the Harry Truman Generation. Often, their roots are in rural America, and they've grown up with a traditional, more rural view of the pastor's role.

The Result

The Need for Significance

One very basic need of every person is a sense of significance. In his book, *The Search for Significance,* Robert McGee emphasizes the importance of this need: "Whether labeled 'self-esteem' or 'self-worth,' the feeling of significance is crucial to man's emotional, spiritual, and social stability, and is the driving element within the human spirit. Understanding this single need opens the door to understanding our actions and attitudes."[5]

There's a subtle difference between self-worth and significance. Self-worth affects who we *are,* that is, our sense of value or personal worth. Good self-worth means we feel good about ourselves. Significance relates

to what we *do,* a sense that what we accomplish has value. Good significance means we feel good about what we do. In essence, we want to believe
that our lives make a difference, that they really count for something. We
do not want to think that we're just taking up space here on planet earth.
Regardless of any difference between significance and self-esteem, both are
critical to our emotional and spiritual health.

Significance and Ministry

Those who aren't mobilized and involved in the ministry of the church
find their significance in other pursuits. Most commonly, they find it in
their work or in leisure time pursuits such as sports or a hobby. They believe
that their lives make a difference because of their expertise in their vocation or hobby. Consequently, as long as this is the case, they may never
become involved in the ministry of their churches. Their private response
is, "Who needs it?"

Those who are involved but are in the wrong place, the round pegs in
square holes, eventually realize that they lack a sense of significance in
their ministry. They begin to wonder if what they're doing will make a difference. Then they question if their ministry and possibly their church
count for anything. The eventual result is burnout and potential disillusionment with the church and possibly Christianity. Often, they not only
join the "unemployed," but the ranks of the unchurched.

The Task of Lay Mobilization

The primary task of lay mobilization is to equip and mobilize laity for ministry. This is the thrust of Ephesians 4:11–12: "It was he who gave some
to be apostles, some to be prophets, some to be evangelists, and some to
be pastors and teachers, to prepare God's people for works of service, so
that the body of Christ may be built up." The local church must be a place
where people are pursued, won, enfolded, discipled, and mobilized for
ministry. The goal is "every member a minister!" Our people need to be
equipped and mobilized for several important reasons.

First, all Christians in the church, whether professional or laypeople,
are happiest and healthiest when they're both equipped and mobilized for
ministry. There needs to be a balance as shown in the two columns below:

Equipped	Mobilized
Consuming	Contributing
Soaking	Serving
Taking in	Giving out

It's good for people to "sit and soak" because that's a legitimate part of the equipping process. In fact, in the two columns above, many of the items in the column on the left are sometimes used in a negative way although they're all essential to the process. Actually, there's a time for God's people to consume, to "sit and soak," to absorb or take in.

A second reason is that problems occur when a person is not involved in either process or is involved in one but not the other. Some aren't "soaking" at all, whereas others are "soaking" and that's all that's happening. Here the task of the church is to correct both problems. In the first situation, our job is to bring people from a state of noninvolvement to one of involvement. In the second, it's to correct an imbalance. Both professional and laypeople typically experience a lack of balance. Laypeople tend to gravitate to the column on the left, and the pastoral staff to the column on the right.

On the one hand, potential lay ministers are equipped but in desperate need of mobilization. They've heard numerous messages on the spiritual gifts and may have discovered their unique gifts, but they aren't using them. They might be compared to a basketball team that's always practicing but never plays any games. After a while, they'll grow weary, lose interest, and either look for another team or retire early.

On the other hand, the pastor and possibly the staff are mobilized to the maximum but are in need of additional equipping or re-tooling. Typically, they begin ministry with some training, but become so overwhelmed with ministry that they don't have or take time for more equipping. As time passes, they need exposure to new ministry ideas. They need to become aware of what others are doing who are effectively ministering to our generation. They're like a basketball team that plays so many games that they don't have time to learn any new plays or develop the different aspects of their game. The result is that they lose a lot of games and grow tired of playing the same old game. The crucial need in both situations is for a healthy balance.

A final reason why all need to be involved is because everyone is a "10" somewhere.[6] God doesn't make mistakes when He creates people, brings them into this world, and then into His kingdom. His design is intentional and with an ultimate purpose in mind, which includes some form of service in relation to the local church. Everyone fits somewhere and the closer they come to that fit, the greater will be their ministry satisfaction and personal feelings of significance. Again, it becomes the task of lay mobilization to help them come as close as possible to their proper fit.

The Solution to Lay Mobilization

The equipping and mobilizing process begins with personal assessment. Assessment is vital in helping believers discover how God has designed them and then how to minister accordingly. The principles covered in chapters 5 and 6 and in *Maximizing Your Effectiveness* not only apply to church planters but also to those who in a lay capacity minister in the local church.

The Preparation for Lay Mobilization

A good lay mobilization program must be planned before it's implemented in the church. This planning process involves several important decisions.

The Philosophy of the Program

The first is philosophical and involves both an issue and an answer.

The issue is twofold. Do you create a structure and attempt to place the people you have into that structure, or do you start with the people you have and design the structure around them? The rationale behind beginning with a structure is that every church requires certain basic core ministries that are necessary for it to function. While these may vary from church to church and tradition to tradition, most consist of such areas as evangelism, worship, preaching, and Christian education. If a new church doesn't have some of these bases covered, then potential members will look elsewhere. For example, families, which make up the backbone of any ministry, will be attracted to a church that has something for the children.

The other option involves starting with the people that God has attracted to the core group and designing the church's ministries around them. The rationale is that God is in control and has sovereignly brought together those who make up the core group. Rather than attempt to force them into a predesigned structure, why not design the structure around them in light of their gifts, temperaments, talents, and so on? Then each will serve in ministries for which they have the right gifts and passion.

The answer lies somewhere in between for church planters. It would be wise to start with a general structure that consists of the ministries that will be necessary to reach a particular target group. People should not be forced into ministries that violate their divine design. While people may have to serve in areas for which they are not designed, this service shouldn't exceed 40 percent to 50 percent of their ministry time. From a practical standpoint, it's not always possible to place people in their precise "ministry niche." Life simply doesn't work that way! However, the church can move too far in the other direction and violate divine design, which will eventually cause ministry burnout.

God sovereignly attracts people with the right designs to staff the necessary programs. In fact, it is fascinating to take the core group through an assessment program and observe the various designs He's brought into the church. If, however, this isn't the case, then the church planter should delay starting a program—and possibly the church—until the right people are available.

There are some options. Either take a passive approach and wait for God to bring them along as new people join the core group, or go out and attempt to recruit the right individuals for the ministry. An example would be quality musicians for a band. Pursue these individuals by talking to other worship leaders and band members. Often God provides through persistent pursuit.

The Design of the Program

A second decision involves the design of the assessment program. If there's someone on the church-planting team who's trained in assessment, then it will be that person's responsibility to make these determinations.

There are several design decisions that have to be made. One concerns the length of the program. The instruction phase, which will be explained below, should last no longer than four to five weeks. Setting aside one to two hours a night a week over a four- to five-week period should be sufficient. This phase shouldn't last any longer than this, unless the interest of the group dictates otherwise.

Another design decision involves the areas to be assessed. These should include spiritual gifts, passion, temperament, leadership role and style, and any natural gifts or talents. In addition, what assessment tools, if any, will be used? The information in chapters 5 and 6 should be most helpful in determining this.[7]

The Recipients of the Program

A third decision concerns those who will be assessed. Probably everyone should be assessed. This sends a clear message to all that the church desires that "every member be a minister." There are people who've never been very active in a church ministry who will be motivated to service as the result of a good assessment program.

Also, most people become excited about the process and require little motivation to become involved. It's a good idea to explain at the beginning that this approach is more developmental than psychological to relieve any anxiety on the part of those who've experienced assessment for counseling purposes.

The Length of the Program

A fourth decision is how long the program should last. Should the program be used initially as the church is planted and dropped later, or should it become a permanent ministry of the church? Here there's little debate. A divine design assessment program is a must for any church that desires to mobilize its laity. It's also an essential ingredient of the assimilation process. It encourages new people to stay and get involved. Consequently, this program should be established for the life of the church. The initial core group should go through it and everyone who joins thereafter. It's wise regularly to evaluate and expand the ministry as the church grows in size.

The Process of Lay Mobilization

A good assessment program will accomplish lay mobilization by taking people through a minimum of three phases.[8]

The Education Phase

First is the education phase, which attempts to help laypeople discover their basic divine design. It consists primarily of two parts: instruction and evaluation.

The instruction portion is necessary to introduce the core group and any new believers to the various areas of assessment. This involves teaching them about such topics as spiritual gifts, passion, temperament, and leadership styles. The aim is to provide them with a general, biblical understanding of these areas. For example, they should know what the Scriptures teach about spiritual gifts in general and the definition and uses of each gift in particular. This may take place over several weeks. Should this process last too long, however, people will begin to lose interest.

At the same time, evaluation also takes place. Each person listens with an "evaluative ear." They're absorbing all the information while, at the same time, evaluating and determining what is true of them. This can best be accomplished both by explaining the various areas and by using selected assessment tools such as a spiritual gifts inventory or one of the personality profiles. The aim is to help people come up with at least an initial feel for their divine design that they can put down on paper. I have written *Maximizing Your Effectiveness* (Baker Book House, 1995) to help accomplish the Education Phase. It instructs believers in the divine design concept and then provides a number of assessments (spiritual gifts inventory, temperament tools, and so forth) in the appendixes.

Of the few churches that attempt some kind of program of assessment, most prematurely conclude with the first phase. This serves only to excite people and then kill their initial enthusiasm. There's another critical stage as well.

The Consultation Phase

The second critical stage involves consultation. Here people meet with a designated staff or layperson who provides personal consultation one on one or in a small group context.

The consultant could be an individual who is a member of the initial church-planting team and specializes in personal assessment. However, this is such a new field that there simply aren't many of these people who are trained and available. Because there's such a need for this kind of ministry, we'll be seeing more assessment people in ministry in the future. We could call them ministers of discipleship or involvement.[9]

Most likely the consultant will be someone on the planting team who enjoys and serves the team in this as well as several other capacities. This person should select and train key laypeople in the church who show a gift or inclination for assessment. They should be allowed to take over this vital ministry. Chances are good that God will provide a gifted layperson who's stronger in this area than the original pastoral staff person. Then as the ministry grows, this person can recruit others as lay consultants.

Regardless, the consultant will accomplish several objectives. The first is to provide individuals with personal help in determining and confirming their designs. This may involve spending additional time helping them through the process and answering their questions or simply confirming the results of the instruction phase.

Once this is accomplished to the satisfaction of both, then the second objective is to aid them in discovering their personal ministry mission. The consultant will help them decide what ministries they're best suited for in light of their individual designs. This objective will be the most difficult and will require some time and expertise.

The Mobilization Phase

The final stage is mobilization. In this phase, the consultant helps believers discover where they can minister either within or outside the walls of the church. This is the stage at which people discover their "ministry niche."

First, the consultant will need to be aware of the various ministry needs within the church body. This information may come from a variety of sources, depending on the size of the ministry. If the church has just been planted, then the source will be the team. If the church is already established, then the information will come from the various ministries within it. Regardless of the source, the team or ministries need to develop job or ministry descriptions for each position in their ministries to guide placement. These would include spiritual gifts, passion, temperament, supervisor, and any other pertinent information. All of this data could be loaded in a computer database so it can be accessed in the placement process.

Next, the consultant will send the person to the one in charge of the ministry. Then it becomes the responsibility of the ministry to orient and equip the person for service. Should things not work out, the person returns to the consultant, who may reassess the individual, make some adjustments in the ministry vision, and then try another ministry.

Should people have ministry missions that don't presently coincide with any of the ministries of the church, then one of two things can happen. The team will need to make a decision as to whether they're ready to start a new ministry. Perhaps they could become involved in a target ministry of the church such as outreach to international students at the local college or street people in the inner city area.[10] Another possibility is to encourage their involvement in some ministry beyond that of the church. It could be a parachurch ministry or possibly a ministry in another church in the area.

A Lay Mobilization Exercise

1. Are you familiar with the method of lay mobilization described by Bill Hybels at the beginning of this chapter? Can you add anything to it from your own personal experiences? Are you satisfied with this approach?

2. Do you agree with the explanation of why so many laypeople aren't involved in our churches? What reasons would you add, if any, to the list in this chapter?

3. In preparation for developing a lay mobilization plan, will you create a structure and attempt to fit people into it, or will you develop the structure around your people? Will you attempt both?

4. Do you like the lay mobilization process that's presented in this chapter? Why or why not? What would you change or add to it?

10

Pouring New Wine into New Wineskins

A Culturally Relevant Ministry

With a smile on her face, a friend gave my wife a sheet of plain, typed paper. She read it, laughed, and passed it on to me. I've read it and chuckled, and now I pass it on to you just as it came to me.

FOR ALL THOSE BORN PRIOR TO 1945

We are survivors!!!!! Consider the changes we have witnessed:

We were before television, before penicillin, before polio vaccines, frozen foods, Xerox, contact lenses, Frisbees and the PILL.

We were before radar, credit cards, split atoms, laser beams and ballpoint pens; before pantyhose, dishwashers, clothes dryers, electric blankets, air conditioners, drip-dry clothes—and before man walked on the moon.

We got married first and *then* lived together. How quaint can you be?

In our time, closets were for clothes, not for "coming out of." Bunnies were small rabbits and rabbits were not Volkswagons. Designer jeans were scheming girls named Jean or Jeanne, and having a meaningful relationship meant getting along well with our cousins.

We thought fast food was what you ate during Lent, and outer space was the back of the Riviera Theatre.

We were before house-husbands, gay rights, computer dating, dual careers and commuter marriages. We were before day-care centers, group therapy, and nursing homes. We never heard of FM radio, tape decks, electric typewriters, artificial hearts, word processors, yogurt, and guys wearing earrings. For us time-sharing meant togetherness—not computers or condominiums;

a "chip" meant a piece of wood; hardware meant hardware; and software wasn't even a word!

In 1940, "made in Japan" meant junk and the term "making out" referred to how you did on an exam. Pizzas, McDonalds, and instant coffee were unheard of.

We hit the scene when there were 5 and 10 cent stores where you bought things for five and ten cents. Sanders and Wilsons sold ice cream cones for a nickel or a dime. For one nickel you could ride a street car, make a phone call, buy a Pepsi or enough stamps to mail one letter *and* two postcards. You could buy a new Chevy Coupe for $600 but who could afford one? A pity, too, because gas was only eleven cents a gallon!

In our day, cigarette smoking was fashionable, grass was mowed, Coke was a cold drink, and pot was something you cooked in. Rock music was a Grandma's lullaby and AIDS were helpers in the principal's office.

We were certainly not before the difference between the sexes was discovered but we were surely before the sex change; we made do with what we had. And we were the last generation that was so dumb as to think you needed a husband to have a baby!

No wonder we are so confused and there is such a generation gap today! BUT WE SURVIVED!! What better reason to celebrate?[1]

Most people who read this little essay laugh, but for different reasons. Some people laugh because it's nostalgic. It reminds them of the "good old days" when life seemed so much simpler and easier. These "Pre-Boomers" make up the generation that preceded the Baby Boom Generation. They are the Harry Truman Generation. Other people laugh because they take much of what is said for granted. They tend to assume that life has always been like it is today. This group consists of the Baby Boom Generation and Generation X.

What all of this depicts is change. Times have changed drastically! And there's more—much more—to come. In terms of information alone, George Barna notes that "We now have only 3 percent of the information that will be available to us by 2010."[2] Someone has said that, currently, the amount of information doubles every five years! Obviously, all this massive change has deeply influenced our culture. Life during the 1940s and 1950s is completely foreign to life as it is in the twenty-first century.

As our world changes, the evangelical church must change as it attempts to communicate the message of Jesus Christ. The cultural leap from the unchurched community to most American churches is too vast. Consequently, our planted churches must be culturally relevant if they're to reach this and future unchurched generations for the Savior. They must be relevant when they begin, and they must remain relevant.

It's also imperative that church planters develop a biblical theology of culture. They must understand that culture in itself is neutral. For example, Adam and Eve lived within a culture before the Fall, and cultural diversity will be with us in heaven (Rev. 7:9–10). However, culture was devastated by the Fall and now may be used for good or bad (a good example is the use of language—James 3:9–10).

There are no less than five principles that will help church planters realize and maintain cultural relevance.

The Principle of Cultural Recognition

In terms of what it values and practices, every church must distinguish between its unique culture and biblical truth.

The Explanation

The Culture of the Church and the Community

While every church exists within a culture—the "world out there"—every church also has its own unique culture—the "world in here." This culture is affected by the general culture of the community in which the church is located—the "world out there." Whether we like it or not, every church is affected to some degree by the culture of its community. The "world out there" is reflected in various ways in the "world in here." Though some Christians resist this truth, it's simply part of living in a community.

The Christian often views the general culture of the community in a totally negative light. It's important to recognize, however, that not everything in the "world out there" is necessarily bad. There are a number of areas that are morally neutral, such as participation in the arts or the pursuit of a particular talent like singing or playing a musical instrument. Ultimately, the question isn't whether we reflect the culture of our community. That's a given! The question is which culture we reflect—that of the 1940s and 1950s or that of the twenty-first century.

Evangelical churches attempt to follow the teachings of the Scriptures and to apply them to what they do in the church as well as at home and in the marketplace. Thus, the "world in here" is a mixture of the application of the Bible to the life of the church and the influence—whether great or small—of the "world out there." Again, the latter can be good or bad (Rom. 14:14–15). The point is that the church's values and beliefs consist of a mixture of scriptural truth and the "world in here."

The Problem

The problem is that over time the church begins to confuse the two and values the style and practices of the "world in here" on an equal basis with eternal biblical truth. This affects choices of clothing, hair styles, music (both instruments and songs), times for the church service, versions of the Bible, the order of worship, the number of services per week, the name of the church, prayers, and pews.

For example, the church may have used an organ for years as the primary instrument in facilitating worship. Many in the congregation become so accustomed to singing with the accompaniment of an organ that they think there's something sacred about this particular instrument. Yet it's only a matter of time before the culture changes, and the organ declines in popularity as a musical instrument in the "world out there." How do churches respond? Most churches continue to use the organ because they now believe that it's a sacred instrument. After all, they've been using it for all these years, so there must be something special about it. As someone once said, "If it was good enough for Paul and the apostles, it's good enough for us!"

The Application

The principle of cultural recognition seeks to help the church distinguish between that which is truly biblical and eternal (functions) and that which is temporal and subject to change (forms). Knowing and understanding this principle is beneficial because it makes us aware of the two categories and allows us to consider change in the second category. Far too many people aren't even aware of the fact that they have placed a church tradition on the same plane as biblical truth. This results in little or no change at all.

Church planters must be aware of this danger from the very beginning. In fact, they must be sensitive to both the culture of the community and the culture of the church. They should not be afraid to make changes in the church that don't violate Scripture. For example, many churches are using guitars and drums in their worship services. While these are morally neutral instruments, they are more in vogue with the "world out there" than organs.

In some areas of the country, when unchurched people walk into a church that still uses an organ, they're "turned off" by it and aren't willing to consider spiritual truth. While they have no problems with the organ as a musical instrument, it's simply not "in." Sometimes the sermon is prejudged as not "in" as well. It would be a shame for an unchurched person to walk away from a service where Christ is proclaimed because a group of people have insisted on using a musical instrument that is merely a part of their tradition.

The Principle of Cultural Adaption

The mature church must be willing to be flexible in areas that relate to its unique culture (the "world in here"), but not in areas that relate to biblical truth.

The Explanation

There are two areas in which a church can adjust in response to changes in the "world out there." It can change what it believes (faith), and it can change what it does (practice).

Changing What It Believes

The first area has to do with the foundational principles of belief and doctrine. The evangelical church for the most part holds to the Scriptures as its authority and the basis for what it believes. Since biblical truth is eternal truth, the church cannot and must not compromise the principles of Scripture.

There are some churches, however, which have chosen to respond to the massive changes in our culture by making changes in the area of faith. In response to pressure from gays and lesbians, many denominational churches have begun to take steps to ordain them as priests. Others are considering softening their stance on homosexual relationships and sexual relationships outside of marriage.

Changing What It Practices

The other area has to do with the church's practices or how it acts on what it believes. This is reflected in its strategies, programs, and lifestyles. Many of these are morally neutral areas where the church has freedom to change and adjust to what is taking place in the "world out there." This is God's way of keeping His church relevant to its culture so that the church can get a fair hearing from those who are not or have never been a part of it. The evangelical church must not change or violate the clear principles of the Scriptures, but it must change and adjust what it does in terms of its programs and strategies if it's to remain relevant.

Sadly, many evangelical churches have refused to do this. Thinking they're maintaining biblical integrity, in reality they're preserving the culture of a bygone era. If you want to know what life was like in America in the 1940s and 1950s, then attend one of these churches because things haven't changed much. Unfortunately, unchurched people walk into these churches and experience culture shock. They're repelled—not by the message of Christ, but by the lack of relevance. They know a dinosaur when they see one! Far too many churches today either aren't aware of or are resistant to such things as copy machines, computers, fax machines, and express mail! Their policy is to wait twenty or thirty years to see if these things are from God or from the devil.

The Application

A Willingness to Be Flexible

The planted church must be willing to be flexible in areas of Christian liberty and the "world in here," especially when it comes to reaching unchurched people. In 1 Corinthians 9:19–23, Paul indicates that while he has various rights within the realm of Christian liberty, he is willing to set them aside in order to reach lost people. This involves moving in their direction. In verse 20 Paul says that he became like those who were under the law in order to reach them with the gospel. This is a reference to the religious Jews of the first century, who would be somewhat parallel to churched lost people today. In verse 21 Paul states that he became like those who weren't under law to reach them as well. This is a reference to the nonreligious Gentiles, who would be very similar to today's unchurched generation.

Why Churches Aren't Flexible

In 1 Corinthians 9:19–23 and 10:23–33, Paul isn't talking about compromising the faith. He's talking about a willingness on the part of the church to be open to change and to adapt its traditions and practices ("the world in here") to reach the unchurched. But many are unwilling to be flexible.

Inward focus. One problem is that a significant number of evangelical churches focus inwardly, not outwardly. They plan their programs around themselves, around their wants and desires. For example, they find it most convenient to meet on Sunday mornings at 11:00 A.M. This is a matter of Christian liberty, and there's nothing wrong with it.

But what if they conducted a survey of unchurched people in their community and discovered that, if invited, these people would come to church but only for the 11:00 service? Would they be willing to give up the convenience of this time slot to reach the lost? Would they be willing to get up an hour earlier, worship at 9:00 A.M., then bring their lost friends to an 11:00 A.M. meeting that is designed to reach them with the gospel of Christ? Would they be willing to give up their favorite place in their pew so a lost person could sit there?

Unrealistic expectations. Another problem is that far too many of our churches expect lost people to behave like saved people—before they've become saved people. We're asking them to adjust to us and the way we do things at church rather than adapting to them and where they are in life.

Many of these people are "traveling incognito" when they visit our services. They don't want to sign, sing, or say anything. They're simply "checking things out." They don't want to be singled out or embarrassed. Yet many of our churches conduct their evangelistic services as if these people were Christians. We speak Christianeze and expect them to understand our language. We use such terms as reconciliation, redemption, and propitiation in our sermons (terms that lost people in the first century understood because they were used commonly in everyday life). We sing older, traditional hymns of the faith that employ such King James verbs as "wert" and "art" and expect them to understand our music. We ask them to sign a visitor's card and stand and introduce themselves so we can know who they are. This is done in spite of the fact that speaking in public is the number one fear of most Americans. Then we wonder why none of our lost visitors ever come back for a second look.

A Clarification

If we truly desire to reach the lost in general and the unchurched lost in particular, we must be willing to be flexible and adapt what we do to them and where they are in life. We need not abandon any biblical principles. We should not schedule a "happy hour" to get to know these people. Nor should we fill our music with popular contemporary themes such as sexual immorality and suicide.

But we can begin to move in their direction in an attempt to reach them with the saving message of Christ. For example, we can demonstrate that we're not a cloistered community by addressing current issues in our sermons. We can present what Scripture has to say about healthy families in contrast to dysfunctional families. We can address the benefits of sexual intimacy within marriage as opposed to outside the marital bond. We can hold out the hope and help found in Romans 6 for those who find themselves in bondage to some addiction.

We can also adapt and move in their direction in terms of our music. Scripture doesn't consecrate a particular musical instrument. The fact that a number of churches today still use an organ or a piano in worship doesn't mean that these are sacred instruments. The church needs to be open to the use of other instruments such as guitars and drums. The fact that secular institutions use these instruments doesn't mean the church can't. Lost people will quickly see that how we use these instruments is different from how the world of secular entertainment uses them.

The same is true of music with a beat. The fact that secular music may have a beat to it doesn't mean Christian music shouldn't. The key is what the church does with the music that has a beat. Certainly, wisdom and moderation are necessary. Most churches, however, have not thought this through and have overreacted in the opposite direction.

An Inconsistency

It's interesting to note that many of these churches are flexible when it comes to reaching young people. They recognize the value of what Paul is saying in 1 Corinthians 9 and 10. They realize that youth ministries that aren't relevant die a quick death. Yet, they draw a line and refuse to apply this principle to the other programs of the church in which they're involved.

It's also interesting that a number of today's pastors who are reaching unchurched lost people in great numbers were formerly in youth ministry. What they've done is to plant innovative churches using the principles they learned in working with and ministering to young people.

The Principle of Cultural Evaluation

The church should regularly evaluate the cultural aspects of its ministry and make whatever adjustments are necessary to stay in touch with the people to whom it seeks to minister.

The Explanation

The Purpose

The purpose of this principle is to keep the planted church on the "cutting edge." A large number of evangelical churches remain anywhere from ten to as many as forty or even fifty years behind the "times." It's important that the church of Jesus Christ not become a memorial to a generation that has passed from the scene long ago unless it's specifically targeting people who were a part of that generation. There's nothing wrong with remembering and valuing some aspects of life as it was forty or fifty years ago, but this should not be done in the church.

The Problem

Pastors who apply the principle of cultural evaluation will involve their churches in regular evaluation. This involvement means change. This will upset people. For some reason most of us don't like change. We like to stick with that which is familiar, the "tried and true."

Yet change is the key ingredient in both salvation and sanctification. To be saved, people must change their thinking about working their way to heaven and accept God's way through Christ. But change doesn't end at the cross. The whole of sanctification involves the process of change. In 2 Corinthians 3:18, Paul writes, "And we, who with unveiled faces all reflect the Lord's glory, are being transformed into his likeness with ever-increasing glory, which comes from the Lord, who is the Spirit." If change is critical to salvation and sanctification, then we must be open to the idea that change could benefit us in terms of what we do in the church.

The Benefit

The merit of regular evaluation and updating of the church's programs and ministries is that the church will grow and expand in its outreach. Without regular evaluation, churches get involved in too many programs and activities. A particular ministry such as a Sunday school class will go on and on even though it may no longer serve the purpose for which it was intended and attracts only a few people. Other programs are begun and eventually the church has far more than it can possibly manage.

The result is that the church adopts a maintenance mentality and shifts into a maintenance mode. Should it have to hire a new pastor, it finds a maintenance person whose ministry is primarily to keep everything running smoothly. This will plateau the church and eventually send it into decline.

The Application

Churches should regularly evaluate their practices but not their faith. Faith is permanent and eternal and isn't subject to change because it's based on an eternal, unchanging God. The same isn't true concerning our practices and how we implement that faith in our churches. But what are we to evaluate, who does it, and how often is "regularly"?

What to Evaluate

The church should evaluate everything it does. Nothing should be exempt. There should be no "sacred cows" that are beyond the scrutiny of good evaluation. This is healthy for the church and prevents various ministry forms from becoming institutionalized and perpetuated eternally. This doesn't mean that everything gets changed all the time, for this would lead to chaos. What it does mean is that constant change is taking place so that the various ministries improve in their effectiveness.

Who Evaluates

The best people to carry out the evaluation process are those involved in particular ministries. The church should give them the freedom to evaluate and innovate within the purview of their unique ministries. If they've been properly placed, then they should know best what their ministries are to accomplish and whether or not they're succeeding. Occasionally, someone might come in from the outside to bring in fresh ideas. These individuals should be under another person who is responsible to make sure that good evaluation takes place. But evaluation is best left to those who are involved in the ministry—who know the ministry well.

How Often to Evaluate

The time when evaluation takes place depends on the particular ministry being assessed. For example, the Sunday morning service should be evaluated weekly. All facets of what takes place should be looked at in terms of such questions as, "How did we do?" and "What can we do better the next time?" This includes not only the sermon, the choice of songs, and how well they were performed, but other things such as the pace of the service.

Other programs involving areas such as Christian education, evangelism, and outreach can be evaluated over a longer period of time. This evaluation should be done at least quarterly and at a minimum annually. It's helpful to implement "shelf-life" ministries. The various perishable items found on the shelves of grocery stores have a shelf-life. A date is stamped somewhere on the item giving the time after which it should no longer be used or consumed. The various ministries in the church could also be assigned a shelf-life of one year. After that time is up, the ministry would have to justify its existence if it's to continue. The basis for this justification would be the quarterly evaluations. The shelf-life of most church ministries ranges from eighteen to twenty-four months unless they're regularly evaluated and updated. After that they need to be either dropped or overhauled.

The Principle of Cultural Exegesis

The church must be a student of the "world out there" as well as the "world in here." If our churches are to remain relevant to our culture, then they must spend time exegeting that culture as well as the Scriptures.

The Explanation

What does the term "exegete" mean and how does it apply to the Bible and to the culture?

Exegeting the Bible

Exegesis involves the skillful application of basic Bible study methods to Scripture in order to understand and present its meaning. It takes time and is critical to the teaching and preaching ministries of the church.

The real importance of exegesis is that it helps us to both discover and communicate divine truth. In times when truth is viewed by so many in our culture as relative, the church must articulate and apply the absolute truths of Scripture to the needs and problems of the contemporary world. The postmodern concept of relative truth leads only to a loss of hope and despair; the concept of absolute, divine truth brings hope and leads to salvation.

Exegeting the Culture

Not only must we know how to exegete the Bible; we must be able to exegete the culture in which we live. A vital aspect of communicating divine truth is the application of that truth to life. This can't take place, however, unless we understand what's taking place in people's lives, both lost and saved. It might seem strange to include Christians as well as the lost. Yet in the 1990s many of our churches are microcosms of the larger macrocosm of the world in general. To study what's taking place in the "world out there" and to address it in terms of God's truth will help add authenticity to sermons—whether they're directed to lost or saved people or both.

First Chronicles 12:32 is a key passage in illuminating this principle. The writer presents the numbers of those who had decided to join David in his battle with Saul. When he gets to the men of Issachar he describes them as those "who understood the times and knew what Israel should do." Apparently this particular group was in touch with what was going on, unlike many of the others. Not only did they understand their times, but they also knew what to do about what was going on.

The Application

How can planted churches exegete the "world out there"? There are at least five ways to accomplish this.

Build Friendships with Lost People

The first involves a practice followed by a problem.

The practice. The practice is to pursue contacts with lost people in an attempt to develop relationships that result in friendships. This means that Christians will have to spend some time with the unsaved and get to know them well enough to understand their needs, hurts, dreams, and aspirations. Every Christian should be doing this with at least one lost person or couple regularly.

The problem. The problem is that far too many Christians have few if any lost friends. They have lots of lost acquaintances, but not many lost friends. In some cases this may be due to a false view of separation. Some teach that Christians should associate with lost people as little as possible; otherwise, they'll become "worldly." Christians may have to work with unbelievers, but they should avoid spending time with them away from the workplace.

Actually, the Savior taught that we're to be *in* the world but not *of* the world (John 17:14–19). If this means that we shouldn't associate with lost people, then we would need to revive the ancient practice of monasticism. Jesus, by example, demonstrated that it's important that we spend time with lost people, that we get to know them and address their needs (Luke 5:27–32; 15:1–2; 19:5–7). At the same time, however, we're not to live like them. The problem that many churches are facing is that their people aren't in the world (they don't know many lost people), yet they're of the world (their behavior is little different from that of their lost neighbors and workmates).[3]

Another reason Christians don't associate with lost people is because they don't appreciate some of their bad habits. For example, most believers prefer not to be around people who use profanity or tell obscene jokes, especially in front of the family. Yet, this need not form a barrier to befriending these people. There are ways to deal with their habits and not lose the relationship. If you take these people aside and explain that you value them and their friendship but ask that they respect your feelings in these areas, most will understand and appreciate your candor. You will come across as authentic.

Listen to the Culture

In his book, *Thriving on Chaos*, Tom Peters suggests that executives develop what he calls "naive listening." He writes, "Listening to customers must become everyone's business. Listening means: (1) hanging out (on their turf), (2) listening naively and with intensity, and (3) providing fast feedback and taking action."[4]

Few of us listen very well to begin with, much less to lost people. This has to stop if we have any desire to reach them. But as Peters indicates, this will take some effort on our part. Not only will we have to listen to them, but we'll have to do so intensely and on their turf. "Their turf" includes, among other things, their areas of interest. The temptation is to pay attention only to things that interest us. Yet we must begin to take an interest in things that matter to them. Often we have these things in common with them. We simply may not be aware of it, unless we ask and listen.

READ, READ, READ!

Read what people are reading. Read the newspaper and know what's going on in the community. Consider subscribing to *USA Today* and know what's going on in the world. Be conversant on matters that affect the community and our world. Read magazines such as *Time, Newsweek,* and *People Magazine.*

Discover what topics are hot and what topics are not. Ask if the sermons on Sundays are addressing any of these issues. Is the church in general dealing with these issues in terms of its programs and ministries? For example, hardly a day goes by that the typical newspaper doesn't have a story or article about various addictions such as drugs and alcohol.

Attempt to read a good novel at least once a year. Select one that has been at the top of the best-seller list. What issues does this work deal with? Is the author sending a message, and, if so, what is it?

Collect and Interpret Demographic and Psychographic Data

The term "demographics" refers to general information about people, such as where they live, their income, their education, their marital status, and so on. The term "psychographics" refers to what these people value and how it has influenced their lifestyles. This kind of information will reveal much about the culture.

There is a lot of excellent information periodically in the newspaper. Other sources are utilities, local colleges and universities, realtors, developers, chambers of commerce, and city planning departments. There are also some professional organizations that provide this information for a price.

Develop and Implement a Community Survey

A good way to exegete a community is to survey it. If you want to know what people are like, then why not ask them? The idea here is to go straight to the source. The only problem is that people aren't always truthful. Nevertheless, the contact with them is invaluable.

A sample survey. The following community survey has been used effectively in starting up new churches among unchurched lost people:

1. Are you currently attending a local church?
2. What do you think is the greatest need in this community?
3. Why do you think some people don't attend church?
4. If you were looking for a church in the area, what would you want?
5. What advice would you give to a new pastor?
6. Would you be interested in more information?[5]

An explanation. Several comments are appropriate. The first question is an attempt to discover if the individual is churched or nonchurched. It's important to ask if people are presently attending a church—*not* if they're members of a church. There's still a significant number of people in America, especially in the South, who are members of churches but aren't attending them.

The second question is designed to identify felt needs from their perspective. While these needs may vary, if enough people are surveyed, there should be some consistency.

The third question will underscore what turns people off to spiritual things. Use their responses in advertising. For example, a number of people will list money as an objection. They claim that all the church is interested in is their money, not them. Another is dull, boring sermons. A well-done, attractive mailer could tell them to leave their wallets at home. Relevant sermon titles might catalyze some interest in spite of their disappointments with sermons in the past, especially if these messages probe felt needs. For example, in the 1990s, when the O. J. Simpson "not guilty" verdict came in, I preached a sermon on God's justice entitled "What God Would Say to O. J."

The Principle of Cultural Homogeneity

The church will not reach everybody but will initially attract those who are culturally similar to those who make up the core group.

The Explanation

What does this principle mean and what problems has it encountered in its application to ministry?

The Definition

The homogeneous principle was developed by Donald A. McGavran, who is undoubtedly one of the twentieth century's premier missiologists and the founder of the Church Growth Movement. The principle states that "Men like to become Christians without crossing racial, linguistic, or class barriers."[6] Lost people are most comfortable with those with whom they feel an affinity.

The Controversy

This has become one of the most controversial principles of the Church Growth Movement. Its critics have attacked it as racist and classist. Yet their reaction is "kneejerk" and due to a failure to understand what McGavran is saying. He is talking about the way lost people think and respond. He's describing the thinking of the unregenerate mind. He's not saying this is the way things ought to be. It's not his contention that this is the way *God* thinks and acts, but it's the way *lost people* think and act. McGavran approaches this principle from the perspective of the lost mind-set and the way things are in this world, not from the perspective of the divine viewpoint or what should be.

The Reality

No church can be culturally neutral. This is because what churches do (preaching, worship, the offering, and other practices) are all culturally conditioned. As I said at the beginning of this chapter, this isn't necessarily wrong because culture itself is neutral (Rom. 14:14–15).

It's also important to note that Paul, who wrote Ephesians 2:11–22 also wrote Galatians 2:6–10, and targeted Gentiles while Peter targeted Jews.

In reality, the church has practiced the homogeneous principle for years as reflected in several areas of its ministry.

Missions. It's a common practice, and a good one, in missions to turn works that have been started by foreign missionaries over to nationals after a period of time. Nationals have a greater opportunity to minister to other Christian nationals and the lost of their country. They understand the culture and the needs, hopes, and aspirations of their people.

Christian education. Most if not all Christian education programs in churches of any size provide classes for singles, couples, adults, young marrieds, youth, children, and newcomers. Why do they do this? Simply because they realize that there's a sense of affinity among some groups. Singles tend to prefer to meet with other singles for a variety of reasons such as commonality of needs. The same is true of couples. Why don't we mix older adults with our high school age young people? They don't share the same interests. Is this wrong? Most think not.

Church planting. Ethnic peoples are attracted to churches started by the same ethnic people. For instance, Koreans are attracted to new churches that have been started by Koreans. African Americans prefer to attend churches started by African Americans. The same is true for Hispanics, other Asians, and whites. And this is particularly true of lost Asians, Hispanics, and whites. Regardless of whether this is right or wrong, it's true. This practice violates Scripture only when these churches exclude people of another culture. A painful example would be the treatment of some African Americans by white churches in America in the 1950s and 1960s.

An Illustration

Mark Platt, a church planter on the West Coast, illustrates the homogeneous principle with a story about a young African American preacher named Larry.

It was Larry's desire to start a church for *all* people. Mark was interested in how he planned to accomplish this goal, so he asked Larry several questions. The first concerned how he planned to preach to this multiethnic congregation. His answer was that he would "hoop," which is a style common to preaching in many African American churches. Next, he asked how he would take the offering. Larry said that they would have an "offering walk," which is a common way to take the offering in African American churches. This involves placing the offering plate at the front of the church and asking people to walk by and place their money in it while the preacher watches. The question we must ask about Larry's church is, "Whom will it attract?" The answer is obvious. We can't escape our roots.

I once had a most interesting conversation with a fellow faculty member's wife. She is a highly educated woman who considers herself to be very open-minded. She was upset that her church didn't have other ethnic people in attendance, especially African Americans and Hispanics. She'd also heard of the homogeneous principle and was adamantly opposed to it. I agreed with her on the first issue regarding the ethnic makeup of her church but not the second concerning the homogeneous principle. So I decided to ask her some questions.

The first was, "So, you want your church to reach out to and attract more people of different races? That's excellent, I agree with you and so does the Bible!" In my second question I asked, "And what are you willing to give up to attract these people to your church? Would you be willing to listen to a different preaching style on Sunday morning? For example, would it be permissible for your pastor to 'hoop' rather than teach with his normal heavy Bible content? Also, would you be willing to involve yourself in an 'offering walk' rather than sitting in a pew and passing the plate? If you want to reach people of other cultures through the worship service of your church, especially lost people, then what changes are you willing to make?" She responded with silence. She wasn't ready to give up the way they "did church."

The Application

Planted churches should recognize that, whether right or wrong, the homogeneous principle is true and is practiced by most lost people. Therefore, they will attract and win best those who are of the same culture and nationality.

The Initial Target Group

Churches will be wise *initially* to target lost people in their communities who are culturally similar. This doesn't mean that they shouldn't minister to people of other cultures should the opportunity present itself. It does mean that it would be a mistake for a white Anglo church to target a Hispanic community if that church isn't willing to make some cultural adjustments in its approach to ministry. For starters, its people could learn Spanish.

Yet it would be far wiser for this church *initially* to target a white Anglo community consisting of people much like themselves. There would be an affinity present that wouldn't be true of the other community. Those who minister, such as the pastor, could then preach in a style that's more natural to them.

The Ultimate Target Group

As the church grows it will attract people from other ethnic groups and become more heterogeneous. Some people are willing to give up their particular style of worship for other values. For instance, some value good Bible teaching to the extent that they'll attend a church of another culture to get it. Some churches have excellent ministries for the hearing- or seeing-impaired that attract and encourage the crossing of stylistic boundaries by ethnic peoples.

Once the church becomes more heterogeneous, it will be able to pursue more aggressively a ministry to people of other ethnic groups. As it attracts some Asian people, it should consider targeting Asian people in the community. Again, when they begin to reach these people, it would be wise to provide either classes or services for them in their own language and style so that they'll attract and reach other lost Asians.

The Principles of a Biblical Hermeneutic

How can church planters know when they may have crossed the cultural line? How can they know when, in their attempts to be relevant to the culture, they may have conformed to the culture and bought into the spirit of the age? The answer is found in applying six key hermeneutical principles to the church.[7]

Form versus Function

In chapter 4, we studied the principle of form and function as an assumption that undergirds this book. There we learned that the Scriptures fix the functions of the church such as evangelism, worship, and giving. Functions are as true in the twenty-first century as they were in the first century. Scripture, however, doesn't dictate the forms the various functions may take. This allows churches the freedom to remain relevant to their culture.

Church planters must be careful to determine whether they are dealing with a function or a form in conducting ministry. For example, must churches have small groups? The answer depends on if they are a form or function. Small groups are a form. The function they serve may be biblical community, evangelism, or worship.

Tradition versus Scripture

A church tradition is a nonbiblical custom or practice (form) that church people attempt to observe, often preserve, and pass on to the next generation. The Bible teaches that traditions can be good or bad. In Mark 7:1–23, Jesus condemns the Pharisees' practice of setting aside funds that could help their parents by declaring them corban (a gift devoted to God). They placed their tradition ahead of scriptural truth. In Acts 17:2–3, Paul observes the custom of entering the synagogue and interacting with the Jews in attendance. This tradition didn't violate Scripture.

How might church planters observe this principle? First, they must distinguish between what is tradition and what is Scripture. Many parishioners confuse Scripture with tradition and cling to the latter as if it was the former. An example is the old-timer who quipped, "If the organ was good enough for Paul, it's good enough for us!" The other is not to place traditions as equal to or above Scripture. This was the error of the Pharisees in the first century and the Roman Catholic Church in later centuries.

The Negative versus the Positive Hermeneutic

The negative hermeneutic teaches that if a custom or practice (form) is not found in the Bible then it's wrong and unbiblical. It may be expressed with such clichés as "Where the Bible speaks, we speak; where the Bible is silent, we're silent." Those who hold to this view condemn the use in church of such things as drama, drums, guitars, and, in some cases, any instrumental music.

The problem with this view is that it's neither biblical nor logical. The same churches have Sunday schools, nurseries, hymnals, pulpits, pianos, even indoor plumbing. Where do they find these practices in the Bible? I prefer the positive hermeneutic. It teaches that though you can't find a practice in the Bible, then it's permissible as long as it doesn't contradict or disagree with the Bible.

Patterns versus Principles

Patternism teaches that the church must not only follow the biblical principles of the early church but its practices or patterns as well. If one of the early church's patterns was to meet on the first day of the week (Acts 20:7?), then twenty-first-century churches must follow suit.

This position is incorrect for five reasons. First, it assumes that all the churches of the first century followed the same patterns. No evidence exists for this. Second, which church's patterns do you follow? The Corinthian church exercised various gifts in the public worship service (1 Cor. 11:26–39). We don't know that others followed the same pattern. Third, there doesn't appear to be enough information to know what the early churches practiced—just "snatches" here and there. Fourth, patternism locks the church into a first-century culture as the Amish have locked themselves into an eighteenth-century culture. Finally, ask, Can we apply a biblical principle? The biblical principle regarding when a church meets for worship is that we are free to make up our own minds (Rom. 14:5–12).

Descriptive versus Prescriptive Passages

Descriptive passages are those in the Bible that describe what took place in the early churches. For example, the church at Troas may have met on the first day of the week (Acts 20:7?). Consequently, some argue from this that the church in all the other centuries must follow suit.

The fallacy with this view is that just because a practice is described in the New Testament doesn't mean that it was mandated by the New Testament. We must not allow non-absolutes of the early church to become binding absolutes for the twenty-first-century church.

Prescriptive passages are those in the Bible that prescribe what ought to take place in the church. Various biblical imperatives, prohibitions, and other indicators help us to identify them. Some examples are the Great Commission, the Lord's Supper, baptism, church discipline, and others.

The Secular versus the Sacred

Since the Middle Ages, many in the Christian church interpret that which takes place outside the church as secular and, therefore, bad. For example, to look to the business community and those who write in this context for insight in conducting church business is sacrilege.

This isn't biblical. Scripture draws no such line that divides sacred from secular or the church world from the business world. The question is, Does what you're doing fall under the lordship of Christ—whether inside or outside the church? Because all truth is ultimately God's truth (either revealed in or outside the Bible—special or general revelation), church planters may learn from the business community much as Moses learned from his father-in-law, Jethro, who likely was an unbeliever (Exod. 18). However, they must be careful to use their biblical training ("theological grid") to evaluate all that they read from these other sources to discern what is, in fact, truth.

An Exercise in Cultural Relevancy

1. When you read "For All Those Born Prior to 1945" at the beginning of this chapter, what did you think? Where you attracted to it, or did it simply amuse you? What does it tell you about the impact of the culture on people regardless of whether or not they're Christians?

2. In the churches you've attended, what are some practices or traditions that you believe have been commonly confused with biblical truth? How has this confusion affected the church?

3. Are you willing to be flexible in areas that involve the practices of the church? Where might this be a problem for you (music, clothing, length of hair)?

4. How do you feel about being evaluated? Have you ever been in a church that regularly evaluated itself? If you have, what were some of the benefits of evaluation? What were some of the problems that developed? How might the latter be avoided?

5. Do you feel like you understand the culture in which you live? Do you have any lost friends, people with whom you spend time away from work? If the answer is "no," what do you plan to do about it?

6. Do you believe that you understand Donald McGavran's homogeneous grouping principle? How do you respond to this principle? Does it have a place in church planting? What is it?

7. Are any of the hermeneutical principles for the church new to you? Have you violated any of these in the past when interpreting matters that relate to the church?

11

Worship That Makes a Difference

A Holistic, Authentic Worship

When I was a child, one of the games we played involved word association. Someone would say a word, and we'd all blurt out the first thing that came to our minds. For a moment, I'd like to play the game with you. The question is, "What first comes into your mind when you hear the words 'worship service'?" Obviously the answer will depend on your experience of worship in the various churches you've attended over the years. Perhaps you think, "That's what we do at our church on Sunday morning at 11:00 A.M." Then again, you may think of the great hymns of the faith, announcements, and a pastoral prayer.

Now I'd like to change the game a little and ask you a second question: "What do you *feel* when you hear the words 'worship service'?" Please note that I didn't ask what you *think* but what you *feel* about these two words. The difference is that the former is a cognitive exercise while the latter is emotive. Do you have warm feelings and pleasant memories, or do you feel bored and a little empty on the inside?

Another interesting approach would be to play this game with Christian laypersons. First, you could ask them what they think when they hear the words "worship service," and then what they feel. Their responses will probably be real eye-openers for those of us who are in the professional ministry and positions of leadership in the church. What we think and feel varies considerably from person to person, colored by our expectations and disappointments.

Finally, it would be most informative to end the game and ask a final question: "Do you value the worship services at your church? Do you look forward to worship on Sunday morning?" The expectations of those who worship and what's actually taking place in many of our churches are far apart.

There is a solution to this problem that involves planting churches that implement a holistic, authentic worship. In explaining what this means and how it works, we need to look first at the problem of inauthentic worship, and then at the philosophy and practice of authentic, holistic worship.

The Problem of Inauthentic Worship

The Problem

The problem in far too many evangelical churches at the end of the twentieth century is that they fail to realize how crucial authentic worship is.

The Typical Service

Ronald Allen and Gordon Borror describe a worship service that is typical of what takes place on Sunday morning at 11:00 in many evangelical churches across America.

> An organ prelude was played, but no one paid much attention. The service began with a reading of a psalm of praise, followed by an urgent plea for Sunday school teachers, presented by a well-intentioned lay leader who needed help. He asked for two or three volunteers to rescue a class of junior boys from running around the parking lot. This presentation was followed by a greeting from a recently returned missionary, who was doing great work in the field but took too long to tell about it. The opening hymn (twenty minutes into the service) had nothing to do with the sermon. After the hymn, the Scripture reading was dropped because there was no time.[1]

This account reminds me of how worship was conducted at the last church that I pastored. The service was normally accompanied by a piano and an organ. For a time we were without a pianist, so we had to depend on the organ. The organist was an elderly lady who was on some medication that made her drowsy. She often fell asleep during my pastoral prayer. This wouldn't have been a problem except that one of her hands would fall and hit the keyboard. I would be waxing eloquent in a great prayer and all of a sudden there would be a loud "bonk"! We eventually grew somewhat accustomed to it. In fact, if it didn't happen, I'd always wonder if she was all right. As I think back over it, this wasn't the problem. The problem was that that was the most exciting thing that happened during our worship time! Unfortunately, there are many who listen to these examples and say, "That describes what's happening at our church on a good morning!"

In light of all the struggles of a small church, we got by. The problem is that from God's perspective, we were offering up "blemished lambs" in response to the perfect Lamb He offered up for us. From a ministry perspective, such a service is totally inadequate when it comes to transforming lives, which is what worship is all about.

The Typical Attitude

The typical attitude in a significant number of evangelical churches, especially on the part of pastors, is that worship is merely the preliminary before the main event—the sermon. It's viewed as comparable to the appetizer before the meal or the "warm up" before the game. In their book, *Worship*, Allen and Borror have sensed this same attitude:

> As pastors, we evangelicals have not been much concerned with worship either. In many of our circles the Sunday morning event is considered a "preaching service" in spite of the fact that the official title in the bulletin reads "Morning Worship." Viewing the preacher's singular act of proclamation as significantly more important than the entire congregation's acts of adoration, praise, confession, thanksgiving, and dedication, is espousing an expensive heresy that may well be robbing many churches of their spiritual assets.[2]

The Result

The result of all this is that worship is poorly done, predictable, boring, and irrelevant. Consequently, rather than attracting people *to* Christ our churches are distracting them *from* Christ. The unchurched visit to "check us out" and don't return. Our young people leave as soon as they finish high school to join the ranks of the unchurched, vowing never to be bored again. One of my students told me that he had invited a lost, unchurched neighbor to go with him to his church. He said that about halfway through the service, his neighbor elbowed him and said, "If I'd had to pay to get in here, I'd be wanting my money back about now!"

But what can pastors and church planters, especially those of us who have had little or no training in the areas of worship and music, do about this? We need to rethink our philosophy of worship before starting a new church. Most likely, we have inherited our present philosophy, and if it's not adequate, then it's imperative that we construct a new one. The solution to the problem of inauthentic worship lies in developing an authentic, holistic philosophy of worship.

A Philosophy of Authentic, Holistic Worship

What's involved in a worship service that's authentic and holistic? What do these terms mean? The answer is found in five key areas that relate to worship.

The Importance of Worship

Churches and pastors must recapture the importance of worship in the life of the church. There are three reasons why.

Worship Is Emphasized in the Bible

Worship is important because the Bible says it's important. In fact, worship is emphasized in Scripture from beginning to end. (In fact, it's mentioned more than preaching!) In his book, *People in the Presence of God*, Barry Liesch presents five worship models that he finds revealed in Scripture. These five basic models are: "pre-Sinai (family worship modeled by the patriarchs), tabernacle-temple, synagogue, Pauline, and worship in the book of Revelation."[3]

Worship Edifies People

Worship is important because, when it's done well, it has the potential to influence people as much or more than the sermon. The goal is for people to be spiritually refreshed, nurtured, and transformed through worship. When this takes place, then Christians are willing to give themselves away in sacrificial service. It's essential that believers' souls be satisfied in worship if they're to function as believer-priests. If something happened to the pastor so that he wasn't able to preach one morning, people should still leave the service with their souls nourished and satisfied as the result of having attended the worship service.

Worship Is Integral to the Church

Worship is important because it's an integral part of what takes place in the service that occurs in most churches on Sunday morning. The people in our churches, their guests, and visitors judge the church on the basis of what happens in the public worship service. This service attracts the largest number of people in most cases and is viewed as the church at its best. Much of the week's preparation time is focused on this one main event. Consequently, it serves as a litmus test for the church as a whole. Most people determine whether or not they want to be a part of the church based on the worship service—even before considering the church's pro-grams and events. If worship is not done well, then, in most minds, this is a reflection on the other programs of the church, and they don't come back for a second look.

The Definition of Authentic Worship

Authentic worship is an active response to God in which we acknowl-edge His great worth. This definition has three important elements.

A Response to God

God is proactive in the sense that He has pursued us as lost people rather than the reverse. "There is no one righteous, not even one; there is no one who understands, no one who seeks God" (Rom. 3:10–11). God's pursuit of us is clearly seen in such great divine events as the incarnation, death, and resurrection of Christ. Once we come to faith in Christ, it's in worship that we respond to Him and what He's done for us. Therefore, worship is to be a responsive experience.

An Active Response

Worship is an event that requires some effort on our part. We don't simply sit in a pew or kneel and wait for something to happen. According to Scripture, there should be an active response on the part of God's peo-ple. For example, in Revelation 5, which is one of the great worship chap-ters in the Book of Revelation, the saints sing (v. 11) and speak (v. 12) to God.

Worship may also include an active physical response. For example, in Revelation 5:8, the saints as well as others in heaven fall down before Christ, who is worshiped as the Lamb. I've noted that in my own worship experience, I pray best when I'm on my knees as opposed to sitting or standing.

It Acknowledges His Worth

In discussing the English word "worship," Allen and Borror indicate that "This term comes from the Anglo-Saxon *weorthscipe*, which then was modified to *worthship,* and finally to *worship.* Worship means 'to attribute worth' to something or someone."[4]

Consequently, whatever we worship—whether an object or a person—we attribute various degrees of worth to that object or person. Of course, the point in Christian worship is that we're attributing supreme or ultimate worth to God. We're acknowledging that of all that we value in life, we value Him the most. We're attempting to elevate above all else His great value and worth in light of who He is and all that He's done.

The Elements of Worship

Adoration

Adoration involves acknowledging publicly and privately the attributes of our God and His great works. This honors God in a most wonderful way. It also involves praising Him for all He's done for us personally. One of the great books of the Bible that is full of examples of adoration is the Psalms (see especially Pss. 33, 36, 105, 111, 113, 117, 135).

Confession

Confession, like adoration, can be both public and private. Here we acknowledge our "dark side" or what the Bible refers to as the "flesh." After celebrating the goodness of God, it's only natural that we gain a deeper sense of our own sinfulness and guilt. Confession is God's provision for dealing with our "dark side." First John 1:9 points out that while it can be personally painful and even embarrassing, our God is pleased when we confess our sins to Him. Not only does it serve to "flush out" our spiritual system, but it sensitizes us to the sin in our lives and makes us more dependent on Him (see Ps. 51).

Thanksgiving

As with adoration, the Psalms also have many examples of worship expressing the giving of thanks to God for all His many benefits. For example, there are individual thanksgiving psalms (Pss. 30, 32, 34, 92, 107, 116, 118, 121, 138). There are also communal thanksgiving psalms (Pss. 65, 67, 124).

Thanksgiving is another way of honoring God. After a sincere time of confession, the natural response is to spend some time expressing our thanks for Him, His forgiveness, and our blessings. These include such things as answered prayer, spiritual blessings, and material blessings.

Commitment

The natural outcome of adoration, confession, and thanksgiving is the commitment of ourselves to Christ and His service, whatever that may be. This commitment involves sanctification. When we begin to understand God's great love and forgiveness in light of our sinfulness, our natural response is to present our bodies as instruments for His service (Isa. 6:8–9; Rom. 6:12–14).

Supplication

Prayer is a time when we talk to God and make requests for ourselves and others within and outside the body of Christ. This is done publicly by one or two people and privately by all who are present in the service. These requests may involve such areas as marriages, ministries, jobs, friends, health, finances, and decisions. Again, various books of the Bible record the prayers of God's great people. Some New Testament prayers can be found in Matthew 6:9–13; John 17; Ephesians 1:15–23; 3:16–21; Philippians 1:9–11; and Colossians 1:10–12. There are some who've noted these prayers and wisely patterned their own after them.

Proclamation

Proclamation is the preaching of the Word of God. Certainly, preaching involves worship in that it, too, is a response to God that acknowledges publicly His great worth. Proclamation could occur at the beginning or middle of a public time of worship, but most often occurs at the end. It's a means for communicating a word from God that heals and edifies His people and saves the lost.

The Result of Worship

A Commitment of Our Lives to Christ

A major effect that worship can have on God's church is to bring its people to a fresh commitment of their lives to Christ.

This is the message of Romans 12:1: "Therefore, I urge you, brothers, in view of God's mercy, to offer your bodies as living sacrifices, holy and pleasing to God—this is your spiritual act of worship." In other words, the commitment of ourselves to the service of Christ *is* worship. Wouldn't it be honoring to Christ if our worship services so glorified Him and satisfied people's souls that they committed their lives afresh to Him each week!

The Importance of Holistic Worship to Authentic Worship

But how does this process happen? Authentic worship is holistic and culminates in a Romans 12:1 experience.

The cognitive aspect. As worship occurs, it first touches the intellect or the cognitive aspect of our being. If, for example, we're singing, then we think about the words and their spiritual meaning and significance. This enables us to understand the songs and prevents us from singing heresy.

The affective aspect. Next, worship touches our emotions or the affective aspect of our being. If we're singing, then the songs influence us emotionally as well as intellectually. We not only understand what we're singing to and about God, but we're feeling it as well. Certainly, we sense David's intense emotions as he worships in the Psalms. Even more so, we sense those of the Savior as He prayed so intensely in the garden before His crucifixion.

The balance. The fact that worship touches both these aspects of our being is important because the result is balance in these two areas of our lives. The temptation is to tilt one way or the other. Some people are very cognitive and approach worship intellectually. The message never gets past their mind. This happens to a lot of seminarians in an academic environment. Others are very emotional and approach worship looking only for a deep emotional experience. They may be singing heresy to God and aren't even aware of it. What's important to them is that they feel something. Holistic worship serves to avoid both extremes by involving both aspects in worship.

The result. When both the intellect and the emotions are involved, the result is a changed life. Again, this accomplishes a Romans 12:1 type of commitment. We begin to love God with all our heart, soul, and mind (Matt. 22:37). Both our heads and our hearts are touched, and through an act of the will we surrender our bodies as living sacrifices to Christ.

The Requirements of Worship

What kinds of things encourage authentic, holistic worship?

Leaders Must Be Worshipers

It takes a worshiper to lead worshipers. Therefore, the leaders in the church of Jesus Christ must be authentic worshipers of Christ. In the past, most pastors involved themselves in public worship through proclamation of the Bible and pastoral prayer. The trend today is toward more pastoral involvement in other areas of worship as well—not so much in leading singing, but in leading the congregation in a time of corporate adoration, confession, thanksgiving, commitment, and prayer.

Such leadership requires an intensive, regular time of private, personal worship on the part of pastoral leaders and all who lead God's people in worship. The leader's private worship becomes public on Sunday morning.

Worship Should Be Culturally Relevant

All that was said in the previous chapter about cultural relevance applies to worship. One of the reasons the youth in so many churches drop out and join the unchurched is because some of our churches are still worshiping much as they did in the 1950s and 1960s.

Young people and unchurched Christians enjoy worship when the form is relevant to them. For example, many prefer contemporary Christian music to the older hymns of the faith. The music seems more upbeat and uses words they can understand. They also prefer instruments that are more popular today such as guitars, other stringed instruments, and drums. In fact, this is good for church planting because it's easier to purchase and learn how to play a guitar than it is to purchase and play an organ.

Worship Must Be Done Well

It's important that the church pursue a "reasonable" excellence in all that it does. This especially includes worship. There must not be any "flying by the seat of the pants." People who sing off key during special music or who play untuned instruments detract more than they facilitate good worship. It comes across as so inauthentic!

It would be better that churches not attempt certain aspects of worship rather than do them poorly. For example, if there's no experienced, reasonably accomplished pianist available, then sing a cappella. If the hymnals are in bad shape or not appropriate to the group, then don't use them. If a slide projector works one Sunday but not the next, repair it or stop using it.

Worship Needs a Proper Environment

One of the difficulties in church planting is locating and keeping an adequate facility in which to meet. It's not advisable to buy land and build too quickly, so church planters may meet in temporary facilities for as long as three to ten years.

It is important to locate the best facility in the target area in terms of cost and other requirements, including seating, lighting, sound, cleanliness, and accessibility. Sometimes church planters overlook these things to their detriment. They must realize that if they target lost seekers, many of them are used to good facilities and will not tolerate a substandard environment.

Worship Must Be Creative and Innovative

One of the real "turnoffs" is worship that's predictable and boring. And it's very important to Baby Boomers and Gen Xers in particular that it be creative and innovative.

Therefore, church-planting teams would be wise to include people with strengths in this area who will take full responsibility for worship. These people could, in turn, recruit and form their own teams of laypeople who would assist and provide fresh insight.

What might creative worship look like on a Sunday morning? Innovative worship consists of such things as skits, drama, audiovisual presentations, creative dance, and the use of video in preaching.

The Practice of Authentic, Holistic Worship

The Philosophy of Worship

The church planter must begin with a significant philosophy of worship. Developing a philosophy of worship involves several steps.

The Vision

The philosophy of worship is derived from a clear, challenging vision for the church. The purpose of going through the envisioning process is to cultivate a vision for the planted church. This is one of the most critical things the church planter will have to accomplish.

What's important to understand here is that the church's vision dictates its philosophy of worship. First, you develop a significant vision, then you recruit a gifted team around that vision. Finally, you develop a unique strategy that will accomplish your vision with that gifted team.

Your philosophy of worship is a part of that strategy. If you don't take the other steps first, then your philosophy may not match and implement the vision. For example, if you developed a more traditional philosophy of worship, and later decided to pursue a vision that included reaching contemporary, unchurched Baby Boomers and Busters, you'd be in trouble! Chances are that you'd fail or at least struggle in the worship phase of the ministry. Once you know your vision, the philosophy of ministry will fall in place naturally.

The Number of Services

The next step in developing a philosophy of worship is to determine the number of services that will take place each week. At issue is the question, "How many services will people attend each week? What is reasonable?" There are several options.

One meeting. It's biblical and reasonable to expect that believers meet corporately once a week no matter how busy their schedules (Heb. 10:24–25).

Two meetings. If you decide to hold a service to reach lost people, then you'll need at least two services or meetings a week. There will be a need to balance the special meeting for lost people with one for believers or else the latter will starve spiritually. Either meeting could take place in a regular service or small group context.

George Barna relates that he met with what he believed to be a highly committed core group of a newly planted church. He discovered that these people were willing to commit up to two blocks of time each week to the church for a total of about four hours per week per person. In addition, they actually expected all of their needs to be met within these two time blocks.[5]

Three meetings. The maximum is three times per week. With the kinds of schedules people are keeping, asking for three commitments a week may push them to their limits. The old traditional approach that committed people come to three services a week, Sunday morning and evening and the Wednesday night prayer meeting, is rapidly disappearing. Willow Creek Community Church attempts to involve people in a Sunday morning or Saturday evening "seeker's service," a new community service on either Wednesday or Thursday evening, and a small group. Yet they have a highly committed group of believers involved in their ministry. Ultimately, you and your core group must decide what's fair and reasonable, and ask people to commit to it.

The Purpose of the Services

Once you've determined the number of services per week, the next step is to decide what takes place in those services. There are basically three options.

The seeker's service. This is a service designed specifically to reach unchurched lost people, in particular, those who are interested enough that they'll come to a public service if invited by a friend. (Some seekers prefer a small group setting.) In this approach, there is limited participation on the part of those in the audience. Much of what happens takes place up front among those who are leading and involved in the service.

This service is a vehicle to help those in the church expose their lost friends to a positive presentation of Christianity. While it may occur on the weekend, it may not attempt to be a worship service. That could take place at another time. Some Christians don't understand the purpose of this type of service and will complain that they haven't worshiped—which probably is the case. It's important to explain to them the purpose of the "seeker's service" and invite them to the service for believers.

However, a seeker service may include worship and lots of it. While lost people may not be able to worship God in spirit and truth, they may eventually come to faith through a well-done worship service. The psalmist alludes to this in Psalms 40:3 and 57:9.

The nurture service. This is a service specifically designed for believers. This meeting is critical for the church if it attempts a separate "seeker's service" because it focuses on worship and a sermon designed to nourish the sheep. It balances the program of the church. A basic mistake on the part of some who attempt to pursue a "seeker's service" is that they pour all their efforts into that service each week but forget or are too exhausted to feed the sheep. The result is that the latter starve spiritually and eventually drift away.

Most unchurched lost people would feel out of place in this service because it's not intended for them. Once they have attended the "seeker's services" and eventually come to faith in Christ, then the next step is to involve them in this meeting for purposes of spiritual nurture.

The average traditional church conducts a nurture service each week. The problem is that they have very little to offer unbelievers in this service. Consequently, they aren't reaching any lost people and many have become what some call ingrown "holy huddles" or "cognitive communities."

The seeker friendly/sensitive meeting. This service is designed to try and reach unchurched lost people and nourish believers at the same time in one service. Both the worship and the sermon attempt to be "seeker-friendly" and to appeal to both groups. For example, the music is usually upbeat and contemporary, while the sermon pursues needs and issues from the Bible in a way that is relevant to both groups. This approach has been used by some traditional churches in an attempt to become more relevant and balanced in their approach to reaching people. The obvious problem is maintaining a balance between evangelism and edification.

For some the use of the term "seeker" in relation to the worship services has become a turnoff. This may be due to a bad experience in a contemporary church. Consequently, in the church I pastor, we have replaced the term "seeker-friendly" with "people-friendly."

The Style of Worship

The next decision in developing a philosophy of worship concerns the style of worship. In particular, much of the focus here is on the music involved in the church's worship. Some important questions need to be worked through in planning and developing the music portion of the worship time:

1. Will the music be traditional, contemporary, classical, or a combination? Will these musical styles be combined in one service or two separate services?

2. What kinds of instruments will be used? Some of the options are the piano, organ, guitar, drums, brass, and synthesizer.
3. Will the songs primarily be hymns, praise songs, choruses, or a combination?
4. Will there be a choir and/or specials?
5. Will the songs be sung from hymnals, from the bulletin or a bulletin insert, or projected on a screen using some type of projector?
6. Will someone lead the music by standing in front of the congregation (a possible distraction) or by playing an instrument? Another option is having several people sing together in front of the church.

The very first question raises the issue of contemporary versus traditional music, which has caused numerous disagreements between the Baby Boomers and Gen Xers and the Harry Truman Generation. Often but not exclusively, the older generations have problems accepting the younger generations' music. A question might prove helpful. What makes music sacred or secular? Different answers exist in the Christian community. One is the fact that some music was written over two hundred years ago in Europe by people such as Martin Luther and the Wesleys. Another is the notes, melody, beat, or the instruments used in producing the music. A third is the words or lyrics of the song. The first answer is culturally elitist and unbiblical. The second is mere conjecture. While it may be a little too simplistic, the last answer makes the most sense.

It's also helpful to realize that today's traditional music was yesterday's contemporary music, and tomorrow's traditional music is today's contemporary music. For example, when Martin Luther wrote some of the church's great traditional hymns, he was writing contemporary music for his generation. In fact, it's rumored that some of the Wesleys' hymns were penned in a tavern! Consequently, this music concerns issues and struggles Christians were facing in the culture of that day.

The key to answering the questions in this list concerns the people who make up the planted church's target group. The worship and music must be relevant to them, or they will not come.

The Preparation for Worship

Long-term Worship Planning

There are several areas that need to be worked through in attempting long-term planning.

A philosophy of worship. Long-term worship planning builds on a philosophy of worship. The philosophy must come first because it forms the foundation on which many planning decisions are based. To attempt to plan without a philosophy of worship is to play "blindman's bluff" with the church's worship services.

The responsibility for worship. The senior pastor or "point person" must take the final responsibility for the church's worship. This is true even if there's a worship person on the team. Worship is so vital to the church's life that the senior pastor must see that it's done well.

A worship team. Long-term worship planning involves recruiting a worship team. The team doesn't have to be large. It may consist of only two people. Regardless, planning in general is better accomplished in a team context because several minds are better and more creative and productive than one.

Key to the worship team is the worship director. This may be a talented, gifted layperson who is a part of the core group or congregation. It could be a professional whom you have recruited for the position. If the latter, I have several suggestions. First, when recruiting this person, be sure to get a good recommendation from someone who is known as a good worship director. Second, if possible, observe the individual in another context.

Where do you find good worship directors? In most urban areas, a network of these people exists. Contact the worship directors in several churches and ask them for names.

A planning retreat. It's helpful to schedule a planning retreat. The "point person" or primary communicator should get away for a week or so and plan all of the sermons or a significant portion for the following year. Once this is accomplished, either the team or the team and the primary communicator should attempt to get away together to plan the worship services around the sermon topics. This could take place once a year over several days or it could take place quarterly for a day or two.

A worship network. Study and network with other churches that share your philosophy of worship. Good leaders are learners in the sense that they never stop learning. In particular, they learn by searching out what others are doing, especially churches that are innovative and open to change. This involvement keeps them on the "cutting edge."

Short-term Worship Planning

Short-term worship planning concerns three areas in particular.

Focus the worship service. It focuses the worship service. You may attempt four or five things in a worship service such as congregational music, a special, announcements, and so on. Is there something that ties them all together? If not, will they detract from one another? As much as possible, worship leaders should attempt to focus the service on one theme or central idea. The key to this is the central idea of the sermon.

Format the worship service. Short-term planning involves formatting the worship service. Each worship service will have a format. This format may consist of the following:

1. A beginning
2. Announcements
3. Chorus/hymns
4. A congregational greeting
5. An offering
6. Special music
7. Special events (such as drama, a video, baptism, and so on)
8. A sermon
9. A conclusion

In formatting a service containing these ingredients, you must make a number of decisions. One is how you'll begin the service. It's a good idea to have three or four different ways to begin and end a service. This prevents boredom. Another is how to handle the announcements. Most would like to eliminate them from the worship service but seldom do. Others make them a minute or two before the service begins. Many newer, innovative churches include a congregational greeting time. This has been effective but is hard on introverts, especially unchurched ones.

Evaluate the worship service. Short-term worship planning includes evaluating the worship service. This should be done by the worship team and the primary communicator, who is most likely the pastor. It would be wise to include several people from the congregation who have an eye and an ear for good worship. It should take place weekly and as soon as possible after the worship service. The team should ask, "How well did we accomplish our purpose? What did we do and what didn't we do well? How can we do it better next week? In light of what we did this week, what will we do next week?"

The Presentation of Worship

Keep the Music All Together

Music in the worship service should be presented in an uninterrupted block of time. It takes time for people to slow down, adjust, and prepare their hearts for worship. People may not be ready to worship until they've sung two, three, or as many as four songs. There should be plenty of singing (six or more songs) in blocks of time. This time can vary from twenty minutes to one or as much as two hours. It's also very important that the transition from one song or hymn to another be smooth or the flow of the service will be interrupted.

Strive for Excellence

Good worship strives for excellence! The constant problem that the church faces is that people have become accustomed to technical sophistication in the marketplace, on television, and in the various arts.

On the other hand, the majority of churches in America are small and pride themselves on their family-type atmosphere that says it's permissible to "fly by the seat of your pants." The problem is that over a period of time this attitude breeds carelessness in the preparation and performance of worship. When people visit who are not related to the "family," especially the unchurched, they see this and don't return.

Churches must not pursue perfection for this is impossible to achieve, but they should attempt to do the very best they can in their worship services. This is because they represent the Savior to a lost and dying world. In this attempt, it's helpful to remember three things. First, something isn't better than nothing. For example, a poor pianist or guitarist isn't better than no pianist or guitarist at all. If they can't play reasonably well, don't use them. Second, do less and do it better. Some people attempt to do too much in a worship service. They try to include too many different events such as a musical special and an audiovisual presentation plus other things. The problem is that the more you attempt, the greater the likelihood that something will go wrong. Finally, rehearsals should be the norm rather than the exception. It's during rehearsals that the "bugs" are located and exterminated.

Involve the Congregation in the Worship Service

This relates primarily to the nurture and "seeker sensitive services," not a "seeker's service." If the church has a choir, its role in the service must be minimal. In some traditional churches the ministers of music or the worship people spend 90 percent of their time working with a choir. The result is that the choir does 90 percent of the worship because the worship leader has no time left to devote to the congregational aspects of worship. If the choir absorbs a lot of the worship leader's time, then it's best not to have a choir. Worship must be congregational, not choral.

Be Aware of Worship Tension Points

An awareness of the various worship tension points will add a dynamic to the worship service that keeps people's attention and facilitates good worship. The following is a partial list of these tension points:

1. Silence versus sound
2. Solitude versus group participation
3. Traditional versus contemporary style
4. Planned versus spontaneous worship events
5. High-tech versus low-tech
6. Complex versus simple worship techniques
7. Platform versus audience participation
8. Celebration versus reflection
9. Talking versus listening
10. Theme versus no theme
11. Intellectual versus emotional
12. Freedom versus control
13. Formal versus casual
14. Personal versus public
15. Vertical (divine element) versus horizontal (human element)
16. Feminine versus masculine
17. Familiar versus unfamiliar[6]

The Preaching in Worship

While the other events in the worship service are often underemphasized, the importance of the preaching event can't be overemphasized. People must hear a clear word from God that is relevant to their lives as they attempt to live from day to day. The following material presents several principles that facilitate excellence and relevance in today's pulpit. These principles assume a working knowledge of preaching in general and sermon construction in particular. It will attempt to build on this knowledge.[7]

Sermons Must Be Interesting Not Boring

One of the biggest complaints from unchurched people, both saved and lost, is that most sermons and preachers are boring. Every church should pass a law that states that it's a crime to bore people with the Bible.

There are several factors that create interest in sermons. The minister should strive to say something interesting at the very beginning of the sermon. Preachers can begin with such things as a personal story, a news event, or a statement from a popular celebrity or sports figure. This immediately tells the audience that the speaker is worth listening to. Once they've gained this interest, good speakers attempt to maintain it throughout the rest of the sermon with illustrations and relevant stories.

Another way to create interest is to preach on topics that are important to and interest the audience, not yourself. There's a constant temptation for preachers to address issues that interest them but may not be of interest to their audience. This is often a fatal flaw in those who have recently graduated from school and are relatively new in the pulpit.

Here the Bible provides an instructive example. It's important to note that some books were specifically written to a particular church in order to answer people's questions such as Paul's letters to the Thessalonians. Others deal with specific problems, such as Corinthians and the prison epistles. Preachers must realize that most audiences aren't interested in who might be the author of Hebrews, the rationale for supralapsarianism, or the robust economy of the Hittites and the Amalekites. They're interested in themselves and everyday life from Monday through Saturday.

Messages Should Touch Felt Needs

The way to capture people's attention is to address their felt needs. Felt needs are the key to unlocking the closed mind and softening the calloused heart. Preachers will be able to communicate almost anything if they speak in terms of the audience's needs, aspirations, hopes, and dreams.

Again, various books of the Bible focus on the needs of a particular church. For example, in 1 Corinthians, Paul targets the church's need for information concerning divisions, marriage and divorce, food offered to idols, spiritual gifts, love, and the resurrection of Christ. He specifically mentions needs in Ephesians 4:29. Some in the evangelical community have responded negatively to the emphasis on addressing felt needs in sermons. This seems strange in light of such passages as Ephesians 4:29 and 2 Corinthians 8:14 and 9:12.

Good speakers know where people hurt. If they don't know, then they make a point of finding out. They may simply ask or conduct an informal survey in the church or local community. They pay close attention to needs addressed by the local media. Finally, they're aware of the common needs that people have as the result of their humanity.

It's best to present these needs in the introduction of the sermon after the audience's interest has been captured. This tells them that not only will you be interesting but that you understand them and the difficulties of life.

Topical Exposition Is a Valid Form of Preaching

Many evangelical schools train students to preach through a book of the Bible. This is called book exposition. The problem is that some present this as the only way or the best way to preach expository sermons. In fact, some seminary graduates feel guilty if they preach a topical sermon.

Actually, there's more evidence in the Scriptures for topical exposition than book exposition. An example would be all the topical sermons in the Book of Acts. Also, the Savior himself used a topical approach, addressing such issues as adultery, greed, money, and hypocrisy. There's no evidence that anyone preached through a book of the Old Testament. This is not to diminish the importance of book exposition, but to put the two in proper perspective and to free preachers up to preach topically or biographically as well as through a book of the Bible.

A problem with book exposition is that preachers often begin with the text rather than with the audience. They study a particular text and then attempt to apply it to their audience whether or not it applies. For example, some pastors may preach through a particular book of the Bible that deals with issues that neither they nor their audiences are currently facing. Consequently, any application comes across as contrived and inauthentic.

An advantage of topical exposition is that it allows preachers to begin with their people. Then they take Bible passages that are relevant and apply them accordingly. Jesus often discerned the needs of people first and then addressed them from the Scriptures. One problem with topical preaching is the temptation to take passages out of context and misapply them to the audience's needs.

Preaching Should Balance Both the Practical and the Theological

In general, most people want to know both what the Bible says and how it works. The two must go together! To emphasize one at the expense of the other does injustice to the Scriptures and the preaching process.

Few people are interested in the Bible and theology as ends in themselves. They want to know how these two relate to their lives. While many are interested in what's going to happen at the end of the age, they're even more interested in what's going to happen at the end of the week!

Therefore, sermons that emphasize "how to" are very popular and helpful to laypeople. For example, a series of sermons on Philippians 4 could be entitled: "How to be Happy in an Unhappy World." The title of a sermon on Romans 12:19–21 might be worded: "How to Right Life's Wrongs." A sermon on divorce could be entitled: "Growing Through Divorce, Not Just Going Through Divorce."[8]

These kinds of sermons are very practical and relevant. They're as heavy on application as on theology. In fact, it's most important that preachers realize that the Bible has a lot to say about everyday life and how to live it. Those who remember this truth and preach accordingly will touch lives with Scripture.

Sermons Should Be Simple and Memorable

Two major points are enough for one sermon; it is acceptable to have three points although this may be pushing it. People can easily remember two points such as a problem–solution approach or a principle–application approach to the text of a sermon. Good preachers realize that the average person in the pew can only remember so much and pay attention for so long.

One way to help people remember sermons is to tell stories—lots of stories that illustrate biblical principles. In fact, this is one of the universal means of communication in many cultures around the world. Everyone loves a story! That's one of the attractions of movies, television, and books. In addition to stories, use lots of illustrations and examples because they'll have a similar effect, especially if they are personal. Be sure to preach from the narrative portions of the Bible. These are very popular today with Generation X. They prefer the narrative over the didactic literature of the Bible because they love its stories.

Messages Should Not Be Too Long

Twenty to thirty minutes is long enough for any sermon. Today's average audience, no matter how great their theological sophistication, probably doesn't hear anything beyond thirty minutes, no matter how important. In some cases, long sermons irritate today's audiences, especially if they're boring and delivered poorly.

A good practice is to study those who make their livelihood by communicating. An example would be the media. Note how they keep people's attention. Often an hour-long television drama is broken up into numerous segments with different plots and characters. This serves to maintain both the audience's interest and attention.

Language Must Be Clear and Contemporary

Often, in a noble attempt to be true to Scripture, some preachers will use lots of biblical terms such as "born again," "repent," "saved," "redemption," "propitiation," and so on. The problem is that these words don't communicate to the average person in the pew and the unchurched guest in particular.

Ordinary people who lived in the first century understood many of these terms because they were used regularly in their culture. For example, the biblical term "redemption" was used of the price paid to purchase or liberate a slave in the local slave market. In fact, the Greek of the New Testament was not a special language but was the common (koine) Greek world language used from about 300 B.C. to A.D. 500.

It is the responsibility of the preacher to contextualize Scripture for today's modern audience. The minister should explain these terms and use contemporary synonyms that convey the same meaning today that they had in the first century. One helpful way to accomplish this is to use a reliable, modern translation of the Bible. Most people today struggle with the King James translation of the Bible. Both the New American Standard Bible and the New International Version of the Bible are true to the original text and understandable to the person in the pew.

Sermons Should Be Creative and Positive

Most people appreciate creativity in the church in general and in sermons in particular. Some pastors have sought to be creative by conducting interviews as a part of the sermon. For example, my former pastor was preaching on the topic of homosexuality in Romans 1. Toward the conclusion of the message, he interviewed a converted homosexual! In a sermon on abortion, he interviewed a lady who had experienced an abortion.[9]

A number of preachers are using other creative means such as the mini-drama and video. A videotape could be used to convey an experience or a situation that illustrates visually some point in the sermon. The drama has many uses. It could come before the sermon and present a problem that the sermon then solves, or it could follow the sermon and demonstrate a way in which the sermon could be applied to one's life.

Positive sermons communicate more effectively in the long run than negative sermons. They let people know what you're for rather than what you're against.

A Worship Exercise

1. What is your primary motivation for going to a worship service? What is your response to the worship that takes place in your church? Why?

2. Critique the worship service at your present church in terms of its strengths and weaknesses.

3. Is the worship at your church authentic or unauthentic? Describe the difference.

4. What is your philosophy of worship?

5. Are you an authentic worshiper of Christ? When and how often do you worship?

6. Do you find yourself making some of the preaching errors mentioned at the end of this chapter? Which ones? Is there some person whom you can trust to critique your speaking?

12

Pursuing Lost People with a Passion

A Biblical, Culturally Relevant Evangelism

Hurricanes can inflict tremendous damage on property and have claimed many people's lives. But, fortunately, when a hurricane is coming various warning signs go up. There are constant weather bulletins, media reports, and special hurricane warning flags that are hoisted to the top of flag poles.

Today there are numerous warning signs about the dark future of evangelism in this country. One sign comes from western Europe. Western Europe has exerted a great influence on North America in numerous ways, including Christianity. In 1997, Dr. Alister E. McGrath, while speaking at Dallas Theological Seminary, noted that England in the eighteenth century was primarily a Christian nation. However, today only 10 percent claim to be churched. McGrath warned that this was because the church stopped doing evangelism and focused its attention on teaching and the pastoral care of its members. In the summer of 1995, I pastored a church in Amsterdam, the Netherlands, where the number of unchurched was around 97.5 percent! So what? The great missionary statesman Donald McGavran stated that "If top priority is not given to effective evangelism by our churches, in two generations the church in America will look much like its counterpart in Europe."[1] While we can't be sure when he said this, I suspect it was two generations ago!

Another warning sign comes from Floyd Bartel. In his book *A New Look at Church Growth*, he writes that "95% of all Christians in North America will not win one person to Christ in their entire lifetime."[2] Obviously, this is a shocking figure. Sixty-five percent would be high, but 95 percent is frightening!

A third warning sign is from George Barna. In *The Frog in the Kettle*, he writes that "In the past seven years, the proportion of adults who have accepted Christ as their personal Savior (34%) has not increased."[3] From this he concludes that what American Christians believe about the Bible apparently isn't significant enough to share with others.

A fourth warning comes from Bob Gilliam. In the mid- to late 1990s, Gilliam, a church growth consultant who works with churches from coast to coast, surveyed more than 500 evangelical churches in 40 denominations over a 10-year period, including more than 130,000 church members. His survey revealed that each year the average evangelical church led 1.7 people to Christ for each 100 people in attendance. If you owned an insurance company, and your salespersons sold a total of 1.7 policies per year, you would be out of business in a hurry!

While numerous signs indicate that there's danger ahead if the established church in North America doesn't change its attitude toward evangelism, there's a solution. That solution is church planting. Peter Wagner believes that "*The single most effective evangelistic methodology under heaven is planting new churches.*"[4] New churches have the potential to pursue lost people with a passion. Consequently, the sixth vital church planting principle involves a biblical, culturally relevant evangelism.

A Culturally Relevant Evangelism

Effective evangelism in the twenty-first century needs to be characterized by cultural relevance. A primary reason why so little evangelism is taking place in and through evangelical churches is because many don't know how to relate relevantly to the growing number of unchurched lost people in America. There are at least three reasons for this problem.

Christians Don't Know Any Lost People

The first reason is that most people in the church don't know any lost people; they don't have any lost friends.

Most Christians Are Isolated and Insulated from the Lost

The primary problem is that most active Christians have, over a period of time, insulated and thus isolated themselves from lost people.

The fact. Believers know lost people in the sense that they may work next to them or live next door to them, but there are no lost people on their list of friends. They simply don't spend quality time with lost people, especially of the unchurched variety. They don't invite lost people into their homes on a regular basis. They don't consistently spend their leisure time activities with lost people. Most often, when they do things with other people, it's with Christians, not unchurched neighbors or workmates.

The exception. The exception is when a lost individual first comes to faith in Christ as Savior. New believers are often so excited about their faith that they make a point of telling the good news of what's taken place in their lives to many of their lost friends. However, they join a church, and, over a period of time, note that others aren't sharing their faith. This is catching! In some churches, these new believers discover that evangelism simply isn't valued. Other important areas are being emphasized, such as social responsibility, physical and spiritual healing, or some program to the exclusion of evangelism.

The result. Eventually, over a period of time, new believers stop sharing the faith, and other priorities in the church take hold. They isolate themselves from unbelievers and spend all their time with believers. They focus on ministries within the walls of the church. This, in turn, serves to insulate them from the lost as well. Soon they no longer have any lost friends, nor do they want any. They prefer to be around believers only.

The Reasons

There are several reasons why all this takes place.

Christians aren't comfortable around non-Christians. The first has to do with our comfort level. Simply stated, we're not comfortable when we're around lost people, often for what seem to be good reasons. Sometimes they use crude language that we aren't used to, and it has a shocking effect on us. We can add to this list the consumption of alcohol and illicit relationships with the opposite sex. And the list goes on!

We need to constantly remind ourselves that the Savior spent a lot of His time with lost people. And they weren't the aseptic religious people of his day, the scribes and the Pharisees, but the sinners and tax-collectors (Luke 5:27–32; 15:1–2; 19:1–10).

Christians expect lost people to behave like saved people. Another reason we shun lost people is related somewhat to the first reason. It has to do with our expectations. We expect lost people to behave like saved people. The very fact that we're surprised when a lost person uses a string of expletives says something about our expectations. To expect the lost to act as though they're saved is totally unrealistic and unbiblical! We must not expect lost people to behave like saved people until they've become saved people.

Churches Maintain Culturally Irrelevant Methods

A second reason why churches can't relate relevantly to unchurched lost people is because they use evangelistic methods that don't fit people and are generally ineffective with unchurched Baby Boomers and Gen Xers.

Methods That Don't Fit People

Some churches want their evangelistic outreach to be more effective but aren't sure how to go about it. Therefore, they look to those who have a reputation for excellence in evangelism and are winning people to Christ. Most churches turn to evangelistic parachurch organizations for their evangelistic methods.

On the one hand, this makes a lot of sense. The idea is that if you want to do something well, then study and imitate those who do it well already. Why reinvent the wheel? On the other hand, the problem with looking to the parachurch for its methodology is that the latter most often attracts gifted people, those with the gift of evangelism, those who use primarily one style of evangelism—confrontational evangelism.

The problem in the local church is that only about 5 percent to 10 percent have the gift of evangelism and are comfortable with a confrontational approach. A case in point is Coral Ridge Presbyterian Church in Fort Lauderdale, Florida. This church is well known in Christian circles for its Evangelism Explosion Program. In fact, some on the church's staff travel and conduct Evangelism Explosion seminars in numerous churches. This is an excellent program that primarily uses a confrontational approach. Yet only about 10 percent of the membership are involved![5]

Methods That Aren't for an Unchurched Generation

Many churches attempt to reach people in *today's* unchurched culture with methods that worked with people in *yesterday's* churched culture. Most of their evangelistic methods are left over from the Harry Truman Generation. The thinking is that if they worked back then, then they should still work today and they will still work tomorrow. This would, of course, be true if our culture never changed. But it does change, and these churches haven't thought through the implications of that cultural change on their evangelistic methods.

There are several examples. In general, evangelistic bumper stickers with the words "Jesus Saves" don't appeal to lost Boomers and Busters. They think this is weird. The use of Christian radio and television isn't highly effective either. The problem is the listening and viewing audience. Who watches Christian television and listens to Christian radio? Christians, not unbelievers! Handing out gospel tracts isn't as effective as it used to be unless they are read by "seekers" who are already interested in spiritual matters. Knocking on doors works in blue-collar areas and the inner city, but isn't as effective in middle- and upper-income white-collar neighborhoods. Citywide evangelistic crusades aren't attracting people—with the exception of those held by Billy Graham. Lost people will attend a Billy Graham Crusade because he has become an American institution and is a man of high integrity.

Churches Have Missed the Unchurched Culture

A third reason why evangelical churches don't know how to relate relevantly to the unchurched generation is because they don't understand the culture. These churches have several false assumptions that need correction.

The Unchurched Aren't Pursuing the Church

Many traditional churches have missed the shift in America from a churched to an unchurched culture. Up until the late 1950s and 1960s, America was predominantly a churched culture. This doesn't mean that much of America was truly born again. But a lot of people were in church on Sunday, both lost and saved. This was due in part to the large number of churches prevalent in America in those days. Also, there wasn't as much for people to do on Sundays other than go to church. Most towns and cities enforced "blue laws," which kept businesses closed on Sunday. There weren't many events that took place on the "Lord's Day" to draw people away from attending a church.

Many churches still live and think in terms of those times. While they're aware that some things have changed, they haven't been able to figure it all out. Consequently, they believe that as long as you hang a "welcome" sign out front, then lost people will flock to the church. The fact that they aren't has them a little puzzled.

The Unchurched Are Secular, Not Judeo-Christian

In the 1950s and 1960s, due to the large number of churches in America, there was a strong Judeo-Christian influence on most institutions and organizations, including public school systems; national, state, and local governments; and the business sector. As the result of a number of decisions by the Supreme Court, this is no longer the case. In fact, many of these organizations are prohibited by law from displaying any Christian symbols or sponsoring public prayer and Bible reading.

All of this has affected the typical postmodern North American Baby Boomer and Buster. While some are hostile, many look upon Christianity as simply irrelevant to them and the times. Therefore, they've adopted a thoroughly secular mind-set. The older Boomers can remember the old days and what church was like, while their children and Gen Xers have little knowledge of Christianity except for that depicted on television and in the movies. Consequently, we may live in the same neighborhoods, cheer for the same teams, and even speak the same language, but our core beliefs and values are worlds apart.

The Unchurched Are More Concerned about Now Than the Hereafter

Most unchurched people focus on the present, not the future. They don't think about eternity because that isn't important. The idea is, to paraphrase one beer commercial, "You only go around once in life, so get all the gusto you can get!" Consequently, these people struggle with such concepts as "delayed gratification." The word "patience" isn't in their vocabulary because it's not found in their dictionary. A 1990s slogan for Burger King advertised "Have it your way, right away!" People want everything and they want it now—whether it's money, sex, or hamburgers.

The obvious result of all this is that people can't have it all, and they can't have it all now. Therefore, they're extremely frustrated and bear numerous deep, emotional scars. This is reflected in high divorce and suicide rates. This generation populates the offices of psychologists and psychiatrists from Los Angeles to New York. Consequently, to reach this generation, the American church will have to show the benefits of Christianity in the here-and-now. It will have to demonstrate in life and teaching that Christianity isn't simply some shallow "pie-in-the-sky-by-and-by" approach to life, but that it addresses the hard issues such as who we are, where we have come from, what we are worth, and why we are here.

The Unchurched Are Process-, Not Event-Oriented

In the first half of the twentieth century, evangelism primarily involved a single presentation of the gospel to lost people. Success involved getting them to say "yes" and pray a sinner's prayer. It was more an event because America at that time was a churched culture where much pre-evangelism had already taken place. Churches didn't have to spend a lot of time discussing the existence of God, the deity of Christ, or the veracity and authority of Scripture. Much of this was already assumed and accepted by the lost. In many cases, they simply needed accurate information regarding how to be saved.

In the 1970s up through the early twenty-first century, all that has changed drastically. With the shift in America from a churched to an unchurched culture and the growing number of first- and now second-generation unchurched lost people, sharing Christ is much more a process than an event. Very little pre-evangelism is taking place. In a post-Christian, postmodern world, people aren't so sure that there's a God. Many believe that Jesus was merely a man or at best a prophet like all the others, and that the Bible is just another book. Consequently, the witnessing process involves a number of "mini-decisions" on the part of those who would come to Christ.

It becomes obvious that our methodology, not our message, must be adjusted to allow for all the changes that have taken place in the culture. The people in Christ's church must have patience with the lost and know some of the biblical answers to the hard questions they're asking. Above all, they need to be willing to love and befriend lost people and build long-term relationships with them that have the potential to result in their salvation.

A Biblically Based Evangelism

While the methodology of evangelism changes and adjusts to the culture, the biblical principles of evangelism remain the same. There are numerous principles of evangelism found in the Bible.

The Principle of Pursuit

The church must pursue lost people, not wait for them to come to it. This principle is found in various passages such as those on the Great Commission (Matt. 28:19–20; Mark 16:15; Acts 1:8). In particular, it's both emphasized and illustrated by the Savior (Luke 5:27–32; 15:1–31; 19:1–10).

In essence, this is the Great Commission—or at least the first of three steps in carrying out the Great Commission. The problem is that not many churches are doing this. Some go into early "evangelistic retirement" while others are merely "reshuffling the Christian deck." A church that's not pursuing and reaching lost people isn't a Great Commission church and needs to reconsider its purpose. The church planter's vision must be to pursue and win lost people.

The Principle of Value

The principle of value says that lost people matter to God. The Savior loves and values them. While it's taught throughout the Bible it's illustrated clearly in Luke 5:27–32, 15:1–31, and 19:1–10. The point is that if the lost matter to God, then they should matter to His church.

But how can we know if they matter to Christ's church? What's the proof? Those of us in His church will begin to love lost people and pursue them individually and corporately as a church. We will invite them into our homes to meet our families and eat with us. We will attend various events together and be available when they go through difficult times.

The Principle of Relationship

We should spend time with and get to know lost people. This principle is illustrated in such passages as Luke 5:29–32, 15:1–2, 19:7, and Matthew 9:9–13. The idea isn't that we're to be *like* lost people; rather, we're to be *with* lost people. Actually, we're to be different from lost people but in a way that attracts them to Christ. While we can't be with them all the time, we can be with them sufficiently long enough to understand them and how they think. The result is that we learn to relate to them naturally.

Again, the problem is that the longer we're saved, the fewer lost friends we have. The result is that evangelism becomes unnatural (sharing with strangers) rather than natural (sharing with friends). We can apply this principle by committing ourselves to relate to a few lost people on a regular basis. This could be a lost single person at work. It could be a lost, unchurched couple next door, or it could be an unsaved international student at the local university. The important thing is that we begin to relate to them redemptively.

The Principle of Need

The church can gain the attention of lost people by addressing their felt needs. Scripture doesn't ignore people's needs (Acts 2:45; Eph. 4:29; Phil. 4:19; 2 Cor. 8:19, 9:12). Again, the key to unlocking the closed mind and touching the calloused heart is felt needs. This principle is found throughout the Scriptures. People responded to the Savior because of their felt need for salvation. Jesus regularly met people's physical needs and used this as an opportunity to meet their spiritual needs. Several books of the New Testament were written to address the needs of various local churches.

Lost people will respond to people, sermons, and programs that authentically present biblical solutions to their needs. Some object to this strategy, arguing that we need to start with a just and holy God and not with a lost and depraved sinner. While this may be the case with some lost people, we have to get their attention first. Many aren't interested in God, but they're interested in themselves. The idea here is to start where they are and patiently take them to where God wants them to be as the Savior did with the Samaritan woman (John 4).

The Principle of Cultural Adaption

The church should adapt its practices, not its faith, to the people it's trying to reach. These practices concern cultural things (the "world in here") like when the church meets, which translation of the Bible it uses, the instruments used in worship, casual versus formal attire, and so on. This principle is taught by Paul in 1 Corinthians 9:19–23 and 10:23–33. It's also demonstrated by Jesus' ministry (see, e.g., John 3–4). In practicing cultural adaption, the church must never change or compromise in any way the clear teaching of Scripture.

We can't expect today's unchurched lost people to come to us on our terms and adjust to the church's unique culture. This simply will not happen. The mature church must be willing to be flexible and put aside its own cultural and individual preferences in order to reach the lost. For example, if lost people will come to our meetings if we dress informally, then we need to take off our ties! If they will come only on Sunday morning at 11:00 A.M., then we need to design a special service for them and meet as believers at another time. If they prefer to park close to our church facilities, we must be willing to park farther away and walk.

The key question here is, "What are you willing to give up to reach lost people?" The Father was willing to give up His Son (John 3:16). The Son was willing to give up His life (Rom. 5:8). Paul was willing to give up his soul (Rom. 9:3). In light of this, the question for us is, "What are we willing to give up?"

The Principle of Receptivity

The church should pursue receptive lost people, those who *might* be interested in spiritual matters. Unsaved people are at different stages in their view of spiritual concerns. This can be demonstrated by a horizontal continuum, with absolute unbelief on the left side and belief on the right side. Most lost people are located somewhere along this continuum. A biblical example that illustrates this concept is the parable of the sower (Matt. 13:1–9, 18–23). The different soils mentioned represent where various people are along the continuum. Those who are receptive to spiritual matters are somewhere in the middle of the continuum, slowly moving toward belief.

Receptive people also vary in their situations. They could be members of our families or our friends. Some may be experiencing unusual stress as the result of physical disability, financial hardship, or a relationship gone bad.

How might we identify these people? In *The Pastor's Church Growth Handbook,* Charles Arn gives us some help. He writes that unchurched people are most responsive to a change in lifestyle during periods of transition in their lives. A period of transition is a span of time when an individual's normal everyday behavior patterns are disrupted by some irregular event that causes stress in his or her life. Some examples would be the birth of a child, a marriage, a divorce, or a hospitalization. Those who undergo this kind of transition are even more receptive when irregular events compound themselves over a short period of time. However, the greater the length of time following a period of transition, the less receptive they will be.[6]

The Principle of Responsiveness

The church should not only pursue *receptive* lost people, it must pursue *responsive* lost people, those who are interested in spiritual truth. We would call these people "seekers." There are several biblical examples of this principle. Jesus instructed His twelve disciples to pursue responsive lost people (Matt. 10:11–15; Mark 6:10–11; 12:34; Luke 9:4–6). Paul pursued responsive people (Acts 13:43–52; 18:1–7). Some individuals who were "seekers" were Zacchaeus (Luke 19:1–10), Nicodemus (John 3:1–21), the eunuch from Ethiopia (Acts 8:26), and Cornelius (Acts 10). The point is that these people are strongly moving toward or are very close to faith in Christ. They must be pursued with a passion.

The Principle of Clear Communication

The church must be careful to use language that clearly communicates biblical truth to the lost. The church of Jesus Christ must realize that it belongs to a unique subculture that is different from all other subcultures, even in the same part of the country. One example of this difference is its language. Those in the church speak a "temple language" or what some call "Christianeze." We use terms such as "believer" and "sister" and "brother" that are used in a different way in other subcultures.

We also use such terms as "repent," "righteousness," and "sanctification" in sermons and lessons. These aren't used or understood by those outside the church. Much of this language comes from the New Testament and was commonly used by the average person in the world of the first century. While people understood these terms in the first century, both churched and unchurched people don't understand them today. Therefore, we must be careful to explain their usage and to find equivalent terms from our culture if we're to communicate the biblical message clearly.

The Principle of Multiple Hooks

The church should use as many methods as possible to reach the lost. When I was in high school, I spent a lot of time hunting and fishing. I soon discovered that if the fish weren't biting, it was a good idea to change my method. For example, early in the morning large mouth bass would often strike at a top water lure cast close to the edge of the shoreline. A little later in the day this wasn't effective. Instead, I would stick a hook through an earthworm and drop it into various submerged stumps to catch perch.

In "fishing for men," it's essential that we keep lots of hooks in the water. Just as it takes all kinds of churches to reach all kinds of people, so it takes all kinds of methods to reach all kinds of people. Different methods work with different people, and some methods change in terms of their effectiveness as the culture changes. If we're open to different methods, we'll reach people with the gospel.

The Principle of Specific, Intentional Prayer

It's essential for the leaders of the church to be intentional in their prayers and to ask God specifically to give His people a genuine desire to reach the lost. In Matthew 9:36, Jesus observes the harassed and helpless condition of the various crowds that approach Him, and He feels compassion for them. Consequently, in verse 37, He turns to His disciples and points out the need for more workers to harvest this large crop of hurting people. In verse 38, He tells them that a solution to this need is to pray and to ask God specifically to send out more workers into the harvest field.

Such crowds are found in abundance in every community. The Savior is teaching that there's a need for believers to find and reach them, but it can't possibly be done by just a few people in each church. There's a need to mobilize the church as a whole. An essential ingredient in mobilizing people for evangelism is intentional, specific prayer on the part of those who are leading those people.

The Principle of Discipleship

The Great Commission demands disciples as well as decisions. There's a general tendency on the part of people to move to one extreme or the other. Some pursue discipleship or some aspect of discipleship such as teaching to the exclusion of evangelism. Others pursue evangelism (decisions) to the exclusion of discipleship. Neither accomplishes the Great Commission, although the latter does get people into the kingdom.

The point here is that authentic evangelism pushes past a mere decision and presses for discipleship. In fact, a disciple of Christ is a more accurate representation of a true decision for Christ. Conversion is meant to be germinal, not terminal, the beginning, not the end, of a closer relationship with Christ.

Both extremes falsely dichotomize the Great Commission mandate. Scripture clearly separates conversion from discipleship in *presentation*. For example, the two are clearly distinguished theologically in comparing such passages as Ephesians 2:8–9 with Ephesians 2:10. These passages are presenting the theology of salvation. However, Scripture doesn't always dichotomize between the two in *practice* as seen in a descriptive passage such as Acts 14:21–22, where the disciples are seen in action. It's the descriptive passages that cause so much confusion in Christian circles in trying to determine correct doctrine. A case in point is Acts 2:38. The key here is to go first to the verses that speak to the doctrine theologically. Then we base what we believe more on theological passages than on descriptive passages.

The Principle of Natural Style

Each Christian has at least one or more natural styles of evangelism.

The Source

Bill Hybels presents this principle in his book *Honest to God?* He got the idea from the Bible! He points out that it takes all kinds and types of Christians to reach all kinds and types of lost people:

> Only a tiny fraction of the unbelievers in this world will be reached by the stereotypical evangelist. The unbelieving world is made up of a variety of people: young and old, rich and poor, educated and uneducated, urban and rural, with different races, personalities, values, political systems, and religious backgrounds. Isn't it obvious it would take more than one style to reach such a diverse population?
>
> That's where we come in. Somewhere in that multifarious group is a person who needs to hear the message of Christ from someone just like you or me. A

person who needs an evangelist of your exact age, career, and level of spiritual understanding, or of my exact personality, background, and interests.[7]

The Styles

Hybels proceeds to list six possible evangelistic styles. The first is the confrontational style demonstrated by Peter with his Pentecost sermon in Acts 2. The second is the intellectual style used by Paul in Acts 17:3. This involves "explaining and proving" that Christ was Messiah. The third is the testimonial style used by the blind man in John 9. Christ had healed him and revolutionized his life. It was all he could talk about! The fourth is the relational style of the demon-possessed person in Mark 5. The fifth is the invitational style. It was used by the Samaritan woman in John 4, who, after she spoke with Christ at the well, went and invited her fellow Samaritans in a nearby city to come and listen to Him. The sixth is the serving style demonstrated by Dorcas in Acts 9.[8] An eclectic approach would involve the use of a combination of these styles.

The Application

Every church with a vision to reach lost people should help people discover their natural evangelistic style(s). This could be a part of the lay mobilizing process mentioned in chapter 9. Evangelism becomes more natural when people share according to their unique style. Combine this with those who have either natural or spiritual gifts in the area of evangelism, and they'll witness from a position of strength and giftedness. This is a gifts-based, style-shaped evangelism.

The Principle of Natural Prospects

The best and most natural prospects for evangelism are one's family and friends. Tom Wolf, the former senior pastor of The Church on Brady in Los Angeles, California, has developed this principle for the church.[9]

The Examples

There are numerous examples of this principle throughout the New Testament. In Acts 10:24 and 11:14, Cornelius has compassion not only for himself, but his family and "close friends." In Acts 16:14, Lydia comes to faith in Christ, and in verse 15 her family does as well. The same is true of the Philippian jailer and his family in verses 30–34. The pattern repeats itself in the situation of Crispus and his family (Acts 18:8), a royal official and his son (John 4:53), a demon-possessed man and his family (Mark 5:19–20), Zacchaeus' family (Luke 19:9), and the household of Stephanas (1 Cor. 1:16).

It's helpful to understand that a household as used in both the Old and New Testaments was much larger than the typical American household of the twentieth century.

> In addition to the men, there were married women and the unmarried daughters, as well as the slaves of both sexes, persons without full citizenship, and "sojourners," or resident foreign workers. If we remember that families had numerous children, and that an Israelite might easily be a father at twenty, a grandfather at forty, and a great-grandfather at sixty, and that the younger brothers of the head of the family, with their descendents, could also belong to a patriarchal family.[10]

Regarding the family in the New Testament, Michel writes, "It is explicitly emphasized that the conversion of a man leads his whole family to the faith; this would include wife, children, servants and relatives living in the house."[11]

The Research

Win Arn demonstrates the importance of the principle of natural prospects in research conducted by the Institute of American Church Growth. The institute asked over 14,000 laypeople the question: "What or who was responsible for your coming to Christ and your church?" One to 2 percent listed a special need, 2 to 3 percent said they simply walked in and stayed, 5 to 6 percent listed the pastor, visitation was responsible for 1 to 2 percent, 4 to 5 percent listed the Sunday school, an evangelistic crusade was responsible for 1/2 of 1 percent, and 2 to 3 percent listed the church's program. Finally, 75 to 90 percent listed a friend or relative.[12]

The Application

Consequently, the church must encourage its people to pursue their natural prospects such as their family, neighbors, and friends with the gospel. These are people with whom they've already formed important, personal relationships. According to the Scriptures and the survey by the Institute of American Church Growth, this is a natural, biblical form of evangelism that gets lasting results.

The Principle of Grace

Grace is God's unmerited favor toward humankind. He does things for us with "no strings attached." Steve Sjogren has written a relevant book on evangelism entitled *Conspiracy of Kindness*.[13] The intent of the book is to encourage believers to do various acts of kindness for lost people with "no strings attached." For example, Christians could wash cars, mow lawns, give away Pepsi, clean car windshields, put money in lapsed parking meters, shovel snow, and many other things with no expectation of return. In fact, an offer of remuneration is turned down. Christians respond, "We're simply attempting to show the love of Jesus in a practical way." When people ask why, it serves as an invitation to witness to them.

These acts of kindness or grace have a staggering effect on lost people. The unchurched think that all the church is after is their money. This proves them wrong in a positive way, and they, not the Christian, initiate a discussion of the gospel.

Developing a Biblical, Culturally Relevant Strategy for Evangelism

Evangelism is best accomplished through a well-designed strategy that pursues lost people. This should be done with both an individual and a corporate strategy of pursuit. The first involves the individuals in the church, and the second involves the church as a whole.

A Strategy of Individual Pursuit

The church should design a strategy of evangelism for its members that takes into account their unique styles and helps them pursue lost people. The following five-step strategy could serve as a pattern.

Examine One's Relational Community

Every person has a relational community. The idea behind this first step is to encourage the people in the church to examine regularly their relational communities, looking for receptive and responsive people who might be interested and sensitive to spiritual matters. A relational community consists of a minimum of three groups.

The family community. The family community consists of the various people who are related in some way to the church member. These people would be grandparents, parents, children, aunts, uncles, cousins, and in-laws. While family ties aren't as strong as they used to be in light of the divorce rate and the growing number of single parents, in many places still "blood is thicker than water." These natural ties provide fertile ground for evangelism. A most helpful exercise in discovering receptive and responsive family members is to draw a family tree and use it for prayer purposes.

The neighborhood community. The neighborhood community consists of the neighbors in the immediate vicinity. Often friendships can be developed within this community that are as strong relationally as those between family members. Consequently, the people in our churches must be encouraged to take every opportunity to develop their relationships with the "people next door." A helpful exercise is to draw a community map with the church member's house in the center.

One problem for a growing number of people in our churches is that they live fairly far from where the church is located. The old parish system, where everyone attended the church in the neighborhood, is long gone. This began to erode with the development of expressways, which allowed people to cover great distances in a short period of time. The result is that some people attend churches that are quite far from where they actually live. This makes it difficult to invite neighbors to church because they're not willing to make the long drive out of their community.

The work community. The work community includes the people that the average church member is in contact with during the week while at work. It often consists of one or two people who may be on the same team and others with whom there's a more distant work relationship. It's helpful for purposes of prayer and spotting responsive people in this community to draw an organizational chart. The problem with inviting these people to church-sponsored events is the same as that for the neighborhood community—distance. The people who make up the work community may live in the opposite direction from where the church is located.

Develop a "Hit List"

As people in the church routinely examine their various communities, they will begin to discover certain people who might be receptive and responsive to Christianity. These are often individuals who are going through a stressful period in their lives. They may be experiencing illness, the loss of a job, or the loss of a family member. These people could be put on a list in the order of their perceived receptivity to spiritual matters. For the sake of memory and emphasis, we could call this a "hit list."

The Masterplanning Group International has developed a similar idea. They actually sell a card that they call a "Ten Most Wanted List." The Group encourages believers to list ten people they most want to see come to Christ. They provide a list of suggestions regarding those who might be on the list and what a person can do to build a relationship with them. Also, the card includes a small tab where all ten names may be listed. This tab can be removed and carried in one's wallet or purse.[14]

Pray for Those on the "Hit List"

Next, the members are asked to pray daily for those people who are on their "hit list." This need not take more than a few minutes of their time and can be accomplished while driving to work or on a lunch break. This serves to help them concentrate on their prayer efforts for the lost and to keep the lost constantly before them.

Most Christians pray to some extent. It may be for a short time daily, or it may only be once a week at the worship service. Regardless, the point is that they don't spend much time in prayer, so they don't experience a lot of answers to prayer. When people begin to pray, God will begin to answer their prayers. The result is a changed attitude toward prayer, a changed life, and new people populating the kingdom.

Cultivate Relationships with Those on the "Hit List"

The fourth step in the strategy is to pursue a relationship with the person or persons at the top of the list. If this person is a recent widow, then you could mow her lawn and help with repairs. You could check up on her regularly to see if she has any needs you can meet. If it's the couple next door, invite them over for coffee and dessert. Invite the husband over to watch a football game and eat pizza. Invite him to go along to the local store to buy fertilizer or a hammer and nails.

In particular, people should look for things they enjoy doing, and do them with lost people. If two women enjoy cooking, they can get together and share recipes and cook up a special meal for their husbands. If they both enjoy jogging or a workout, they could jog together or work out together at the local health club. If neighbors enjoy playing board games, invite them over for popcorn and a game of Monopoly.

Discern Their Needs and Look for Times of Receptivity

Finally, as people in the church get to know those in their relational communities, the latter will begin to divulge their felt needs. When a person is hurting in some way, it's difficult to hide it. These are ideal times to talk about spiritual things.

God often uses physical or emotional pain in a lost person's life to get attention and catalyze spiritual interests. Christians need to be alert to these times because they're periods of potential receptivity and response to Christ. And it's at these times that a person in the church could implement evangelism. Using an invitational style, they might invite the lost person to a neighborhood Bible study or a special church service for "seekers." If it's a confrontational style, this is the time to confront gently. If it's a testimonial style, this is an opportunity to testify concerning all that God has accomplished through Christ.

The church needs to initiate this strategy for individual pursuit at the point of membership. When most people join a church, they're making a commitment to that church. They've decided they want to be a part of that body and are at a point of high commitment. In the membership process, they would be asked to draw up a family tree, a community map, and an organizational chart for work. Next, they could develop a "Hit List" or a "Ten Most Wanted List." This would be an excellent start toward implementing the strategy on a personal basis.

A Strategy of Corporate Pursuit

It's imperative that every church with a Great Commission vision develop a corporate strategy for pursuing lost people in general and unchurched lost in particular. This involves two areas.

Develop a Unique Strategy of Evangelism

Not only should individual members be involved in evangelism, but the church as a whole should be involved as well. This is primarily the responsibility of the pastors and their teams who need to design a specific strategy that fits their church and their particular target group in the community.

This strategy is usually reflected in the church's programs. If you want to know what a church values, then examine its programs. Churches that value social action have numerous programs designed to help various groups in the community such as the poor, the homeless, and the unborn. Churches that value Bible knowledge have programs that primarily involve a strong teaching ministry. They're marked by Sunday school classes or small groups taught by excellent teachers.

Churches with a Great Commission vision must establish innovative, relevant programs that balance evangelism and edification. In essence, this process is accomplished by first developing the strategy and then designing the church's programs around that strategy. The strategy in its simplest form is twofold and consists of evangelism and edification. The next step is to design several programs to accomplish evangelism and several programs to accomplish edification.

Churches that God is blessing are balanced in their approach to evangelism and edification. They're both reaching lots of lost people and discipling a significant portion of them. And each of them has developed a strategy on which their programs are based. For example, Willow Creek

Community Church, located near Chicago, Illinois, has a seven-point strategy. Their entire program, including the now popular "seeker's service," is designed specifically to implement that strategy.

Encourage and Help People in Their Personal Evangelism Efforts

A corporate strategy that balances evangelism and edification encourages the people in a church or beginning core group to share their faith individually. This needs to be reinforced by other efforts as well. People will need constant encouragement from the pulpit. Pastors who value evangelism will communicate that in their sermons. The church will need to sponsor evangelistic classes that help people discover their evangelism styles and share their faith. The church could encourage the leaders of small groups to take their people through this training. Also, small groups could be created specifically for the purpose of reaching lost people.

An Evangelism Exercise

1. Do you have any lost friends? How much time do you spend with lost people, not including those you work with or members of your family? If you spend little time with lost people, then list some of the reasons.

2. Why are so few Christians and churches reaching lost people today? Do you know of any exceptions?

3. Using the biblical principles of evangelism listed in this chapter as a checklist, which are characteristic of your evangelism efforts and those of your church?

4. Draw a map of your neighborhood with the houses or apartments that immediately surround your house or apartment. Place people's names on it appropriately and use this as a means to pray for opportunities to relate to them. Do the same for your relatives using a family tree, and for people at work using an organizational chart.

5. What were the circumstances surrounding your coming to faith in Christ? Did they involve a relationship with a friend or relative? If so, what does this tell you about the effectiveness of friendship evangelism?

13

The Bigger We Get, the Smaller We Get

A Robust Network of Small Groups

Over the past twenty to thirty years much ink has been spilled concerning the gap between the Baby Boom Generation and the Harry Truman Generation. Yet the biggest gap the Boomer Generation feels is within itself. The Baby Boom Generation has been described as "a relationally vacuous generation struggling in their ability to form lasting relationships."[1] As Paula Rinehart writes in *Christianity Today*, "Their lonely statistics speak for themselves. They are 500 times more likely to be single than their parents were, and even half of those who marry will probably divorce."[2]

One reason for this problem according to Michael Morris, an Episcopalian priest, can be found in the Boomers' desire to lead a life of anonymity. He writes, "Most live in their own isolated boxes in the suburbs, a thousand miles away from family, in communities in which they feel no roots.... They are plagued by loneliness—yet driven by demanding jobs and competing family needs. Underneath all that activity is a deep longing for a connection with God that seems real and intimate."[3]

Churches with a Great Commission vision often grow big in a hurry. On the one hand, this is exciting because lost people are accepting Christ and populating the kingdom. On the other hand, for a generation that prizes honesty and disclosure on an intimate level, this growth doesn't seem so good. Will the church of Jesus Christ have to choose between one or the other? Or is it possible to have the best of both worlds?

Here church planting provides some help. The seventh vital church-planting principle concerns a robust network of small groups. This principle can be summed up in the words "The bigger we get the smaller we get." To accomplish a Great Commission vision, churches must not only reach lost people, but also develop a robust network of small groups. One must be balanced by the other for healthy church life. There are several considerations that can help church planters initiate such a program in the new church. The first three provide the rationale for the program; the others provide help in organizing and starting it.

Small Groups Are Biblical

Small groups were an integral part of the early church and vital to its life.

The Size of the Early Church

The various churches in the Book of Acts were large in comparison to the typical North American church. For example, the church in Jerusalem began in an upper room with about 120 people (Acts 1:12–15). In response to the preaching of Peter it grew almost immediately to 3,120 members (Acts 2:41). Acts 2:47 tells us that the church *continued* to grow (Luke uses the Greek imperfect tense, which indicates continuous action). Then, Peter preached a second sermon and the number of men alone grew to be about 5,000 (Acts 4:4).

The early church and the apostles underwent great persecution. As a result the apostles were scattered into other areas such as Judea and Samaria (Acts 9:1). Ultimately, God used this persecution to spread the gospel according to His plan stated in Acts 1:8. The result is that the apostles and Paul, in particular, planted churches in Judea, Samaria, Asia Minor and Greece. Many of these churches beginning with the Jerusalem church grew into large, citywide congregations (Acts 2:41, 47; 4:4; 5:14; 6:1, 7; 9:31, 35, 42; 11:21, 24, 26; 14:1, 21; 16:5; 17:4, 12; 18:8, 10; 19:26; 21:20).

The Structure of the Early Church

The large size of the churches in Acts presented some obvious problems in terms of ministry.

The Problem

A conservative estimate of the size of the Jerusalem church alone was 20,000 to 25,000 people. It could have been much larger and so could some of the other city-churches that were planted later. How was the church to minister to and care for all these people?

The apostles and elders solved this problem by structuring the churches around both large and small groups. Acts 2:46 indicates that the Jerusalem church met in a large area in the temple (Solomon's Colonnade according to Acts 3) and in homes. Acts 5:42 indicates that the church continued to meet "in the temple courts and from house to house." Finally, in Acts 20:20, Paul says that he taught in Ephesus "publicly and house to house."

Large Group Meetings

It would appear that the large city-church meetings were used primarily for three purposes.

Evangelism. Large group meetings were used for evangelism (Acts 4:4; 5:42). This meeting took place in the temple in the portion called Solomon's Colonnade (Acts 3:11). It was a large area where a number of people could gather as indicated by the response to Peter's sermon in Acts 4:4. Apparently, the church moved into the area at a certain time, used it temporarily, and then moved on. With persecution, these meetings may have occurred infrequently or not at all.

Preaching. A second purpose of large group meetings was for preaching (Acts 20:20). The text gives no clues as to where this preaching took place.

Teaching. Teaching was also accomplished in the large group meetings. Acts 5:42 suggests that such meetings were tied closely to evangelism and the fact that Jesus was the Messiah. This teaching was public and consisted of anything that was helpful to the church (Acts 20:20).

Small Group Meetings

The small group meetings or house churches had a variety of purposes, all of which contributed strongly to developing a vital sense of community.

Provision. According to Acts 2:44–45, small group meetings served to meet people's material needs. Acts 4:32–37 indicates that people were willing to sell their possessions to provide for those who for various reasons had nothing.

Communion and Worship. These meetings also served as a place where Christians broke bread (Acts 2:46), which could be a reference to communion, and worshiped (Acts 2:47).

Evangelism. In Acts 5:42, Luke indicates that a purpose for small group meetings was evangelism.

Prayer. In Acts 12:12, Peter escapes from prison and interrupts a prayer meeting that was taking place in a group.

Encouragement. In Acts 16:40, we see that Paul used small groups for encouraging other believers. These meetings, of which there were probably many, took place primarily in people's homes (Acts 2:46; 5:42; 12:12; 16:40; 20:20).

The Purpose of Small Groups

The one major, all-encompassing purpose for small groups is the transformation of a person's life or life change through biblical community. The broad sweep of the Scriptures indicates that God's people are to be constantly changing and growing more and more like Him (Lev. 20:7; Col. 1:28–29; 1 Peter 1:15-16). This process is commonly referred to in theology and the Bible as sanctification. But there's some confusion as to how this takes place in the context of the local church.

An Assumption

Most people assume that life change takes place as the result of the pastor's preaching ministry in the church. Certainly, a major purpose for preaching is to encourage the transformation of a person's life. The problem in many churches, however, is that this is either the primary or the only vehicle for implementing life change. I call these pulpit-driven churches.

The reason this is a problem is because preaching is only one of many ways to facilitate life change and it's not necessarily the best way. There are no less than four reasons why. First, we discovered in chapter 2 that church attendance in general and attendance of the worship service in particular is down. And those who do attend, don't attend every week. Second, the average attender forgets 90 percent to 95 percent of what he or she hears within seventy-two hours. Third, people may make a decision in response to a sermon but rarely a commitment. What's the difference? A decision is short-term in effect, while a commitment is long-term. Finally, if the church is sermon-dependent, then the preacher better be a good communicator. Average or mediocre won't do!

Pause for a moment and join me in an experiment. I would challenge you to reflect on how long you've been a Christian. Let's assume ten years. Next, attempt to calculate the number of sermons you've heard during the period of time you've been a Christian. If you've attended a traditional church where the pastor preaches three times a week, you'll discover that you've heard a lot of sermons over the years! Let's assume only one sermon a week for 12 months a year which comes to 48 sermons a year. If we multiply this times 10 years, we come up with 480 sermons. Are you surprised?

Now here's the question. How many of those sermons have had a major impact on your life? When I've conducted this experiment with students in a seminary classroom or with people in a local church setting, the answer is usually somewhere between one and ten. Most, however, remember less than five significant sermons.

Another question is, "Did you come to faith in Christ as the result of hearing an evangelistic sermon or the witness of one or two individuals?" While some Christians could answer that it was a combination of the two, statistics indicate that 75 percent to 90 percent of people come to faith in Christ through a significant relationship with another person. It would seem that the sermon doesn't have the life-changing qualities that so many today take for granted.

Some important variables exist. First, the ability of a sermon to affect a Christian's life will vary according to the giftedness and capabilities of the person in the pulpit. This will range from high impact to little or no impact. Another variable is the fact that consistent exposure to sermons can and usually does have a cumulative effect. While we may not think they're affecting our lives because we can't recall very many that have, the Spirit has been using bits and pieces of various sermons over the years to bring about some life transformation.

The Reality

The reality is that life change takes place most often as the result of a significant relationship with either an individual or a small number of individuals in community. Let's conduct a second experiment. The chances are good that if you're reading this book, you've committed your life to service and ministry for Christ. This may have happened only once for you or it could have happened several times over the years since you've become a Christian. Now consider the circumstances surrounding your commitment to Christ. The question is, "Was it the influence of the life of one or a few significant people in your life?" Most people indicate that this, indeed, was the case.

Let's conduct one last experiment. Take a moment and recall the circumstances surrounding the time when you accepted Christ. The question is, "Was it the result of the witness of one or two significant people in your life?" When I've conducted this experiment, in most cases the answer has been, "Yes." Again, this is confirmed by Win Arn's survey and the various passages presented in chapter 12.

The obvious conclusion is that if churches expect their people to grow spiritually and mature in Christ, then they'll need to provide ways to facilitate that growth. One of the primary means that God has used since the days of the early church to accomplish growth is some type of small group ministry. Therefore, churches that take seriously the Great Commission mandate will have a robust network of small groups.

The Advantages of Small Groups

Small Groups Aren't Limited by Facilities

Most churches, no matter where they're located, struggle at some point with their facilities. Planted churches usually experience problems with locating adequate temporary facilities. It's not easy to find the kind of place that's necessary to accommodate all the ministries of a new church, including such things as a nursery, classroom space, and adequate parking. Another factor is the cleanliness of these facilities.

Even when a church has purchased or constructed its own building, there continue to be problems. There are the usual problems with maintaining the existing facilities, which face all churches. A significant number of churches today are losing people and becoming smaller. They meet in facilities that have become too large. Some churches are growing and struggle with where to put all their people. Most likely, the planted church will have to face the latter situation.

A decided advantage of a robust network of small groups is that the new church doesn't have to worry about locating and renting additional facilities. They can meet just about anywhere at a wide variety of times. For example, they can meet in someone's office, a home, or even outdoors in good weather. They have the option of meeting in the same place, or they can vary the location of the meeting from time to time.

Small Groups are Geographically Expandable

Not only are small group ministries not limited by facilities, but they're also not limited by location. While they can meet where the primary congregational meetings take place, they don't have to. They're geographically expandable. They can meet just about anywhere they want. In fact, one way to reach your neighbors is to locate a small group ministry at your house and to invite the people next door.

Geographically expandable small groups also facilitate the planting of branch churches. Some of these small groups that are located at some distance from the church could provide potential future sites for the planting of other churches in those areas of the town or city. While most churches begin with a single core group, which itself is a small group, another strategy is to plant a church by starting several small groups and bringing them together once or twice a week for evangelism and worship.

Small Groups Promote Biblical Community

It's difficult for people who meet in large groups to get to know one another. These kinds of meetings are designed to facilitate corporate evangelism, preaching, and teaching, not the development of biblical community.

Authentic biblical community is what takes place when Christians implement the biblical imperatives and exhortations that affect how they relate to one another. An example is the "one another" passages. Fifty-nine times the Bible exhorts believers to minister in some way to one another. Twenty-one times (one-third) they exhort us to love one another. Others that fall somewhere under the capstone of love are the following:

"be at peace with each other" (Mark 9:50)
"be devoted to one another" (Rom. 12:10)
"honor one another" (Rom. 12:10)
"accept one another" (Rom. 15:7)
"have equal concern for each other" (1 Cor. 12:25)
"serve one another in love" (Gal. 5:13)
"be kind and compassionate to one another" (Eph. 4:32)
"consider others better than yourselves" (Phil. 2:3)
"admonish one another" (Col. 3:16)
"encourage one another daily" (Heb. 3:13)
"each one should use whatever gift he has to serve others"
    (1 Peter 4:10)

These and other exhortations are all elements of biblical community that are realized best in a small group context. This was true of the ministry of Christ in the first century as He worked with the twelve to change the world. It was also true of the church (Acts 2:46; 5:42; 8:1-3; Rom. 16:5; 1 Cor. 16:19). And it is true of Christ's disciples and His church in the twenty-first century.

Small Groups Encourage Lay Ministry

Repeatedly and in various ways, Scripture promotes lay ministry in the local church. One way is through the exercise of spiritual gifts (1 Cor. 12–14). Another is by equipping laypeople for ministry (Eph. 4). A third is the ministry of believer-priests (1 Peter 2; Rev. 5).

There are numerous commands and exhortations in the New Testament regarding lay ministry. The large number of "one another" passages encourage believers to do things to or for each other. For example, in 1 Thessalonians 4:10, Paul tells the church to "love each other" and in 1 Thessalonians 5:11 to "encourage each other."

The question is, "How do we implement these commands and 'each other' passages in the church?" Most people note them mentally and attempt to apply them when possible. Small group meetings and ministries provide an ideal community in which these may be implemented and consciously pursued.

Small Groups Aren't Limited by Finances

The cost for operating most churches ranges from minimal to exorbitant depending on the size of the church and its buildings. The rule is simple: the larger the church, the greater the operating costs. These expenses include such things as the purchase and maintenance of facilities and vehicles and the provision of staff salaries.

While the cost of operating most churches is significant, the cost of conducting a small group ministry is minimal if any. The leader is usually a layperson who isn't paid. Neither are there any vehicles or facility expenses. In fact, it's possible to conduct small group ministries without incurring any costs whatsoever. In many cases, some small groups charge only for supplies or for coffee and donuts.

Small Groups Decentralize Pastoral Care

In the traditional cultural model, the pastor is expected to provide pastoral care for the people in the congregation. In fact, this is where we get the title, "pastor." This model works as long as the church has less than one hundred members. Once a church begins to grow beyond this figure, pastoral care needs to involve more than one person.

Many of the early churches were megachurches. How did they solve the problem of pastoral care? Evidently, they used a different model. Much pastoral care took place in and through small group communities. Two examples of this are found in Acts 2:44–45 and Acts 4:32–37. In essence, those in the various house meetings took care of their own. It's imperative that as a planted church begins to grow that it establish small groups. Otherwise, there will be a breakdown in the pastoral care component of the church, which could have tragic results (see Acts 6).

Small Groups Facilitate Leadership Training

One of the reasons why 80 percent to 85 percent of the churches in America are plateaued or in decline is because of a lack of adequate leadership. One solution to this problem is the small group ministry. Small groups can be used as proving grounds and incubators for training new leadership in the church.

One of the problems in the training of leaders is that much of it takes place in a classroom. Rarely do people have the opportunity to actually lead until they've completed the class or even a degree from a school. The best leadership training takes place in actual life. Indeed, the "proof of the proverbial pudding" is what happens when the prospective leader is placed in charge of a group. This kind of training can best be accomplished in the local church through its small group ministries. Those who've proved their leadership abilities could adopt intern or apprentice leaders for whom they take responsibility. When they believe the new leader is ready, the group could split and the new leader takes the new group.

Small Groups Promote the Assimilation Process

One of the problems many churches face in terms of growth is how to keep people from "slipping out the back door" of the church. This involves what church growth people call the assimilation process. Often one of the major reasons people leave a church is because they're searching for significant relationships that the church doesn't provide. In time, they look elsewhere.

Participation in a small group should be a requirement for membership in the church. When people join a church, it is usually at a high commitment point in their lives. They're willing to make commitments that they might not make at another time. Once they put down some roots in the group, they become assimilated and aren't likely to leave the church unless some other problem should surface. Usually, the longer they're in the group, the more committed they become to the small group concept and the more they become assimilated in the broader church community.

The Organization of Small Groups

There are several ways a small group can be organized.

Small Groups Can Be Organized According to Geography

One way to organize a small group program is on the basis of geography or where people live in the community. Those people who live in the same area of the community come together at some central location and form a small group. Once the group is established, other people in the area are invited to join as well. As new people join the church they're assigned to a small group on the basis of where they live in the community. As people move to new areas or new people come into the church from those areas, new groups are formed there as well. This also has the potential to facilitate church plants in those communities.

While this is a viable option for the church, most groups don't organize according to geography. In fact, most organize on the basis of affinity. People, no matter where they live in the town or city, are attracted to one another on the basis of such things as age, occupation, common interests, and needs.

Small Groups Can Be Organized According to People's Schedules

The large group meetings of the church occur at certain designated times that are deemed as best for the entire church or for a specific target group. The traditional meeting time has been on Sunday morning at 11:00 A.M. As the culture has changed and the "blue laws" in many areas of the country have been eliminated, this may no longer be the best time for every church. Yet most churchgoers set 11:00 A.M. aside in their minds because the church has been meeting at this time for so long. For them, this is the "Lord's Day." As mentioned earlier in this book, some churches are so intent on reaching lost people, they've given 11:00 A.M. over to their target group for a "seeker's service." They hold a believer's service for themselves at another time.

Unlike the large group meetings of the church, the small group meetings aren't limited to a specific time of the day or week. They can meet once or twice a month or even weekly. And they can meet at practically any time during the day. The determining factor is the time schedules of its participants. The question is, "When can we all meet?" This flexibility allows people who are on difficult work schedules to meet with others during the week even though they may work all day Sunday or on Sunday mornings.

Small Groups Can Be Organized Around Common Interests

The large group meetings of the church usually have a specific purpose for meeting. It could be for evangelism, worship, preaching, or teaching. Large group meetings may be targeted at believers, unbelievers, or both. These purposes usually remain consistent throughout the life of the church. While change may and should take place, it's usually within these purposes and not beyond them.

The small group program of the church can be used for these same purposes and for other purposes as well. Many programs are organized around people's common interests. These interests consist of such things as prayer, outreach, family, singles, support, caring, and Bible study. Some programs consist of target group ministries, which attempt to reach specific peoples with the gospel such as the cults, the elderly, the poor, international students, and others.

Small Groups Can Be Organized
Around Dependence Problems

For years the church of Jesus Christ has all but ignored some major social problems. These problems include addictions, co-dependency, eating disorders, sexual abuse, depression, dysfunctional families, and pornography.

A large group meeting can address these problems only in a sermon or forum approach, which at best deals with the problem "at a distance." The small group program of a church can focus specifically on one of these problems and deal with it more directly as well as provide support for those experiencing them. Today more and more churches are beginning to move in this direction, much to the delight of church-goers and those outside the church. This may or may not involve some kind of therapy. Most groups wisely avoid the latter and are there more for support.

Small Groups Can Be Organized for Specific Ministry Tasks

Some churches organize their small group programs with a wide variety of options. These may be dictated by the church. In some situations various groups may come into existence on their own for specific purposes determined by those who make up the group.

Another option for a church is to use its small groups for specific ministry tasks either within or outside the church itself. These might consist of such tasks as outreach, worship, teaching, building and grounds, drama, or children's ministries.

The Basic Ingredients of Robust Small Groups

Lyman Coleman and the people who are a part of Serendipity have established themselves as leaders in the field of small groups. Their work in this area has performed a great service for the church at large. They present three basic ingredients for small groups and point out that these must be kept in balance in any small group if it's to remain healthy and accomplish its purpose.

Bible Study/Nurture

The first ingredient—which Coleman calls the "basic building block of an effective small group"—is Bible study for the purpose of spiritual nurture. These Bible studies can focus on any number of areas or issues. In reality, the "sky's the limit." Any healthy small group is based in some way on the nurturing and instructive qualities of Scripture, not on the opinions of those people who make up the group. There's more involved than Bible study: "'Too much of a good thing' can lead to spiritual indigestion."[4] For example, if the church is already strong in teaching the Scriptures (during the worship service or in Sunday school), then it must not make this time simply another Bible study.

Group Building/Support

The second ingredient concerns building the group. This involves developing group trust. The group must strive to become a trusting community if it seeks to develop biblical community. According to Serendipity, group building involves a fourfold process. History giving requires that group members tell their personal "stories" (roots, spiritual journey, and dreams) to the group. Dallas Seminary uses life maps (mentioned in chapter 6) in spiritual formation groups as one means for accomplishing this purpose. Gift awareness and affirmation involves sharing gifts and receiving affirmation from others regarding the same. Goal setting concerns asking what each group member needs to do or why that person is in the group. Fellowship and building depth in ministry consists of caring and accountability.[5]

Mission/Task

Bible study and group building aren't enough by themselves. Serendipity believes there's one more ingredient that's necessary—the mission or task of the group. Essentially, this mission is ministry to others: "The most natural form of outreach is to reach out to others who have a similar need for support and bring them into the group. But a group that concentrates exclusively on ministry (like most committees in the church) often ends up with burnout."[6]

Determining the Role of Small Groups

What is the role of small groups in the overall ministry of the church? Will it be a church of small groups or a church with small groups? What's the difference? In the former, small groups are the primary ministry of the church. While the church will have a worship service with preaching, the primary emphasis is on the small groups program. Everyone is encouraged to involve themselves in a group. Carl George and Ralph Neighbour are strong advocates of this emphasis.

In the latter, however, the groups are just another ministry of the church. They are valued on the same level as a Sunday school program, Awana, and any other programs.

Determining the Purpose of Small Groups

What is the purpose for the small groups within the larger ministry of the church? How do they fit in? There are no less than three choices, each of which has its advantages.

To Minister to the Needs of the Church

Small groups can meet the basic, general needs of the church that can't be met in a large group setting. This is an eclectic approach and might include a wide variety of such needs. For example, small groups can serve as a means for assimilating new members into the church; they can be used for mobilizing the laity for ministry; they are vital to developing future lay leadership and potential staff leadership; and they provide an excellent vehicle for communication between the staff and the larger church body. Other examples of needs are pastoral care, fellowship, support, community, and accountability.

To Balance the Ministry of the Church

Another approach is to use the small group program to balance the other ministries of the church. Churches may find that their large group meetings don't cover all their "ministry bases" but leave a vital base uncovered. Consequently, small groups are designed and implemented to cover that base. For example, some churches may have only one large group meeting a week and use it for either evangelism or edification. In these churches, the small group program is established to provide the other missing ingredient. If the large group meeting focuses on evangelism, the small group focuses on edification (or vice versa).

I pastor Northwood Community Church in Dallas, Texas. We use our small groups program to balance our other ministries. We provide a large group meeting on Sunday as a "people-friendly" event where we not only worship but preach biblical messages that address the needs of both the believer and the unbeliever. Prior to this service, we provide a Sunday school program for all ages that focuses on in-depth Bible study. We've developed our small group ministry to provide biblical community that includes pastoral care. These components are not found in our other ministries.

To Perform the Pastoral Care of the Church

A third approach to small group ministries is to use them to provide for the basic needs of people on a pastoral care basis. This is often a function of small groups in larger churches. As noted earlier, it's not possible for the senior pastor of a large church to provide the pastoral care for all the people in a large church.

Consequently, small groups are established and function as mini-churches to provide this pastoral care component. The key factor in this approach is that the leader of the group and/or others in the group must be able to shepherd and minister to people's needs much as the pastor would. In effect, they all function as lay pastors of small flocks within the church itself. Therefore, it's critical that churches that adopt this approach recruit and thoroughly train their mini-church pastors since they play such a vital role in each small group.

The Leadership for Small Groups

Good leadership is critical to the success of any small group program. There are three questions that must be answered in establishing well-led small groups.

Who Are the Leaders?

While the pastoral staff may want to lead a small group in order to remain "in touch" with the people in the church, the leadership of the small groups must be the responsibility of the lay leadership within the church. God raises up gifted and capable lay leaders to function in these capacities. This is the concept behind the analogy of the church and the human body in 1 Corinthians 12–14. This provides for the best use of lay leaders in contrast to sitting on church boards that meet once a month to administer the affairs of the church.

Initially, in a planted church, the core group may be small and the pastor will lead it. As it grows and splits into other small groups, qualified laypeople should assume leadership responsibility. Eventually, the pastor will shepherd and train these lay leaders in a small group context of their own.

Where Will They Come From?

Small group leaders must be recruited. The key in the planted church is to recruit qualified people to lead the initial small groups. It's very important that planted churches start a small group program as soon as possible. If there are no qualified leaders, then they must delay beginning the church. While these qualifications vary from church to church and the purposes of the groups, the initial qualifications could be those found for elders and deacons (see 1 Tim. 3:1–13; Titus 1:5–9) or those listed in Acts 6:2–5. These qualifications serve only as a starting point and are probably too strict for many who would lead a community.

Once the initial small group leaders have been selected, then it will become their responsibility in conference with the pastor to recruit and train other apprentice leaders to assume the leadership of future small groups. As the initial small groups grow and divide into other small groups, they could lead the new groups. Another option is for them to recruit their own small groups from the people who make up the growing congregation.

How Will They Be Trained?

One of the problems numerous small group programs experience is either poor small group leadership or constant turnover of leaders. The solution to this problem is regular leadership training. The fault in so many programs is that we recruit willing and capable small group leaders, train them initially for the position, and then promptly abandon them. There are several ways in which this training can be accomplished.

The Apprentice/Intern Model

The first model involves an apprenticeship or intern program. Here the leaders of the small groups take responsibility for this training. The idea is that experienced leaders recruit apprentice or intern leaders from the congregation at large, their own small group, or other small groups and give them "on the job training."

The 6+6+6 Model

Another approach is the 6+6+6 Leadership Training Model developed by Serendipity. This plan begins with an initial six-week program for those who wish to serve as leaders. A pilot group is led by a trainer who uses a six-week course from the Serendipity New Testament. During the second six weeks the potential leaders practice teaching and are evaluated by the trainer and the other potential leaders. This, in turn, is followed by one more six-week period during which those in the pilot group start their own groups. The trainer continues to supervise these leaders but not as closely as before. The trainer meets with them once a week as a group to answer questions and to deal with specific problems.

The Metachurch Model

A third approach is the metachurch model developed by Carl George in his excellent book *Prepare Your Church for the Future* (Revell). This model includes the apprentice/intern model above and is led by a pastor or staff person who meets at least once a month with the leaders and provides continual training in VHS. The "V" stands for vision and relates to vision casting. Here the leader or pastor attempts to keep the vision before the leaders. The "H" stands for "huddling" and involves nurturing the souls of these leaders. The "S" is for skills and concerns the continual development of established skills and the acquisition of new skills needed for ministry in the groups.

The Organization of a Small Group Ministry

Every ministry in a church must be organized if it's to function and minister efficiently. The organization of the small group program in the church must help leaders assume responsibility for a manageable number of people.

An Organizational Model

An excellent model for this organization is found in Exodus 18. At the beginning of the chapter, Moses attempts to counsel and advise approximately 2 million Israelites on a one-on-one basis. His father-in-law, Jethro, wisely advises Moses to select other capable men from among the people "and appoint them as officials over thousands, hundreds, fifties, and tens." They are to bring only the most difficult cases to Moses. The result is twofold: an emotionally healthy Moses and a satisfied ministry constituency. This model provides an excellent example for organization in today's church in general and small groups in particular.

The Application of the Model

Large Churches

Most large churches, which are still growing, probably have already implemented this model or something similar to it. If a church has grown very quickly over a short period of time into a large but poorly organized ministry, it could benefit immensely by adopting this organizational model.

New Churches

This is an ideal model for the planted church as well. A new church could adopt it at the very beginning and continue to use it for the life of the church. Even if the church becomes a megachurch, the model simply expands with the growth of the church.

Implementation

To implement this organizational model, the church will need to determine the ideal size of its small groups. Each group should be led by a lay pastor. Someone will need to take responsibility for these groups and their lay leaders as they begin to grow and divide. This could be a person on the team who is a specialist in small groups and one or two other areas. It could also be a gifted layperson. This person would be the primary leader and could work with and cultivate the lay leaders of each group.

Once there are five groups of from seven to twelve people, this leader should be replaced by a second leader and begin to cultivate other groups of seven to twelve people with lay leaders until they, too, reach five groups and the process repeats itself. These five groups are very close to Moses' group of fifty. Eventually, as the program grows, the primary leader will build a network of leaders, who, in turn, develop other leaders. In this manner, it's possible for the primary leader to lead hundreds, and maybe even thousands according to the growth of the church.[7]

Developing a Small Group Ministry

The church planter and the team will need to develop a small group ministry for the new church. There are eight steps in this process.

The Role Step

First, they must decide how big a role the small groups program will play in the overall ministry of the church? Will it be a church *of* small groups or a church *with* small groups? That is, will small groups be the primary thrust of the church or just one of many programs of the church?

The Purpose Step

Second, the team must decide the purpose for small groups in the church. Will small groups be used to meet some of the general needs of the church that can't be met through the large group meetings? Another option is to use small groups to balance or complement the other major ministries in the church. Small groups can also be used as the primary means for pastoral care.

The Organization Step

The next step will be to decide who will be responsible for the small group ministry. There are several options. One person could be the pastor of the church. Ultimately, the pastor is responsible for the ministry regardless of whether or not someone else has direct responsibility. Another person could be a team member. A third option would be a part-time professional person who isn't a part of the ministry team but has some time available and the skills and abilities to work with the program. A fourth option would be a layperson in the church who has the gifts and capabilities to handle the program.

The Participation Step

This step involves a decision on the part of the team as to how many people in the church they desire to see involved in the small group program. What is the numerical goal? What is the desired percentage of involvement? This could range anywhere from 25 percent to 125 percent if it's to be a church *of* small groups.

This decision is important for two reasons. First, it will demonstrate how committed the leadership of the church is to the small group concept. For example, a numerical goal of 125 percent congregational involvement doesn't seem very realistic. However, the use of this figure in sermons and conversation communicates to the flock a strong pastoral commitment to the program. Second, it will determine how strongly the pastoral team emphasizes the program. Any program of the church that has more than a 50 percent rate of involvement should and will be pushed hard by the team.

The Recruitment Step

It's not possible to begin and maintain a small group program without people.

Purpose

The purpose for the recruitment step is to locate and involve people. The only limit on the various ways to recruit participants is the imagination and creativity of those leading the program. The point is that there are all kinds of ways to interest and implement people in small groups.

Methods

Perhaps one of the best ways to recruit people is through "satisfied customers"—lay leaders and other participants who are already involved in a group and are delighted with its ministry in their lives. People who are both ministering and being ministered to are excited people who make great recruiters. They want to tell others what's happened in their lives so that these people can benefit as well.

Another way to recruit people is through advertising. This involves such things as a clever note in the church bulletin, a special bulletin insert, a verbal announcement, a well-done skit, and posters strategically placed on the walls of the facility. These catch people's attention and "grab" their interest.

There are other recruiting methods as well. The church could require involvement in a small group as a condition for membership. It could set up an attractive small group booth in a highly visible place such as the lobby or at the main entrance to the sanctuary or the church building.

The Training Step

The sixth step involves determining how the lay leaders will be trained. Several methods have already been mentioned. One is the apprentice or intern model. Another is Serendipity's 6+6+6 model. And a third is the metachurch VHS model that includes the apprentice/intern model.

The Administrative Step

This seventh step is taken by the small group itself, not those who are setting up the program. The group will need to decide such administrative matters as are necessary to accomplish the purpose of the program. These consist of when the group will meet, how long they'll meet, where they'll meet, confidentiality, and any attendance requirements.

The group needs to deal with three other important issues as well. First, the group will need to select a host or hostess. The leader can't be expected to lead the group and be the host at the same time. The second issue involves child care. The group will need to determine how they'll care for young children during the time the community meets. While this latter point may seem trivial, the issue of child care can hamstring the entire small group program of a church! Third, the group will need to decide for how long they plan to meet as a group. I would suggest they covenant for nine months (September through May). Then give people the option to move to another group. If the group decides to meet through the summer, then they can recovenant for two more months.

The role of those responsible for setting up the program is to make sure that these administrative matters are accomplished and to provide any assistance necessary to help the groups make these decisions. They might ask that all the groups agree to sign a covenant in which the above administrative matters are written down for purposes of accountability.

The Evaluation Step

Constant evaluation is necessary if the program is to improve and make necessary corrections. A number of decisions need to be made here.

Who?

First, who will evaluate and who will be evaluated? All those who are involved in some sort of leadership role should be evaluated. They, in turn, must also be involved in evaluating others. The pastor or the ministry team could evaluate the leader of the small group program. The leader of the program could evaluate the lay leaders (or vice versa). The lay leaders could evaluate their apprentices.

When?

Another decision involves when this evaluation takes place. The pastor's evaluation of the group leader could take place quarterly. The group leader's evaluation of the lay leaders could be on a quarterly basis as well. Lay leaders need to evaluate their apprentices weekly or whenever they lead the group.

What?

A third decision would concern the criteria for evaluation. They should be kept as short and simple as possible. They could involve such questions as: What am I not doing well? What am I doing well? How can I do it better next time?

A Small Group Exercise

1. What were the circumstances surrounding your coming to faith in Christ? Did it involve a relationship with one or a few people or was it in the context of a large group such as a worship service? Is the same true of your commitment to minister for Christ whether as a professional or layperson?

2. Have you ever been involved in a small group program? If yes, was this a part of a church or parachurch ministry? How many churches are you aware of that have a robust network of small groups?

3. What were some of the advantages and disadvantages of any of the programs you may have been involved in? How might this information help you in planning a program for a planted church?

4. Are you personally convinced of the need for a small group program in the planted church? Why? If you're convinced, then how strong is your commitment to this program (weak, strong, very strong)?

5. What effect does age have on a person's commitment to a small group program? Do small groups appeal more to those of the Baby Boom Generation or the Harry Truman Generation? What might this tell you about planning a small group program for a planted church?

Part 4

The Process of Church Planting

The novice farmer must not give in to the temptation simply to walk out into a field and broadcast seed in all directions. While that seems the most natural thing to do, it would spell disaster. There are several steps that must take place prior to the planting of the crop. First, the true farmer will prepare the soil. The rule is that you don't drop seed into soil that's not been well prepared ahead of time. Second, good farmers know that they're farmers. While farming is strenuous, often exacting work, most love the land and what they do with it, and find that they're naturally attracted to the work. They may complain a lot about their conditions, but they would have it no other way. Third, astute farmers know what crops they want to plant. They're well aware of what they can plant, and when and where they can plant it.

Once all these decisions have been made and the soil prepared, then it's time to begin the actual planting process. The seed is sown. As it begins to sprout and grow it will be watered, fertilized, and sprayed with a pesticide to protect it from various insects. Eventually, it will be harvested, packed in some way, and taken to market where it will be sold to the highest bidder.

The actual planting of a church also involves a process. Once church planters have thought through certain key issues (Part 1), know that they are, indeed, designed to be church planters (Part 2), and have decided what kind of church they're going to plant (Part 3), the remaining task is to begin the process of church planting (Part 4). Whereas, these other parts have focused on the why, who, and what of church planting, this part concerns the "how" of church planting. It involves six stages, which are analogous to the human birth process: conception, development, birth, growth, maturity, and reproduction. Part 4 will cover all these stages, but will focus primarily on the first three because these early stages have proved to be where church planters need help the most.

14

We're Going to Have a Baby!

The Conception Stage

It would appear that I've abandoned Bill and Betty Smith! If you recall from chapter 2, Bill was challenged by his seminary professor to consider church planting. He and Betty, his wife, accepted that challenge, and together they've worked through all the material presented thus far in this book. How do I know all this? I'm the proof! And while Bill and Betty Smith are fictitious names, there are hundreds of Bill and Betty Smiths who within the past few years have gone through a similar process. Now Bill has completed seminary and the Smiths are ready to begin the process of actually starting the church. Where do they go from here?

An essential question in church planting is, "Where do you begin?" The answer: at the same place where a couple planning a family begins—"at conception."[1] The conception stage commences with the genesis of the idea of planting a church. Just as a baby is conceived in its mother's womb, so the idea of planting a church is conceived in a person's mind. For the seminarian, such as Bill Smith, this could take place during seminary. Actually, it's possible that much of the conception stage could take place while a person is still in seminary! Regardless of one's circumstances, once the idea is conceived, what happens next? What steps should Bill and Betty or anyone else for that matter follow? What events need to take place?

The conception stage of church planting is where you begin to apply the information gained in the prior parts of this book. It consists of eight consecutive steps: discovering the church's core values, developing a mission statement, conducting an environmental scan, developing a vision, developing a strategy, implementing that strategy, planning for ministry contingencies, and evaluation.[2]

Before we look at the first step, we need to consider the place of prayer in starting a church. Actually, the first step is prayer. Before we attempt to plant a church anywhere, it's imperative that we spend hours on our knees in prayer. In fact, it would be wise for church planters to recruit personal intercessors who will pray for them, their teams, and the entire planting endeavor on a constant basis.[3] Church planters, however, should not regard intercessory prayer as the first step because that might influence people to emphasize it only at the beginning of the process. Instead, it must be encouraged *throughout* the process. We can't place enough emphasis on prayer! It is best to view the church as an infant who is constantly dependent on and surrounded by the air of prayer. Just as a person needs a constant supply of oxygen throughout life in order to survive, so the new church will need a constant supply of prayer throughout its life if it's to survive.

Discovering Values

The process of church planting begins with the discovery of the church's core organizational values. The reason is that the ministry's values answer the basic, fundamental question, Why do we do what we do? Core values are the essence of what makes a great church. These values will determine the outcome of all the other steps that make up the conception stage of church planting.[4]

The Importance of Core Values

Why is the discovery of the organization's core values so important?

First, values determine a church's ministry distinctives. No ministry is alike. All are different in some way. Some churches focus on teaching while others focus on evangelism. The determiner in either case is the values.

Second, your values dictate people's personal involvement in the church. Thus, church planters can spare themselves and their churches much grief by communicating their values to all who consider becoming a part of the church before they come on board. Encourage those with similar values to join the team and those with different values to look for another church more in tune with their values.

Third, core values communicate what's important. They signal your ministry's bottom line. They make it clear to all what you stand for—what you believe is God's heart for your church.

Fourth, the church's values help you embrace positive change. Change has become a constant all across North America, and this change has had a great impact on churches, some of it for good and some for bad. The key question to ask is, Does this change agree with or contradict the ministry's core values?

Fifth, the values affect the church's overall behavior. They shape the entire organization. They dictate every decision that you make and determine every dollar you spend. Values are foundational to your behavior, the bottom line for what you will and won't do.

Sixth, your values inspire people to action. The shared beliefs of both the leaders and the followers are the invisible motivators that energize people to take action.

Seventh, core beliefs enhance credible leadership. All leaders are values-driven, and the ministries they build reflect those values. Leaders with good values build ministries of high integrity.

Eighth, your values shape the ministry's character. They are the qualities that make up and establish an organization's character, and that character determines how the organization conducts its ministry.

Ninth, values contribute to ministry success. It's the organization's ingrained understanding of its core beliefs more than its technical skills that makes it possible for its people to be successful in ministry.

The Definition of Core Values

I define a planted church's primary values as its constant, passionate, biblical core beliefs that drive its ministry. This definition has five key elements.

First, core values are constant. Once you have determined your church's core values, they should not change appreciably. Should you come up with a different set of values each year, the result would be chaos.

Second, values are passionate. Just as vision is a seeing word, so passion is a feeling word. A set of good core values touches the heart and elicits strong emotions. You feel strongly about them.

Third, values are biblical. The core values found in a Christian organization such as a planted church should be biblical. The true test of a credo or values statement is, Is it biblical? That doesn't mean that it has to be found in the Bible. It does mean, however, that it shouldn't contradict the Bible.

Fourth, values are core beliefs. People use various synonyms for values: *precepts, principles, tenets, standards,* or *assumptions.* I'm not convinced that all these terms properly equate with values. Regardless, a study of values concerns not just any beliefs but your primary or core beliefs. A belief is a conviction or opinion you hold to be true based on limited evidence or proof. It isn't a fact so much as it's a conviction that a number of people hold to be true.

Fifth, values drive the ministry. Finally, it is your core beliefs that drive your ministry. Values are translated into behavior. They are the deeply ingrained drivers behind all of the church's behavior. This includes such vital areas as the decisions made, money spent, risks taken, problems solved, goals set, and priorities determined, plus many other things.

The Kinds of Values

We can further refine the above definition by analyzing the different kinds of values that your planted church may hold. There are five.

One kind is conscious versus unconscious values. The credo or values of your church exist at both a conscious and unconscious level. Most probably fall under the latter. Leaders must discover and articulate the church's primary values so that all may know why they're doing what they're doing whether good or bad.

A second is shared versus unshared values. I am convinced that the degree to which you'll experience success or failure in your church planting endeavors depends on whether your core people share the same values. Shared values foster high levels of loyalty, lead to consensus on key decisions, promote a strong work ethic, and reduce levels of stress, along with other benefits to the ministry.

Another is personal versus organizational values. Each church planter has a set of personal organizational values. One of my assignments for my pastoral students at Dallas Seminary is to discover their organizational beliefs before they go into a ministry. Those who take an established church need to discover that church's credo and make sure that their values align with the church's. Otherwise, the honeymoon for both will be short-lived, and one or the other will sue for divorce. Church planters, however, bring their personal values to the planted church. Their values will become the church's values. That's one of the many advantages of church planting.

A fourth kind is actual versus aspirational. Leaders and their churches have both actual and aspirational values. Actual values are the beliefs they own and act on regularly. Aspirational values are the values that the church planter or church doesn't presently own. It's important that the leader distinguish between the two or risk losing credibility when drafting a values statement. For example, to state that the church values evangelism when no one has come to the faith hurts the church's integrity.

A fifth is good versus bad values. Not only will a ministry have good values, but it will have some bad values as well. This is true of every ministry—there's no escaping it. Bad values are bad beliefs such as prejudice, intolerance, the abuse of power, and so on. What's important is that the church become aware of those values and begin to do something about them.

The Discovery of Your Values

Church planters can discover the core values of their church by discovering their own core values. Several techniques will aid you in your values discovery.

1. Now that you have a definition of a value, take a sheet of paper and brainstorm what you believe are your key beliefs.

2. Collect and study various church's values statements or credos. Those that catch your eye are probably your values. I have provided my church's credo at the end of this section to get you started. I have also listed a number of credos in the appendixes of *Values-Driven Leadership* (Baker Book House).

3. Take the following abbreviated Core Values Audit. (A more extensive audit is found on page 185 of *Values-Driven Leadership*.)

Core Values Audit

Directions: Rate each of the core values below from 1 to 5, 1 being the lowest and 5 the highest.

___1.   Godly servant leadership

___2.   A well-mobilized lay ministry

___3.   Bible-centered preaching/reaching

___4.   The poor and disenfranchised

___5.   Creativity and innovation

___6.   World missions

___7.   Passionate evangelism

___8.   Authentic worship

___9.   Intercessory prayer

___10. An attractive facility

___11. The status quo

___12. Strong families

___13. Cultural relevance

___14. Seekers

___15. Other:

Write down all the core values—no more than ten—that received a rating of 4 to 5.

The Development of Your Core Values

Once you've discovered your values, it's time to develop them. This involves writing your values statement or credo. You should publish this credo and make it available to those who are a part of your ministry or desire to be. Figure 1 presents the credo that we developed at Northwood Community Church in Dallas, Texas.

Figure 1
CORE VALUES STATEMENT
Northwood Community Church

The following presents the core values of Northwood Community Church. We desire that they define and drive this ministry in the context of a warm and caring environment.

Christ's Headship
We acknowledge Christ as the head of our church and submit ourselves and all our activities to His will and good pleasure (Eph. 1:22–23).

Bibllical Teaching
We strive to teach God's Word with integrity and authority so that seekers find Christ and believers mature in Him (2 Tim. 3:16).

Authentic Worship
We desire to acknowledge God's supreme value and worth in our personal lives and in the corporate, contemporary worship of our church (Rom. 12:1–2).

Prayer
We rely on private and corporate prayer in the conception, planning, and execution of all the ministries and activities of this church (Matt. 7:7–11).

Sense of Community
We ask all our people to commit to and fully participate in biblically functioning small groups where they may reach the lost, exercise their gifts, be shepherded, and thus grow in Christlikeness (Acts 2:44–46).

Family
We support the spiritual nurture of the family as one of God's dynamic means to perpetuate the Christian faith (2 Tim. 1:5).

Grace-Orientation
We encourage our people to serve Christ from hearts of love and gratitude rather than guilt and condemnation (Rom. 6:14).

Creativity and Innovation
We will constantly evaluate our forms and methods, seeking cultural relevance and maximum ministry effectiveness for Christ (1 Chron. 12:32).

Lost People
We value unchurched, lost people and will use every available Christ-honoring means to pursue, win, and disciple them (Luke 19:10).*

Mobilized Congregation
We seek to equip all our uniquely designed and gifted people to effectively accomplish the work of our ministry (Eph. 4:11–13).*

Ministry Excellence
Since God gave his best (the Savior), we seek to honor Him by maintaining a high standard of excellence in all our ministries and activities (Col. 3:23–24).*

*Aspirational values

Developing a Mission

Once the church planter or the church planting team has discovered and clearly articulated the planted church's core values, the next step in the conception stage is to develop a mission statement.[5]

The Importance of the Mission

The church must have a mission for several reasons. *First, the mission dictates the ministry's direction.* It provides a compelling sense of direction. It serves to focus the church's energy, and, most important, it answers the directional question, Where are we going?

Second, the mission focuses on the church's function. Here it serves to answer the functional question, What are we supposed to be doing?

Third, it spells out the congregation's preferred future. Someone has observed that the best way to predict the future is to create it. That's the function of the mission statement.

Fourth, the mission provides a template for decision making. Like a template, it provides a pattern or guide that defines what the church will and won't do.

Fifth, the mission inspires church unity. It serves as a point around which the people can rally for the cause.

Sixth, it shapes the church's strategy. The mission answers the question, What? The strategy answers the question, How?

Seventh, a good mission enhances ministry effectiveness. Someone once said that all good performance starts with a clear direction.

Finally, it facilitates evaluation. The mission is the criterion or standard by which one evaluates a ministry.

The Definition of the Mission

The church's mission is a broad, brief, biblical statement of what it's supposed to be doing. It has five vital components.

One component is breadth. Unlike a church's vision, the mission is broad. It needs to be all encompassing, overarching, and comprehensive.

A second component is brevity. Peter Drucker says that it should be short enough to fit on a T-shirt. Thus, it must pass the T-shirt test.

A third component is that it's biblical. That is, it must agree with the Scriptures. For example, God's mission for Moses is found in Exodus 3:10: "So now, go. I am sending you to Pharaoh to bring my people the Israelites out of Egypt." Christ's mission for the church is the Great Commission (Matt. 28:19–20).

A fourth component is that it's a statement. It's imperative that the church planter write out the church's mission in the form of a mission statement.

A final component is that the mission is a statement of what the church is supposed to be doing. In a business sense, it articulates what business we're in.

The Development of a Mission Statement

The following is a four-step process for developing a mission statement that's tailor-made for your planted church. Work your way through each step by answering the questions.

Step 1: What are you supposed to be doing according to the Bible? Three mini-questions will help you answer this question. Are you in a church or parachurch ministry? If the former, then Christ has already predetermined your mission (the Great Commission). Whom are you attempting to reach or serve? And how will your ministry serve or reach these people?

Step 2: Can you articulate your mission in a written statement? Here are the mini-questions: What specific words best communicate with your people? (This will help you personalize it for your unique congregation.) Do your people understand what you've written? Does your format convey well your mission? Here are several mission formats that will help you shape your statement. Which works best for you?

The mission of (ministry's name) is to _____.

Our mission is to _____.

(Ministry's name) seeks to _____.

Step 3: Is your mission statement broad but clear? Is the statement broad and all-encompassing? Is the statement clear and understandable?

Step 4: Is the mission brief and simple? Here are the mini-questions: Does your mission pass the T-shirt test (brevity)? Have you expressed it in one sentence? Is it memorable?

A Sample Mission Statement

I pastor Northwood Community Church, located in Dallas, Texas. The following is Northwood's mission statement:

> The mission of Northwood Community Church is to develop people into fully functioning followers of Christ.

This statement calls for several observations. First, since we are a church, our mission is the Great Commission as found in Matthew 28:19–20 or Mark 16:15. However, rather than simply quoting one of these passages, we have personalized it to fit who we are.

Second, we are attempting to reach people—lost and saved—in the Dallas metroplex. We left the term "Dallas" out in favor of brevity.

Third, we will serve people by developing them into fully functioning followers of Christ. The latter is our definition of a disciple. Disciples at Northwood are characterized by the three Cs: conversion, commitment, and contribution.

Fourth, we have placed this statement on the bulletin cover underneath the logo. I comment on it often from the pulpit, and we go over it every time we hold a newcomer's class. We have also placed it on church business cards and distributed them to our congregation. So our people understand it well.

Finally, it obviously passes the T-shirt test, and most of our people have it memorized.

The Communication of the Mission Statement

Once you've drafted a dynamic mission statement, you must communicate it to your people. There are several ways to accomplish this. One is to preach on it periodically (at least once a year) and to refer to it in your sermons. Another is to put it on your bulletin masthead. A third is to print it on a business card and pass it out to your people. Ask them to keep it in their wallets or purses. A fourth is to develop a logo. You should develop a logo for the church regardless. The question is, Do you want the logo to represent the entire church or to communicate the mission or the vision?

Conducting an Environmental Scan

The third step in the conception stage is to conduct an environmental scan.

The Purpose of the Environmental Scan

The environmental scan helps the church planter and the team avoid the peril of the ostrich. It poses the question, What's going on out there? Unlike the proverbial ostrich, who buries its head in the sand, the church needs to remain alert as to what is going on in the world surrounding it—to understand its times (1 Chron. 12:32). The danger for too many church ministries is that over time they become inward-focused and lose all perspective as to what is taking place in their culture and their national and international environment. The result is cultural irrelevance.

Consequently, though it's step three in the process, you will continue from this point on to conduct regular scans so as not to lose touch.

The Contents of the Environmental Scan

The environmental scan involves two particular environments: the general environment and the church environment.

The General Environment

The general environmental scan enables the church to address the trends and practices of the world in which its people live and work. This includes the international, national, and local scenes. The scan covers trends in at least five areas.

The first are social trends. You will need to keep abreast of the trends and practices in the areas of gender, family, health, crime, race, aging, athletics, the generations (Builders, Boomers, and Busters), psychographics, and demographics, as well as others.

The second are technological trends. This covers the information revolution, computers, communication, the environment, medicine, genetics, energy, warfare, robotics, transportation, entertainment, education, and other technological practices.

The third are economic trends. This includes the national debt, the federal deficit, the trade deficit, inflation, taxes, Social Security, the effects of downsizing, and so on.

The fourth are political/legal trends. This covers the legislative and judicial processes, Supreme Court decisions, elections, church–state issues, the White House, zoning issues, and other such trends.

The fifth are philosophical/religious trends. These include secularization, privatization, pluralization, relativism, naturalism, postmodernism, and so forth.

The Application. Select what you believe are the most important trends in each of the five areas above that will affect your church. Make a diagram like that in figure 2. Place each trend in the "Trends" column and your response in the "Response" column. You may address these trends in your sermons. They will also affect your strategy.

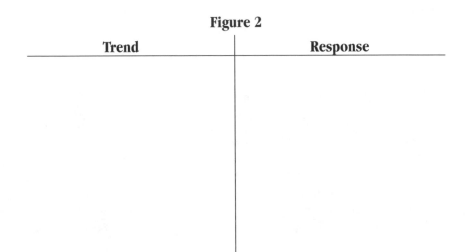

Figure 2

Trend	Response

The Church Environment

The church environmental scan keeps the church planter abreast of the trends, practices, and programs of international, national, and local churches. It's a way of keeping track of what God is and isn't doing in our world. The purpose of the scan is not to mimic the entire program of another church, but to learn from those areas that God is blessing.

The Application. Create a diagram like that in figure 3. Then identify the particular church in the left column and the trend in the right column. One example is Yoido Full Gospel Church in Korea. It's the largest church in the world. What we learn from this church is how to minister to people individually in a large church context. This church's answer is small or cell groups. You put the name of the church in the column on the left and cell groups in that on the right.

Figure 3

Churches	Trends
International Churches	
National Churches	
Local Churches	

Developing a Vision

The fourth step of the conception stage is the development of a vision.[6]

The Importance of a Vision

A vital element is the church planter's vision for his or her ministry.[7] A vision is different from the mission and is important for several reasons.

First, the vision communicates where the church is going. It's the function of the mission statement to help plan where the church is going. However, the vision is a communication tool that functions to help you communicate where it's going.

Second, the vision provides a snapshot of the church's direction. Whereas the mission statement is a statement of the ministry's direction, the vision provides a picture or snapshot of that direction. People need to see it in their head as well as see it on paper or it won't happen.

Third, the effect of the vision on the church is to challenge your people to accomplish the ministry whereas the job of the mission statement is to clarify what that ministry is.

Fourth, the purpose of the vision statement is to inspire people to greater efforts for God. It motivates or energizes activity. The mission statement informs them of those efforts.

Fifth, the vision touches the emotions. It's source is the heart. The mission is a "head thing." It affects the intellect.

Finally, the vision is unique to every church. It spells out all the particulars. You see people, facilities, and land. The mission is broad and general. Most churches should share essentially the same mission—the Great Commission.

The Definition of a Vision

An organizational vision is a clear, challenging picture of the future of your ministry as it can and must be.[8] This definition has six essential ingredients.

First, a vision is clear. People can't act on information they don't understand. The goal is that everyone in the church understand the vision so that they can clearly articulate it.

Second, a vision challenges. Once a vision is conceived and born, it may die a quick, untimely death. If the vision doesn't challenge the people, then there is no vision but a collection of lifeless words on a sterile sheet of paper.

Third, a vision consists of a mental picture. Vision is a "seeing" word. A good vision probes people's imaginations and conjures up positive pictures, images, and memories in their minds.

Next, a vision relates to the future. A vision is what is seen in the future regarding the ministry of the church. It concerns the exciting possibilities that the future holds, a picture of what we want the church to become.

Fifth, a vision can be. A significant vision has great potential. A vision "can be" in the sense that it's possible. It's not some "wild-eyed" dream, but based squarely on the bedrock of reality.

Finally, a vision must be. A critical sense of urgency exists about a vision. It has even been known to keep people awake at night!

The Development of a Vision

Once church planters realize the importance of a vision and have arrived at a clear, working definition, they need to give birth to a vision. In birthing a vision, we must ask two important questions: Who develops the vision? How do you develop the vision?

Who Develops the Vision?

The first question is a personnel question. It attempts to determine the participants in the envisioning process.

Initially, the pastor of the new church is the "point person" who is responsible for birthing the ministry vision. The pastor-leader must cultivate the vision, not someone on the staff or the core group. While good pastor-leaders listen to their constituency, it's their responsibility and not that of the constituency for developing a powerful, coherent vision for the new work. In so doing, they'll be viewed as the true leaders of the ministry. If they attempt to shift this responsibility to someone else, then it will affect the congregation's perception of who is leading the church.

How Do You Develop the Vision?

The second question moves from a personnel to a process question. Now that we know *who* is primarily responsible for birthing the vision, we need to understand *how* that process works. This involves six events, which take place in cycles and not necessarily in this order.

1. Envisioning prayer is prayer that specifically focuses on the development of a vision. An example would be Nehemiah's prayer in Nehemiah 1:4–11. Church planters should devote time to this kind of prayer.

2. Small visions don't motivate. Church planters must not think small. Paul indirectly exhorts us in Ephesians 3:20 to both ask and think big: "Now to him who is able to do immeasurably more than all we ask or imagine."

3. In the process of developing a vision, you will generate lots of ideas. Write them down! This is a brainstorming process. Put on paper what God is putting on your heart. Write down everything that comes to mind. Later you can determine what is and isn't important.

4. Peruse this material and attempt to organize it. This serves as a skeleton for ideas that can be fleshed out later. Some of the "bones" or contents could include the following: a statement of the purpose for the church, some of the values, the strategy, the target group, the place of ministry, as well as other features.[9]

5. The visionary and others might probe the dream with numerous questions. Is the dream clear? Is it challenging in the sense that it inspires people to action? Does it create mental pictures? Is it future-oriented? Is it both realistic and stretching?

6. The developmental process, like good soup, must be given lots of time to sit on the back burner and cook. Give the process adequate time.

It could take place quickly, but most often it comes together over a period of time.

What Does a Good Vision Statement Look Like?

Good vision statements can take numerous forms. One of the best examples is Dr. Martin Luther King Jr.'s "I Have a Dream Speech." You can find it and other samples in my book *Developing a Vision for Ministry in the Twenty-first Century*.

Figure 4 presents the vision statement that we developed at the church that I pastor—Northwood Community Church—in Dallas, Texas.

Figure 4
NORTHWOOD COMMUNITY VISION

Vision is not about reality or what is. Vision is all about our dreams and aspirations or what could be.

At Northwood Community Church, we envision our sharing the good news of Christ's death and resurrection with thousands of unchurched friends and people in the metroplex many of whom accept Him as Savior.

We envision developing all our people—new believers as well as established believers—into fully functioning followers of Christ through people-friendly worship services, Sunday school, special events, and most important small groups.

We envision becoming a church of small groups where our people model biblical community: a safe place where we accept one another and are accepted, love and are loved, shepherd and are shepherded, encourage and are encouraged, forgive and are forgiven, and serve and are served.

We envision helping all our people—youth as well as adults—to discover their divine designs so that they are equipped to serve Christ effectively in some ministry either within or outside our church. Our goal is that every member be a minister.

We envision welcoming numerous members into our body who are excited about Christ, experience healing in their family relationships and marriages, and grow together in love.

We envision our recruiting, training, and sending out many of our members as missionaries, church planters, and church workers all over the world. We also see a number of our people pursuing short term missions service in various countries. We envision planting a church in America or abroad every two years.

We envision a larger facility that will accommodate our growth and be accessible to all the metroplex. This facility will provide ample room for Sunday school, small groups, Bible study, prayer, and other meetings. While we do not believe that "bigger is better," numerical growth is a by-product of effective evangelism. Thus, we desire to grow as God prospers us and uses us to reach a lost and dying world.

This is our dream—our vision about what could be!

Designing a Strategy

Once a church planter has discovered and articulated the church's core values, developed a mission statement, conducted an environmental scan, and developed a powerful, significant vision, the next step in the conception stage is to develop a general, overall strategy.

Each of the prior steps will exert some influence on the strategy. The values will dictate what does and doesn't go into the strategy. The mission will give direction to the strategy while the vision will picture and energize it. The environmental scan will update the planter on current cultural trends and provide sample strategies from other churches as examples.

A mistake that many aspiring church planters make is trying to model their new ministries after some highly successful contemporary church. This is the product approach. While this may work, the failures far exceed the successes. Rather than attempt to duplicate a successful church product, it's wise to pursue the process of strategy development. Following a process will result in a unique product or ministry model that is tailor-made for your unique ministry situation.

This process includes five ingredients that answer five core questions. First, Who are you trying to reach? The answer involves discovering your target group. Second, How will you reach your target group? The answer is to design a specific working strategy to reach them. Third, Who will take part in reaching this target group? The best answer is a ministry team. Fourth, Where will the church meet? Where is the best place to reach our target group? The answer is your facilities. Finally, How much will it cost to reach the group? The answer involves finances. You must raise and manage well your financial resources.

Discovering the Target Group

The first ingredient in the strategy process is to decide whom you're going to reach. There's a certain amount of naiveté in this area. For example, many seminarians think that they'll go out into the world and reach everybody! The desire to reach everyone in general, while very noble, could result in reaching no one in particular. The problem is that this isn't only naive, it's unrealistic! While we should be willing to minister to everybody, the truth of the matter is that no church can minister to everybody! Once a particular group of people opts for a particular style of worship and preaching, it has already limited itself culturally in terms of its potential congregation. My chapter on culture explained this.

Discovering your target group involves two stages. The first is determining the group, and the second is locating it.

Determining the Target Group

Church planters must, like Paul and Peter, determine whom their exact target group will be. This involves four areas.

Identify the Target Group. The first is to identify your particular target group by answering in order each of the following questions.

Will you target lost people? Church planters must answer this question honestly. Most evangelical churches would answer in the affirmative. After all, who would vote against evangelism? But in reality, according to an article in *Christianity Today,* 80 percent of the churches in America that are growing are experiencing transfer growth, not conversion growth.[10] They're merely "reshuffling the Christian deck."

Christ's Great Commission mandate begins with reaching lost people. Any church planter who starts a church today must catch a strong vision for reaching lost people or forget about starting a church and become a part of one that's reaching the unsaved.

Will you target unchurched lost people? Lost people can be divided into two groups: those who are churched and those who are unchurched. There are still a significant number of lost people in parts of America such as the South and the "Bible belt" who attend a local church. While the new church will want to reach these people, it should not include them in its target group. Consequently, when the church-planting team comes into a new area, they can assure any pastors who might feel threatened by their presence that they have no intentions of "stealing sheep."

Then whom will they target? The obvious answer is the unchurched lost in the community. We refer to them at Northwood Community Church as Community Charley and Cathy. These people are "fair game" for church planters.

Will you target people like yourself? No church can reach everybody. This is because there is no church that can conduct all the ministries necessary to meet everyone's needs. Therefore, this raises the question, "Whom will we reach?" The realistic answer is the people who are most like those who make up the church's core group.

Those who are attracted to the new church initially and for several years after are usually close to the church planter/pastor in terms of age, marital and family status, and other socioeconomic factors. This is an example of the homogeneous grouping principle covered in chapter 10. Since people, both lost and saved, think and act in this manner, it would seem wise to reach out to them initially because they're the ones who will be most responsive.

Will you target receptive people? The principle of receptivity, covered in chapter 12 on evangelism, tells us that some people will be more receptive to the new church than others. People who are naturally like us will be attracted to us. They'll feel an affinity with us. There are also others in the community whom the Holy Spirit has been convicting (John 16:7–11) who are interested in spiritual matters. They will be open to the new church as well and might be willing to break the homogeneous principle to get some answers to their questions about spiritual things.

Will you target needy people? The key to unlocking the closed mind and touching the calloused heart is to address people's felt needs (2 Cor. 8:14; 9:12; Eph. 4:29; Phil. 4:19). Then you should use them, in turn, to address their spiritual needs. As the Savior demonstrated, hungry lost people listen better to the gospel when they've met their physical need for food.

Consequently, the church planter must realize that the way to penetrate and gain the attention of a community is to address positively its felt needs. Barna writes:

> If we expect the Christian Church to attract more people, we will have to become more sensitive to their felt needs. The competition of the local church is not other churches down the street. It is television, sleeping in on Sunday, the weekend special at Bloomingdale's, games and picnics in the park and so forth. As people's lives become more tense, their time more valuable, and their skepticism about the influence and benefits of the church more confirmed, attracting people will be more difficult.[11]

The question is, "What are the community's needs?" Generally speaking, every community will have certain broad basic needs and specific needs. The first consists of those needs that the community shares with all other communities across America as reflected in Maslow's hierarchy of needs. The second consists of certain needs that are unique to a community. For example, a particular community may depend heavily on a certain industry to bolster its economy.

Another question asks, "How can we discover these needs?" One way is to survey the target group. Simply stated, this involves asking them what their needs are. In addition, a good source is the media such as radio and television news. Another way is to observe the target group. This may involve moving into the community and spending some time there. A fourth answer is to use demographics and psychographics.

Gather Information on the Target Group. Once you've identified the target group, next you'll need to gather as much information as possible about that group. In particular, determine who they are (demographics) and what they want out of life (psychographics).

Who are the people in your target group? Demographic information provides details on the people who make up the target group. A demographic study will give the following information about people in the community: age, sex, race, population, number and types of households, median income, level of education, occupation, and purchasing power.

What do the people in your target group want out of life? Psychographic information presents what people are searching for in life. A psychographic study seeks to discover the target group's basic attitudes, wants, needs, and values that affect their lifestyles.

Church planters can obtain this information in several ways.

1. Ask people for the information. This would involve conducting some kind of personal survey.
2. Move into the area and begin to observe the people.
3. Read local periodicals and newspapers since they give this kind of information.
4. Read material on psychographics. An excellent periodical is *American Demographics Magazine*. Though dated, two good books are Arnold Mitchell's *The Nine American Lifestyles*[12] and Tex Sample's *U.S. Lifestyles and Mainline Churches*.[13]
5. Obtain professional help. An organization that provides this service is Percept. It's a Christian organization that's aware of church planting and the kinds of help church planters need. It also supplies both demographic and psychographic information.[14]

This material relating to psychographics and demographics will prove vital to targeting and reaching the lost people in a community. It will affect almost every aspect of the new church—from marketing the church to the kinds of sermons that are preached on Sunday.

Construct a Profile Person. Third, you'll use this important information to construct a profile of a target individual. This profile person could be a man or a woman and could be given a name. Several churches have done this. For example, Willow Creek Community Church has created a profile person they call "Nonchurched Harry." Saddleback Community Church has created "Saddleback Sam." My church targets "Community Charley and Cathy."

This profile person could be a cartoon character with a specific identity. This character could be dressed in clothing that's typical of the community and even have something in its hand such as a tennis racquet or a golf club.

The profile person will serve to facilitate communication among the leaders, the team, and people in the church and aid in focusing the church's efforts. The profile person's name or picture reminds everybody of whom the church is focusing its ministry on.

Determine the Kind of Church That's Necessary to Reach Your Target Group. Fourth, you should ask the following questions. *What kind of pastor should lead your church?* In light of the target group, what kind of person would be able to minister to them most effectively? Take into account such factors as age, education, family, and so on.

What kind of people should be in your core group? These people should be committed, caring, friendly, and warm but not "smotherers."

What kind of meetings should you have? The kinds of meetings would be those which people in the target group will attend. Also, consider such factors as the meeting's purpose, time, structure, frequency, and size.

What kind of sermons should you preach? This would concern such areas as topics, length, interest, needs, hopes, dreams, and aspirations.

What kind of worship should you implement? In terms of the target group, a certain style of worship should be implemented. This involves such areas as contemporary versus traditional worship, musical instruments, and choirs.

What kind of programs should you sponsor? There are certain basic programs that are common to all churches such as an evangelism program. However, specific programs should take into account the particular needs of the target audience. For example, if the target group consists of young families, then programs need to be designed accordingly.

Locating the Target Group

Once the church planter has determined who the target group is, the second stage in designing a ministry strategy is to discover where that group is located in the community.

The strategy is to target urban, suburban, and rural areas for new churches. A key aspect of a geographical strategy for church planting is to target specific areas for new church starts—in particular, the urban and suburban areas of the country.

The majority of people in the world today now live in cities. Demographers forecast that by the year 2000 Mexico City will have close to 30 million inhabitants. Approximately 60 percent of the people who live in the state of Colorado live in the Denver metropolitan area. Peter Wagner indicates that 74 percent of Americans lived in urban areas as early as 1976.[15] Thus, the world's cities have increasingly become "fertile ground" for the gospel. In fact, in his book *Apostles to the City,* Roger Greenway writes that "The only conclusion we can reach is that at no time in history has it been more true than now that he who wins the city, wins the world."[16] This shouldn't surprise us because Paul targeted strategic urban centers (a total of twenty-three cities!) on his first three missionary church-planting journeys.

What about the other areas such as rural America? What typically happens is that information flows from the urban areas to rural areas. In other words, to reach urban areas is to reach rural worlds as well. For example, Paul targeted the city of Ephesus (Acts 19:1), which was known as the "gateway to Asia." The result was that after two years of intense church planting, the gospel had spread throughout Asia (Acts 19:10). Consequently, if we desire to reach America with the gospel, we must start with our cities but must not neglect rural America.

The method for targeting urban areas is demographics. In the book *The E-Myth,* Gerber writes, "Demographics is the science of marketplace reality. It tells you *who* your customer is."[17] The importance of knowing the target group can't be overemphasized. A church can't reach people it knows nothing about. There are five reasons why working with demographics is important to church planting.

1. It aids in locating people in general and a target group in particular in the community, country, or world.
2. It assists church planters in analyzing and understanding the target group. For example, it analyzes the group in terms of its income, education, age, race, sex, housing, and occupation.
3. It aids in detecting population shifts and new growth areas. This is immensely helpful to church planters in targeting new growth areas where there are fewer churches and people are more open to spiritual matters.
4. It helps in determining where to locate a church. Once planters know their target community, demographics will help them deter-

mine the best place in that community to establish a physical base of operations.

5. It brings credibility and confidence in church planters and their ministries. When people who might support the new work with their money and prayers see a strategy that involves demographics, they realize that the church planter is a competent, credible person.

There are essentially two sources for locating demographic information. Local sources are the primary source for demographics because they provide the most accurate information. They consist of public libraries, chambers of commerce, city and county planning offices, zoning boards, realtors and real estate organizations, universities, colleges, public schools, utility companies, newspapers, commercial developers, door-to-door surveys, and telephone surveys.

National sources include various professional organizations that provide this information for a price. These are secondary sources that should be confirmed by some kind of backup from one or two local sources. Some examples of these organizations are CACI Source Products of Fairfax, Virginia; National Decisions Systems of Encinitas, California; Panoramic Area Ministry of Pasadena, California; Urban Decisions Systems of Los Angeles, California; and Percept of Costa Mesa, California, who focuses on churches. Data can also be obtained from organizations such as McDonalds. Call their regional headquarters and ask for the research department. There is a charge for their information.

A valuable periodical is *American Demographics Magazine*. It's usually loaded with important, practical material that's helpful for any church ministry. Since it costs approximately fifty dollars for a one-year subscription, it might be wise to use the copy at the local public library.

Church planters can do a lot of their own demographic work by following five steps.

First, determine where in the world you want to plant a church. (Let's assume for the sake of an example that it's somewhere in the United States.)

Second, determine where in the United States you desire to plant a church. This would include both the state and the particular city. *American Demographics Magazine* is most helpful for those who are open to going anywhere in the United States because periodically it publishes a list of the top fifty fastest growing metropolitan areas in the country. Church planters could pray about this list and see if God directs them to start a church in one of these areas.

Third, determine where in the city you want to plant a church. This is the step where the target community is identified. A helpful way to accomplish this is to find the target group and information about them in CACI's most current edition of *Sourcebook of Demographics and Buying Power for Every Zip Code in the U.S.A.* This can be purchased from CACI Source Products of Fairfax, Virginia, but it's expensive. Therefore, use a copy in the local public library. Locate the zip code that is listed in this source and then find the same zip code in *The ZIP Code Atlas and Market Planner* (also available from CACI or the library). The latter source will give the exact geographic area in the city and the community in which the church is to be located.

Fourth, do a feasibility study of the target community. Appendix B contains an excellent feasibility study done by Carol Childress for a potential church in Kingwood, Texas. A good feasibility study consists of the following material. (Follow along in the Kingwood study.) First, there should be a statement of the purpose for the study such as planting a church. Next, there should be a community profile presenting the population, housing, education, occupation, and income of those who live in the target community. Third, there is a lifestyles and values profile based on a psychographic study. Fourth is a list of area churches. Fifth is a list of potential meeting sites. Sixth, there is a pastoral leadership profile that predicts what kind of pastor would be best for the community in terms of education, skills and abilities, experience, age, and marital and family status. Seventh is a list of possible core group members and families. Eighth, there is an assessment of the future growth potential of the area.

Obviously, the usefulness of demographics depends on their accuracy. Good material results in good decisions, while bad material results in bad decisions. Primary demographics are the most reliable. The reason is because they are gathered by church planters at the actual site of potential location and ministry. This assumes, of course, that the planters know what they're doing. Secondary demographics are less reliable because they're gathered by others such as a professional company that might be located on the other side of the country. Most likely, they get much of their information from the census, which is taken every ten years. The longer the time since the last census, the less accurate will be the information. Consequently, any demographic studies must be confirmed by actually visiting the potential target area and doing some work yourself.

Developing a Specific Working Strategy

Once the target group has been identified and located in the target community, the second core ingredient in designing the broad ministry strategy is to design a more specific working strategy to reach them where they are. This answers the all-important question, How will we reach our tar-

Figure 5

Engel's Scale

God's Role	Communicator's Role		Man's Response
		−8	Awareness of Supreme Being but no Effective Knowledge of the Gospel
General Revelation	Proclamation	**−7**	Initial Awareness of the Gospel
		−6	Awareness of the Fundamentals of the Gospel
Conviction		**−5**	Grasp of the Implications of the Gospel
		−4	Positive Attitude toward the Gospel
	Persuasion	**−3**	Personal Problem Recognition
		−2	Decision to Act
		−1	Repentance and Faith in Christ
Regeneration			**New Creature**
	Followup	**+1**	Postdecision Evaluation
		+2	Incorporation into Body
Sanctification	Cultivation	**+3**	Conceptual and Behavioral Growth
		+4	Communion with God
		+5	Stewardship
		. . .	Reproduction Internally (gifts, etc.) Externally (witness, social action, etc.)

Rejection

Eternity

get group? The specific strategy attempts to design a unique, more refined strategy tailor-made for the particular community. To develop the working strategy, you should think through the following areas.

Designing a Working Strategy to Accomplish the Great Commission

In developing a specific strategy to reach the target group with the Great Commission, you must remember that our contemporary culture is process-, not event-oriented. Evangelism must be biblically and culturally relevant. What this means is that people in the twenty-first century aren't as pre-evangelized as those in the early twentieth century. Consequently, most will take longer to think through the gospel and its implications and accept Christ (six to twelve months).

Coming to faith in Christ can be viewed as God's moving a lost person across a continuum from one extreme (no knowledge about Christ) to the other extreme (maturity in Christ). Faith in Christ would be somewhere in between. This continuum is well represented by Engel's scale, pictured in figure 5.[18] The point of all this is that a good strategy will take this process into account.

An easy way to think about it is in terms of three levels. Level 1 represents an unconverted person, level 2 is a converted person, and level 3 is a committed Christian.

The object of the strategy is twofold. First, we desire to move level 1 people (unconverted) to level 2 (converted) and then to level 3 (committed). Second, we want to move level 2 people (converted) to level 3 (committed). Commitment is crucial. Eighty percent to 85 percent of American churches are reeling from nominal Christianity. If new believers fail to become committed, they soon drown in the waters of nominal Christianity.

The Stages of a Specific Working Strategy

A specific strategy consists of four stages that accomplish the Great Commission: the mission statement, goals, action steps, and a visual.

The first is a restatement of the church planter's mission. Since the mission statement is primarily a planning tool, it's important that it appear first. It answers the question, What are we supposed to be doing? The church's answer is "to make disciples" (Matt. 28:19–20). The strategy answers the question, How will we make disciples?

The second stage is the goals. You derive the goals from the mission statement. Often, for the church they will be the traits or characteristics of a disciple.

The third stage is the action steps. They are the steps that you take to accomplish the goals. Each step repeats the goal and then provides one or several strategies to accomplish the goal. These strategies will include various programs such as small groups, a Sunday school, a prayer ministry, community service, and others (see below).

The fourth stage is a visual. You would be wise to develop some type of visual that will help people visualize and understand your working strategy.

An Example of a Specific Working Strategy

Figure 6 is a condensed, edited version of a working strategy that my leadership team developed at Northwood Community Church in Dallas, Texas.

Figure 6

STRATEGY STATEMENT
Northwood Community Church

Every strategy implements a mission. So this strategy begins with a restatement of our mission.

Mission

Our mission is to be used of God in developing people into fully functioning followers of Christ.

Fully functioning followers have three characteristics (the 3 Cs):

1. Conversion to Christ (they know Christ as Savior).
2. Commitment to Christ (they are committed to grow in Christ).
3. Contribution to Christ (they serve the body, share their finances, and seek the lost).

Goals

The strategic goals (to realize our mission):

1. To see people converted to Christ (to interest in *becoming* a disciple).
2. To bring people to a commitment to Christ (to become a *committed* disciple).
3. To equip people to make a contribution to Christ (to become a *contributing* disciple).

A Fully Functioning Follower of Christ

Steps

The specific action steps to accomplish our goals:

The following three action steps are vital to our plan to move people from prebirth to maturity. The steps are represented by using the visual of a three-legged stool. Each leg represents a level of commitment. The range is from level 1 (the least commitment) up to level 3 (the maximum commitment).

1st Leg: Conversion to Christ

Goal: To lead people to faith in Christ and active involvement in the church (to interest in becoming a disciple). Luke 15:1–10, 19:1–10; Col. 4:2–6; 2 Tim. 4:4; 1 Cor. 14:22–25.

Strategy #1: A "people-friendly" large group meeting at 10:45 A.M. on Sunday to interest unchurched lost and saved adults and young people in becoming Christ's disciples. It will include the sermon, drama, celebrative worship, and a regular presentation of the gospel.
Strategy #2: Other events to minister to lost and saved people and assimilate them into the church such as Vacation Bible school, men's and women's ministries, aerobics, Pioneer Boys and Girls Clubs, Awana, Sports events, community events, and others.

2nd Leg: Commitment to Christ

Goal: To bring people to a commitment to Christ (to become a committed disciple). Col. 1:28; Eph. 4:12–13; 1 Tim. 4:7–8; Heb. 6:1–3. (What does a committed disciple look like? The answer is found in Acts 2:41–47.)

Strategy #1: Discipleship Small Groups (fully functioning communities)

Lay leaders will oversee small group communities who help one another become more like Christ. Meeting twice a month, these communities will could include the following: shepherding, studying the Bible, exercising spiritual gifts, biblical community, accountability, prayer, and evangelism.

Strategy #2: Christian Education

Christian education consists of a children and adult's Sunday school, a nursery, and children's church. The adult's Sunday school consists primarily of classes that will cover more in depth than the sermon or groups topics that are vital to commitment and spiritual growth.

3rd Leg: Contribution to Christ

Goal: To equip people to make a contribution to Christ (to become a contributing disciple). This involves three things: serving the body, sharing your finances, and seeking the lost.

Strategy #1: Serving the body (Eph. 4:12).

A staff or lay Minister of Involvement will use our Sunday classes to assess our people and provide the necessary information for them to discover their divine designs (required of new members). The staff or lay minister will match the people with the church's ministries for which they are best suited according to their design.

Strategy #2: Sharing our finances (Acts 2, 4; 2 Cor. 8–9).

We will use the Sunday service, the Sunday school, and the small groups to teach our people the biblical principles that will help them to handle their finances in a Christ-honoring way.

Strategy #3: Seeking the lost (Luke 15; 19:1-10).

We will provide classes in evangelism so that our people will understand the importance of evangelism, discover their style of evangelism, and how to share their faith with the lost. We will involve our people in missions abroad as well as at home. We will plant churches as we grow.

Other Examples of a Working Strategy

Two other examples should prove helpful in developing a strategy. The first is the 7-Step Philosophy of Ministry of Willow Creek Community Church, represented in figure 7. The strategy begins at the top with a horizontal continuum that represents the various stages of spiritual growth, ranging from those who are hostile to spiritual things to those who are living a balanced Christian life. This continuum parallels that of Engel's. Below the continuum are the seven steps that move a person from one end of the continuum to the other.

Another excellent strategy is the one developed by Rick Warren, the pastor of Saddleback Valley Community Church located near Los Angeles, California. It's found in figure 8 and is pictured as a baseball diamond with four bases. The object of the strategy is to move an individual around the bases. Moving from home plate to first base is knowing Christ. Moving from first to second is growing in Christ, moving from second to third is serving Christ, and moving from third to home plate is sharing Christ.

Other Programs for a Specific Working Strategy

When designing programs that accompany action steps, it's most helpful to keep apprised of what other churches who share the same vision are doing. (The environmental scan should help you with this.) The following are some programs that have proved highly effective in action steps that implement a Great Commission strategy.

Targeting the relational community. This particular program was covered in chapter 12 on evangelism. It is an important program for evangelism in any church because it attempts to involve those in the church in reaching out to others who are a part of their relational community, such as neighbors, workmates, and family members. Some other programs may be used along with it such as direct mail. However, they may cease to be used at a point in the life of the church, whereas targeting the relational community will always be practiced.

This is at the very heart of what Willow Creek Community Church is doing. In fact, their program depends on people inviting their lost, unchurched friends who are a part of their relational community to a weekend "seeker's service."

Direct mail. This program involves sending some kind of mailer to the homes of people who are in the new church's community. The purpose is to attract a lost, nonchurched person to a service or a small group meeting. This is a good method for smaller core groups because it doesn't need a lot of people to accomplish it. However, an effective program could prove costly. The new group may want to send a mailer from two to four times a year. Good times are early in September, early December, before Easter, and in early summer.[19]

Early in its ministry, Saddleback Valley Community Church used direct mail very effectively in attracting a number of unchurched lost people to its services. Some of my former students have used this program very effec-

Figure 7

Willow Creek's 7-Step Philosophy of Ministry

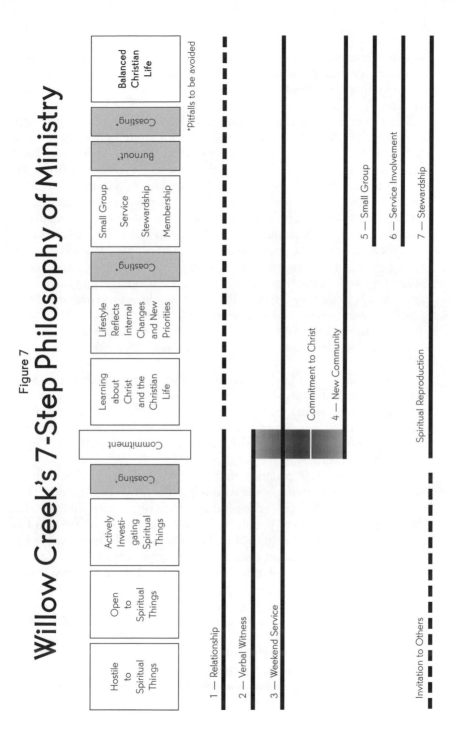

| Hostile to Spiritual Things | Open to Spiritual Things | Actively Investi-gating Spiritual Things | Coasting* | Commitment | Learning about Christ and the Christian Life | Lifestyle Reflects Internal Changes and New Priorities | Coasting* | Small Group Service Stewardship Membership | Burnout* | Coasting* | Balanced Christian Life |

*Pitfalls to be avoided

1 — Relationship

2 — Verbal Witness

3 — Weekend Service

Commitment to Christ

4 — New Community

5 — Small Group

6 — Service Involvement

7 — Stewardship

Spiritual Reproduction

Invitation to Others

tively in attracting unchurched people to a new church. They make sure the mailer is attractive and accurately targets their community. They're convinced that this is the best way to attract lost people in spite of the cost involved.[20]

Telemarketing. Some church plants have used a telemarketing program. Perhaps the best known and one used most for church planting is "The Phones for You!" program developed by Norm Whan in California. People in the core group call every household in the target community to invite them to church. The telephone call is followed up by several letters and one final call to encourage those who have responded to follow through.

Community service. This approach seeks to provide programs that meet the various needs of the community according to Galatians 6:10: "Therefore, as we have opportunity, let us do good to all people." It could involve the new church in teaching sewing, crime prevention, aerobics, self-defense for women, and simple auto repair classes. The church might also offer certain events like a fitness fair, a 10K run, a weight-lifting contest, a "red apple" day for teachers, and a rocket club for children. Finally, the church might sponsor a MOPS (Mothers of Preschoolers) or DADS program. Unchurched people respond to these programs because they target their felt needs.

High attendance Sundays. Some churches select two to four Sundays or more each year and sponsor a special event on those Sundays. The people in the group are encouraged to invite those in their relational communities. The event could feature a testimony by a popular Christian personality or sports star. Often they feature a musical program performed by a professional musician.

A prayer ministry. A program that has proved effective is that which solicits prayer needs from people who live in the target community. This can be done either through the mail or by canvassing the neighborhoods. These requests are given to people in the new church who will pray for a given period of time. Then they'll make a contact with the person who submitted the request for an update and any new requests. Eventually, through these contacts, a relationship develops and there are opportunities to present the gospel.

A welcome wagon. In this program, the church will obtain a list of all the new people moving into the target community. Next, they'll either write a letter or send a team of people to welcome them to the community and invite them to the church. Often, with the latter approach, the visiting team may bring them a gift such as an apple pie or a liter of Coke.

This program attempts to reach people at a time in their lives when they might be open to spiritual matters and coming to a church. Ezra Jones

Figure 8

Saddleback's C.L.A.S.S. Strategy

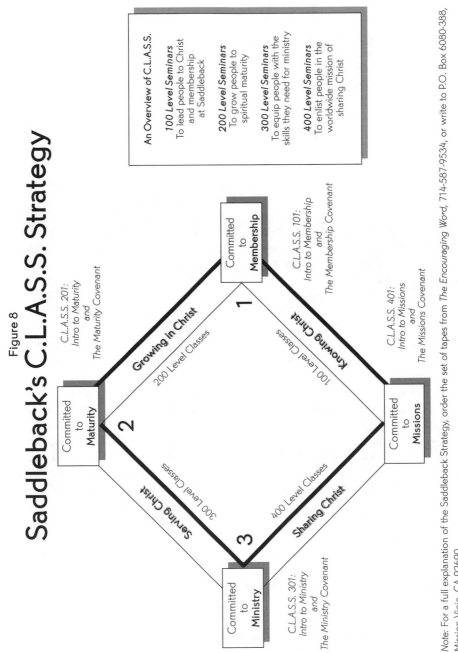

An Overview of C.L.A.S.S.

100 Level Seminars
To lead people to Christ and membership at Saddleback

200 Level Seminars
To grow people to spiritual maturity

300 Level Seminars
To equip people with the skills they need for ministry

400 Level Seminars
To enlist people in the worldwide mission of sharing Christ

Committed to Membership

C.L.A.S.S. 101:
Intro to Membership
and
The Membership Covenant

C.L.A.S.S. 201:
Intro to Maturity
and
The Maturity Covenant

C.L.A.S.S. 401:
Intro to Missions
and
The Missions Covenant

Growing in Christ
200 Level Classes

Knowing Christ
100 Level Classes

Committed to Maturity

Committed to Missions

Serving Christ
300 Level Classes

Sharing Christ
400 Level Classes

Committed to Ministry

C.L.A.S.S. 301:
Intro to Ministry
and
The Ministry Covenant

1
2
3

Note: For a full explanation of the Saddleback Strategy, order the set of tapes from *The Encouraging Word,* 714-587-9534, or write to P.O. Box 6080-388, Mission Viejo, CA 92690.

notes that most people moving into a new area will either find a new church or become confirmed nonchurchgoers within the first three years.[21]

"*Farming.*" This is a regular visitation program developed by Mark Platt, who works with Conservative Baptists in the area of church planting. He got the idea from a young real estate salesman in Simi Valley, California. Basically, the church-planting pastor consistently visits the people in his target area. What Platt discovered is that after repeated visits, the pastor wins the right to be heard and people respond. The secret to "farming" is consistency. It takes at least six visits before people even begin to recognize the pastor. This calls for at least one visit a month.

But where does a busy church planter find time to make all these calls? Platt spent only two hours a day in visitation. The result is that he covered five hundred homes per month. He reports that in one six-month period he had over fifty families visit the church as the result of "farming."

Media. A program that has been used for many years to communicate the message of the church has been the media such as the newspapers, radio, and television. There are several problems with the typical approach to the use of the media. The first is the cost, especially those associated with television. The second is the fact that the media has typically reached more Christians than lost people. For example, most churches advertise on the church page of the newspaper. The only problem is that unbelievers and especially the lost don't read the church page. Most churches place advertisements on Christian radio stations. But who listens to Christian radio stations?

The media is still a good place to advertise and can be used to reach unchurched lost people. However, the church might place its advertisements in some part of the newspaper other than the church page. The church could use an ad with a cartoon character that highlights an upcoming sermon that addresses the felt needs of lost people in the target area. Have the newspaper run the ad in the sports section if you desire to target men. Broadcast radio advertisements on the most popular non-Christian station in town. The church might also inquire if there is any free public service time available.

Another possibility is to volunteer to host or conduct a religious talk show on a popular, local non-Christian radio station. Begin the program by addressing a particular problem or felt need in the community and then show what Scripture says about the issue. Provide time for listeners to call in with questions.

The key to discovering and designing a program for an action step is creativity. Allow the team some time to be innovative and think creatively about programming. "Brainstorm" together. Discern what God is blessing in the country and in your area, especially in churches that are reaching lost people. Attend conferences and stay on the "cutting edge."

Recruiting the Right Personnel

After you've developed your working strategy, the third ingredient in developing your overall strategy is to recruit the people who will help you plant the church and implement the working strategy. This step answers the question, Who will be involved in reaching the target group? Far too many church planters attempt to start their churches by themselves or with the aid of a small core group. A much better option is to conceive or recruit a dynamic, gifted church-planting leadership team who will "own" and have a major role in realizing the dream. While the process may already be under way, this is the point in the strategic planning process where you must address the issue of personnel. But even if it begins here, it does not end here but becomes a never-ending process as you will always be recruiting personnel.

Why Recruit a Team?

There are two strong reasons for recruiting a church-planting team. The first concerns the importance of a team ministry and the second is the advantages of that ministry.

The Importance of a Team Ministry. A team approach to ministry is important for several reasons.

Christ ministered through a team. Christ chose to accomplish His ministry on earth using a team approach. This is important to note because He is God and the all-powerful Creator of the universe. Therefore, He doesn't need mortal men to do His work. Yet, instead of doing it alone, He chose to work through a band of fallible, inept disciples (Mark 6:7).

Paul ministered through a team. Paul did not attempt to carry out the Great Commission vision alone, but ministered through a team. It consisted of people such as Barnabas (Acts 11:22–30), Mark (Acts 13:2–3, 5), Silas (Acts 15:40), Timothy (Acts 16:1–3), Luke (Acts 16), and others (Acts 18). Also, Acts 19 and 20 mention Erastus, Gaius, Aristarchus, Sopater, Secundus, and Tychicus.

New Testament ministry was team ministry. Though not a biblical imperative, the ministries of Jesus and Paul demonstrate that New Testament ministry was team ministry. Lyle Schaller indicates that the key to reaching a new generation is starting churches, but to be effective it requires teamwork: "Starting a new church is one of the loneliest jobs in the world. I wouldn't do it unless I were part of a team."[22]

The Advantages of a Team Ministry. There are several advantages to ministering in a team context, especially if you recruit those who can lead the ministry to the next level of excellence.

Multiple Ministry. First, a team brings together several individuals with multiple gifts, talents, and abilities. This results in a more diverse ministry menu. When we look at all the gifts described as belonging to the body of Christ (Rom. 12; 1 Cor. 12; Eph. 4), we wonder why anyone would want to attempt a ministry all alone!

More Ministry. Second, a simple but often overlooked fact is that a team can accomplish more than an individual. Ecclesiastes 4:9–10 says, "Two are better than one, because they have a good return for their work: If one falls down, his friend can help him up. But pity the man who falls and has no one to help him up!"

Self-ministry. Third, a team can minister to itself. This also seems to be the point in the passage above from Ecclesiastes: "If one falls down, his friend can help him up."

How to Recruit a Team

The second question concerns the team recruitment process. It requires us to ask what we should look for in potential team members. The following four qualifications are "musts."

Character. The number one qualification for any person on a team is godly character. Such passages as 1 Timothy 3:1–13, Titus 1:6–9, and Acts 6:3 set the standard. These passages teach that there are various character qualifications for leaders in a team context in the church.

Vision. Another qualification for team ministry is vision. As Biehl and Engstrom assert, "A team forms around a dream. No dream, no team."[23] But not just any dream. It's critical to the success of the ministry team that they have the same dream. When a diverse group of people come together on one team, there's great potential for disagreements and splits. The secret is to bring them together under the same vision. When they commit to the same vision, they begin to see how their different gifts, talents, and abilities blend together to accomplish that single vision.

Values. A third qualification is common or shared values. As noted above in the section on values, the core values drive the ministry. They dictate every decision and determine every dollar spent. In short, they're vital to an effective ministry team. A team that doesn't share the same core values will disintegrate quickly and painfully.

Design. A fourth qualification concerns the potential team member's divine design. It includes such things as spiritual gifts, passion, temperament, leadership role and style, and natural gifts and talents. You should carefully examine each member's design early in the recruitment phase. For example, it's possible that two, three, or even more on a team could have many of the same elements in their design. Consequently, the team would lack the diversity it needs to minister effectively to a diverse group of people.

Where to Recruit a Team

The School Campus. A number of schools train men and women for various roles and positions in vocational Christian ministry. These range from unaccredited short-term schools to accredited graduate seminaries.

The Local Church. Another excellent source for recruiting teams is the local church. A major obstacle, however, for the contemporary church in America is that not enough churches are involved in starting new works. Again, as Peter Wagner has pointed out, church planting is one of the best methods of evangelism known today.

These churches, like the seminary campus, will also provide fertile soil for recruiting church-planting teams. As the church adds professional staff and implements an intern program, and as gifted laypeople surface, all could be recruited and trained within the church to extend its ministry through establishing new churches. In this role, the church would serve as an incubator for future new church leadership teams.

What Kind of Teams?

Temperament. An important factor in recruiting a team is the temperament of the individuals who will make up the team. Here we need to ask the configuration question, What are the best temperament combinations for recruiting and developing gifted, significant church-planting teams? The best way to answer this question is to examine briefly the information on temperament from the *Personal Profile* and the *Myers-Briggs Temperament Inventory (MBTI)* (see chapter 6). It must always be kept in mind that these inventories are merely tools. They are to be used as helpers not final determinants of who functions where on a team.

The Personal Profile. In chapter 6, we looked at how the DiSC model relates to developing effective teams for church planting. The best team leaders are those with either a High *D* and a secondary *I*, or a High *I* with a secondary *D*. The next best combination for those in the "point" positions is a High *D* or High *I* in combination with either a secondary *S* or *C*. A third possibility, though not as strong, would be either a High *S* or High *C* in combination with a secondary *D* or *I*.

Another issue that is affected by temperament is how the various combinations relate to one another in terms of effectiveness in the work environment. The Performax Company, which publishes the *Personal* and *Biblical Personal Profile,* has developed a compatibility chart that shows the various degrees of compatibility of the DiSC temperaments with one another in the areas of social interaction and work tasks.

This chart indicates that the two best temperament combinations for accomplishing a work-related task is the person with a High *D* or one with a High *I* teamed with a second person with a High *S.* The next best combination is a person with a High *S* working together with another who's a High *C.*[24] It's important to observe two things. First, as indicated earlier, the High *D*s and *I*s benefit a team the most by functioning or leading in the "point position." Second, the High *S* temperament serves in all three team combinations (rated as excellent) as the best possible backup person on the team. In other words, the High *S* temperament makes for excellent team compatibility in accomplishing a work-related task.

This doesn't mean that other temperament combinations can't get the job done. What it does mean is that, all things being equal, these temperaments function best in these positions and relationships in a task-oriented team environment.

The *Myers-Briggs Temperament Indicator (MBTI).* What are the most effective team combinations in terms of temperament according to the *MBTI*? Four preference choices exist in terms of temperament according to the *MBTI.* The first is extraversion or introversion *(EI),* the second is sensing or intuitive perception *(SN),* the third is thinking or feeling judgment *(TF),* and the last is judgment or perception *(JP).* (If these preferences seem a little vague at this point, turn back to chapter 6 and read the brief description of them.)

How do these preferences and their combinations affect recruiting teams for church planting? From her work in the field of temperament combinations, Myers concludes that the stronger teams consist of people who scored differently on the *MBTI,* showing a preference for either sensing *(S)* or intuition *(N),* or for thinking *(T)* or feeling *(F)* but not both. They should be alike on at least one other preference. In other words, they should both show a preference for either extraversion *(E)* or introversion *(I)* or for judgment *(J)* or perception *(P).*

In working with the *MBTI,* Roy M. Oswald and Otto Kroeger wisely add the following caution:

> One caution: the more the staff members differ in type, the better able they will be to minister to a diverse congregation; but it will be more difficult for

them to communicate and get along with each other. This is a trade-off. Be aware that when differences in type abound on a parish staff, more time and energy must be applied to maintaining support and communication.[25]

Personnel. In addition to temperament, a second factor in recruiting and developing a team for church planting is to think in terms of personnel. This would include such things as the number of team members, their roles or functions on the team, and their giftedness.

The two-person team. On the basic two-person team an effective combination would be a leader and a manager. The leader would be the one with the spiritual and natural gifts of leadership (Rom. 12:8) and possibly the spiritual gift of faith (1 Cor. 12:9), which involves vision. The manager would be the person with the spiritual and natural gifts of administration (1 Cor. 12:28). This team, most likely, would function better than two leaders or two managers teamed together.

The three-person team. Lyle Schaller believes that all church-planting teams should include at least three people: a pastor, an evangelist, and a music specialist. He also suggests a five-person team that would, in addition to the three just mentioned, include someone to minister to families with children and a person responsible for developing church life.[26]

The three- to five-person team. Willow Creek Community Church is encouraging three- to five-person teams according to certain spiritual gifts. For example, they strongly encourage teams that are led by someone with the gift of leadership. The other two members consist of a teacher and a programmer. Ideally, there would be two additional members: a youth worker and an administrator.[27] The teacher in the Willow Creek strategy would teach the believers at the New Community services during the week. The programmer would be responsible for what takes place in the various congregational services such as the drama and worship.

Perhaps the best way to determine the right combination for the team is to consider the church's ministry strategy. For example, if the team desires to plant churches that reach lost people, then they'll need an evangelist. If they want good worship, they'll need someone gifted in music. If they desire a church with an emphasis on small groups, they'll need someone with gifts and experience in small group ministry. The most effective leadership teams for planting growing churches for the twenty-first century will be those with three to five persons who combine many of the following gifts and abilities: leadership, administration, faith (vision), evangelism, preaching, teaching, worship, small groups, youth and family, and counseling.

Doctrinal Agreement. Your team will need to be in agreement on basic Bible doctrines and potential doctrinal issues. You would be wise to write a doctrinal statement for the church early in the conception stage. Then you'll use it too as a guide for team selection. I would suggest that in the essentials, there be unity, in the nonessentials, liberty, and in all things love. The question, of course, is, What are the essentials?

Church planters also need to decide where they stand on potentially controversial doctrinal issues such as tongues, divorce, women's role in the church, political involvement, and other similar issues.

Mini-bios. Once you've recruited your team, ask each to develop what I refer to as a "mini-bio." It is a brief statement that identifies who the person is and gives information about his or her family, ministry training, areas of expertise, and other pertinent information. A picture also adds a nice touch. The purpose of the "bio" is to introduce the team to those interested in some way in the church plant.

Board of Reference. The team should meet together and develop a board of reference. It will consist of people who have worked with the team and/or with individuals on the team and can recommend them on the basis of their character and past performance.

The days of the specialist pastor who attempts to minister without a team in the context of the typical church are numbered. If these church plants survive, most will remain small and drain the leader's energy and the sponsor's finances. Organizations and denominations would be wise to send out one church-planting team, consisting of four or five people, and invest in it rather than four or five separate individuals to plant four or five separate churches.

Locating the Ministry's Facilities

The fourth ingredient in developing your working strategy is to locate a place for the church to meet. The question is, What facilities are necessary and best for reaching your target group?

Here the age-old maxim "form follows function" applies. The facilities must align with the working strategy. If your strategy dictates a Sunday school program, then the facilities must have adequate rooms for classes. If you target people with infants, you must have a nursery. If you have a worship service, then you'll need a place to hold that service.

I deal more in depth with facilities in the development stage (chapter 15). There we'll look at the characteristics of a facility such as location, appearance, visibility, accessibility, size, cleanliness, and many others. We'll also probe the prospects for a good facility such as a school, public center, storefront, movie theater, and other places.

You should consider the possibility of remodeling. You might find the right facility in a good location, but have to remodel it to suit your needs.

Some have the option of purchasing land and a facility or purchasing land and building a facility. If the former, be sure to ask lots of questions and be on the lookout for hidden costs and problems. I knew of one five-acre piece of land that was for sale in a new, growing suburb. It looked like a fantastic deal. However, the city wanted a least one acre of the land for a second road, and the buyer would have to pay for it. Also, a Mormon Stake (church) had bought the adjoining property. The agent handling the property didn't volunteer this information until the church discovered it and asked him about it point blank.

Raising the Ministry's Finances

The fifth ingredient in developing your specific working strategy is to ask, How much will it cost to reach our target group? The answer is twofold. This involves raising and managing your financial resources.

Raising the financial resources. For you to raise adequate financial resources for yourself and the ministry, you need to determine your precise financial needs. The way to accomplish this is with a budget that reflects most accurately the costs of your ministry community. Your budget will consist of such items as salaries; housing (rent or mortgage plus utilities); insurance (liability and health); automobile; rent or lease for meeting facilities and an office; facility improvements; office supplies, furniture and equipment; Sunday school curriculum; and equipment such as sound, musical instruments, lighting, and chairs.

The next step is to raise those funds. I have covered the topic of fund-raising in chapter 3. It's important here to note that many denominations have discovered the need for church planting and are providing help for those who desire to plant churches through them. Some will match the funds that the church planter raises and others will even match every dollar raised with two dollars. In addition, a few churches have caught the vision to plant and fund new churches. Consequently, at this point—if not earlier—you need to decide (if you're not already with a denomination) if you want to affiliate with a particular denomination. You would also be wise to seek out a parent church.

Managing the financial resources. Once you've raised the necessary funds for your church planting ministry, you need to properly manage those funds. This involves such practices as receipting gifts, using several people of known high integrity to collect and count any offerings, living by the budget, and at least a yearly audit of funds. The public is all too aware of the televangelists in the 1980s and 1990s who misappropriated the funds given by well-intentioned people to their ministries. They're looking for integrity in this area, and we must not disappoint them.

Implementing the Strategy

After you have developed your overall strategy, the sixth step in the conception stage is to implement the same. The greatest problem in developing an overall ministry strategy is implementation. Church planters can catalyze and articulate a fresh innovative, powerful strategy, but somehow may never get around to implementing it. They fail to follow through. Thus, it dies a quick death for lack of implementation.

It's imperative that we take action if we want to translate the vision into the very fabric of the organization. We must make it happen. To fail at this point in the conception stage is as demoralizing as getting to the goal line but not scoring, or getting to the marriage altar only to change your mind. The implementation step consists of six key ingredients.

Determine Specific Actions

The first key ingredient is to determine the specific actions you need to take to accomplish the strategy. You can't implement the entire strategy all at once. Thus, you must ask, What are the specific actions we must take at the beginning to afford the greatest impact? They will be four or five. At Northwood Community Church, our target group was primarily Baby Boomers with children. Consequently, it was imperative that we bring our Sunday school program "on line" as soon as possible (see figure 9 below). These people wanted something good for their kids.

Formulate Specific Priorities

Once specific actions are identified, the second ingredient is to prioritize them. This serves to focus our resources, energy, finances, people, and creativity. Again, at Northwood, our number one priority was our Christian education program.

Decide on Specific Deadlines

The third ingredient is to decide when the action should be accomplished. Assign each action a specific month and year.

Assign Responsibility

The fourth ingredient is to assign responsibility to someone for the implementation of the specific action. You ask, Who is the best person to carry out this assignment?

Communicate the Specific Priorities

The fifth key ingredient is communication. Here you ask, Who needs to know about these specific actions? People need to know what you're implementing if they are to "buy in" and be involved in any way in its implementation.

Schedule a Monthly Implementation Review

The final ingredient is an MIR (Monthly Implementation Review). This allows the church-planting team to review the monthly operational performance of the ministry and to assure accountability.

Identifying Ministry Contingencies

The seventh step in the conception stage is to identify the ministry contingencies. The question is, How do we handle the pleasant and not so pleasant surprises that will come our way while on the ministry journey? Emergency and crisis situations happen. Unprepared people react poorly and make bad decisions that serve only to further aggravate the situation.

These contingencies may be good events (opportunities) such as a large gift of money, a sudden growth or influx of people, some positive publicity in the local newspaper, a revival, and other events. Most are jeopardies that could destroy the new church plant such as a church split, the sudden resignation of the lead pastor, an economic reversal, a staff sexual affair, an accusation of sexual harassment, the sexual abuse of a child, a kidnapping, a serious accident, and many others.

The solution is to brainstorm these potential opportunities and jeopardies and be ready for them if and when they happen. Some are preventable. For example, to prevent the possibility of the sexual abuse of a child in the nursery or a Sunday school class, the church would be wise to have at least two or more workers available. Some jeopardies aren't preventable, so you must be ready when they occur such as a heart attack during the worship service. In this situation, you must train your ushers to aid the person who has suffered the attack.

Figure 9

STRATEGY IMPLEMENTATION
Northwood Community Church

Just because we have a well-developed strategy does not mean that it will happen automatically. Once we have developed our ministry strategy, we must implement it. Strategy implementation involves the formulation of strategic priorities and specific actions. The following are ours.

Priority One: Christian education program

Develop a Sunday school program, nursery, and children's church that provide Christian education for all the people in our church.

Actions	Deadlines	Responsible Persons
1. Recruit Pastor of Christian Education		
	November 1999	Tom Stanley
2. Recruit teachers, helpers, and a director		
	December 1999	Greg Holmes
3. Train teachers, helpers, and the director		
	January 2000	Greg Holmes
4. Remodel rooms where necessary		
	January 2000	Greg Holmes
5. Implement Christian education program		
	February 2000	Greg Holmes

Evaluating the Ministry's Performance

The final step in the conception stage is evaluation. Few churches formally appraise what they are doing. That doesn't mean, however, that evaluation doesn't take place. People are constantly judging whether or not they like their Sunday school class, their small group leader, last Sunday's sermon, and so forth.

For churches to grow and improve, they need to conduct regular evaluations. This practice makes sure the ministry regularly recognizes people's strengths and contributions to the church as well as their weaknesses and failures. While most don't like evaluation, it allows the church to confront problem people and problematic performances that otherwise go ignored. Rather than hurt ministry morale, our system has encouraged it. It reminds us to reward people and forces us to deal with our problems.

The rule is: what gets appraised gets done. To accomplish good appraisal, you must answer the following questions: Who evaluates? Whom and what do they evaluate? How often do they evaluate?

Appraisal is based on and works off each person's job or ministry description. First, each individual needs to have a ministry description that spells out clearly his or her responsibilities. The evaluation is created from and based on that.

At Northwood Community Church, we've implemented a 360° evaluation program. Each one on the board evaluates the board as a whole, each member on the board (including the pastor who is an elder), and the staff. The board chairman sits down and discusses the results with each. Also, each person on the staff evaluates everyone else on the staff plus the board. I, as the senior pastor, review the results with each. All also evaluate themselves with a self-appraisal. We do this three times a year.

This appraisal process allows everyone to know their assessed strengths and weaknesses. We try to applaud the former. This might involve a raise and promotion for a staff person. We look at the weaknesses, discuss them, and ask the person to work at improvement. This lets them know where they stand. Should the individual not improve, then we could potentially dismiss him or her after a time. Should the latter occur, then the person is well aware of the problem and reason for dismissal. Often, these people resign before the church releases them.[28]

This chapter has covered the basic steps that church planters must take to put the new church in place. However, this is only part of the battle. Zig Ziglar says that 15 percent of the reason why you get, keep, and move ahead in a job is determined by your technical skills and job knowledge. The other 85 percent rests with your people skills and people knowledge. I'm convinced that this is doubly true of ministry. You can accomplish all that's in this chapter and more, and fail due to a lack of people skills. What's the message? Work hard at relating well to people. Let the Spirit help you (Gal. 5:22–23).

A Conception Stage Checklist

_____1.   Recruit an intercessory prayer team

_____2.   Discover your core values and develop a credo

_____3.   Develop a mission statement

_____4.   Conduct an environmental scan

_____5.   Develop a vision statement

_____6.   Develop a logo

_____7.   Design a strategy

_____8.   Determine a church plant location (demographics and psy-
hographics)

_____9.   Write a brief doctrinal statement

____10.   Determine a theological position on controversial topics
such as tongues, divorce, women's role in the church, etc.

____11.   Recruit and train a staff team

____12.   Write "mini-bios"

____13.   Develop a budget

____14.   Raise finances

____15.   Investigate possible denominational affiliation

____16.   Locate a parent church

____17.   Recruit a board of reference

____18.   Anticipate and prepare for contingencies

____19.   Develop ministry/job descriptions

____20.   Design and produce evaluations

A Conception Stage Worksheet

1. Have you discovered your core values and developed a mission, vision, and a strategy for the same? Have you done this on both a personal and a congregational level?

2. How much time do you spend each day in prayer for the church? Have you recruited an intercessory prayer team to pray for you and the ministry?

3. The enemy in church planting as well as other ministries is discouragement. Have you faced it yet in any of your ministries? How did you handle it?

4. Are you convinced of the need for developing a ministry team? If so, who are some potential candidates for your team? Where might you locate other team members? How many people would you want on your team? What would each do?

5. What kind of people would be in your target group? Are they lost or saved? If they're unsaved, are they unchurched? Are they a lot like you in terms of affinity? What methods might you use in attempting to reach them?

6. What kind of ministry contingencies might you face? How do you plan to deal with them?

15

Childbirth Classes

The Development Stage

While in seminary, Bill Smith worked his way through much of the conception stage. He's developed his core values, a mission, and a strong, significant vision statement that involves pursuing and reaching unchurched lost people. He has also recruited two other men at seminary as part of a gifted, aggressive church-planting team. While all three men possess different gifts and abilities, they're strongly committed to each other and to the accomplishment of the same vision to reach the unchurched. They've also outlined a ministry strategy to accomplish their dream: they've focused on a target group of people who are much like them, located that target group in a particular community, and outlined a specific working strategy to reach these people. One final important event has also transpired. All three have just completed their seminary training and received their degrees. Where do they go from here? What's the next step in the process of church planting?

The second stage in the process of starting a church is the development stage. The primary purpose of this stage, as with a newly conceived child in the womb of its mother, is to prepare this new life for its birth (the third stage). The new church faces two potential problems at this point. On the one hand, it could start too soon and the birth will be premature. On the other, it could wait too long and be delivered past term. How long, then, should it take? What time is necessary to prepare for birth? In most cases, this ranges from three months to a year, depending on whether or not there's a pre-existing group of interested, committed Christians in the target area.

The primary issue concerns what takes place during the development stage. What does the new church need to accomplish to become ready for its birth in the target community? In other words, what happens between conception and birth?

Gathering a Core Group

A church can't exist without people! The development stage assumes that there's someone to be developed. Consequently, the development stage begins with the gathering of an initial core group of people who are interested in starting a new church. This will involve either a "cold start" or a "hot start."

Gathering a Nonexistent Core Group

What is a "cold start," what are its advantages and disadvantages, and how is it accomplished?

A Definition

A "cold start" involves gathering a nonexistent group of believers. There are Christians already living in the target area, but they may not know one another and they're not meeting together for the purpose of planting a church.

Bill Smith and his team have targeted a particular community in an urban setting where they don't have any contacts. Most likely, they've been praying over a list of the fastest growing metropolitan areas in America as listed in the *American Demographics Magazine,* and God has directed their hearts to this one. They've completed a feasibility study on the area and have determined their target community. The next step is to move into the area and begin to locate and raise up a core group of interested, relatively mature Christians.

It's also possible to move into the area and primarily target lost people. However, this would require that time be set aside to develop them because of their initial immaturity. The planting of the church may have to be delayed until these new believers are ready.

The Advantages and Disadvantages

There are both advantages and disadvantages to gathering a nonexistent core group.

An advantage. One of the definite advantages of this approach is that the people who become involved "join you." The result is that they grant you the authority and the necessary power to lead them. They're committed to your leadership and values from the very beginning of the work. In contrast, when pastors take established churches, they "join them." At the beginning they aren't given the authority and power to lead these people. The new pastor has to earn it, which takes time and providence.

The disadvantages. There are several disadvantages to this approach. The first is that you can't get started "long distance." You have to move into the area first in order to make contacts with the people. The second disadvantage is a result of the first. This approach takes a lot of time and patience. Discouragement is likely to set in unless a lot of good contacts are established early.

The Methods

There are several ways to make contact with potential core group members in a target area.

Prayer. The first and most important is to get on your knees before the sovereign God of the universe and ask Him to help you raise up the right people for the new church. Ask Him to put you in the right places with the right people at the right times.

The constituency of a school. Second, if the church planters are seminary or Bible college graduates, they could ask the school to write a letter to its constituency in the target area informing them of the new church and encouraging them to contact the team. If the school will release the names, then the planters could make the contacts themselves and assess any interest in the new work.

Parachurch. Another approach is to make contact with any parachurch organizations in the area. Some examples would be Christian Businessmen's International, Campus Crusade for Christ, or Young Life. Explain the church's vision and strategy and see if there's any interest. Often parachurch groups will share the same vision and will be delighted to help a church that desires to reach out to lost, unchurched people. These organizations can provide the names of contact people in the community as well as encourage their own people to come your way.

"Cutting-edge" churches. A fourth approach is to contact a high-impact, "cutting-edge" church and share with it your vision. Once you feel you've gained their confidence, ask if they have any contacts in the target community. They might be willing to send some of their own people your way. Often there will be people who write them from around the

country desiring to find a similar church in their community. These contacts can be valuable.

Advertising. Place an ad in the church page of the community newspaper explaining the vision and plans to start a church. Since Christian people read the church page, you will stir up some interest. I used this method effectively in planting my first church. You could also send out a letter of explanation to the community. While this may create a lot of interest, one drawback could be a negative response from other pastors in the area.

Networking. I use this term to cover several areas. As you circulate in the community, you will come in contact with Christians in general and unchurched Christians in particular (John 1:39–45). You'll come across them at the mall, grocery store, soccer practice, and elsewhere. Ask, Who do you know who isn't going to church anywhere? You could recruit people by conducting a neighborhood survey. Regardless of where you find them, invite them to the core group.

Gathering an Existent Core Group

What is a "hot start," what are its advantages and disadvantages, and what is a good method for working with it?

A Definition

A "hot start" involves gathering and working with a group that has already come together in some locale before the church-planting team arrives on the scene. There are several potential "hot start" situations. The first is a group of people from a mother church who desire to begin a daughter church. They might be Christians who live and have been meeting together in the same community located a substantial distance from the church. Rather than drive all that distance, they could begin a church in their own community. In a similar fashion, a mother church might desire to plant a daughter church in a particular community and recruit some of its people who live in that community to form the core of the new church.

Another situation involves a group of people without a mother church who are located in an area of the country where there aren't many evangelical churches. They could contact the placement office of the seminary, who, in turn, will put them in contact with the church-planting team.

The Advantages and Disadvantages

The advantages. The most obvious advantage in this situation is that not as much time is required to locate and recruit people to make up the initial core group. In general, they're already in place. Also, if there are enough people in the initial core group, they may be able to come up with a strong financial package.

The disadvantages. There are several disadvantages. The core group might have a different vision and different core values from that of the church-planting team. For example, they may be more interested in having someone come and teach them the Bible than in reaching their lost friends and neighbors. The critical issue here is whether they're willing to "own" the new vision and share the values. Another is that the church planters are "joining them," especially if they've been in existence for a period of time. Thus, it might take longer to gain their allegiance.

Whether a "hot" or "cold start," look for people who are what I refer to as "magnet" or "attractor people." These are individuals or couples who have strong people skills (often high *Is* on the *Personal Profile*) and have developed large or multiple webs of relationships in the community. Their presence contributes to quick growth and strong outreach into the community.

My experience with "hot starts," along with that of other church planters, is that within a year or two the initial core group will often leave the church. This is because some don't understand the sacrifice that it takes to plant a church. They're simply looking for a Bible study. The greater problem is that many will not share the same values, mission, and vision. Consequently, in time, they will be replaced by those who do. Therefore, it's most important that church planters take great pains to explain repeatedly to their initial core groups the church's values, mission, vision, strategy and other vital concepts.

A Method

But what does the church planter or the planting team do when they first meet with an existent core group? What's their agenda? What are the kinds of things they should discuss? The purpose of the first meeting is for the leader to get to know the core group and to assess if they're the right match for this team. The following considerations should determine the tenor of the first meeting.

Allow for a large block of time. It's important that there be plenty of time for discussion and interaction between the team and the core group. One possibility is to get away together for a weekend in a place where there will not be a lot of interruptions. Children should be left with a baby sitter.

Get to know one another. There should be sufficient time to get to know one another. This will help in bonding and developing a sense of community. Both the team and the core group could give some information about themselves. Participants should make a point of visiting with one another during breaks and the evenings and mornings when people are relaxed and together. Playing a game of volleyball or some other team sport is a good "mixer" that will help accomplish this goal.

Ask lots of questions. The more questions you ask, the better you'll be able to assess the situation and the existent core group.

1. Find out about the origin of the group, their backgrounds, and their beliefs.
2. Determine the group's purpose, vision, and felt needs. Most important is their core values. What is their vision, and do they have the same vision? What are their values and are they shared? Do you share their values? Before this meeting, you might ask each person in the group to listen to a tape or view a video that communicates your vision. Determine if they're open to it or not.
3. Is there a need for this church? The answer is always, "Yes," but it's important for them to verbalize it.
4. How serious are these people about starting a new church? Try to determine their level of commitment.[1]

Secure a commitment. The commitment of the existent, potential core group is critical if a church is to be planted. They must make a strong commitment to the new work and the team. In order to secure a commitment, three things must be done.

First, discuss the nature of the commitment. The core group must realize the need for a commitment. It's vital to the ultimate realization of the vision. The level of commitment is important as well. The group must make the strongest of commitments to the new work. It's not to be treated simply as another optional Bible study. Commitment involves the whole family. Husbands and wives must both be committed to the new church. Commitment involves their time, talents, and treasure. How much are they willing to give to the new work?

Second, discuss the areas for commitment. Spend a significant amount of time discussing the core values, mission, and the vision and the strategy to accomplish that vision. This should lead to a discussion of what kind of church will be planted. Will it be a seeker-type church, or primarily focused on Christians? If so, what does that mean and what is involved? Consider other topics for discussion such as the importance of a commitment to personal, spiritual growth; a commitment to excellence; the doctrinal stance of the church; the structure of leadership; and the team's position on such issues as the role of women, the place of the sign gifts, divorce and remarriage, and involvement in political issues.

Third, call for a commitment. Eventually, both the team and the core group will need to make a decision whether or not to proceed with starting a church together. Both groups may need time to discuss this among themselves. Try to allow some time for this while all are still together. This will provide time in which to answer any questions that may surface. It's possible that both groups will decide to commit to the new work before the weekend is over. Otherwise, more time may be needed to discuss the matter. Take no longer than a week.

Regardless of the time, if the decision is affirmative, several things must be done. First, ask who has decided to be part of the core group. Next, ask these people to write on a piece of paper how much money they're willing to commit to the new work. Finally, have them complete a commitment card with their names, addresses, and financial commitments.

Cultivating a Core Group

The potential core group is now an official core group, and the church-planting team is ready to move on. What happens next? The second phase of the development stage is to cultivate the new core group in preparation for the birth of the church. The cultivation stage has much in common with pouring cement. You're able to dictate the shape it takes, but remember that it hardens quickly. And once it hardens, it's hard to change.

Assessing the Core Group

One of the very first things the team must do is to assess the people who make up the core group. This is an exciting process that answers the question, "Whom has God sovereignly brought together?" This should be the responsibility of a particular person on the team who is assisted by the other members of the team.

The team should assess all who make up the core group, including their spiritual gifts, passion, temperament, leadership roles and styles, and natural talents, gifts, and abilities. I have written *Maximizing Your Effectiveness* (Baker Book House) for this very purpose. Most likely, this will be new to all the people in the group. This will help all involved become delighted and excited about what God has done in their lives. They will also be anxious and motivated to implement their gifts in a ministry in the new work.

Implementing a Strategy

Once you've assessed the core group, the team will be able to begin to implement the strategy and establish its programs. Determine your programs in light of the people God has provided. Don't attempt to institute programs unless God has provided the people who are gifted to lead and implement them.

You may not be able to implement the entire strategy up front. That's okay. This may not occur until the birth stage or after. Do what you can with the people God gives you. Determine which programs will help the group reach the lost people in their relational community. For example, you might begin a "seeker friendly" Bible study. Another decision concerns the edification of the group. It will be necessary for the group to meet together for worship and Bible study. How many meetings a week are reasonable for the core group? As little as one or as many as three? The team should have already thought through much of this in the conception stage; however, some adjustments will need to be made in light of the people in the core group.

Meeting Corporately with the Core Group

There should be a regular weekly meeting of the entire core group that's led by the point person on the planting team. If the church has a large, well-endowed core group of people, then the church's strategy may include a "seeker's service" for the lost and a believer's service for Christians. Eventually this meeting will become the believer's service. If the strategy is to have only a "seeker-friendly" service, then it will become that service.

Initially, this corporate meeting will serve to orient the group to the vision, mission, and values of the church based on the Scriptures, although it will include time for worship. It's important that the team's values become the core group's values. In this meeting, the pastor, as the primary vision caster, will teach on such concepts as the following: the Great Commission vision; a strong servant-leadership; a well-mobilized lay army; a culturally relevant ministry; a holistic, authentic worship; a biblical, culturally relevant evangelism; and a robust network of small groups.

Selecting and Training Lay Leaders

Not enough can be said about the importance of lay leadership to the new church. The church-planting team simply can't do it by themselves. Whether the new church survives and accomplishes its vision will depend on its ability to recruit and equip quality lay leaders.

Recruiting Lay Leaders

The church-planting team should begin to recruit lay leaders as soon as possible. Actually, this process begins at the initial meeting with the potential core group. The team should discern which individuals have already gravitated toward leadership in the group.

The basic requirements for leadership in addition to natural and/or spiritual leadership gifts will be character, vision, and influence, undergirded by good core values. Determine which individuals in the group walk with Christ on a consistent basis. Everyone attempts to look good at the first few meetings, but how do they respond when there are problems and differences of opinion? Also, determine who has "caught" the vision and share the values. If people do not yet "own" the vision and values, they're not ready for leadership. Godly people who have a vision will attract followers.

Training Lay Leaders

There are several methods for training lay leaders. These were discussed in the chapter on small groups. A good method is to train leaders both corporately and individually. One member of the church-planting team, probably the point person, could assume the responsibility for training the leaders as a group. They could meet once or twice a month and use the method developed for the metachurch model involving vision casting, huddling, and skills building (VHS). Then each person on the team could disciple the lay leaders, meeting individually once a week.

The ultimate purpose for recruiting and training these leaders is for service and ministry to the church body (Eph. 4:11–12). It isn't intended to make them members of a lay elder or deacon board or have them sit on a board that makes decisions concerning administrative matters. The church-planting team will either be the elders or the equivalent to the elders and will take care of these matters. The lay leaders will be training to lead small groups or other ministry groups in the church. It's most important that this be clarified in the early meetings with the core group before a final commitment is made to start the church. If you decide to have a board comprised of laypeople, then select those who have proved themselves by leading well their small groups over a significant period of time such as one to two years (1 Tim. 5:22).

Implementing a Small Group Program

As we saw in chapter 13, a robust network of small groups is vital to the life of the church. While they, like the corporate meeting, are an important consideration in designing a strategy, they're so important that they need to be singled out for special attention. They were critical to the early church (Acts 2:46; 5:42; 20:20). They're just as vital to developing a sense of biblical community in the contemporary church.

The Timing

Since this program is important to the new church, it should be implemented as soon as possible. Ask everyone to become part of a small group. If people object, chances are good that they don't understand the vision and values, or they're not yet ready to be a part of this particular church. The only delay in implementing this program might involve allowing sufficient time to train the leadership for the small groups. Once this training is underway, then the groups can begin.

The Leadership

The leaders for these groups will be recruited and trained initially by the church-planting team as mentioned above. They will not need to be fully trained before they actually begin to lead a group. In fact, an important aspect of their training will be to involve them in the leadership of a group while they're being trained. Then they'll have an opportunity to implement what they're learning in their large and small group training sessions.

The Strategy

It's possible that the core group will be small enough at the very beginning that it starts as an independent small group led by the point person on the planting team. However, as it grows, it should regularly divide and form new small groups led by trained lay leaders with apprentice understudies. If the initial core group is large, then it will need to break up into smaller groups. As these groups grow, they, too, should divide and form new groups. In the latter case, the point pastor may lead one of these groups or lead only one that consists of the lay leaders of all the other groups.

Advertising the Church

During the development stage the new church formulates its advertising program. It will need to decide if it should seek professional help or attempt the program on its own. If the team knows very little about how to advertise, then they'll need professional counsel. Some churches have become creative and innovative in their advertising, and are willing to give some help in this area.

Before an advertising program is undertaken, several things need to be accomplished.

A Sense of Direction

A sense of direction is critical to the new church. It must not only have a shared set of values, but it most also have a shared mission and vision. This accomplishes a number of things for the church, such as giving it common direction, providing it with motivation, and encouraging unity. You should have developed the values, mission, and vision statements and written them down. If this wasn't done in the conception stage, then it must be done no later than the development stage. These will be an integral part of the advertising program.

A Strategy

The team should have already decided how they plan to accomplish the mission and vision. The ministry strategy, as explained in the conception stage (chapter 14), will accomplish the mission and strategy. Without this knowledge, it will be impossible to conduct an effective advertising program.

A Budget

Good advertising costs money. There are some techniques that don't cost a lot of money such as hand delivering a brochure or inviting a friend to attend a service. However, there are a lot of advantages to implementing a telemarketing or direct mail program, and this will involve some expense. Consequently, the team and the church will need to decide how committed they are to advertising and the degree to which they'll use it as a means to attract unchurched people to the new church. (My view is that it's vital.) Next, they'll need to make this a part of the budget.

A Team

It would be most helpful to assemble a team of people in the core group who could handle the church's advertising. The team could be made up of people who are either in the field or know something about advertising. They could be responsible for collecting ideas from other churches with good advertising programs and developing a program of advertising for the new church. They might also have some good ideas on how to raise the necessary funding to cover the costs of the program. Be sure to select a team leader.

Administering the Church's Affairs

Not only is leadership important to the new church, but the management and administration of its affairs are also necessary.

Managing the Finances

The new church will need to establish a credible, efficient financial control program. This will involve such things as establishing the church's financial policies; raising, collecting, monitoring, and disbursing its funds; and a yearly audit. It is essential that the financial program be "squeaky clean." The church must avoid doing anything that might cast doubt on its financial integrity.

Evaluating the Team, Leaders, and Programs

Evaluation is critical to the growth and improvement of the ministry. A regular program of evaluation should be implemented by the developmental stage. The evaluation process should involve those on the church-planting team, the lay leadership, and the various programs of the church. The key is to develop "agreed upon" job or ministry descriptions and base the evaluations on them.

Monitoring Attendance, Growth, and Finances

Since numerical growth is usually an indicator of whether the church is making progress toward the accomplishment of its vision, the leadership team will need to monitor its attendance, growth, and finances. Records should be kept of who's involved in the ministry and the weekly attendance and any giving at the various ministries. The team should begin to look for patterns in attendance and giving. For example, does attendance and giving go down in the summer but increase in the fall? If so, what can be done to change this pattern?

Naming the Church

More than likely, the group will be ready to select a name for the church early in the development stage if it hasn't taken place already. Most people in the core group will want to identify themselves with a name. This will also be necessary if the church decides to incorporate. Names are very important to people, especially to the unchurched. I say more about how to select a church name in the next chapter.

Incorporating the Church

The team will need to make a decision regarding the incorporation of the church. They'll need to check with the state as to what its requirements are for incorporation. Often an attorney or a certified public accountant can provide information and assistance. If finances are limited, then ask for help from the mother church or a recently incorporated church in the area. In many states, incorporation protects individuals in the church from any lawsuits that might be brought against the church. You can sue an incorporated church for its assets, but not its people for their individual assets. Also, incorporation or its equivalent is necessary to gain IRS tax exemption.

Locating a Place to Meet

The group should constantly assess its needs. This involves monitoring attendance and growth to determine if the present facilities are adequate. Project when the church might need to relocate and where, and begin to look for future relocation sites in the target area.

Preparation of the Facilities

Most churches aren't in a position to begin their own facilities. They'll have to rent the facilities of a school, a business, strip mall, a daycare, or some other organization. In most cases, they'll need to arrive early and prepare the facilities for worship, child care, and nurture programs. This requires the efforts of a team of "unsung heroes" who are willing to come early and stay late in order to accomplish this task.

Planning for the Future

The church that doesn't plan for the future may not have a future. Since the development stages prepares the church for the next stage, that of birth, then the team should be planning ahead. There are numerous factors that must be worked through in order to birth the new church.

Growing the Core Group

The team has gathered the core group and is in the midst of cultivating the same. The third phase of the development stage is to grow the core group. The term "growth" is used here in the sense of numerical growth—in particular, both conversion and transfer growth. The object of the church is to reach people, and this must begin in the development stage. In fact, the church will not be ready for the birth stage until it reaches a numerical size that's sufficient to sustain its birth. Growing the core group involves evangelizing unbelievers and recruiting believers.

Evangelizing Unbelievers

The church's vision and a critical core value should be to reach lost people and unchurched lost in particular. This vision has been used as a means to recruit many of the people who make up the new core group. They're present because they've made a conscious decision to "own" the new church and what it represents. In their minds, they see their relational community coming to faith in Christ, and they're excited and motivated to get on with it.

Thus, the church-planting team must strike while the proverbial iron is still hot. Not to act will result in losing valuable momentum toward weaving the direction (mission and vision) into the very fabric of the church. The twofold strategy that was developed in chapter 12 should accomplish this.

Implement a Strategy for Individual Evangelism

Two things are necessary to accomplish this.

Assume personal responsibility. People in the core group will need to assume personal responsibility for pursuing the lost people who make up their relational community.

Preparation for this should begin in the initial meetings following the formation of the core group. Core group members should understand that their relational community consists of their family, workmates, and neighbors. They need to think about the people who make up these communities and make a list of those who might be receptive to spiritual truth. Often it's helpful to draw a family tree, an organizational work chart, or a map of the neighborhood immediately surrounding their houses.

Develop a strategy. Next, they should develop a strategy to reach these people. The one in chapter 12 is a good one.

1. Put responsive people on a "hit list."
2. Pray daily for them.
3. Cultivate relationships with these people.
4. Look for times of receptivity to spiritual truth and reach out accordingly.

Initial training will help people discover their individual styles of evangelism. Most laypeople view evangelism as confrontation. Consequently, since many aren't good at confrontation, they don't share their faith. They must become aware that there are other styles and then discover their own if they're to be effective in sharing the gospel.

Implement a Strategy for Corporate Evangelism

Not only will people need to be involved individually in evangelism, but the church or core group needs to be involved corporately. Basically what this means is that the core group will need to have a corporate strategy for evangelism.

Most likely, this will involve ways in which the entire core group can assist individuals in their evangelistic endeavors. For example, the church could implement a "seeker-friendly" Bible study as a vital part of its program. The pastor or someone on the team could lead this study. This would provide a meeting to which people could invite their lost friends to hear a positive presentation of true Christianity. Later, this might develop into a Sunday morning or Saturday night "seeker's service."

Recruiting Believers

The vision of the new church is not to steal sheep from the other churches (transfer growth), but to win sheep from the community (conversion growth). At the initial planting, however, the new church will need a group of mature believers as an important part of its foundation. This may involve some transfer growth initially. There are basically two sources of mature believers for the new core group.

The Mother Church

The first and best source of mature, committed believers is the mother church. In fact, the best way to plant a church is through the efforts of a mother church. The advantages are numerous, one of which is the provision of a core group of people.

Some mother churches are so committed to church planting that anyone in their church is subject to being recruited for service in the daughter church, even the staff. Other parent churches will either train as staff the church-planting team or provide staff members to assist the new group with certain vital ministries such as music and youth.

Christian Friends and Acquaintances

Another source of mature believers consists of the Christian friends and acquaintances of the people who make up the core group. As those who are a part of the group "catch" the vision for planting the church, they should be encouraged to share that vision with their Christian friends. The result is that others will "catch" the vision and be attracted to the new church as well.

The problem, most likely, is that these individuals will be part of another church in the community. That church may not be open to the idea of losing its people to a new church, especially if it's plateaued or in decline and hurting financially. Therefore, the new group may be criticized and accused of "sheep stealing." Perhaps one way to defuse this response would be to encourage these potential core group members to meet with their pastors and explain what's taking place and why they're getting involved in a different ministry.

The development stage involves gathering, cultivating, and growing the new core group. Its purpose is to prepare that group for the birth of the church, which is the next stage in the process of church planting. This stage is the subject of the next chapter.

A Development Stage Checklist

_____1.   Recruit a potential core group

_____2.   Communicate values, mission, vision, and strategy

_____3.   Begin core group meetings

_____4.   Implement divine design discovery

_____5.   Identify and train lay leadership

_____6.   Implement small groups

_____7.   Network through the core group

_____8.   Locate a place to meet

_____9.   Set up a bookkeeping system

___10.   Open a bank account

___11.   Determine equipment needs

___12.   Purchase and/or rent equipment

___13.   Develop an advertising strategy

___14.   Recruit teams (worship, drama, and others)

___15.   Develop a constitution and bylaws

___16.   Pursue incorporation

___17.   Network with key people in community (lost and saved)

A Development Stage Worksheet

1. What preparation needs to take place in your own life before you'll be ready to lead a core group through the development stage? Do you have the requisite skills and knowledge? For example, do you know how to conduct assessment and implement small groups? Are you prepared spiritually to lead a core group? Where and when will you get this training?

2. This chapter stresses the importance of planting a church with the help of a mother church. If you're not planning to work through a parent church, then explain why.

3. Do you see yourself as involved initially in a "cold start" or a "hot start"? What are the advantages and disadvantages of your kind of start?

4. Of the potential ways to contact believers in a community, which are feasible in your situation?

5. Think through the seven critical areas of cultivating a core group. What ideas might you add to each area?

6. How might you handle accusations of "sheep stealing" from pastors of churches in your targeted area?

16

It's a Baby!

The Birth Stage

Bill Smith and his team are excited. Things have progressed unusually well. While they've implemented a "cold start," Christians in their community have responded enthusiastically to their dream of planting a church to reach the unchurched in the Northeastern part of the United States. They quickly gathered a sizable core group of fifty adults and are currently in the stage of cultivating and growing this core group. What thrills Bill most is the fact that these people are inviting their lost friends to a "seeker-driven" Bible study, where fifteen have accepted Christ over a five-month period of time. This would bring the total to sixty-five adults. In addition, the core group has made a strong financial commitment to the new church, which has provided a decent financial package for the team.

Now it's time to ask the question, "Where does the church go from here? What's the next stage of church planting?" The answer to these questions is the birth stage. This is the stage where the new church goes "public" with its first meeting. It's at this point that the church is ready to pursue its geographical community (those in the target area) in addition to its relational community (the friends and acquaintances of its people). The primary purpose of this stage is to provide an opportunity to pursue and reach the geographical community for the Savior. From the perspective of the community, this is where the church is born. Up until this time they have probably not even been aware that there's a new church in the area. Now all that will change. The birth stage consists of five steps that are necessary to prepare for the first "public" meeting or the "birth event" of the church.

Knowing When to Start

The first step for the growing core group is knowing when to start. While much of the development stage is general preparation for the birth stage, the question is, "When does the development stage end, and the focused preparation for the 'birth event' begin?" The problem is that most start too soon. People tend not to feel that they're a church unless they're involved in a large group worship service. Resist this pressure. At least three ingredients make up the answer to this important question.

The Elapsed Time

The first ingredient involves the amount of time that has elapsed from the initial gathering of the core group to the "birth event." Much depends on whether the church was initiated with a "hot" or "cold" start.

The "Hot Start"

On the one hand, the "hot start" involves gathering a core of committed believers from a group of people who've already come together in some locale for the general purpose of starting a church. When this is the case, the development stage might be relatively short, probably three to six months. This will depend on the amount of time and preparation the planting team puts into the new work during the conception stage and any problems that might surface during the development stage.

In his book, *Church Planting for a Greater Harvest,* Pete Wagner essentially agrees with this estimate:

> It takes nine months for a human baby to develop. Experience has shown that this might be a little too long for the nucleus building phase of a new church. If the proper planning is done and a competent feasibility study produced, it is well to plan for a nucleus building phase of four to six months. A longer period might have been called for in the past when we did not have today's know-how. But any church planter who is up-to-date on the field should have the techniques to make it happen in four to six months.[1]

The "Cold Start"

The "cold start" involves gathering a core of committed believers in a community where the planting team doesn't have any prior contacts. The team will have to raise up an interested group of Christians by making a lot of initial contacts in the target community. This situation can be more difficult and may add several months to the length of the development stage.

It could take three months to a year in this situation to get to the "birth event." It will take even longer for the "lone wolf" church planter who goes into a target area and attempts to build a core group with lost people who are won to Christ. The "lone wolf" approach is not the best because New Testament ministry is team ministry and core groups need to be formed with solid, mature believers.

The Number of People

Not only is the amount of time that has elapsed during the development stage an ingredient affecting the "birth event," but the number of people who are in the core group is an important consideration as well. Veteran church planters suggest several different sizes.

Ten to Twelve Seed Families

Donald MacNair, an adjunct professor at Covenant Theological Seminary, the coordinator of Theological Education for the Presbyterian Church in America, and the director of Churches Vitalized, is a church planter and has written a book entitled *The Birth, Care, and Feeding of a Local Church*.[2] He believes that at least ten to twelve families are needed before a church can proceed with what he calls phase 2, which lasts from nine to twelve months.[3]

This was excellent advice for those who were planting churches in the 1950s through the early 1970s when MacNair wrote his book. At that time, America was a churched culture and it was easier to gather an interested core group of people. Today the culture is predominantly unchurched and people are slower to respond. Consequently, if the core group desires to grow and reach a lot of people for Christ, it should wait until it's larger before it attempts the "birth event." Most likely, ten to twelve seed families will not be enough people to "staff" the various positions needed to accomplish the first "public" meeting.

Fifty to One Hundred Adults

In *Church Planting for a Greater Harvest*, church growth expert Peter Wagner suggests that the church needs to decide how large it wants to grow. If it desires to grow larger than 200 people, then it should have from 50 to 100 adults in the core group before it goes public. He writes, "If the long-range plan for the church is to be under 200, the critical mass can be as small as 25 or 30 adults. However, if the plan is for the church to grow to over 200 that is too small. The critical mass should be between 50 and 100 adults."[4]

You must keep in mind that some variables could make a difference in this figure. One is the geographical location of the new church. An urban church plant would require a larger core group, whereas a rural plant might allow for fewer people. Wagner indicates that another variable is the group's "collar color." He writes, "There may well be many variables that determine ideal nucleus size, but I am so far aware of only one study. It suggests that for a blue-collar, working-class church you can start near the lower end of the range, but for a professional, white-collar church you do better toward the top part of the range."[5]

More Than Fifty People

Wagner cites some research from the Southern Baptists that indicates that the size of the core group at birth may affect the new church's ultimate survival. He writes, "Research by the Southern Baptist Home Mission Board has shown that Southern Baptist churches going public with under 50 have three times the rate of failure as those that start with over 50. It wouldn't surprise me if this applied to most other denominations as well."[6]

Jim Dethmer, a former pastor at Willow Creek Community Church in northwest Chicago, says that if you desire to plant a seeker-driven church as Willow Creek has done, then you need more than fifty people. He advises that seeker-driven churches need at least one hundred people in the core group, a sizeable church-planting team in place, and from $100,000 to $150,000 in the bank.

The Conclusion

The conclusion from all this information and research is the general rule: *the bigger the better.* Critical mass is essential. If you want to break through the 200 barrier and other growth barriers (which is the position of this book), you need a minimum of fifty adults before you go "public." And the more people you have in the core group beyond fifty adults, the better your chances are of reaching a significant number of lost people for the Savior.

The Particular Sunday

A final ingredient that can help in determining when the core group is ready to have its first public meeting is the particular Sunday on which that event will be scheduled. Over the years, it's become evident that certain Sundays on the calendar are better than others for attracting unchurched people from the target community.

Easter Sunday

Unchurched people are more likely to go to church at certain times of the year. While this may vary from community to community, good times are Christmas, Mother's Day, possibly Father's Day, and Easter. Of these four, one of the best has proved to be Easter Sunday. Many church planters have concluded that if a lost, unchurched person is going to go to church at all, then the most likely time is Easter. This may be because Easter is observed internationally as well as nationally and people are given time off from work or school. At this time, their thoughts often turn naturally to spiritual matters.

Since this is the case in so many communities across America, a good time to have the first public "birth meeting" is on Easter Sunday. The church could mark Easter Sunday on its calendar and then go back three to six months if it's a "hot start" or longer if it's a "cold start." This would help the church-planting team determine when they might want to gather the initial core group and the length of time for the development stage.

A Special Sunday

If Easter Sunday isn't feasible, another approach is to create a special Sunday and have the "birth event" on that Sunday instead. This could take place on practically any Sunday on the calendar except those covered in the next category. We implemented this strategy at the last church I pastored. In order to give our people an opportunity to invite their lost, unchurched friends to our church, we held what we called a "Fall Harvest" and a "Spring Celebration." We advertised these two events and planned for lots of food, fun, and fellowship. The result was an excitement in the air and a lot of new faces in the pews.

There are numerous other possibilities. For example, some churches feature a "Celebration of Friendship" Sunday to which everyone brings a person who's a friend and a part of their relational community. Other churches might invite a special speaker such as a radio, television, or sports personality. Some will feature a contemporary Christian music group. In fact, the only limit on what you can program is your imagination.

Holiday Sundays

While Easter Sunday may be the best time for the first public meeting of the new church, several other Sundays have proved to be the worst times for this meeting. Some of these Sundays fall on holiday weekends. When a holiday falls on a Monday, the three-day weekend becomes an ideal time to take a trip. Consequently, people often leave town or tend to stay at home. The worst Sundays for the "birth event" tend to be Memorial Day, Veteran's Day, Thanksgiving, Superbowl Sunday, and July 4.

Other bad Sundays in particular are "time change" Sundays. These are the Sundays each year that are affected by daylight-savings time. We either set our clocks forward or backward to allow for the time change. Most have found this to be a low attendance Sunday in their churches.

Choosing a Name

Another step in preparing for the first "public" meeting is the naming of the church. Many new church starts will do this as early as the conception or development stages. The point here is that if the church hasn't yet selected a name, now is the time to do so.

Some will delay this decision because they don't believe that choosing a name for the church is important. Using one of his characters, Shakespeare once asked, "What's in a name?" The answer in church planting is, "Everything!" Enough research has been done to indicate that people, even unchurched people, pay attention to church names. A number of factors should be considered.

The Target Group

One factor to consider in choosing a name for a church is the target group or the people whom the church has singled out for evangelism. The setting in which the group and the church are located will influence this.

An Urban Setting

Presently, denominational labels such as Baptist, Methodist, Presbyterian, and Episcopal have not attracted people in an urban setting. Whereas denominational loyalty was strong in the 1940s and 1950s, it was not in the 1990s. Some predict that the early twenty-first century will be a postdenominational age. People, especially Baby Boomers and Busters, are more interested in what churches have to offer them than in denominational affiliation.

In fact, in some unchurched areas of the country, such as the Northeast, the Northwest, and the West Coast, denominational affiliation can work against a new church. Saddleback Valley Community Church near Los Angeles, California, is a Southern Baptist church. However, many of the unchurched who attend don't know this. One of my students planted a Southern Baptist Church in Washington State. He used "Baptist" in the name but removed it a year later because of the negative effect it had in the unchurched community.

A Rural Setting

What we have just observed about church names in an urban community may be reversed in many rural communities, especially in the South. One of my students wrote a master's thesis on planting churches in rural east Texas. He discovered that people there viewed churches without denominational affiliation as either charismatic or a cult.

The Community

Another factor to consider in choosing a name for the church is the particular community in which it's located. The church may want to use the same name in combination with the term "community." For example, the Southern Baptist church mentioned above, Saddleback Valley Community Church, is located in the Saddleback Valley area around Mission Viejo, California. Another example is Willow Creek Community Church. The church I pastor is Northwood Community Church. Using the term "community" was very popular in the 1980s and 1990s across denominational lines. It communicates warmly and inoffensively in unchurched areas of the country and imparts a sense of identity with the actual community.

Some Suggestions

First, if your desire is to reach lost people and unchurched lost in particular, then you might want to consult with them regarding a church name. Initially, put yourself in their shoes and create names that would appeal to them. Once you and your people have decided on several, ask some unchurched lost people which names they would choose and why. This should prove most illuminating.

Second, keep the name as short as possible. It should be easy to spell and pronounce. An exception might be a name that's commonly known in the area such as the name of a community or a major road or highway.

Third, be careful to avoid names that could alienate people. Some names are pejorative.

Fourth, while there's no reason to be ashamed of what you believe, it's wise not to put your doctrinal statement in your name. For example, avoid names such as Faith Independent Closed Communion Predestinarian Bible Baptist Church, Pentecostal Fire-Baptized Holiness Church, or the First

Two-Seed-in-the-Spirit Predestinarian Baptist Church. Most unchurched people don't care what you believe. They care more about who you are!

An exception might be some rural areas where pride and tradition are important parts of the people's religious heritage. An example would be the hills and mountains of southern Tennessee where people have historically been Southern Baptists and Freewill Baptists.

Fifth, don't use names that have potential to be misunderstood. These could be names that those who've been Christians for a long period of time might recognize but an unbeliever wouldn't. One example would be the use of the term "Catholic" in the name of a Protestant church such as Zion Catholic Church or Redeemer Catholic Church. Another example is the use of the term "reform." Some people hear this term and the first thing that comes to mind is a reform school.

Other names that can be misunderstood are Mennonite, Moravian, and, even in some cases, Evangelical Free Church. Not that there's anything wrong with these names! In many cases each has a rich heritage that's traceable back to Europe and a group of Christians who held to the faith in spite of intense religious persecution. Again, the issue is how an unbeliever responds to these names. Would some not come to our churches because of the name? In an area of Christian liberty such as the name of a church, we as mature believers must be willing to defer to the lost people we're attempting to reach. If our name unnecessarily offends or brings a negative response, then there are too many other good names we could adopt in order not to make this an issue.

One final term that appears in some names is "metropolitan." This term is often used in urban areas in an attempt to include a large number of people. But churches that use the term "metropolitan" should be aware that there's a group of homosexual churches that commonly use the name Metropolitan Community Church.

Finally, there are some names that have the potential to communicate negative impressions. One example is the term "memorial," which may be used of a church that's named in memory of a person. The problem here is that it reminds unchurched people of death or even a memorial service for someone who's just died.

Another example is the name of a church that I spotted one day on a drive through rural East Texas. Apparently, a Baptist pastor, Paul Powell, who's from that part of Texas, also spotted the same sign. I'll let Paul tell you the story.

> But many of our churches mirror the despair of the age rather than proclaim the hope. I was driving down the highway the other day and saw a sign with

an arrow pointed down a country road that said, "Little Hope Baptist Church—3 miles." I thought to myself, My soul, I'm glad I'm not the pastor of that church. If I were, my first action would be to start a movement to change its name. I would have them call it: "Big Hope Baptist Church" or "New Hope Baptist Church," or "Living Hope Baptist Church," or "Coming Hope Baptist Church" or "Everlasting Hope Baptist Church," or "Glorious Hope Baptist Church," or "Flaming Hope Baptist Church"—anything but "Little Hope Baptist Church."[7]

Now to be completely fair to this little church, someone told me that it's located in a small rural community called Little Hope. In this situation, the name doesn't sound so bad except to those who live outside the community of Little Hope. However, in terms of reaching the lost in general, Powell makes the point as he continues the story.

The only name worse than "Little Hope Baptist Church" would be "No Hope Baptist Church." That's exactly what many of our churches are presenting to the world today: little or no hope. . . . If we hold up hope, our despairing world can be reached.[8]

Locating a Place to Meet

Along with knowing when to start and choosing a name, the new work will need to locate a place suitable to hold its first public meeting and its subsequent meetings.

The Characteristics of a Location

In church planting and church renewal, there are a number of characteristics that should be thought through in terms of site selection. It would be a shame if people avoided a church because of a lack of one of these characteristics. Use these characteristics as a checklist to be reviewed quarterly if not monthly.

Appearance

A critical characteristic of a good facility is its appearance. It affects two groups of people.

The core group. A facility's appearance affects congregational self-esteem. Most people view their church and its facilities as a reflection on themselves, and in many ways it is. People intuitively want what they identify with to look good, whether it's their cars, houses, or church facilities. When they don't, it may indicate that the people themselves are struggling in their present situation. They may have lost their sense of pride and don't care anymore.

Some people in a church with declining facilities get used to leaks in the roof and peeling paint on the walls. They learn to tolerate these conditions. However, others in the church don't. Consequently, when there's a big push to invite their friends to the services, they politely say, "No thanks." They'd be too embarrassed, especially the young people. They don't want their lost friends to see where they go to church. While they may understand, their lost friends wouldn't.

Lost people. The other group who is affected is lost people. Keep in mind that many of today's unchurched lost have high expectations due to the pursuit of excellence in the marketplace and the media. If the facilities are in poor condition, they simply will not come, or they'll come only once and reject the message because they reject the facilities.

A good approach in selecting the facility is to see it through "lost eyes." We must ask ourselves the question, "What would lost people in our target group expect when they arrive at our church on Sunday morning or Saturday night? If they were responding to a direct mail campaign, would they take one look at our facility and drive back home, or would they stop and come in?"

Visibility

The visibility of the building is a second characteristic that affects location. Can the building be seen? When people drive by, can they see the facility? Sometimes the storefront church simply blends in with all the other storefronts.

What can a church do to gain greater visibility? It should attempt to locate in a place where it's not simply one of many buildings. A location along an expressway is ideal because the building can be seen by all who use that expressway every day. Often a sign will help. It can catch people's attention and direct it in a positive way toward the building.

Accessibility

Whereas the second characteristic concerns seeing the building, the third concerns finding the building. How easy is it for people to locate the facility? The ideal location would be near a major artery such as an expressway or a busy road. The church would be both easy to see and easy to locate. While this may appear to be a major obstacle for the new church in terms of cost, keep in mind that at this stage you're renting, not purchasing facilities. Consequently, there's a good chance that you can rent a building such as a public school or a place in a shopping center that's quite accessible to the community.

Size

The facility and grounds should be the right size for the vision of the core group. The building must be large enough to hold a significant number of people (one to four hundred or five hundred) who might respond to a mailer. At the same time, if it's too large, people will feel overwhelmed by the facility. They will develop a feeling of insignificance.

Ezra Earl Jones recommends that a church consider locating on three to five acres depending on its growth goals. He believes that three acres are adequate for a church of eight hundred to one thousand members. If it expects to grow larger, then he recommends five acres.[9] The need to provide adequate parking affects much of this. Consequently, with the ability of telemarketing to attract lots of people and today's transportation-oriented culture where many families have at least two cars, it is preferable to rent a building on approximately three to five acres.

Why so big when the group is small? The church may stay in rented facilities for three to five years. It is best that it not have to move too many times during this period. The church needs to have enough room for future expansion.

Cleanliness

Cleanliness isn't next to godliness, cleanliness is godliness! Dirty facilities reflect negatively on a congregation. Pastor Bill Hybels of Willow Creek Community Church believes this is so important that not only are the facilities regularly cleaned each week, but nicks and scratches are repaired and painted as well.

There are two areas to focus on in particular. They're the nursery and the women's bathrooms. As new parents, one of the first things that my wife and I checked in a church was its nursery facilities. And the number one thing we looked for was its cleanliness. I've heard horror stories of rat droppings on the floors and roaches crawling across soiled linen in the cribs! No parents would want to leave their baby in such a situation. Consequently, it would be foolish to expect the same of sophisticated unchurched people. The other area is the women's bathrooms. These, like the nursery, must be immaculate.

Location

An obvious but often overlooked characteristic of a temporary facility is its location in the community. Someone in the business world once said that the three most important elements for a successful business are location, location, and location! The simple rule in church planting is that you must locate in a building that's in your target community. If a church desires to be identified with a particular community, it must locate in that community.

The church also needs to take into consideration the location of the people in the core group. While they should be willing to be flexible and perhaps drive a little farther, they shouldn't be inconvenienced. In fact, some of the lost people who'll come to the new church will be from the core community's neighborhoods—especially if it's a new area.

The church should also be alert to any nuisances in the area. There could be an airport nearby that often diverts its traffic over the church building, making it difficult to hear on Sunday mornings. Also, there could be a pharmaceutical plant or a paper mill in the area that emits noxious odors. The way to find out about these possible problems is to ask people who live or work in the area near the building under consideration.

Potential Programs

A seventh characteristic is how conducive the physical plant is to the planned programs of the church. A building should be evaluated in terms of its possibilities for a nursery, classrooms, and worship.

Every church must have a nursery for infants and small children. Is there a room that could function well as a nursery? Does it look and smell clean, and would it be easy to keep clean? Churches must also provide some rooms for Christian education. People are most concerned about what kind of education their children are getting in church. They often decide for or against a church on this basis. Finally, is there adequate space for congregational worship? Will people be able to see and hear well? Are the lighting and acoustics adequate?

Cost

Sometimes churches fail to take into account all the expenses involved in renting and using a building for their meetings. They may look at the rental costs alone and fail to anticipate other costs. For example, what will the utilities cost? What is an adequate amount of insurance? What renovations will be necessary to prepare the building for church services? Is the sound system adequate? Will cribs, tables, chairs, and other items have to be purchased? All of these factors—and more—must be taken into consideration.

Storage

A ninth characteristic that is often overlooked by church planters is adequate storage space. Often churches are started in buildings such as schools, where folding chairs, cribs, portable signs, and tables must be put away after the services are over. If adequate on-site storage is not available, then what does the church do? Usually, most facilities have some room available; however, it's best to discuss this with the landlord and reach an agreement before moving into the facility. Some landlords have a way of dragging their feet after a contract has been signed.

Should there be no on-site storage space, there are some other alternatives. One is to obtain permission to place a small portable building on the site. Another would involve the purchase of a vehicle such as a midsize truck, which could be used for storage and to transport the contents to the building each Sunday. Of course, either alternative would involve additional cost to the new church.

Signs

Not only is it important to advertise the church, but it must have some way of identifying itself visually in the community, if not during the week, then at least on Sunday mornings. One of the ways most churches accomplish this is with a sign.

There are several ways that a new church can accomplish this in temporary facilities.

Build a sign. One is to build a collapsible wooden sign. In my first church plant, we put together two four-by-eight feet sheets of plywood with hinges at the top and legs at the bottom. A sign painter volunteered his time, and we had a sign. On Sunday mornings, we simply lifted it out of storage, and placed it in front of the building where we met. After the service, we reversed the process and placed the sign back in storage until next Sunday.

Purchase a sign. Another approach is to purchase a vinyl or canvas sign. Most sign shops have the capability to produce these at a reasonable price. There are several advantages. The first is storage; all you have to do is carefully roll it up. You could even keep it in the trunk of someone's car. Another is placement. You can place signs anywhere. Some churches mount the canvas on two poles and put the sign out by the road so everyone who passes by sees it. Others will drape them over the sign for the building in which they're meeting. For example, if it's a school, then on Sunday morning, place the vinyl over the sign for the school so that, in effect, their sign becomes your sign for the morning or evening.

Parking

Another factor to consider is parking. The size of the entire facility and grounds should be big enough to include adequate parking. Sometimes those in the target group may drive two or even three cars to church on Sunday morning: his, hers, and the kids! If people can't find a place to park their cars, then they'll not attend the church. Most will drive through the lot, and if no parking spaces are available, they'll drive back home. Some people are nervous and are looking for reasons to talk themselves out of coming to church. Let's not make it easy for them by failing to provide adequate parking!

Several alternatives exist for facilities with small parking lots. Sometimes the best facility doesn't provide adequate parking. When this is the case, ask the core group to park in the remote areas and leave those spaces close to the building for guests. Another alternative is to ask core group families to come in one car and park it in a lot adjacent to or nearby the facility. Finally, the core group could park some distance from the building, and a van could shuttle people back and forth.

Reputation

The twelfth characteristic of a good location is the facility's reputation in the community. You may question this one, so I must tell you a story. When I first accepted Christ in college, I attended a new, small church that was located in a rented facility that obviously had been built originally for a church. This new church didn't grow, and hardly anyone in the neighborhood came to any of the services. Later, we learned that every bizarre religious group that came to town rented and used this facility. The neighborhood was suspicious of us for good reasons.

Before renting a facility, especially a former church building or a public community center that's located in a neighborhood, ask the people living near the building about its past history and occupants. Some locations are haunted by the "ghosts of Christmas past," to borrow a line from Charles Dickens.

The Prospects for a Location

One of the questions that all church planters need to ask is, "What are some potential places where our church could meet until we find a permanent facility?" There are several possibilities, all of which are affected by the church's vision and strategy and its target group.

A School Building

In *44 Questions for Church Planters,* Lyle Schaller indicates that public schools are one of the three most commonly used temporary places for new mission churches.[10]

The reason for this is obvious. Most schools are set up to provide the various facilities that a church needs. There's usually an auditorium for large group congregational worship and lots of classroom space for a Christian education program. However, there are some disadvantages to using a school building. One is that some school districts will allow the church to use their facilities only for a limited period of time, often one year. Another is that the church will not be able to use the building during the week. This results in having to "set up" and "take down" certain things each week, such as chairs, cribs, or a sound system. Also, it could mean renting other facilities for office space during the week at extra cost to the church.

A Church Building

Another possibility is using or renting a church building.[11] A number of ethnic church plants meet on Sunday afternoons in an existing church's facilities. If the existing church is the mother church, then there may be no cost involved for the daughter church.

Another possibility is to rent the facilities of a church such as the Seventh Day Adventists who meet on Saturdays. There are several advantages to this approach. One is the available facilities such as the nursery, auditorium, and classrooms. Others would be the advantages of parking and a sound system. Some disadvantages could be a possible bad reputation in the neighborhood on the part of the church that owns the building, a location that's not close enough to that of the target group, the design of the building itself, and a poorly maintained facility.

A Public Center

Public centers include recreation centers, community centers, or day care centers. These centers usually are very open to renting their buildings or rooms to churches, especially those that are privately owned. Also, most people in the community are aware of their locations.

There are some disadvantages. Often public facilities are difficult to clean and maintain. Each group that rents the facility may be responsible to clean up after themselves; consequently, the facility may be poorly cleaned if at all. Also, these centers are not always set up conveniently for the church in terms of a place for a nursery and a large group meeting. In addition, there may be inadequate parking space, and the church might have to purchase its own sound system.

A Storefront

Often a good choice for the location of the new church is a storefront, especially one that's located in a shopping mall in the center of the target community. These malls are usually frequented by young and old alike. They provide the church with lots of visibility in the area because of the location and because the church has use of the front during the week as well as on weekends. The church could minister to the community by offering special programs during the week such as counseling services or a neighborhood crime watch. The only disadvantage might be the cost.

A Movie Theater

Another good option is a movie theater. This will provide an auditorium with a stage, screen, and sound system already in place. Also, theaters are often located in shopping malls where there's high visibility and lots of parking. Schaller notes that some theaters contain several rooms of different sizes that can be used as the church grows larger.[12] The disadvantages are the lack of space for a nursery and a Christian education program. Also, the new church will not have the use of the facility during the week, and its time of use would be limited to Sunday mornings prior to the start of the first show.

Several churches have used theaters in the past. One example is Willow Creek Community Church. One of its early meeting places was in a theater in Palatine, which is located near Chicago, Illinois. One of my friends has begun a church in an older, well-known fine arts theater located near a university in the downtown area of Denton, Texas. They call the new church "Sunday Morning on the Square." They've cleverly used this location in all their advertising to attract the unchurched in the community. For instance, one of their mailers looks like a piece of film and contains the following: "If life has you feeling like a rebel without a cause, check out the new feature at the Fine Arts Theater." Another says, "If your life's dreams seem to be gone with the wind, check out the new feature at the Fine Arts Center."

Other Possibilities

New churches have sometimes used hotels, motels, bank buildings, YMCAs and YWCAs, and funeral homes. Each of these have both advantages and disadvantages. Perhaps the most questionable facility is the funeral home. On the one hand, they have some excellent facilities for congregational worship because so many have chapels. On the other, the idea of meeting in a funeral home could discourage a significant number of unchurched people who are looking for an excuse not to attend. However, a clever marketing ministry in the church might be able to use a location in a funeral home to the church's advantage much as the Denton church plant used the Fine Arts Center.

Publicizing the Meeting

If the new church is going to have an impact for the Savior in its target community, then it will have to make its presence known to that community. A fourth step in preparing for the "birth event" is publicizing the meeting. Far too many established churches fail to make their presence in the community known to the unchurched. They assume people know they're there. This, of course, wouldn't apply to the church plant because it doesn't as yet own a permanent facility for people to drive by.

So what does the new church do? This is where marketing and advertising come in. The primary purpose for the birth stage is to encourage and help a church with an "invasion mentality" to reach to its community. There are two primary ways to accomplish this.

Reaching the Geographical Community

The first and primary way is to publicize the church in its geographical community. In order to accomplish this, the church will need to have a strategy and a method.

The Strategy

The church-planting team is already aware of the importance of publicizing the new plant in the target community and has made a decision to do so in the conception stage. Early in the development stage, the team will need to develop a strategy as to how the new work will publicize itself in the community.

The problem. One of the problems that churches which have adopted the "birth event" approach have experienced is a sizable drop-off factor. They'll advertise the opening day event and spend a lot of money doing so with the result that a considerable number of unchurched people in the community will show up. The problem is that a significant number, as many as one-third to one-half and even more, don't come back the following Sunday![13]

They haven't been offended by the gospel or the sermon. Rather, they simply aren't in the habit of going to church! That's one of the reasons why they're unchurched! Those with a "herd mentality" who do return the following Sunday wonder what happened to all the people and might not come back themselves the third Sunday.

Some solutions. The team must develop a strategy that encourages people to come back the following Sunday as well. One strategy that doesn't work is to attempt each Sunday to top what took place the previous Sunday. For example, "We had a great day last Sunday, but wait until you hear who'll be here next Sunday!" This appeals to the wrong motives, and it's just a matter of time before the entire strategy crashes.

Rather than pour all of its efforts alone into one meeting on the first Sunday, the church should focus attention on the first three or four Sundays. An example of one church that did this is Kensington Community Church near Detroit, Michigan. On the first Sunday, the church attracted people in the community through newspaper ads and a direct mail campaign. But it didn't stop there. Early in the following week, it passed out numerous brochures in the target community located around the church's facility publicizing the next Sunday. Finally, the church asked their core group to invite the people in their relational communities to come on the third Sunday. To some degree this helped minimize the drop-off problem.

Another technique is to encourage people who visit to return on the following Sunday. There are several ways to accomplish this. One is to invite them verbally to return next Sunday. At the end of the service, you could say, "If you enjoyed the service today, and God used the message to touch your life, then why don't you come back next Sunday?" You might add the following: "If you think you might need a reminder, then leave us your phone number on the card in your bulletin, and we'll give you a quick call on Friday or Saturday."

Another way is to preach a short series of sermons on a highly relevant, need-oriented topic. The first Sunday you begin the series and invite everyone to come back for the second part in the series. Perhaps you could leave something hanging at the end of the sermon that will be resolved the next Sunday. You could work in a story that raises a conflict that will be resolved the next week. This might also be accomplished with drama.

An additional technique is to celebrate the birth event on Palm Sunday, one week before Easter. The very fact that the following Sunday is Easter might encourage the unchurched to return. You could remind them that next Sunday is Easter and encourage them to come back for the second part of the series of sermons you've just begun.

The Method

Once the team has developed a strategy, it will need to decide on the methods it will use to implement the strategy. The Kensington Community Church, for example, selected three methods to accomplish their strategy of bringing people back on successive Sundays: newspaper ads, a direct mailing, and a hand-delivered brochure.

The two methods that seem to reach the greatest number of people are direct mail and telemarketing.

Some favor using direct mail because it doesn't require a large core group and it's screened demographically to avoid those who are not in the target group. The church could send a letter to the community, or pass out a brochure about the church or a birth announcement similar to that parents sent out to announce a new baby. One great disadvantage is the cost of the program, and another is the possibility that the post office may not deliver the mail at the right time.

The team might prefer to use a telemarketing program instead of direct mail. Key factors in making this decision are the cost, the community, and the core group.

If the new church isn't able to reduce the costs of a telemarketing program by the use of a phone bank or a significant discount from a printer, then the program may not be cost-effective.

Some communities have been over-telemarketed. Thus, people in these areas don't respond well to a phone call, especially if it comes during the evening meal. They view it as an invasion of their privacy!

The core group may not be large enough to make all the calls necessary. The average response to a telemarketing campaign is one person per one hundred calls. Consequently, if the church's goal is to have two hundred people at the first service, it will have to make twenty thousand phone calls. If a group of volunteers could make one thousand calls in an evening, it would take twenty evenings to make all the necessary calls. A small group of people would quickly burn out in attempting to accomplish this.

Advertising in the newspaper is another favorite method for publicizing the church in the target community. The ad would need to be placed in the part of the paper that the target group reads. Cost would also be a factor. However, it's possible that the local paper would feature a story on the church and run it the week prior to the "birth event." This would be free publicity. The article should appear in some place other than the religious section of the paper if you're targeting lost and/or unchurched people—they tend not to read the "church page."

Reaching the Relational Community

While the primary emphasis is usually placed on reaching the geographical community, the church may also use this event to reach its relational community as well. This, too, consists of a strategy and a methodology. Now is a good time for core group people to invite those in their relational communities to visit the church.

The Strategy

An important part of the church's strategy for reaching unchurched lost people is to encourage its core group to pursue their lost friends. The church can't reach its target community simply by using a direct mail or telemarketing approach alone. The people who make up the church must develop significant relationships with those in their relational communities. Some churches use this approach as the primary means for contacting and reaching lost people. In fact, it's the best approach for long-term results. Most churches may use a mailer or telemarketing approach at the beginning, but eventually use these strategies less as they grow. The one approach that can be used throughout the life of the church is individual members reaching their relational communities.

Early in the development stage, the church-planting team will need to impart the vision for reaching nonchurched lost people. Next, they'll need to help the core group develop a strategy to accomplish this. The five-step strategy found in chapter 12 on evangelism is an excellent one. It focuses on those who make up people's relational communities (family, co-workers, and neighbors). These are the most natural prospects for evangelism and the easiest to reach. The five steps are the following: examine the relational community, develop a "hit list," pray for those on the list, cultivate a relationship with them, and discover their needs and look for times of receptivity. All of this could culminate with an invitation to the "birth event."

The Method

The core group can use various methods in developing significant relationships with the lost people in their communities.

Mutual participation. One involves doing things together. Our tendency is not to spend any time with lost people because their lifestyles are so different from our own. We simply don't feel comfortable around them, so we avoid them as much as possible. The core group will need to get over this and pursue and spend time with these people. They should do things together, like jogging, aerobics, cooking, sewing, traveling, and dining.

Open homes. Another method is to invite these people into our homes for coffee or to share a meal together. This could be preliminary to doing other things together. They would be able to use this time to discover what they have in common and might enjoy doing together. The conversation might go like this: "Bill, you enjoy playing golf? Well, so do I. Let's get out and hit some balls together. What are you doing this Saturday?"

Other methods. Some other methods involve helping people in the community during times of personal need, involvement in mutual events such as neighborhood clean up, or inviting them to an informal Bible study or MOPS event at your house. Pastor Steve Sjogren provides over three hundred such events in his book entitled *Conspiracy of Kindness*. Actually, the only limit to these methods is the creativity of the core group.

Planning the Meeting

The first meeting and the ensuing meetings are so important that you should plan them carefully. While this may not be the last step, it must be one of the steps in the birth stage. This is because first impressions are lasting impressions. This planning should focus on at least four areas.

Focus on the Service

The team and the church should place extra effort into planning the service because the Sunday morning worship service is what most people in the community will attend. It will serve as the litmus test as to whether people will come back the next week.

The Sermon

The sermon must be a word from God that addresses the audience in terms of its felt needs. It must also be relevant and interesting. It could be the first of a three- or four-part series. An example would be a three-part series entitled "Dealing with the Three Deadly Emotions: Stress, Anger, and Depression." The first sermon would be entitled "The Solution to Stress." The second would be "How to Defuse Your Fuse," and the last one "How to Defeat Depression." Such sermons should be based squarely on the Scriptures and can serve as "hooks" to bring people back next Sunday.

The Music

The music must be done well. Only the best musicians and vocalists from the core group or a parent church should be included in the service. A professional performer could be invited to perform at this meeting in light of its importance. The degree to which this event is targeting lost, nonchurched people (seeker-driven) will determine audience participation. Most unchurched people aren't used to singing and come more to "check things out" than to worship. (However, note that David viewed worship as an opportunity to reach others—Pss. 40:2; 57:9.) Consequently, most of the singing could take place up front on the stage and should be performed by accomplished vocalists.

The Drama

Like the music, if you choose to use drama, it should be performed well. The use of a good four- to six-minute mini-drama to introduce the sermon will surprise and delight most unchurched people. The worship team should rehearse several times with everyone present, including the sound person.

Don't try to do too much in the service. The more you attempt, the greater the likelihood that something will go wrong. A few events done well are better than many events poorly done.

The Greeters

Locate greeters in at least two places. Some could stand in the parking area and direct people to the front entrance of the building. Keep in mind that they're the first people associated with the church whom the guests will see. They must smile and be friendly. If the crowd is large enough, they may need to direct traffic. Other greeters should stand at the entryway to the building where they smile, shake hands, greet people, hand out bulletins, and give directions. It would be most helpful if several people are available to take parents with infants and young children to the nursery.

Focus on the Facility

Everyone should make a special effort to arrive early. Make sure the facilities are spotless. If you anticipate a problem, then bring some cleaning equipment. Check out the auditorium, the bathrooms, and the nursery. Also, determine how well the sound equipment is functioning. The service depends to a great degree on everything operating efficiently. A lot of failures are due to faulty equipment.

Also, determine if you can use the facility in some way to enhance the "birth event." For instance, if the facility has one, then it's a nice touch to serve coffee and possibly donuts in the foyer. Station some people there so that they can meet other people and answer their questions about the church and its programs. Also, you could set up an information booth or table in the foyer. Finally, be prepared for any facility emergencies. Chances are good that something will go wrong!

Focus on the Nursery

You want to reach young couples and most of them will have small children. Therefore, you have no choice but to provide a nursery for their children. Remember that the parents will be paying close attention to the condition of the nursery. They'll be asking questions such as, "Is the nursery clean?" "Is the nursery safe?" "Do they have enough workers to watch all the kids?" "Are the workers friendly and do they love children?" "Do I feel good about leaving my infant or child here while I'm in the service?" If you have a registered nurse in the church, ask that she or he be available or even serve in the nursery. Also, advertise her or his presence so that couples are aware of it. It will make a significant difference in their attitude about leaving their child in the care of the nursery.

Focus on Children's Ministries

If the church has a Christian education program that will be advertised and attended by the children of unchurched couples, then plan to do more than just baby-sit them. It's important that children have classes specifically designed for them. The church will look ridiculous if it advertises programs for all the family but can't provide for children. Whether or not the family returns the following week may depend on how well their children liked the classes. Often parents ask their children three questions: "Did you like it?" "Did you learn anything?" "Do you want to go back?"

Some church planters conclude that once they've completed the birth stage they're no longer a planted church. Yet there is a fourth stage in church planting: the growth stage. It's essential that churches that want to influence a significant number of unchurched lost people in their target communities focus on growth following the birth stage.

A Birth Stage Worksheet

1. In light of the information covered in this chapter, when is the best time for your church to start? Is it a "cold start" or a "hot start"? How many people will you want in your core group? What is the best Sunday for you to begin? If you've chosen Easter Sunday, have you considered starting the Sunday before Easter?

2. Have you chosen a name for the new church? If not, when will you choose a name? If you have, what is it? Is it a good name in light of the factors mentioned in this chapter? Why or why not?

3. Have you found a location for the church? If not, when do you plan to locate a potential site? If you have, what kind of grade (A–F) would you give the location according to the twelve characteristics in this chapter?

4. In light of your budget, how will you publicize the "birth event" in your community? Do you have any ideas on how you will encourage new, unchurched people to return the following Sundays?

5. Have you developed a strategy to reach your relational community? If not, when will you do this? If you have, what are some of the methods you'll use?

6. Have you thought through the four areas regarding the planning of the first meeting? What applies to your situation and what doesn't? What might you add to this section?

17

Feed Them and They Grow!

The Growth Stage

"Three hundred people actually showed up at our first meeting!" exclaimed Robert Andrews, one of the new church's promising lay leaders. "I expected a decent crowd, but not that many people." It wasn't that anyone doubted that God could do it. The question was, would He do it for them? But it happened. The new church sent out thirty thousand mailers and three hundred people from the target community responded—approximately one percent. Nobody could believe it! Nobody, that is, but Bill Smith and the church-planting team. The team and a number of lay leaders had gathered together at a restaurant after the "birth service" for a late lunch to celebrate what God had done. There was a lot of back slapping and hand shaking. Everyone had smiles on their faces. A sense of destiny hung in the air, a feeling that God was going to do something big in the community through these people in this church.

The core group had grown from sixty-five to ninety people. Some were Christians who came because they liked the vision. They had lots of lost friends whom they wanted to see come to Christ. Some were lost people who accepted Christ through the ministry of the "seeker's Bible study." These ninety people launched the first public meeting of the church and were simply delighted at the response. They were aware that not everyone would be back the following Sunday; yet they anticipated another good crowd because it would be Easter Sunday and many of their unchurched friends indicated they would come for Easter. But what will happen after Easter? The church is off to a good start in the community, but what will sustain its growth? What is to keep it from plateauing at around two hundred people?

The next stage in the church-planting process is the growth stage. While numerically growing churches may not necessarily be healthy, most healthy churches are growing numerically. Numerical growth isn't the goal or mission of a Great Commission church; it's the byproduct of a Great Commission mission.

You must understand from the very outset that leaders in general and church planters in particular can't make a church grow. That is God's work. The biblical principle is that some will plant and others will water, but God makes churches grow (Mark 4:26-29; 1 Cor. 3:5–7).

The growth stage is a critical time in the church's life that will determine its ultimate size in terms of numbers. The church will either reach a certain level—the 200 barrier—and plateau, or it will push through this barrier and continue to grow. There are certain growth factors that church planters and their teams should be aware of that will help their churches to continue healthy growth and minimize growth inhibitors. This chapter covers six of these church growth factors, most of which have already been intentionally implemented in the earlier stages. This chapter isn't meant to be an exhaustive treatise on church growth. The goal is to cover four of the more important church growth principles and two that may be overlooked. All of the principles are important to planted churches.[1]

Leadership for Growth

Leadership is a critical factor for growing churches, whether newly planted or established. This leadership includes not only the senior pastor but the church-planting team and the church's lay leadership as well. Leadership begins with the senior pastor or point person on the team. If this individual isn't in favor of growth, then it simply will not happen. But what kind of point people are favorable toward growth? Who are they, and what must they do to facilitate church growth?

Who Grows Churches?

Gifts

Several spiritual gifts naturally facilitate growth, and they're found in most pastors of growing churches.

Leadership. The first is the gift of leadership (Rom. 12:8). Peter Wagner writes, "But I have observed that pastors who tend toward being leaders, whether or not they also are administrators, will most likely be church growth pastors."[2] Leaders have vision that provides a sense of direction and the motivation to move in that direction.

These pastors not only have the gift of leadership, but they are also strong servant-leaders. They do not work under a lay elder or deacon board, but lead these boards as leaders of leaders. That's why they are "point persons." Lyle Schaller has made the same observation: "The pastor must be willing to accept and fill a strong leadership role and serve as the number-one leader in the congregation."[3]

Faith. Another spiritual gift is faith (1 Cor. 12:9). This gift is not exactly the same as vision but it enhances the visionary capacity of Christian leadership. Wagner believes that faith is so important to church growth that he devotes an entire chapter to it in *Your Church Can Grow.*[4] Faith helps pastors want the church to grow and believe that it will. Faith overcomes the fear of failure and helps pastors take risks for Christ's kingdom.

Evangelism. A third gift is evangelism (Eph. 4:11). Obviously, a person who strongly desires to see lost people come to the Savior and pursues the same will grow churches. Not only will such leaders reach lost people themselves, but in church-planting situations they exert a strong influence and encourage others to do the same. Their example is infectious!

Temperament

As with spiritual gifts, so there are certain temperament types that are found in pastors of many growing churches. Peter Wagner observes much the same. In *Leading Your Church to Growth,* he writes,

> The fifth and final limitation on how strong a given pastor's leadership role can be is highly personal. It depends on the temperament of the pastor himself or herself. Some pastors are take-charge people, and some could never bring themselves to take charge. . . . I myself feel that each of us needs to regard ourselves as a product of God the Creator. He has not created every pastor for pastoring a large, growing church.[5]

Church growth pastors tend to display similar patterns on both the *Personal Profile* and the *Myers-Briggs Temperament Inventory (MBTI).*

The *Personal Profile.* Leaders who go out and plant churches or help established churches grow significantly are usually High *D*s in combination with a secondary *I* or a High *I* in combination with a secondary *D.*[6]

D type persons like to get immediate results, love a challenge, and are catalytic. They tend to be quick decision-makers who question the status quo, usually take authority, and are good at managing trouble and solving problems. They are risk-takers who are task-oriented and are "upfront," "out front" kinds of people.

I type individuals like to be around people, and are articulate and motivational. They tend to generate lots of enthusiasm, enjoy participating in a group, and genuinely desire to help other people. They are very people-oriented, and, like the *D* profile, they are risk-takers who don't like the status quo and are "upfront," "out front" kinds of people.[7]

There are some other potential combinations that characterize growth pastors. These would be either a High *D* or a High *I* in combination with either a secondary *S* or *C*. While these aren't as strong as the *D-I* combinations, they show an inclination toward growth. Those who are High *S* or *C* tend not to function as well at leading churches to growth but work better on a team led by a High *D* or *I*.

The *Myers-Briggs (MBTI)*. Those who are strong church growth pastors usually show either an *NT* or an *NF* on their profile.[8] The *N* indicates a preference for intuition. These people are visionary and tend to focus on the future and the exciting possibilities that the future holds. The *T*s show a preference for making decisions based on logic and objective analysis, whereas, the *F*s prefer to make decisions based primarily on values and people-centered concerns. Extroverts *(E)* also have an edge on introverts *(I)*. What all this means is that leaders with the *NT* or *NF* pattern should be in the point position on the ministry team if the team wants the church to grow and reach lots of people.

This type of person should not be an after-thought. He or she must become the team leader at the very beginning of the process—in the conception stage. The field of church growth has been very helpful in discovering what kinds of pastors grow churches. The problem is that this information comes too late for many churches. They already have a person in place who doesn't have the temperament for growing a church, and it's already plateaued. Church planting allows us the luxury of starting with these kinds of people.

What Do They Do?

Now that we understand what kinds of leaders God has "wired" for growing churches in terms of their gifts and temperament, we need to examine what they do. Such leaders function as ranchers more than shepherds.

The Shepherd

Our culture has deeply affected the pastor's function in the church. Over the years, the rural model that was effective during the first half of the twentieth century has influenced the typical role of the North American pastor. This role is typically that of a shepherd of a small flock of people. Consequently, most traditional churches expect their pastors to visit regularly church members in the home and the hospital, marry couples, bury those who die, and preach sermons on Sunday morning.

While there's nothing wrong with these things, how does a pastor in a church of two thousand accomplish all this? The simple answer is that it's impossible! The reality is that churches with these kinds of pastors rarely break through the 200 barrier and most have less than one hundred people. Why? The reason is because one person cannot shepherd effectively more than one hundred people. There simply aren't enough hours in the day!

Again, it's most important to note that this is a cultural model not the biblical model. Scripture doesn't present a model. It presents biblical principles that characterize a model. Consequently, we must evaluate and change the cultural model as necessary so that it's more in touch with the culture in which it's implemented.

The Rancher

Those who pastor larger, growing churches also serve as shepherds. They usually shepherd a small group of people that consists of the staff and the board. However, they function primarily as ranchers in relation to the rest of congregation. In *Leading Your Church to Growth*, Wagner summarizes this role: "in a church led by a rancher the sheep are still shepherded, but the rancher does not do it. The rancher sees that it is done by others."[9]

Several characteristics distinguish ranchers from shepherds in growing churches:

1. Ranchers primarily minister *through* people and train them to do the work of the ministry. Shepherds minister *to* people, and they, themselves, attempt to do the work of the ministry.
2. The rancher has a broad view of ministry, and sees it as involving leadership and other functions as well as pastoral care. The shepherd limits ministry primarily to pastoral care along with preaching and teaching.
3. Ranchers believe that God wants people to minister in the body of Christ because they're capable of doing so. Shepherds believe that they, themselves, are the most qualified to minister in the church because most people aren't capable of serving others in the church; they haven't attended seminary.

4. Ranchers believe that they are dispensable in the sense that if they become incapacitated, they have trained others to carry on the work of the ministry. (Eph. 4:11–12; 2 Tim. 2:2). Shepherds make themselves indispensable. If they become incapacitated, the church struggles without them.

5. Ranchers realize that they can't control all that takes place in the church; thus, their leadership is characterized by a decentralized power. Shepherds feel they must have a say in all that takes place in the church; consequently, their leadership is characterized by a centralized power.

6. Ranchers prefer to be on the cutting-edge of what's taking place in ministry, whereas, shepherds prefer the status quo.

Vision for Growth

If a new church is to grow, then the people who make up the church, and its lay leaders in particular, must have a strong vision for growth. If they don't want the church to grow, then it doesn't matter who the pastor is or what the pastor does. It simply will not happen.

Negative Growth Factors

There are a number of negative growth factors associated with people in established churches that have prevented these churches from experiencing any substantial numerical growth. Three of these factors are fairly common. They are presented in the context of church planting so that the church-planting team will be aware of them and prevent them from surfacing in the new church. Should they surface, then the team will recognize them quickly and deal with them before they cause any damage.

A Family Atmosphere

The first common negative factor is the desire to maintain a family atmosphere in the church. At first, this may sound strange. The question is, "Why wouldn't we want our church to be one big family?" Lyle Schaller answers this question in *The Small Church Is Different:*

First, the strong commitment of the members to one another, to kinfolk ties, to the meeting place, to the concept that the congregation should function as one big family and the modest emphasis on program tend to reinforce the single-cell character of the small church. When combined with the intergenerational nature of the typical long-established small church, these forces tend to enhance the caring nature of the fellowship, but at the cost of potential numerical growth.[10]

A large number of the smaller American churches are basically family clan churches. They're a small group of people who love and care about one another. They may also be related to one another. While there's nothing wrong with people caring about one another, these people have missed the Great Commission mandate. They're not pursuing, evangelizing, and edifying lost people. These small clans exist exclusively for themselves. It's all inreach with no outreach.

A Comfortable Community

A second negative factor is the desire on the part of people to maintain a certain level of personal comfort in their lives. One of the problems in many of our American churches is the pursuit of a "comfortable Christianity." In response to an invitation to involvement, far too many would respond, "Church is great as long as all I have to do is show up every week and put something in the offering plate. When I've done this, I've done my part! Please don't ask me to do anything else; that's not my job, and I really don't have the time to help."

We must face the fact that today's typical churched persons place a high priority on personal comfort. They've developed their own comfort zones and strongly resist any attempts to be moved out of them. They don't share their faith because that could lead to confrontation, which makes them uncomfortable. They don't reach out to new people because the latter might reject them, and that would make them very uncomfortable. In short, any change is threatening.

In the field of church planting, many people who catch the vision will move out of their comfort zones and work hard initially to grow the church. But once the church is established and growing, and purchases or builds a facility, some tend to relax their involvement. Their ultimate goal is to return to their comfort zones.

A Powerful Person

A third negative factor is one layperson or a group of laypeople in the church who desire to control much of what takes place in the church. This could be an affluent person, a board member, the spouse of a board member, or even the board itself. Most often their motives are noble. They want to control things so that liberalism doesn't creep into the church or to protect the people in the church from young, zealous pastors who want to change things.

If the church begins to grow, the chances of maintaining control are slim indeed. These people argue that, "New people don't understand these things. They don't understand how we work around here. They don't realize how we've always done things. Furthermore, they tend to side with the pastor." They realize that they can only control a small, loyal group of people. When new people come into the church, they'll be loyal to the pastor who's probably had an influence on their lives. Consequently, these powerful people strongly resist any efforts toward church growth.

Positive Growth Factors

Church planters can do several things both to facilitate a positive attitude among their people toward growth and to prevent some of the negative factors from occurring. The first positive growth factor is broad and general and the other three are specific and designed to counter the three more common negative factors covered above.

Cast a Single, Clear Vision

Casting a clear, significant vision is critical to facilitating a positive attitude toward church growth. Vision is important to any church, whether planted or already established, because it provides direction and motivation as well as other important elements.

Implement Small Groups

The church that implements a robust network of small groups at the very beginning avoids the problems encountered in the family clan church. It allows its people to have the best of two worlds. On the one hand, the small group provides the kind of loving, caring community that the family clan seeks to protect. On the other hand, it provides this community in the context of a Great Commission mandate. The new church isn't only reaching in through its groups, but it's reaching out through a Great Commission strategy.

Mobilize a Lay Army

Another specific factor that encourages church growth is a well-mobilized lay army. The church-planting team takes the core group through an assessment process early in the development stage. This brings about a change in attitude concerning the pursuit of personal comfort. The discovery of one's divine design and place of ministry motivates Christians to step outside their comfort zones and get involved in ministry. They're excited about the fact that God has uniquely designed them with spiritual and natural gifts, passion, and temperament. This is all new to most of them, and they have a burning desire to serve and discover what God can accomplish through them.

Train Lay Leaders to Minister

A third factor that enhances church growth is training lay leaders to minister in the new church. The new church should be planted with the understanding that the pastoral team will handle the church's administrative affairs. The purpose for this is to free lay leaders from such affairs so that they can lead and minister to the church body. Some will lead specific ministries such as a music or outreach ministry. Others will lead and serve a small group. Regardless, they'll minister within the context of their giftedness (see 1 Cor. 12–14).

This system also prevents one person or group of people from taking control of the church. First, they never get into these control positions to begin with. Second, it gives lay leaders power and authority, but this is exercised effectively within their individual ministries, not over other's ministries or the entire church! Consequently, the final result is that lay leaders are busy serving Christ, and the church experiences the necessary freedom to expand and grow.

Staffing for Growth

A third critical factor for growing churches involves the people who make up the team that is supposed to lead the church to growth. Two questions directly affect church growth: How many people should be on the team? Who are they?

How Many?

If you were to ask the pastor of any church with over one hundred attenders whether they had enough people on staff, undoubtedly the answer would be a resounding, "No!" This is because so many churches across America are understaffed. In terms of church growth, Lyle Schaller writes, "If measured in simply quantitative terms, the majority of the large congregations are staffed to remain on a plateau or decline in size. They are not staffed to grow!"[11] This of course raises the obvious question, "How do you staff for growth?"

The ratio. In dealing with the topic of staffing for growth, Schaller begins by talking about staffing for a plateau. He indicates that a church that plans to remain on a plateau should have one staff person for two hundred people attending an average worship service, two staff for three hundred people, three staff for four hundred people, and so forth up to eight hundred. Then he suggests that a church averaging four hundred at worship have the equivalent of four full-time staff members if it desires significant growth.[12] Others seem to indicate as well that staffing for significant growth involves having a minimum of one staff person for every one hundred people attending the average worship service.

The problem. The problem for most established churches that desire to grow is that they're staffed for a plateau at best and for a decline at worse. When they discover the above information, they have to scramble to try and come up with the right staff person and enough money to hire that person.

Planting churches using teams helps circumvent this problem. A team ministry is biblical and provides other gifted people for mutual ministry and encouragement. It also enables a church to staff for growth. The church-planting team could begin with two or as many as four or five people on staff. Consequently, by recruiting a team consisting of two or more people, the new church will be staffed to grow far beyond its initial size and will probably grow at a faster rate as well.

The question. An important question for church planters to ask is, "What is our vision for growth? In terms of this community, how big could this church become?" If the vision is to plant a church that will reach a significant number of people, then the leadership should consider recruiting a team of four or more staff people from the inception of the church. While only a few churches have been started with a sizable team, these have achieved significant growth in a short period of time.

Who?

Not only is the ratio of staff to congregation important to church growth, but the individuals who make up the staff team are critical as well.

The Source for Staff

One question in staffing a church is, "Where do you find the right people to join the team?" Initially, for church planters the team may be recruited on a college or seminary campus. The potential point person begins to share a vision and others are attracted on the basis of that vision.

Another source is the staff or congregation of a mother church. However, once the church is born and has been in existence for a while, where does it find its staff?

Inside the congregation. Team members can be recruited from the congregation. The advantages are that you know these people and whether or not they'll be a good fit. Many will have been with you from the beginning of the church. They've caught the vision and have been around long enough to prove their character and to display their gifts. The disadvantage is that they've come up in the present paradigm or way of doing things and may not be very innovative.

There are several excellent examples of this approach to staffing. One is Hoffmantown Baptist Church, located on the outskirts of Albuquerque, New Mexico. Norman Boschoff, a Dallas Seminary graduate, is the pastor. In his system, any person in the church can attain a staff position. They begin by working with a neighborhood group. As they're successful they move up until they qualify for a full-time position on the staff. Another example is Willow Creek Community Church, which also recruits from within the ranks. In fact, many growing churches tend to follow this method.

Outside the congregation. Another approach is to recruit staff from outside the congregation. The advantage is that these people bring fresh, new ideas to the team that can bring positive change and benefit the ministry as a whole. In *Discovering the Future,* Joel Arthur Barker writes the following:

> How often has an important innovation in technology, or business, or education, or any field where there are rules and regulations, come from the established practitioners? Rarely. . . . So, where is the logical place for innovation to come from? The edges, the fringes, where there are outsiders who do not know that "it can't be done."[13]

Both are valid methods for recruiting staff for the church. Churches should use the method that best fits their particular circumstances.

The Criteria for Staff

You should consider the following important criteria when going through the process of staff selection.

Personal character. The first and most important is character. The question is, "Does this person walk with God?" A person's character forms the foundation upon which ministry is built. As character goes, so goes the ministry!

Ministry vision and values. A second criterion concerns the ministry vision and core values. Here the question is, "Do they 'own' the church's vision and values?" When people on a team have the same vision and values, they appreciate those who are different and recognize the contribution they make to the ministry as a whole.

Different design. A third criterion involves a different design. It's important that you staff to your limitations. God didn't gift and design us to do everything. We must view those areas outside our designs as limitations not weaknesses. Leaders should minister in areas where they're strong and recruit others to minister in their areas of limitation. Therefore, you should look for people whose gifts, talents, and abilities are different from but complement your own.

Loyalty to the pastor. Peter Wagner adds a fourth criterion for staff selection: devotion to the senior pastor.[14] If, for some reason, a staff person can't be loyal, then that individual should move on. Loyalty doesn't mean being a clone of the pastor but respecting the pastor. It's impossible to work well with leaders you don't respect.

Mobilization for Growth

A fourth growth factor concerns the mobilization of the people in the church. Peter Wagner refers to this as "lay liberation" and calls it one of the vital signs of the church.[15] He writes, "Pastors of growing churches, whether they be large or small, know how to motivate their lay people, how to create structures which permit them to be active and productive, and how to guide them into meaningful avenues of Christian service."[16]

Who Mobilizes the Laity

The Point Person

The ultimate responsibility for lay mobilization in the church falls on the point person of the team. While this could be the responsibility of another person on the team, team leaders should be able to take people through the assessment process. This is because the process, not the idea, is a relatively new concept to the church. Initially, they may not be able to find anyone else who understands the process. Most likely, they'll conduct the ministry until they've trained another leader to take their place.

A Staff Person

In the "cutting-edge" churches of the twenty-first century there will be staff specialists who will function primarily in this capacity. It's possible that this kind of specialist could be a part of the initial church-planting team. However, there should be someone on that team who can serve in a variety of roles, one of which would be as a mobilizer of the laity. The goal of this staff person is to train laypeople to take over the church's lay mobilization program.

A Layperson

Of course, another good option is to train a gifted, capable layperson to serve in this capacity. We must not forget that God has equipped laypeople in such a way that many of them can accomplish ministry-related tasks far better than those who are paid to do so. In fact, in this particular ministry, you're mobilizing laypeople to mobilize laypeople!

How to Mobilize the Laity

The Past

In the 1960s there was a revival or an awakening to the importance of the ministry of laypeople and the exercise of their spiritual gifts. Pastors like Ray Stedman of Peninsula Bible Church in Palo Alto, California, began to teach and write about the importance of laypeople and the gifts to the local body of Christ. They not only taught on the spiritual gifts, but also conducted body life services where people in the congregation could publicly exercise some of their gifts.

The Problem

The problem is that now we've developed a good theology of the gifts, but not a practice of the gifts. There's been lots of good exposition from the pulpit concerning the biblical teaching on the topic, and there may be some time set aside in the services for the exercise of the gifts. However, there's been little, if any, help given to people in terms of discovering their gifts and then implementing them in the ministry of the church as a whole.

The Solution

In the 1980s, this began to change. Churches such as Willow Creek Community Church in suburban Chicago began to develop methods to mobilize the laity. In particular, Pastor Bruce Bugbee developed the *Networking* program, which proved highly effective in mobilizing numerous laypeople in the Willow Creek congregation.[17] In fact, it may serve as the prototype for many of the lay mobilization programs in the churches of the twenty-first century.

The Program

A good assessment program consists of three phases.

The first is the education phase, where laypeople receive biblical and practical instruction on spiritual gifts, passion, temperament, and so forth. The purpose of this phase is to help them discover their unique divine design.

Next is the consultation phase. Here laypeople meet with either someone from the staff team or a trained lay leader who helps them analyze and synthesize the results. The purpose of this stage is to make sure people have correctly analyzed themselves, answer any questions, and discuss some possible ministries in the church.

The last phase is the mobilization phase. In this stage, the consultant helps believers discover where they can minister either within or outside the church body. Then, laypeople are assigned to a specific ministry that will train them for that particular service.

It's important in church planting that you institute this mobilization program early in the process. You should implement it in the development stage with the initial core group. Then you can take everyone who identifies with the group from that point on through the process. This should be a requirement for membership in the church because it sends a loud, early message that the people who are a part of this local body are here to "stand and serve," not just "sit and soak."

Assimilation for Growth

An important factor that is often overlooked in terms of church growth is assimilation. Most newly planted churches will attract a lot of new people through the front door. The problem is that many will eventually exit through the church's back door.[18] Assimilation focuses on ways to involve people in the church so that there will be fewer people who leave.

The Characteristics of Assimilation

Win Arn, a church growth expert with Church Growth, Inc., lists eight characteristics of what he calls an "incorporated member."[19] These are also characteristics of an assimilated person and are very helpful in developing some methods for assimilation. The characteristics are as follows:

1. New members should be able to list at least seven new friends they have made in the church. (These friendships could be, and often are, with other new members.)

2. New members should be able to identify their spiritual gifts.
3. New members should be involved in at least one (preferably several) roles/tasks/ministries in the church, appropriate to their spiritual gifts.
4. New members should be actively involved in a small fellowship (face-to-face) group. Many churches keep their new member groups together indefinitely.
5. New members should demonstrate a regular financial commitment to the church.
6. New members should personally understand and identify with the goals of the church.
7. New members should attend worship services regularly.
8. New members should identify unchurched friends and relatives and take specific steps to help them toward responsible church membership.[20]

Some Methods for Assimilation

An Atmosphere of Acceptance

One primary method for assimilating new people is to make them feel accepted.

The research. In *The Pastor's Manual for Effective Ministry,* Win Arn writes the following:

> New research underscores *why people select one church over another.* "A good church location" was only tenth on a list of sixteen. "My spouse was a member" was fifteenth.
>
> The *number one reason* people select a church today is: "I felt accepted."
>
> Dr. David Jones, a researcher in Jackson, Mississippi, says, "persons are looking for a group of individuals who will first and foremost make them feel accepted" (*RD Digest,* 1/85). This #1 reason is in contrast to the predominant reason researchers found people attended church in the 1950's and early 1960's. A generation ago Americans attended church most often "for the benefit of our children." But in Jones' study, this reason was listed only eighth.[21]

The responsibility. Creating an atmosphere of acceptance by making people feel accepted is the responsibility of the entire core group or church. No one person can accomplish this all single-handedly. In the planted church, this must be ingrained in the core group's thinking early in the planting process. It should be fully discussed and implemented in the development stage.

A Newcomer's Class

A newcomer's class helps not only in communicating vision but also in assimilating new people. Most often the class is directed at returnees or regular attenders who are interested in the church.

The purpose of this class isn't the same as in most churches. It shouldn't focus on the church's doctrine such as the meaning of baptism and the sacraments or any denominational distinctives. Neither should it be a Bible study or an opportunity for spiritual growth. That's not to say that these things aren't important. In fact, they'll be covered later. The problem is that some of the people attending might not yet be Christians.

The purpose for the newcomer's class is to tell people what the church is all about, what it expects from those who want to be a part of it, and to answer any questions. The content of each class would include most of Arn's characteristics of an "incorporated member." The term "vision" should be added to the seventh characteristic and it should be moved to the top of the list. The desired result of the newcomer's class should lead to the next method, a new member's class.

A New Member's Class

A number of the people in the newcomer's class will desire to become a part of the church. Invite them to attend a new member's class or small group.

In the 1980s, a number of churches moved away from having a church membership. Some argued against it because membership isn't found in the Bible. Others may have done it because some denominations place undue emphasis on membership. Yet membership can be used to the church's advantage in terms of assimilation. This advantage is found in the requirements for membership.

Those requirements are mostly contained in Arn's characteristics. Since most people who are considering joining a church are at a reasonably high point of commitment in their lives, they need something to commit to. These characteristics form the object of their commitment.

Commit to the vision and goals. First, they need to commit to the vision and goals (characteristic #6) of the church, which is the Great Commission mandate. You could ask everyone to develop a "hit list" consisting of those people who make up their relational communities (characteristic #8). Their job is to begin to pray for and gently pursue these people.

Join a small group. Second, each person should agree to be part of a small group (characteristic #4). This group would be one source for the seven new friends Arn mentions (characteristic #1). If the affinity is good among those in the new member's class, then they might form their own small group, depending on the church's purpose for small groups. This small group would also provide a means for monitoring the members' worship attendance (characteristic #7) as well as their spiritual condition as a whole.

Experience the assessment process. Third, each will enthusiastically go through the assessment process. It might be accomplished with or apart from their small group. This would not only help them determine their spiritual gifts (characteristic #2) but their entire divine design. Usually, the result of this process is a natural desire to become involved in a ministry of the church (characteristic #3).

Support the ministry. Finally, it's at the time of membership that the church explains its financial expectations (characteristic #5). Some churches make the mistake of addressing their financial needs repeatedly in the worship service. This is a real "turn off" to unchurched people. Rather than attempting this when people are merely "checking out" the church, it should be done when they've decided they like the church and genuinely desire to be a part of it.

Organization for Growth

One other factor affecting church growth that's often missed is the general organization of the church.

The Role of the Staff

The Problem

Currently, in most churches across America, the staff (which consists primarily of one pastor since the majority of churches are small) and the committed lay leaders of the church join together as a board once or twice a month to take care of what are mostly the administrative matters of the church. These may range in importance from the future ministry direction of the church to such things as how much money to spend on supplies. Most spend the bulk of their time on matters relating to the latter!

Since many lay leaders have grown accustomed to churches that are organized in this manner, they assume that these board meetings are what ministry is all about. They tend to see their ministries in the church primarily in terms of functioning on the board. However, even if they didn't view ministry this way—and some don't—these meetings are often so time-consuming that there's little time left in their busy schedules for anything else.

The Solution

Since the ministry of laypeople is so valuable, and they have such little time available for it, one solution is to let the staff take care of these matters. There are several advantages to this approach. Usually the church employs pastors and their staffs, depending on the size of the church, on a full-time basis, which allows them to spend more time in the areas of administration. They have also been trained in church administration and generally know what to do.[22] If they haven't been trained, or when they don't know what to do, they know where to go to get answers.

The Role of the Laity

The Problem

Those who have grown up in churches that have adopted the rural cultural model for ministry are convinced that they aren't capable of ministering to anyone. They believe that in order to minister to people, church leaders must first go to college and then to seminary. Therefore, when they're in need of ministry, they expect the pastor or at least a staff professional to call on them. A layperson might visit and minister more effectively than the staff person, but in their minds this doesn't count! It was nice but not the real thing. If the pastor doesn't visit me, I've not been visited!

The Solution

In a world that's quickly moving toward urbanization, we must abandon the rural ministry model for a more practical, relevant model that focuses more on biblical principles. Probably the best model is one that puts most of the administration in the hands of the staff and places the ministry in the hands of the laypeople.

The principle. Scripture indicates that the entire body of the church is to be involved in the ministry of the church. First Corinthians 12–14 clearly teaches that all believers in the body of Christ have spiritual gifts and are necessary to the life and vitality of the church. A healthy, growing body is one that places a balanced emphasis on all the gifts and the involvement of all the people in the ministry of the church.

The practice. The following are several ways to facilitate lay ministries in the planted church. The first involves a philosophy of ministry that values lay ministry. The lay ministries are constantly lauded and given high visibility in the church. The key slogan is "Every member a minister." The second is an ongoing program of assessment so that laypeople can discover their "tools" and places for ministry (their ministry "niche"). The third is that the church must not start ministries until God raises up qualified laypeople to lead and staff them. The fourth is that these lay leaders have the authority to lead their ministries with only minimal rules and outside interference. They "own" their ministries, not some board.

The information on church growth in this chapter isn't meant to be exhaustive. The purpose is to stress some of the more important factors and some that are often overlooked in terms of church planting. This is because this book isn't simply about planting churches, but about planting *growing* churches. The two go hand in hand. Church planters must not only be familiar with church planting, but must also study and know the principles and practices of biblical and sociological church growth.

A Growth Stage Worksheet

1. According to this chapter, are you the kind of leader who grows churches? What are your spiritual gifts? What is your temperament? Are you a shepherd or a rancher?

2. If you're the kind of leader who grows churches, then what should your position be on a church-planting team? If you're not, then what should your position be?

3. Do you want to see your church grow larger than two hundred people? If your answer is yes, then what size team will you recruit?

4. As you think through the ministry and programs of the new church, are you emphasizing any gifts in particular? If so, what are they? Would you consider your ministry balanced in terms of the gifts of the Spirit?

5. How do you plan to assimilate people in the new church? When will you begin this assimilation process? Does your process include all of Win Arn's assimilation characteristics?

6. What role will the laypeople in the church play in the leadership of the church? Who will be the ministers (do the ministry)? Who will be the administrators (do the administration)?

7. How much do you know about the field of church growth? How many books have you read in this area? What do you plan to read in the future?

8. What church growth principles are you aware of that weren't covered in this chapter? How might they apply to church planting?

18

I'm No Longer a Kid!

The Maturity Stage

Bill Smith gives credit to God every time he's asked about it. The church has been in existence for twenty months and it already has three hundred people attending the morning worship service! It barreled right on through the so-called 200 barrier as if it didn't even exist. Each week the church picks up more and more people. Some are still coming as the result of the mailers that were sent to the target community before Easter. Others are coming because of word of mouth; the new church has gained a growing, positive reputation in the community. Most of these are unchurched, lost people who are curious.

Those in the initial core group and others who joined them have invited a number of their unchurched friends, and about half of those who have responded have accepted Christ as Savior. This has resulted in some changed lives and the rescue of a number of failing marriages. While some in the original group were a little tentative at the beginning, now they're sold on the vision and committed to the future of this church. In fact, many have begun to ask when the church is going to purchase some land and build a facility.

Currently, this church is in the growth stage; it is quickly approaching the maturity stage. Actually, one stage does not abruptly end and then the other stage begins. Instead, the growth stage blends into the maturity stage. Regardless, in the maturity stage the planted church is growing spiritually and numerically. If it's a daughter church, then it's ready to survive on its own. Therefore, it's in the early stages of "weaning" itself from the mother church. Most likely, it's been in existence anywhere from twelve to twenty months or more. Its ministries are expanding, and the church is in the process of developing additional ministries in order to implement the strategy more effectively.

This chapter on the maturity stage covers three topics. The first topic is the maturing planted church. The second is the leadership of a relatively new maturing church. The third topic is the land and permanent facilities of the church. This discussion will give some direction to those in Bill's church and others in similar situations as to when a church should seek permanent facilities and the various decisions they'll have to make in doing so.

The Description of a Maturing Church

A healthy planted church reflects the seven principles of church planting outlined in chapters 7–13. Yet these are merely raw principles, concepts you apply to the future church, the church of the twenty-first century. Here we'll take a brief look at six of them as they've been "fleshed out" in the actual ministry of the planted church.[1]

The Great Commission Vision

A crucial factor in the life of any church is its vision. A new church can be adversely affected by the loss of its ministry vision. What happens in some planted churches, especially those that grow quickly, is that in the midst of all their success they lose sight of their vision. It gets lost in the shuffle, or left behind in all the "busyness." The casting and the content of a church's vision are of critical importance.

The Casting of the Vision

It's crucial that the vision of the church remains clear and that everyone in the church knows where it's going. This is the responsibility and primary ministry of the point person on the ministry team (most likely the senior pastor) as the "keeper of the vision." This person should be regularly sending "fresh waves of vision" throughout the church, constantly clarifying and recasting the church's direction and function according to the Scriptures.

The Content of the Vision

The vision is still the Great Commission (Matt. 28:19–20; Mark 16:15). The church continues to work very hard at pursuing, evangelizing, and discipling lost people.

The positives. The church as a whole is targeting and reaching its community through advertising, direct mail, and telemarketing. However, as it grows it will not use these methods as much as at the beginning because the church's growing reputation in the community and the networking of its people will attract others.

The negatives. This doesn't mean that all is well. The church has lost a few people along the way. For example, some joined the church only to discover that they're not comfortable with the vision. They really don't appreciate youthful offenders from the community who keep showing up in their teens' small groups. As one person said, "I bring my child to church to escape all the kids on drugs, and guess what? They're at the church too!"

A Well-Mobilized Lay Army

So far the church has managed to solve most of its unemployment problems. This is because it has been able to implement an assessment program to recruit and equip a well-mobilized lay army.

The Leadership of the Program

At the beginning, the primary pastor or leader on the team conducted the assessment program. However, God has brought along several talented and gifted laypeople who as a team have taken over the program and are operating it without the pastor. Actually, one of the individuals is extremely gifted and has gone through the training for the *Personal Profile* and the *Myers-Briggs Temperament Indicator (MBTI)*. This person has been a consultant in the marketplace and presently heads up the church's assessment team.

The Success of the Program

The church-planting leadership team is pleased with the success of the assessment program. At the inception of the church, they led most of the ministries of the church. Now laypeople lead the majority of the ministries.

Presently, there are about seventy to eighty ministry roles available for every one hundred members in the church. Church growth expert Win Arn notes that

> There should be at least 60 roles and tasks available for every 100 members in your church. A role or task refers to a specific position, function, or responsibility in the church (choir, committee member, teacher, officer, etc.). Any fewer than 60 roles/tasks/ministries per 100 members creates an environment which produces inactive members.[2]

Consequently, the church has more roles/tasks available than the minimum, which is good. However, the problem is placing people in those roles. This is where the assessment program has been so valuable. It's managed to place a large number of people in 80 percent of its ministry roles.

A Culturally Relevant Ministry

So far one of the characteristics of the church that has impressed a number of the unchurched lost people in the community is its relevance. This is because someone in the church has taken responsibility for this area.

The Responsibility

The church's ministry is characterized by relevance because the leadership team has taken the responsibility to see that the church remains culturally relevant to the community. They've made a point of exegeting the community as well as the Scriptures. In fact, they've set aside regular times to discuss what's taking place in the culture of the target area and how this can be addressed in the church's strategy.

Also, the senior pastor has asked the staff to visit at least two new paradigm churches each year and to observe what those churches are doing in the staff's area of ministry (this is part of the environmental scan). This experience will help them to keep up with new breakthroughs and with what other churches are doing.

The Results

The cultural sensitivity has brought about some mixed results. One is that the ministries are constantly changing and developing. This has caused some problems because people, in general, don't like change. Just about the time they've settled into a ministry, it changes. Consequently, the ministry team is rethinking this issue, and most likely will not make so many changes in the future over so short a period of time.

Another is the fact that the church has begun to take on a more heterogeneous complexion. While at its inception the church primarily attracted people like those who made up the core group, this has begun to change with the rapid expansion of the maturing church.

An Authentic, Holistic Worship

Undoubtedly, it's the worship and the music in particular that have attracted a large number of people to the new but maturing church. Again, this is because someone in the church has taken responsibility for this ministry.

The Responsibility

Initially, the church struggled in terms of the worship program because it lacked a strong leader. There was no worship person on the ministry team. A layperson had volunteered to help out until someone more qualified came into the church. In answer to much prayer and a lot of networking, God located the right person for the ministry. At first, he was part-time, but he proved to be so valuable to the total worship program that the church found the funds to hire him full-time.

He presently focuses most of his attention on congregational worship. Some have suggested that he start a choir. However, planning and coordinating the worship service every week take so much time that this hasn't been possible. He also agrees wholeheartedly with the leadership team in their commitment to congregational worship before choral worship.

The Results

The success of the worship program and its leader has brought several positive results.

First, there's much variety in the worship of the church; it hasn't become predictable and boring. It remains authentic and holistic; God touches people both intellectually and emotionally. Many made a fresh commitment of their lives to Christ as a direct result of the worship program.

Second, the people who perform for the worship service have shown steady improvement since the church was first planted, and there are more of them. The leadership's emphasis on the pursuit of excellence has begun to pay off. Good vocalists and musicians attract other good vocalists and musicians. The result is that the worship has been first-class in terms of the kind of quality that honors God. Lost people come and they're impressed.

A Biblical, Culturally Relevant Evangelism

The church is growing not only as the result of some transfer and biological growth, but because of evangelism growth. In fact, at times the conversion ratio (the comparison of those who've come to faith through the church with those Christians who are transferring into the church) is as high as 50 percent, which is excellent in comparison to most of today's churches.

The Methods

The church's primary method for evangelism is training people to reach their relational communities (neighbors, co-workers, and family). This process is begun at membership and encouraged through the small group program. It's also facilitated by either a "seeker-driven" or a "seeker-friendly" service or small group.

The church has also developed an evangelism ministry led by one of the individuals who was reached through the "seeker's services." This person has developed an evangelism team that works with the new member's class. Presently, they're also developing an evangelism training program that all the church's small groups will take for one month out of each year. The emphasis is on helping everyone in the group discover their unique evangelism style and then develop a strategy to implement that style.

The Result

The primary result of this program is that more people are coming to faith in Christ primarily because Christians are networking with their lost friends. In fact, the church has had to cut back on its publicity program because the ministry is attracting a large number of visitors due to the effect of this networking.

A Robust Network of Small Groups

The small group program has proved to be the real life-changing aspect of the church because of the leadership of the groups and the various small group programs offered in the church.

The Leadership

The small group programs have become popular because the leaders of the groups are well trained and have an excellent ministry record. This is due largely to a twofold training program. First, the leaders intentionally pursue other potential leaders from their particular small groups or the congregation at large. These people receive on-the-job training, serving in the groups as apprentice small group leaders.

Both the leaders and their apprentices attend a small group training session each month. The leader of these sessions casts the vision for the program, meets with the people, and helps them acquire the various skills necessary to lead effective small groups. The results speak for themselves.

The Programs

The number of small groups continues to grow rapidly. In fact, the demand outstrips the supply. No sooner is a new apprentice leader trained, than that leader is assigned a group. The church's goal is ten groups for every one hundred members. According to Win Arn, this is excellent:

> There should be at least seven groups in your church for every 100 members. The consequence of too few groups for members to build meaningful relationships is a high rate of inactives exiting through the back door. Creating an effective group life is a fundamental building block upon which growth and incorporation depend.[3]

In addition, a number of specialized small groups are starting to appear along with a lay counseling program. Most of these are for seekers and for people who've been through significant emotional problems such as abuse, co-dependency, drug addiction, alcoholism, and various compulsions.

The Leadership of a Maturing Church

Now that we've seen what a maturing church looks like, next we must ask, "What does the leadership of a maturing church for the twenty-first century look like?" This concerns a description of the leadership of the church on the pastoral, staff, and lay levels.

The Pastoral Leadership

Pastoral leadership is the leadership of the point person on the team, the primary pastor or senior pastor.

The leader of this church is neither a tyrant nor a despot, like some claimed who wanted to share that leadership at the beginning. While they've moved on to other churches that are plateaued and struggling, this pastor has led his church to spiritual maturity and growth. He blends integrity with strength. Each day he carves from his busy schedule one to two hours for vital worship and intercessory prayer.

This pastor is a rancher over the church and a shepherd of those on the board, the staff, and the small group leaders. He pours his life into and reproduces himself in these people. Yet, they're also influencing his life as well.

This pastor works closely with the staff, whom he values highly. They truly consider themselves a team. This doesn't mean that they don't have disagreements. The key is that they've learned to work through them.

Amazingly, this pastor also finds time for unchurched people. He has the gift of evangelism and, like a magnet, has a way of attracting lost people. When he is not spending time with his family, he is playing racquet ball with a lost neighbor or someone he has met at the health club.

The Staff Leadership

The staff are very important to the ministry of this church. This is because of who they are and what they do in the ministry of the growing, maturing church.

Who They Are

The staff should function and qualify as New Testament elders with a few exceptions (some of the younger members of the team). The Scriptures teach that the elders in the early church were similar to those full-time people on a church staff.[4] Thus, they must meet the qualifications for elders as found in 1 Timothy 3 and Titus 1. However, several laypeople with wisdom and the extra time also help direct the church.

What They Do

While they make up the pastoral team led by the point pastor, they, themselves, lead lay teams. For example, one is the worship leader who has recruited an excellent team of people that have involved themselves in various ways in the worship of the church. This person spends time with the team not only planning and rehearsing, but also in studying the Scriptures and praying together. Another individual is in charge of the mushrooming small group programs and functions in much the same way.

The Lay Leadership

This church isn't top heavy. You won't find all the leadership in the church at the top or on the professional level. You'll find it at the lay level as well. Indeed, one key to the success of the ministry has been the leadership of its laypeople. This is reflected in who they are and what they do.

Who They Are

The church's lay leadership consists of a lot of Baby Boomers. This is because Boomers planted the church, and they have a natural affinity for other Baby Boomers. However, some older leaders are now involved as well, especially in ministries directed toward the older people in the community.

These people aren't elders or even considered to be elders of the church. The staff team and a few laypeople are the equivalent to the elders in this church. However, for church planters who believe in lay elders, now is the time to appoint lay elders or have the congregation vote them into office. Appointing lay elders too soon can result in all kinds of leadership problems that strongly affect the planting of the church. In 1 Timothy 5:22, Paul warns us not to appoint elders (staff or lay) too quickly. In Acts 14, it would appear that he waited at least a year before appointing elders in the churches he planted on his first missionary or church-planting journey.

What They Do

The role of lay leadership is primarily that of ministry. Most are involved in "home-based" ministries. Again, these are the ministries that function primarily within the "four walls" of the church such as small groups, counseling, and teaching. While the majority of those in lay leadership are serving in the "home-based ministries," there are a growing number of people who are leading "target ministries." These are ministries designed specifically to reach certain target groups of people in and outside the church's community, many of whom will not come to be ministered to within the "four walls" of the church. Examples are street people, gangs, single parents, unwed mothers, gays, and those with various addictions.

The Facilities of the Maturing Church

So far the church has met in temporary facilities. This has been by design. The staff team desires to reach many in the community for Christ. Yet they realize that if they attempt to purchase land and build a facility too soon this will limit the ultimate size of the church. As Pastor Rick Warren at Saddleback Community Church near Los Angeles says, "It's a case of the shoe telling the foot how big it can get!"

However, it's in the maturity stage (two to five years) that the church will need to make a decision regarding permanent facilities. By this time the leadership should have some idea as to the church's ultimate growth potential. The church's growth will have either slowed down or still be increasing rapidly. Again, this is a major decision in the life of the church because facilities affect the ultimate size of the church. Actually, this decision consists of at least three aspects: permanent versus temporary facilities, new versus used facilities, and where to locate geographically.

Permanent versus Temporary Facilities

The Advantages of a Permanent Facility

There are several advantages to purchasing or building a permanent facility. First, it communicates permanence and stability to those in the target community. This affects the church's longevity in the community. Second, a permanent facility allows the church to be in control, not a landlord. As long as another person or organization actually owns the building(s) and the property, the church doesn't have the final say regarding what can be done with those facilities. Some facilities, such as a storefront, can be physically altered to fit the church's needs while others, such as a movie theater or a school, can't. Third, a permanent facility ends the "set up" and "take down" process that must occur every week in a temporary facility. This process has a long-term demoralizing effect on the people who serve in certain ministries of the church such as the nursery and the Christian education areas. They never have their own "nesting space" where they can leave their "stuff" and find it again the following week.

The Disadvantages of a Permanent Facility

First, there is the cost of permanent facilities. Over the past three decades, the church has witnessed rising costs in terms of land and facilities. The cost of land in most new, growing areas of urban and suburban America today can be high. Second, there is the disadvantage of the "people factor." Not only does the purchase of property and the construction of buildings on that property cost a lot of money; it puts that money into "brick and mortar," not people. The point is that if that money were invested in a staff team, part-time personnel, and other people-related areas, then the church would benefit more from a ministry perspective. Third, once a facility is built, its size limits the church's future growth in that area. Zoning laws in every community declare that a church can only build to a certain extent on their existing property. In most areas, there are also strict guidelines for allowing maximum space for parking cars.

New versus Used Facilities

If the church decides to reside in temporary facilities, then it doesn't have to make any further decisions about land and buildings outside of those affecting the rented facilities. However, if the church decides to purchase a permanent facility, then it will have to make a second decision. This involves whether the permanent facility will be new or used.

The Advantages of a New Facility

First, a new facility carries with it a natural attraction. The latest styles in construction and design communicate that the future is here, inside this building. Come and experience the latest and the best in this facility.

Second, a new facility enhances the congregation's esteem. People tend to identify with the facilities in which they work and worship. The feeling is that these facilities not only represent the place where I work or go to church, but to a certain extent they represent me because I've chosen to identify with these places. Consequently, they say a lot about me and who I am.

Third, the church can design a new facility to meet its unique needs. Every church is different in some way from every other church. This isn't necessarily bad because the same is true of people, and churches consist of people. If they were all alike, things would become awfully boring! Also, it takes all kinds of churches to reach all kinds of people.

However, these differences mean that each church has its own unique needs. Often the design of its buildings reflects these needs. If the church emphasizes a Sunday school program with large classes, it will need large rooms to accommodate those classes. If it opts for a small group approach, then the rooms can be smaller but more numerous. If, in the worship service, the church projects the words of its songs on a screen as opposed to using hymnals, then it will need to allow for front or rear projection in its design.

The Disadvantages of a New Facility

First, a new facility is the most expensive way to go. The problem here is that some churches risk going into heavy debt in order to cover these costs. If the church should fail to grow, or if the pastor should suddenly leave, the people may be left in a vulnerable position financially. Second, once you've finished the facility, you can only expand and add onto it so many times. Also, the number of services reaches a point of saturation so that the church can't grow any larger numerically. A third disadvantage is urban sprawl. Not too far from Dallas Seminary where I teach, there's a beautiful, large church facility. The auditorium has room for several thousand people. The baptistry is ornate and lined with large slabs of expensive marble. The only problem is that only about two hundred people gather there every Sunday, and baptisms are rare. What happened? After the church was built, the neighborhood changed from suburban-urban to an inner-city complexion. A large but poor ethnic community developed in the immediate area around the site, and the people who lived in the area and attended and supported the church moved to suburbia.

The Advantage of a Used Facility

The advantage essentially is the cost factor. While purchasing used facilities is sure to be relatively expensive in today's economy, it isn't nearly as expensive as putting up a brand-new building. Therefore, when comparing costs, there's really no comparison. This is why the only option for a number of less affluent churches is the purchase of some type of used facility whether it's a church facility or some other.

It's interesting to note that churches in some areas are exercising all kinds of creativity in terms of purchasing used facilities, especially when an area experiences a real estate recession. Some buy vacant shopping centers. Others buy failed restaurants or smaller office buildings.

The Disadvantages of a Used Facility

While it's much cheaper to purchase used facilities, several disadvantages come with this option. First, there are some initial costs involved in occupying a used facility. The general rule is that the cheaper the purchase price for the facility, the greater will be the costs for occupying that facility. For example, the older the building, the more it will be in need of repairs before occupancy. A second disadvantage is the possibility of a poor reputation in the community. Some buildings may have been occupied by a cult or questionable organization so that people in the area will avoid the church.

A Conclusion

Having examined the factors mentioned above, the question becomes, "What should a growing, maturing new church do?" Should they remain in a temporary facility or move to a permanent one? If they move, should they erect a new building or purchase a new one?

The evidence indicates that the advantages of a permanent facility outweigh those of a temporary one. In *Growing Plans,* Lyle Schaller writes, "Most of the congregations that chose to avoid owning and operating their own meeting place eventually concluded that the disadvantages outweighed the apparent advantages."[5]

Not only is a permanent facility advantageous, but a *new*, permanent facility is even more advantageous. If the new church can come up with the funding, then the advantages of a new facility outweigh those of a used facility.

Again, the key is to give the church enough time to get an idea of how big it will become. Not only does this give the leadership a feel for the ultimate growth of the church, but it allows the church to expand to a size necessary to raise sufficient funds to purchase the land and new facilities that will allow for present and future expansion.

Locating Geographically

In the process of purchasing a new, permanent facility, the church will need to decide where to locate in the target community. You need to keep several factors in mind when making this choice.

The Core Group

One factor is where the people who make up the core group are located geographically. You should locate the church ideally in the midst of the core group community or reasonably near them and definitely in the target community. First, if the core group lives too far away, then it will be difficult for them to invite unchurched, lost neighbors and community friends to the church. These people might come once or twice, but the fact that they are unchurched means that they're not in the habit of going to church. Consequently, if they have to travel very far from home, they'll probably not make the effort.

Second, if the core group lives too far away, they will find it difficult to drive a long distance to church. Over a period of time, they'll discover that the drive becomes longer and harder. Win Arn presents some research on the driving time of people to church that affects both groups. His work indicates that the maximum drive time for most people is fifteen to twenty-five minutes.[6]

Third, if the core group doesn't live in the target community, that community will tend to view them as outsiders. They will not see them as a viable part of their community and will reject them and the church.

Other Churches

Another factor in locating the church is the other churches in the vicinity. In some areas of the country, such as the Northwest, this isn't a problem because there aren't very many churches. In the South, it can be a major factor.

As much as possible, the church should be located far away from other churches for two reasons. First, it eliminates any spirit of competitiveness and accusations of sheep stealing. Second, it increases the chances of reaching those in the immediate community of the church. However, if the target area is heavily churched but unreached by those churches, then the church may locate not far from other churches, especially if they're other than evangelical churches.

Urban Sprawl

A third factor in locating the new church is the direction of urban sprawl. Wise leadership will attempt to determine if the area will change rapidly in the next few years. If the answer is, "Yes!" then they'll need to decide if this will affect the church's target group. They've chosen this site for the purpose of reaching a distinct target group. Will this change in the next twenty to thirty years? If so, what will happen to the church and the possibility of reaching its target group in the process of that change?

A Maturity Stage Worksheet

1. If you were to look back on the church you hope to plant five or ten years later, what would you see? Describe what vision comes to mind.

2. As you think about this church, what church-planting principles (vision, evangelism, relevance, and so forth) surface in your mind? What impact have they had?

3. Considering the advantages and disadvantages of a temporary facility, which would you choose? Why? What about a permanent facility? Why?

4. In light of the advantages and disadvantages of a new facility, which would you choose? Why? What about a used facility? Why?

5. If you feel the advantages favor a permanent, new facility, how soon would you attempt to obtain one? Why?

6. Of the various factors for locating the church in a target community, which seem most important to you? Why?

19

Let's Have a Baby

The Reproduction Stage

The words "Don't forget your roots" had somehow lodged themselves in the recesses of Bill Smith's mind. His church-planting professor had said them often in seminary, and now the time has come to realize them in his ministry. The church is almost three years old, and is averaging four hundred people in attendance for the past month. The growth has slowed only a little, finances are good, and the church is investigating the purchase of a large piece of land near their present facility.

Bill is having problems sleeping at night. The last time this happened was back when he was in seminary, contemplating the planting of this church. What's keeping him awake? It's his dream about reaching the entire city. In fact, when he moved to the suburb of this large city in the Northeast, his vision was to "take" the entire city for the Savior. Having planted the church, he believes that now is the time to start another. His desire is literally to circle the city with "cutting-edge" Great Commission churches and to use them to finance and plant other churches in the inner city, certain rural areas, and in other parts of the world. Consequently, in his prayers, he isn't asking God if they should plant another church. That's already been settled long ago. His prayers focus on exactly when and where they should locate the next church.

At this point, Bill's church is growing and is mature enough to begin the process of planting daughter churches at strategic locations around the city—an integral part of any church's ultimate vision. Therefore, a vital aspect of the church's future ministry isn't only to carry out the Great Commission mandate, but to plant church-planting churches (churches that will also carry out the Great Commission mandate both at home and abroad).

This is the reproduction stage. It's not meant to be a separate, distinct stage from the growth and maturity stages, but could be concurrent with the first and should begin somewhere in the latter. It involves not only planting churches all over the large metropolitan areas of America, but planting churches in other countries as well. This stage focuses on three areas: the reasons for, the time of, and the process of reproduction. It's designed to help established, maturing churches know why, when, and how to parent new churches.

The Reasons for Reproduction

In order for a growing, maturing planted church or an established church to start a daughter church, it must think carefully about its reasons for desiring to reproduce itself. People will want to know why the church wants to start another church. Some will ask, "Why should we start another church? Aren't there already enough churches around here?" There are three important reasons for doing so: the need, the examples, and the advantages.

The Need for Reproducing Churches

Few Churches Have the Vision

Few churches have a vision for reproducing themselves through starting other churches. Many are plateaued or in decline. For those that are plateaued, the emphasis is maintenance, and for those who are dying it's survival.

Not many churches in America have taken the initiative to birth churches. Many simply aren't interested. They would perhaps like to start a church, but feel that their church isn't ready yet. While this is probably true, "some day" never becomes "today." Others have helped start daughter churches, but at the initiative of the group of people who desire to form the daughter church. After the church is planted, it's "business as usual."

Regardless of the reasons, I have written *Vision America* (Baker Book House) as a tool to help these churches and their pastors catch a vision for church planting in North America and abroad.

Few Churches Are Reaching the Cities

All over the world in general and America in particular there's a strong movement of people from rural to urban areas. In *Your Church*

Can Grow, published in 1976, Peter Wagner indicated that 74 percent of Americans live in urban areas.[1] This figure has not diminished any over the years.

If the church of Jesus Christ envisions reaching North America and the world, then it will have to reach its cities. The problem is that few churches are reaching the cities and even less are thinking about it. There are some exceptions. For example, one pastor planted a church in Rockwall County located east of Dallas, which grew to a large size rather quickly. However, it has not remained only in Rockwall County; it has circled the Dallas metroplex. First, it planted a church in north Dallas county, which is also growing quickly. Second, it planted one in south Dallas county, and then one in west Dallas county. Next, hopefully, it will plant churches abroad. As these churches grow and plant other churches, they'll have a strong impact on the entire metroplex and ultimately the world.

Most Churches Resist Change

A third need for established churches to plant other churches is the fact that it's so difficult for them to change. Some indicate that of the 350,000 churches that existed in America in the decade of the 1990s, 100,000 closed their doors. Probably even more will close in the twenty-first century.

The problem. The problem is that most of these churches were started prior to the 1960s and developed their ministries in the context of a churched culture. With the shift from a churched to a nonchurched culture, these churches are no longer reaching their communities. The problem is compounded by the fact that some of these churches aren't aware of what's happened, and those who are, in general, aren't willing or able to make the changes necessary to influence their communities. This is because none of us like change; it makes us uncomfortable. It's so much easier to remain cloistered in our comfort zones. Therefore, rather than change what we're doing, we argue that what we've done in the past will also work in the future, and the ministry begins to die.

A solution. A number of the people who leave these churches aren't necessarily opposed to implementing new ideas and ways of doing things. They're opposed to doing them in their own church but would be open to seeing them implemented elsewhere. Consequently, pastors who take established churches and see themselves as change agents need to do two things. First, they must become experts on change. This means reading everything available on the topic. They must be patient and realize that it's difficult to sew a patch of new, unshrunk cloth on an old garment without badly tearing the garment (Matt. 9:16). Second, they should consider implementing their new ideas and methods in new daughter churches where they can pour new wine into new wineskins (Matt. 9:17).[2]

The Examples of Reproducing Churches

Even though not enough churches are reproducing themselves through daughter churches, there are some good examples of churches that have done this in the past, and there are some notable examples that have a vision for accomplishing it today.

The Church at Antioch

Perhaps the best example of a church that reproduced itself through planting daughter churches was the church located in the city of Antioch in Syria. The missionary journeys described in the Book of Acts were vital to the spread of Christianity. However, these were largely church-planting ventures that came out of the church at Antioch.

What's important to observe here is how the early churches such as the one at Antioch understood the Great Commission mandate. Jesus said, "Make disciples!" The Antioch church accomplished this through sending out two missionary church planters who started a number of daughter churches in Asia Minor, Macedonia, and Achaia. What better way to spread the gospel than to plant a number of significant churches in the areas targeted for evangelism. Is there any reason why established churches or growing, mature planted churches shouldn't follow suit?

Some Modern-day Examples

Not all of the churches in America have missed the opportunity of reproducing themselves.

Saddleback Valley Community Church. One notable example is Saddleback Valley Community Church. Pastor Rick Warren began this church in 1980 as a home Bible study with seven people. Today the church is one of North America's largest, and a majority of its people have accepted Christ as the result of its ministry.

But Warren hasn't "forgotten his roots." In an article in 1988 on the church, Sherri Brown wrote, "Church growth extends beyond the immediate church, Warren believes. When the church began in 1980, he proposed they start a church a year. To date they've started nine churches—eight of which have continued and grown to be self-supporting. They plan to start ten more churches the next year."[3] Warren's vision is to spread

Great Commission churches across much of Southern California. The results for Christ will be phenomenal.

Others. There are many others as well. Notable is Calvary Chapel of Costa Mesa, California, which has spawned more than 250 daughter churches across Southern California and the continent. The average size of most of them is between 200 and 300; however, thirteen average more than 1,000 worshipers on a Sunday.

Spring Branch Community Church while under the leadership of Joe Wall sprinkled the Houston, Texas, landscape with as many as twenty daughter churches.

The Advantages of Reproducing Churches

There are numerous advantages to reproducing daughter churches for both the mother church and daughter churches. This section will focus on some of the latter.

Finances

One of the major problems in planting a church is financing the venture. The costs can be high for a core group, especially if it pursues its community through a mailer or a technigrowth program. Some planted churches have the momentum to implement the vision but are slowed in the process because of a lack of funding.

This is where a sponsoring mother church can be an extremely valuable asset. It can give strong financial assistance at the very start and then cut back each year until the new church becomes financially self-supporting. A church's commitment to reaching its community and others can be measured by its financial commitment to church planting.

Core Group

Another advantage is that the mother church may supply some or all of the people who make up the initial core group. This might include some key, necessary lay leaders as well as followers.

This could take place in several different contexts. It would be the case if the new church is not too distant geographically from the sponsoring church. In fact, the new church might locate in a community where a number of members live who have been driving a significant distance to attend the sponsoring church.

It could also be the case if the new church was geographically distant from the mother church. For example, Willow Creek Community Church, before they discontinued directly planting churches, allowed their interns to recruit laypeople in the church for their church-planting teams. Keri Kent writes,

> However, interns are not making public appeals within the church to recruit their teams. "It's based on natural relationships," Bugbee says. "We've given them the freedom to share their vision with those they are ministering to. A year from now, I wouldn't be surprised if they (each) took 25 or 30 people. Eventually, it would be great if they (a team) took 100 people with them."[4]

The result of this aggressive approach was that laypeople got involved in a team and, if necessary, moved to some other large metropolitan area and planted a church there. Again, Kent writes, "Some have given up jobs and homes in the Chicago suburbs to move to another part of the country to be part of a new church."[5]

Accountability

A third advantage is that the sponsoring church can provide necessary accountability for the new work. This will affect several areas. One is the corporate finances of the new work. Are they using financial gifts from individuals and the sponsoring church as intended? Another is the matter of moral integrity, especially in the area of sexual promiscuity. Is anyone on the staff of the new church struggling in this area? A fall here will destroy the new church. A third area is the staff's family life. Are they balancing their time in planting the church and their time with their families? Some have allowed the new church to be their mistress or replace their families!

Encouragement

A fourth advantage surfaces during times of discouragement in ministry. Those involved in any ministry for the Savior will face times of discouragement. Unfortunately, it comes with the job. Even Paul, who was a church planter par excellence, faced times of intense discouragement (2 Tim. 4).

Here is where the mother church can be extremely helpful. It's most difficult to face discouragement alone. The senior pastor or the person assigned to the new church can serve as a comforter and source of encouragement to counter these times of discouragement.

Prayer

Those who plant churches without a sponsoring church must recruit intercessory prayer warriors. This is because the battle isn't simply that of determining where to find the necessary physical resources to get the job done. The battle is being fought in the spiritual realm (Eph. 6:10–19). Often when seminary students go into ministry and experience a lot of success initially, something always goes wrong! This is the result of spiritual warfare. We need to remember that one of the primary weapons against Satan and his forces is prayer (Eph. 6:18–19).

Credibility

A sixth advantage is credibility. At issue here is the credibility of the new church. How do people who might get involved in some way know that the work is legitimate? How might people distinguish this work from some "fly by night" operation? These are the questions that people will be asking, and they're good questions that demand an answer.

This could prove difficult for the church-planting team without a mother church. Churches in this situation should form a board consisting of people who can recommend the church to those who don't know it. Also, a degree from a known theological institution grants limited credibility. However, some church planters have neither.

The best solution is the sponsoring church. When a known, established church births another church, it conveys its credibility to that work.

Counsel

A seventh advantage is the availability of counsel from those on the staff of the parent church. One of the problems in ministry in general and church planting in particular is the knowledge problem. Often leaders find themselves in positions of having to make important decisions but not knowing what to do. The problem is compounded in church planting because so often the church planter and the team are recently out of school and don't have a lot of pastoral experience to fall back on. This is where the counsel of a seasoned senior pastor and church staff can be of much benefit to the daughter church.

Talent

An eighth advantage is that the new church may have access to talented individuals in the mother church. A problem for new churches, especially at the time of inception and later at the "birth event," is coming up with enough good talent to put together a quality worship time. Too often the church attempts to use people who by their own admission are mediocre vocalists or instrumentalists with dire consequences.

The sponsoring church can alleviate this problem by making its talented people available to the new church. A church that is rich in talent isn't able to use all that talent all the time. Therefore, someone could serve by performing in the new church each Sunday. This might include the help of the staff worship leader as well.

Personnel

A ninth advantage is in the area of staff and ministry personnel. Most new churches tend to be understaffed or their staff may be inexperienced. Consequently, the sponsoring church can make their staff available to help with the new work. The worship leader could advise and offer limited services as mentioned above. The youth person could help set up a youth ministry and be available for advice and training. A few churches hire trained people in these capacities and then loan them to the new churches until they're "up and running." This reflects a strong commitment on the part of those churches to the Great Commission mandate.

"Shared Events"

A tenth advantage of having a mother church is "shared events." A complaint often heard from people involved in the new church is that they or their children miss some of the programs and events they experienced in the sponsoring church.

One solution to this problem is for the daughter church to continue to participate in some of those programs or events. For example, every year a number of the churches in Dallas sponsor a family camp or a ski trip to the mountains in Colorado. Some of the families in these churches have made this a family tradition to be observed every year. The new church could join the parent church for this event. In time, the new church will grow large enough to sponsor it on their own, but until then, they can share this time with the other church. This could relate to other events as well, especially those affecting adolescents in the new work.

The Time of Reproduction

Now that we've looked at some of the reasons for parenting a daughter church, the next question concerns when this should take place. What is the best time to plant a church? Several considerations should prove helpful to the mother church in answering this question.

The Size of the Parent Church

One consideration is the numerical size of the mother church. How big should the parent church be in order to plant a new church? Is there an ideal size?

A Perception

The perception among most if not all churches considering church planting is that they're not big enough to start a new church at their present size, no matter what it is. The ideal size is always larger than they presently are.

This same perception can affect the church not only in terms of its size but in other areas as well. For example, the same argument could be mounted in terms of finances. The church may feel that it does not have quite enough finances to start a new church now, so it decides to wait until next year or the year after. However, the ideal amount will always be larger than what the church presently has! And, at this rate, the church will never become involved in birthing new churches.

A Survey

In the summer of 1984, *Leadership* conducted a survey of its readers, asking them to share what they had learned about mothering new churches.[6] Here are some sizes and comments regarding these sizes from the parent churches that still apply even in the twenty-first century.

One church planted a new church with 18 people. The pastor responded, "Also, I'll begin with Bible studies and wait until we have 40 in regular attendance before launching the new church. We started with 18 and now have about 70–80" (Foursquare, California).[7]

Another church planted a church when they had 20 people. They commented, "Start with a larger core group (we had 20). This was very tiring when trying to fill even the basic needs" (independent, Illinois).[8]

A third church didn't disclose its size when it parented its first church. However, it suggested, "You need at least 75 people to function as a complete body" (nondenominational, Illinois).[9]

A fourth church planted when they had 150 people. Their comment was, "Wait until we have a larger congregation. We had 150 at the time" (independent, California).[10]

It would appear from this brief sampling that there's no ideal size at which to begin a new church. Each church in the survey states that, in retrospect, it should have been larger—whether it consisted of 18 people or 150 people. This would seem to indicate that churches that have parented a church as well as those that are considering the same are still under the perception that the ideal size at which to start a church is always larger than their present size—regardless of what that size may be.

A Conclusion

There doesn't seem to be any ideal size at which a mother church should be before it starts another church. In general, all agree that the larger the size of the church, the easier it is to plant another church. Yet if these churches had not started when they did, they would never have reached the ideal size they were looking for, and would not have started their daughter churches.

Perhaps the size of fifty or larger might be a helpful suggestion although there is no hard evidence for this particular size. However, Peter Wagner indicates that a planted church needs a core group of at least fifty people or more before going public if it desires to grow larger than two hundred people.[11] This figure is helpful to a church that has a vision to plant other churches. If it keeps planting churches before it reaches fifty, then it will be delayed in reaching the birth stage, and this will hinder its ministry long term.

Regardless, the idea that we can't plant a church yet because we're not big enough isn't valid. The church must remember that this perception will always be there regardless of its current size. If it has more than fifty people, then it needs to take a step of faith and parent a new church.

The Growth of the Parent Church

Another consideration in terms of the best time to plant a church is the growth of the parent church. At issue here is whether the parent church is growing, plateaued, or in decline.

The Growing Church

Certainly an ideal time at which to plant a church is when the parent is experiencing numerical and spiritual growth. Many examples exist from both the first century and the twentieth century.

The Plateaued or Declining Church

It's not too difficult to understand that growing churches should plant other churches. But what about the 80 percent to 85 percent of churches in America that are either plateaued or in decline? Should they consider starting new churches?

Most of these churches tend to be focused inward not outward. They're concerned with getting themselves off their plateau or turning their situation around. However, what most don't realize is that one means of accomplishing this is parenting a church. Gary Carter, the pastor of Eastwood Fellowship Baptist church in Saint Thomas, Ontario, believes that churches, like gardeners, must prune themselves for growth if they desire to continue to grow.[12] If they don't, then one or two things may happen: stagnation or accidental pruning. The latter refers to people in the church who take the initiative and split off on their own.

But how can a church know when to prune itself, and what effect will this have? Carter writes the following:

> Thus, when a church has not seen recent growth, it may be a signal that it is time to prune—by planting a daughter church. Such a move is likely to stimulate the church to new heights by breaking in on established relationships and patterns in a positive way. Growth will be spurred again by the recent memories of how the sanctuary used to be full. Everyone will know that these pews are now empty because the church selflessly gave people to the daughter church. A holy dissatisfaction will engender enthusiasm to fill those places once again. The new-found momentum may take the mother church to the next plateau that previously seemed out of reach.[13]

The Conclusion

It would appear that church planting should characterize a church regardless of whether it's growing, plateaued, or in decline. The evidence seems to indicate that parenting a church is only natural for growing churches, and is important to plateaued and declining churches that desire a new direction. Consequently, a church can know that it's time to become a parent by the very fact that it's either growing, stagnant, or dying.

The Process of Reproduction

A parent church may know all the reasons for starting another church, and when to do so, but not know how to go about accomplishing it. The result of this kind of effort most often is no child or a lot of unnecessary pain in the process of birthing the child. Either has the potential of giving church planting a bad reputation in the eyes of the congregation, which discourages any future attempts at having another child. This raises the question, "How does a church go about birthing a daughter?" No less than six steps make up the process.

Praying for Daughter Churches

Precede the birthing of any church with much prayer. Prayer must permeate the entire process. This prayer begins with the leadership team but includes the entire church.

The Leadership Prays for Daughter Churches

A church will never rise above its leadership. If the leadership of the church isn't committed to church planting, the membership will not be committed. If the leadership doesn't pray for daughter churches, the membership will not pray for daughter churches. The leadership must set the example for the congregation.

The Church Prays for Daughter Churches

You should cast the vision for church planting in such a way that it will motivate people to pray for the project. It's not realistic to expect everyone to share the same burden and to pray to the same extent, but the goal is to have some people praying all the time.

One way to involve the congregation in praying for daughter churches is to encourage them to become involved in these churches. Those who plant these churches, whether interns or others, could spend a certain amount of time in the church recruiting both a core group and prayer support for the venture. Leith Anderson has encouraged this approach, which he calls the "head-hunter" approach, in his church in Eden Prairie, Minnesota.

Another way is to recruit special daughter-church prayer teams. These would consist of people who have expressed an interest in church planting and missions. The primary purpose of these groups is to pray for specific daughter churches long before they're conceived and long after they've been weaned.

Casting the Vision for Planting Churches

Another step in starting a daughter church is casting the vision for the same. If the vision isn't cast, chances are good that it will not happen. The two issues here are the time and methods for accomplishing this.

The Time for Vision Casting

The church needs to cast the vision for another church all the time. Church planting is the primary if not the only vehicle for the evangelization of America. Therefore, any church plant should have as a part of its ultimate vision the planting of other churches. It must not forget its "roots."

A mother church should begin to cast the vision for daughter churches long before it's in a position to start them. (The best time is at its own inception.) The result is that people will not be surprised when the time comes and the church begins to move in that direction. In fact, if the vision is cast properly, the people will grow impatient with the church, and their constant complaint will be why it's taking so long to become a parent.

The Methods for Vision Casting

The methods for vision casting are much the same as those enumerated in chapter 14. They include such things as the pastor's example, the sermon, visual images, brochures, and audio- and videotapes.

Identifying a Target Group

A vital step in parenting churches is the identification of a target group. This involves a specific group of people in a specific community whether they're close to or a long distance from the church. The general procedures for accomplishing this are found in the strategy section of chapter 14. They consist of the following:

1. Identify a unique target group.
2. Gather information on the target group.
3. Construct a profile person.
4. Determine the kind of church necessary to reach this target group.

However, a sponsoring church brings another dimension to the process, especially if the target group is in the same city. First, in light of its location, it can gather the necessary demographic and psychographic material firsthand. Second, it can supply the people who'll make up the initial core group. This could be a sizable number of people who live beyond the normal driving distance to the church and desire a church with the same vision in their area of the city. However, it could also consist of any cluster of people from the church who desire to target a particular area of the city where they live.

Selecting and Equipping a Leadership Team

Everything rises or falls on leadership. *Who* is as important as *how!* The right person in the right position with God's blessing usually gets the right results. The right person in the wrong position gets the wrong results. The parent church that understands this can play an important role in the success or failure of the future church. An aspect of this role is the selection and equipping of a church-planting leadership team.

Selecting the Leadership Team

Chapters 5 and 6 describe how God has designed each person in a unique way for leadership and ministry. Chapter 14 has a special section on team ministry that includes some instruction on how to select the individuals who make up the team. This selection process involves a consideration of godly, Christ-like character, vision, values desire, and design.

Equipping the Leadership Team

Once they've selected the team, the parent church can serve that team by equipping it for the ministry that's ahead. There are at least two ways accomplish this task, depending on the size of the church.

One approach is to set up an internship program. This could be arranged in conjunction with a Christian college or seminary. This would be a good approach for a smaller church that has only limited funds available. The advantage for students is that they receive a small stipend and room and board from the church plus they meet the graduation requirements of the school. Consequently, they hit the proverbial two birds with one stone.

Another approach is to place potential church planters in staff positions in the sponsoring church. They would serve the church in a full-time capacity, including preparation for church planting. They would be paid full-time and could recruit a team from among the congregation. Once they leave, other church planters could take their places. This is a good option for larger churches.

Recruiting a Committed Core Group

Another very helpful step in parenting a new church is the recruitment of a committed core group of people who will form the nucleus of the new church. If the mother church can accomplish this, it will save the church-planting leadership team the time of having to build a core group in the context of a "cold start." But who will make up the core group, and how will they be recruited?

The Source of the Core Group

The primary source for the nucleus will be those in the congregation. They're a good source for several reasons. First, they'll already have the vision. Second, there will be clusters of people who live beyond the average driving distance to the church (fifteen to twenty-five minutes). These people are already aware of how long it takes to get to church and will probably be interested in something closer to home. The church should chart where its people are located geographically and look for its clusters. Third, these potential core group people are accessible. The church will discover who they are and then will have the ability to communicate regularly with them.

The Recruitment of the Core Group

The question the church must answer is, "How will it recruit its people to form a new core group?" It should follow two steps.

Cast the vision. The first is to prepare the soil by planting the vision. The vision of the mother church from its very inception has included the planting of daughter churches. Thus, the vision should already be well established. Indeed, the church has cast the vision so well that people in the congregation are "chafing at the bit" to become involved in a church plant to reach unchurched lost people.

Ask for volunteers. The next step is to ask for volunteers to be a part of the new work. This has proved to be a simple but highly effective method. A survey of parent churches conducted by *Leadership* in 1985 indicated that three-fourths of them followed this approach.[14] According to Dean Merrill, "The vast majority of these turned out to be permanent transfers, not temporary aids. In the case of Oak Grove Church, Milwaukie, Oregon, for example, '75 members came for a one-year commitment; 72 remained.'"[15] This continues to be a good step in the twenty-first century.

Financing the Future Church

An important step in nurturing new churches is for the church to help in the area of finances. It should work through at least four areas: the amount of money, the source of that money, what the funds are to be used for, and how long the support should last.

The Amount of Money

You must ask, "How much money does the mother church need to provide in order to plant a daughter church?" There is, however, no set figure. Each situation is different because leaders plant churches in different places under different circumstances.

In *Leadership,* Dean Merrill provides encouragement: "Mothering a new church is not as costly as we had expected."[16] He continues, "Few investments totaled more than $25,000 (excluding real estate purchases).

Many daughter congregations were started with as little as $5,000. *Some start-ups required no money at all* from the mother church treasury."[17]

However, the pattern seems to be that the more money the church is willing to invest coupled with good leadership, the greater the return on that investment. An example is Hope Chapel in Hermosa Beach, California, which has started thirty daughters in the past twelve years. Merrill quotes the pastor, Ralph Moore:

> "We spent $3,000 in our first attempt back in 1973. And we were only 125 people at the time. Lately we've been spending in the high twenties with a proven leader, and the daughter church ends up with usually 100+ people in six months." In mid-1983 Moore ventured out himself, with 40 others from the 2,700-member mother church, to plant a new Hope Chapel in Kaneohe, Hawaii. A year later, attendance was running above 400.[18]

Of course, these figures don't include costs for the acquisition of land and facilities. The church will need to determine if it desires to become involved in this aspect of financing.

The Sources of Money

Several different ways exist for a parent church to fund new church starts.

The first is to create a special fund for church planting that is outside the church's regular budget. It would depend on the gifts of people in the congregation who are interested in seeing a network of daughter churches in the area.

The second is the missions budget. Planting churches is definitely an aspect of any church's missions program. You would designate funds in the missions budget specifically for new churches.

The third is to make it a line item in the regular budget. This would serve to give it special treatment and would communicate the church's commitment to it.

The fourth concerns the part of the budget that includes salaries. You would designate and use funds here for the salaries of the church-planting team.

The Use of the Money

You may use the money for a variety of necessities. At the top of the list would be salaries. In Merrill's *Leadership* survey, the most common provision was for salaries.[19] Another common use would be for renting appropriate facilities. After facilities and salaries, other possibilities include such areas as publicity, mailers and brochures, sound equipment, lighting, curriculum, Bibles, and so forth.

The Length of Time

The important question here is, "How long should the church help or support the daughter ministry?" The objective of the new work is to become self-sufficient as soon as possible, so the answer to the question is, "As long as necessary but not for very long."

A suggestion. The parent church should probably make a three-year commitment with hopes that it will not take this long. If it should take longer than three years, then something is probably wrong. The exception to this might be some ethnic works and some plants that target special groups such as the cults and other religions.

A survey. In the *Leadership* survey, Merrill asked the question, "How long was the road to self-supporting status, and thus an independent existence?"[20] The answer was the following:

> Two-thirds of the daughter churches in our survey had reached that milestone in an average of 20 months. The median time, however, was only 12 months, and almost a fifth of the sample reported being on their own financially from Day 1. By contrast, a few cases reported receiving outside aid as long as ten years.
>
> The other third of the respondents were still working toward self-sufficiency and had been doing so for an average of 30 months. The clear preference, of course, was to end this phase as soon as possible, because "as long as the parent is helping to pay the bills," says John W. Fogel, an Alliance pastor in Fulton, New York, "the new church is not totally independent."[21]

The average. The average appears to be somewhere between twenty to thirty months. The median time would be closer to twenty months. This should give encouragement to both planted churches who desire independence and parent churches who desire to see them become independent and self-supporting as soon as possible.

It's most fitting that this book end with this chapter emphasizing the need for planted churches to reproduce other dynamic, biblically based churches—in short, to plant church-planting churches. This ties in with the vision in the Book of Acts. It's to encourage and equip individual Christians and churches to seed American soil with relevant, significant Great Commission works that will assault and crash through the gates of Hades (Matt. 16:18). This is to take place at home and abroad. Not only are we to sow new works to reach the various people groups here on the North

American mission field, but these, in turn, can sow churches on the mission fields of other countries. The vision is for the world! This has been the means through which God has accomplished revival in the past and will be for the future as well. The question is, "Will you become a part of this vision?"

A Reproduction Stage Worksheet

1. How big is your vision? Do you plan to reach a community, a city, a country, the world?

2. Does your vision for church planting include the reproduction of future daughter churches in the area, this country, or overseas? Why or why not?

3. Are you aware of any churches other than those mentioned in this chapter that are parenting new churches? What are they doing? How might this knowledge help you do the same either now or in the future?

4. What are your personal feelings about helping a new church in the area of finances? Does the idea of taking funds away from your church seem a little frightening? How do you think people in your church will feel about this?

5. How do you feel about people leaving your church to become part of a new church? Would you be willing to let a church planter recruit some of your people? Which people? Would they include staff and board members? How about substantial givers?

6. Have you ever considered leaving your church and becoming a part of the daughter church? How would your spouse and family feel about this?

7. How much time would/do you pray for daughter churches? What specifically would/do you pray for? Is God answering your prayers? How?

Appendix A

Addresses for Resource Material

Discover Your Gifts and Spiritual Gifts Workbook
Church Development Resources
2850 Kalamazoo Avenue
Grand Rapids, MI 49560

Spiritual Gifts Analysis
McCart Meadows Baptist Church
2729 Sagehill Drive
Ft. Worth, TX 76123

Team Ministry: Spiritual Gifts Inventory Questionnaire
Church Growth Institute
P.O. Box 4404
Lynchburg, VA 24502

Role Preference Inventory
Masterplanning Group International
P.O. Box 952499
Lake Mary, FL 32795

Appendix B

A Sample New Church Feasibility Study

Sand Creek Village Site
Kingwood, Texas

June 20, 1988

Prepared by

Carol S. Childress
Church Extension Research and Development Section
Baptist General Convention of Texas

Used by Permission

Purpose of the Study

The purpose of this study is to assess the potential of a proposed new church in Kingwood to be located on property at the intersection of Kingwood Drive and Willow Terrace Drive in Sand Creek Village.

The study, along with accompanying planning model, can be used as a valuable tool in the planning process for the new church including the development of appropriate ministries and programs to meet the needs of the area population. In addition, the pastoral leadership profile section can serve as a resource in the selection of a pastor who is indigenous to the community.

Sources for the study include demographic data from National Decision Systems (updated as of December, 1987) and the Friendswood Development Company, school enrollment data from the Humble Independent School district, additional planning and development information from Friendswood Development

Area Population Growth
Sand Creek Village Site

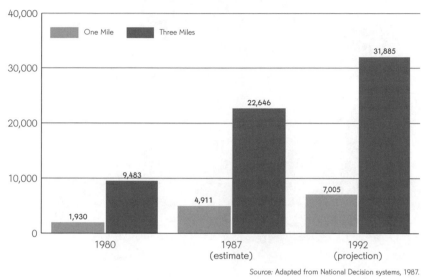

Source: Adapted from National Decision systems, 1987.

Company, and church data from a telephone survey (May, 1988) and the 1987 Uniform Church Letter for existing Baptist churches in the area.

Community Profile

Kingwood, located 22 miles northeast of downtown Houston off U.S. Highway 59, is one of the premier master-planned communities in the United States. Developed by the Friendswood Development Company and King Ranch, Inc., the 13,000 acre subdivision is organized around individual villages which are self-sustaining and provide the necessary community services. While single family homes are predominant, there is also multi-family housing in addition to retail and commercial trade areas.

According to Randy Creech, Marketing Manager for the Kingwood project, the estimated population of the entire subdivision as of March, 1988 was 34,942. Development is expected to continue into the next decade with a projected 1990 population of 40,316 and 63,857 in the year 2000. Friendswood Development Company averages selling between 550 and 600 lots a year for the construction of new houses in Kingwood.

While data is available for one and five mile radii, for purposes of this study, *the area under consideration will be defined as a three mile radius from the intersection of Kingwood Drive and Willow Terrace Drive in the Village of Sand Creek.*

Area Population Ethnicity
Sand Creek Village Site

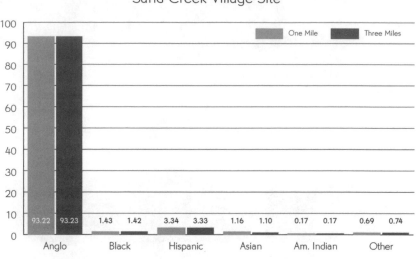

	One Mile	Three Miles
Anglo	93.22	93.23
Black	1.43	1.42
Hispanic	3.34	3.33
Asian	1.16	1.10
Am. Indian	0.17	0.17
Other	0.69	0.74

Source: Adapted from National Decision systems, 1987.

Population

The population of the study area in 1980 was 9,483. The 1987 estimated population was 22,646 and the projected population for 1992 is 31,885.

An estimated 93.23% were Anglo, 1.42% Black, 3.33% Hispanic, 1.1% Asian, and .92% Other. According to enrollment records for schools in the Kingwood community, the student population is 97.6% Anglo, .8% Hispanic, .4% Black, and 1.2% Other, primarily Asian.

The 1987 estimated median age of the area was 28 and the average age was 29. The largest single segment was 35–44 (18.98%) followed closely by 45–54 (12.72%) reflecting the stability and maturity of the population. Children under the age of 14 accounted for 28.78% of the population.

The following are 1988–89 school enrollment projections obtained from the Humble ISD for schools in the area:

School	1988–89 Projected Enrollment
Deerwood Elementary	734
Greentree Elementary	694
Willow Creek Elementary	340
Creekwood Middle School	1,193

According to Friendswood marketing data, residents move to Kingwood from (in order): other states, primarily the Northeast and Midwest; other parts of Texas; and Houston.

Housing

The dominant housing type in the study area is single family, accounting for 93% of the total housing stock. Another 5.06% is multi-family. A total of 89% of the housing stock is owner occupied.

Housing values in the individual Villages of Kingwood range from the upper $50,000's to in excess of $1 million. According to the Kingwood Marketing Manager, over one-half of all the houses sold in Kingwood exceed $150,000 in price. Houses in Sand Creek Village, where the new church site is located, and the adjacent Kings Point Village, range in value from $160,000–$250,000. Other houses in Kings Point and the adjacent Fosters Mill Village range in price from $240,000 to $1,000,000.

The majority of remaining property in Kingwood available for future residential development lies to the immediate northeast and southeast of the new church site. Friendswood Development Company is projecting to sell 556 lots in the next 18–24 months and lots are not sold unless there is a contract for construction of a house.

According to Karen J. Collier, Public Information Officer for the Humble Independent School District, the school district has considered the area's growth in their long range planning and a new elementary school, Willow Creek, will open this fall. Located immediately south of the site on Willow Terrace Drive, the school will have a projected enrollment of 340 K through 5 students.

Education

The area has a very high level of educational achievement. According to the Friendswood Development Company's most recent new homeowner's survey (February, 1986), the average adult male had completed 16.2 years of education and the average adult female 15.0 years. The villages near the new church site had the highest educational achievement in Kingwood. The importance of quality education to the community is also reflected in the high standards of the school system and the outstanding academic achievement of the student population.

Occupation

According to the same Friendswood survey, the primary employment center for every village except one was downtown Houston. Many of the residents are employed by energy-related companies in executive and managerial capacities. Only one-third of the wives are employed outside the home in contrast to the national figure of one-half. According to the 1980 Census for the area, 80% of the employed adult population were engaged in white collar occupations.

Household Income

In 1987, there were an estimated 6,895 households in the area with an average annual household income of $63,783. The median income was $56,823. Over one-fourth (26.2%) of the households had incomes in excess of $75,000. Another

Education of Area Population (1980)
Sand Creek Village Site

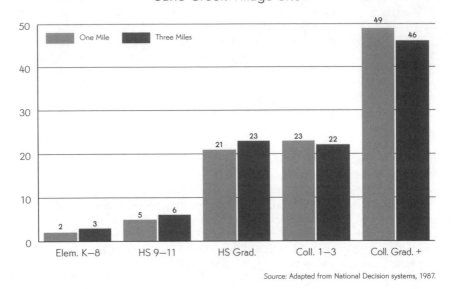

Source: Adapted from National Decision systems, 1987.

32.6% had incomes between $50,000 and $74,999. Only 5% of the households had an income less than $15,000.

Lifestyle and Values Profiles

The previous demographics of the area reflect the lifestyle and values profiles of the households and population.

One-half of the households in the area can be classified as "suburban wealthy" and characterized by their affluence, high valued homes, high level of education, and location in a top metropolitan area. Residents are employed in high paying profession/managerial and technical/sales jobs. The heads of households are generally over 35. There is a large number of teenagers still at home as well as children in college ("empty-nesters"). Family and career are important to these households.

Another 41% of the households can be classified as "suburban affluence" and characterized by their high household income, property values, education level and mobility. Generally younger than "suburban wealthy," these households are located in the new suburbs of the southwest and have a higher concentration of ages 30–34. Well educated, they are career conscious and employed in white collar jobs, many with the new "high tech" companies of recent years.

Based on the previous information, it is not surprising that the major values profile of the population is "Achiever." A total of 41% of the population, twice

1987 Household Income
Sand Creek Village Site

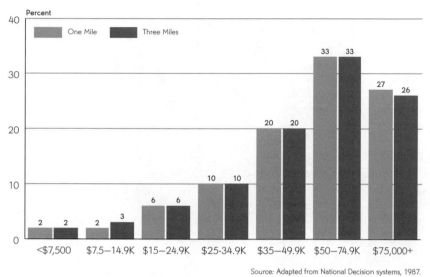

Percent

| | One Mile | Three Miles |

<\$7,500: 2, 2 | \$7.5–14.9K: 2, 3 | \$15–24.9K: 6, 6 | \$25-34.9K: 10, 10 | \$35–49.9K: 20, 20 | \$50–74.9K: 33, 33 | \$75,000+: 27, 26

Source: Adapted from National Decision systems, 1987.

the national average, has this profile. "Achievers" are well educated, and success and career oriented. Leaders among the American public, they take risks when it is necessary to achieve their goals. Their chief characteristic is confidence in themselves and their abilities.

The second highest values group in the study area are classified as "Socially Conscious." Highly educated, they are considered liberal in their social and political ideals. Heavily involved in community and civic events, they are often considered "single issue" or "cause" people being concerned with the environment, poverty, racial or social injustice, etc. This group also has the highest number of dual income families. Almost 23% of the area population is classified as "Socially Conscious," again, a number that is twice the national average.

The final values group of any significance in the area population is "Belonger" at 19%, a figure one-half of the national average for this group. "Belongers" are older, conservative, trusting, and enjoy strong linkages to their community. They are not risk-takers. Their chief characteristic is that of belonging or fitting into a group and the most important group to them is their family.

Existing Churches in the Area

According to the 1987 Kingwood Newcomer Guide, there are 24 congregations of various faiths in the area. Kingwood, First Baptist, and Forest Cove Baptist

1987 Area Population by Age
Sand Creek Village Site

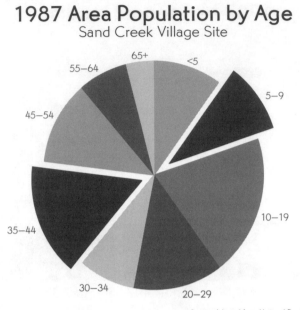

Source: Adapted from National Decision systems, 1987.

Church are the only existing Southern Baptist churches in the immediate area. Strawbridge United Methodist Church is located within two blocks of the new church site and the First Presbyterian Church is nearby. Also nearby is a site designated for an additional Catholic church.

The following are the results of a June, 1988, telephone survey of existing congregations in the community:

Name of Church	Attendance (Sunday AM)
Church on the Rock	50
First Church of Christ, Scientist	450
Church of Christ of Kingwood	350
Episcopal Church of the Good Shepherd	250
Evangelistic Temple North	150
First Presbyterian Church of Kingwood	350
Forest Cove Baptist	589
Grace Church	89
Holy Comforter Lutheran Church	140
Kings Church	70
Kingwood Christian Church	60
Kingwood Community Church	250
Kingwood Faith Fellowship	100

Kingwood First Baptist	541
Kingwood United Methodist Church	700
Kingwood Victory Christian Center	55
North Forest Christian Fellowship	60
North Lake Houston Christian Church of Kingwood	80
Strawbridge United Methodist Church	148
TOTAL SUNDAY MORNING ATTENDANCE	4,482

Using the March, 1988, population estimate of 34,942, the survey indicates that only 12.8% of the study area's population was churched.

Description of the Site

The present site is an 8.914 acre tract located in east Kingwood and bounded to the south by Kingwood Drive, to the north by Rocky Brook Drive, to the east by the Kingwood greenbelt, and to the west by Willow Terrace Drive. Access to the site is excellent by virtue of the southern boundary being Kingwood Drive, one of the major thoroughfares in the entire development.

Heavily wooded and located adjacent to both the greenbelt and a beautiful residential area, the site will require careful master planning to take advantage of the topography while obtaining the maximum use of the land area for a church plant.

There are plans to build a bridge across Lake Houston and when completed, it will provide access to the subdivisions in Atascocita for additional outreach.

The P and I balance on the loan for the property is $303,934. As of August, 1987, the appraised value of the property was $725,000.

Possible Meeting Sites

Approximately one-quarter of a mile south of the property is the new Willow Creek Elementary School scheduled to open in the fall of 1988 which would be the closest temporary meeting site. Other nearby schools are Greentree and Deerwood Elementary Schools.

Humble ISD policy is to permit the use of school buildings as temporary meeting sites for a period of two to three years with demonstrated evidence that the church is making progress toward obtaining a permanent facility. Mr. John Ennis of the Humble ISD (540–5020) is the contact person from whom to obtain additional information concerning the lease of school property.

Appropriate Pastoral Leadership

Compatibility of the founding pastor to the community is one of the most important factors in the development of a new mission/church. Based on the demographics of the area, it would be advantageous if the founding pastor had the following characteristics:

Education: College and Seminary including graduate degree if possible
Abilities and Skills:
   Pastoral experience in successful church plant or a record of growth in an
      established church
   Ability to relate well to executive and professional people
   Understanding of affluent population needs and values
   Catalytic leadership style
   Personal evangelism skills
Age: Mid-thirties to early fifties
Marital Status: Stable marriage, preferably with children

Possible Core Group Members/Families

An analysis of the membership directory of Kingwood, First Baptist indicates that there are 28 families living in Sand Creek Village (6.8% of the total families in Kingwood, First) and three additional families living in King's Point Village, the two closest villages to the site.

   Additional core group member/families might come from the Forest Cove Baptist Church.

Assessment of Growth Potential

Due to a number of factors, the potential for successful development of this site as a new mission/church is excellent.

   The site is more than adequate in size and has excellent access from Kingwood Drive, a major thoroughfare. Its location is in the growth area of Kingwood and the future construction of the bridge across Lake Houston will open additional areas to the south for potential outreach and membership.

   Possible temporary meeting facilities are nearby at the new Willow Creek Elementary School or Greentree and Deerwood Elementary Schools.

   There is a strong existing population base and growth projections indicate the population is expected to almost double in the next ten to twelve years or by the year 2000.

   There are at least 28 Baptist families already living in the area and are potential core group members.

   With the appropriate pastoral and lay leadership, an effective new church can be planted that will impact this area for the Kingdom.

Notes

Introduction

1. Lyle E. Schaller, *44 Questions for Church Planters* (Nashville: Abingdon, 1991), p. 78.

2. Win Arn, *The Pastor's Manual for Effective Ministry* (Monrovia, Calif.: Church Growth, 1988), p. 16.

3. Ibid.

4. George Gallup, Jr., *The Unchurched American—10 Years Later* (Princeton, N.J.: Princeton Religion Research Center, 1988), p. 2.

5. Kennon L. Callahan, *Effective Church Leadership* (San Francisco: Harper & Row, 1990), p. 13.

6. C. Peter Wagner, *Church Planting for a Greater Harvest* (Ventura, Calif.: Regal, 1990), p. 11.

7. "Church Planting: A Bold New Approach to Evangelism in the 90s," *Ministry*, Summer 1991, p. 2. This is a publication from Reformed Theological Seminary, Jackson, Mississippi.

8. Unfortunately, most of this criticism has come from well-meaning Christians.

Chapter 1

1. C. Peter Wagner, *Church Planting for a Greater Harvest* (Ventura, Calif.: Regal, 1990), p. 11.

2. George Barna, *The Frog in the Kettle* (Ventura, Calif.: Regal, 1990), p. 115.

Chapter 2

1. Win Arn, *The Pastor's Manual for Effective Ministry* (Monrovia, Calif.: Church Growth, 1988), p. 41.

2. Ibid., p. 43.

3. Jackson W. Carroll, Douglas W. Johnson, and Martin E. Marty, *Religion in America: 1950 to the Present* (San Francisco: Harper & Row, 1979), p. 13.

4. Constant H. Jacquet Jr., ed., *Yearbook of American and Canadian Churches, 1988* (Nashville: Abingdon, 1989), p. 261 compared with the *Yearbook of American and Canadian Churches, 1996*, ed. Kenneth B. Bedell, pp. 251–52, 255–56. I have rounded these figures off.

5. "Missions Memo," *Missions USA*, July–August 1988, p. 2.

6. Jacquet, *Yearbook 1988*, p. 261, compared to Bedell, *Yearbook, 1996*, p. 254.

7. Carroll, Johnson, and Marty, *Religion in America*, p. 16.

8. Ibid.

9. C. Peter Wagner, *Church Planting for a Greater Harvest* (Ventura, Calif.: Regal, 1990), pp. 14, 16.

10. Ibid., p. 12.

11. Lyle E. Schaller, *44 Questions for Church Planters* (Nashville: Abingdon, 1991), p. 20.

12. Helen Parmley, "Adding Up Membership," *Dallas Morning News,* October 19, 1991, p. 38A.

13. Ibid.

14. Arn, *Pastor's Manual,* p. 16.

15. Schaller, *44 Questions for Church Planters,* p. 17.

16. "Church Planting: A Bold New Approach to Evangelism in the 90s," *Ministry,* Summer 1991, p. 2.

17. George Gallup Jr., *The Unchurched American—10 Years Later* (Princeton, N.J.: Princeton Religion Research Center, 1988), p. 2.

18. Ibid.

19. Ibid.

20. "U.S. Attendance at Services Down in Poll," *Dallas Morning News,* May 28, 1994, p. 43A.

21. "Church Growth Fine Tunes Its Formulas," *Christianity Today,* June 24, 1991, pp. 46–47.

22. George Barna, *The Frog in the Kettle* (Ventura, Calif.: Regal, 1990), p. 142.

23. Ibid.

24. "Study Disputes Accepted Figure," *Christianity Today,* November 8, 1993, p. 60.

25. Gallup, *Unchurched American—10 Years Later,* p. 3.

26. Jack Sims, "Baby Boomers: Time to Pass the Torch?" *Christian Life,* January 1986, p. 24.

27. Ibid.

28. Gary L. McIntosh, "Baby Busters," *McIntosh Church Growth Network,* August 1990, p. 1.

29. Judy Howard, "Back in the Fold," *Dallas Morning News,* May 25, 1991, p. 41A.

30. An excellent book on postmodernism is Dennis McCallum, ed., *The Death of Truth* (Minneapolis, Minn.: Bethany House, 1996).

31. "Latter Day Struggles," *U.S. News and World Report,* September 28, 1992, p. 73.

32. Jacquet, *Yearbook 1988,* p. 262, compared to Bedell, *Yearbook 1996,* pp. 252, 254.

33. Barna, *Frog in the Kettle,* p. 141.

34. Ibid., p. 140.

35. "Schaller Says SBC Must Decide about New Church Starts," *Biblical Recorder,* June 15, 1991, p. 8.

36. *National & International Religion Report,* May 6, 1991, p. 2.

37. Larry Lewis, "The 15,000 Campaign," *Missions USA,* July–August 1991, p. 34.

38. Wagner, *Church Planting for a Greater Harvest,* p. 7.

39. Ibid., p. 11.

40. Win Arn, "Church Growth and Church Age Are Related," *The Win Arn Growth Report,* Pasadena, Calif., vol. 1, no. 21.

41. Schaller, *44 Questions for Church Planters,* p. 22.

42. Ibid., pp. 22–23.

43. "Churches Die with Dignity," *Christianity Today,* January 14, 1991, p. 69.

44. Barna, *Frog in the Kettle,* p. 115.

45. C. Wayne Zunkel, *Growing the Small Church* (Elgin, Ill.: David C. Cook, 1982), p. 48.

46. R. Dwayne Conner, *Called to Stay* (Nashville: Convention, 1987), pp. 10–11.

Chapter 3

1. Dallas Willard, *The Spirit of the Disciplines* (San Francisco: Harper & Row, 1988), pp. 130–31.

2. In reality, though limited, the student's financial state while in seminary is usually better than two-thirds of the rest of the world!

3. In planning and raising funds, most often the Savior allows church planters to raise most but not all of their support. While the entire process is a faith venture, He wants them to step out in faith and trust Him for the remaining necessary support.

4. This concept will be developed further in chapter 7 of this book. However, it's treated in depth in my book, *Developing a Vision for Ministry in the Twenty-first Century* (Grand Rapids: Baker, 1992).

5. Much of the following information was developed by my friend and former student, Clayton Hayes.

Chapter 4

1. George Barna, *The Frog in the Kettle* (Ventura, Calif.: Regal, 1990), p. 115.

2. Some Bible colleges such as Moody and Multnomah continue to remain strong in evangelism. In fact, the president of Multnomah, Joe Aldrich, has written two excellent works on evangelism: *Life-Style Evangelism* and *Gentle Persuasion,* both published by Multnomah Press.

3. Lyle E. Schaller, "Megachurch!" *Christianity Today,* March 5, 1990, pp. 22–23.

4. "Church Growth Fine Tunes Its Formulas," *Christianity Today,* June 24, 1991, p. 47.

5. Barna, *Frog in the Kettle,* pp. 136–37.

6. Jackson W. Carroll, Douglas W. Johnson, and Martin E. Marty, *Religion in America: 1950 to the Present* (San Francisco: Harper & Row, 1979), p. 16.

7. Barna, *Frog in the Kettle,* pp. 142–43.

8. I have written a book on hermeneutics for pastors and the church

that explores this and other issues of what the church can and can't do. *The Pastor, Hermeneutics, and the Church* (Grand Rapids: Kregel Publications, 1999).

9. I deal briefly with this important topic in chapter 9 of *Developing a Vision for Ministry in the Twenty-first Century* (Grand Rapids: Baker, 1992).

10. James M. Kouzes and Barry Z. Posner, *The Leadership Challenge* (San Francisco: Jossey-Bass, 1987), pp. 137–38.

Chapter 5

1. Here I'm using the term "soul" as Gen. 2:7 does of man as a complete whole, a total being, including both the material and immaterial aspects of his being. According to Scripture, man *has* a soul but also *is* a soul.

2. The idea of using the term "limitations" rather than "weaknesses" is the suggestion of Dr. William Lawrence who is the executive director of the Center for Christian Leadership at Dallas Theological Seminary.

3. Charles C. Ryrie, *The Holy Spirit* (Chicago: Moody, 1965), p. 83.

4. This material on gift-mix and gift-cluster is heavily influenced by Robert Clinton's *The Making of a Leader* (Colorado Springs: NavPress, 1988).

5. Ibid., p. 92.

6. Ken Voges and Ron Braund, *Understanding How Others Misunderstand You* (Chicago: Moody, 1990), p. 39.

7. Ibid., p. 70.

Chapter 6

1. The argumentation for this is found in my master's thesis for the Department of New Testament Literature and Exegesis, "The Relationship of

Pastors and Teachers in Ephesians 4:11" (Th.M. thesis, Dallas Theological Seminary, 1978).

2. This profile is not available to the general public. It can be purchased from some counseling and/or consulting organizations. Call the Carlson Company at 1-800-653-3472 for information as to someone in your area who may provide you with this tool. You'll find a similar tool in *Maximizing Your Effectiveness* (Baker).

3. Ken Voges and Ron Braund, *Understanding How Others Misunderstand You* (Chicago: Moody, 1990).

4. Bob Phillips, *The Delicate Art of Dancing with Porcupines* (Ventura, Calif.: Regal, 1989).

5. This inventory isn't available to the general public. You would need to take it through a professional counseling center, a consulting organization, or the departments of education or psychology at a nearby college or university.

6. David Keirsey and Marilyn Bates, *Please Understand Me* (Del Mar, Calif.: Promethean, 1978). If you don't need the book, I would suggest that you order The Keirsey Temperament Sorter. It costs only 25¢. You may order it from Prometheus Nemesis Book Company, P.O. Box 2748, Del Mar, CA 92014 (1-800-754-0039). You'll find a similar tool in *Maximizing Your Effectiveness*.

7. Roy M. Oswald and Otto Kroeger, *Personality Type and Religious Leadership* (Washington, D.C.: Alban Institute, 1988).

8. For more information, contact Mr. Paul Williams at P.O. Box 9, East Islip, NY 11730–0009.

9. Ibid., p. 30.

10. Ibid., p. 35.

11. Ibid., p. 38.

12. Ibid.

13. Ibid., p. 69.

14. Ibid., p. 68.

15. Ibid., p. 69.

16. Ibid., p. 41.

17. Ibid., p. 81.

18. Ibid., pp. 40–41.

19. John P. Kotter, "What Leaders Really Do," *Harvard Business Review,* May–June 1990, p. 103.

20. Ibid.

21. Ibid., p. 104.

22. Ibid.

23. Ken R. Voges, *Biblical Personal Profile* (Minneapolis: Performax Systems International, 1985), p. 7.

24. Voges and Braund, *Understanding How Others Misunderstand You,* p. 70.

25. Voges, *Biblical Personal Profile,* p. 7.

26. Voges and Braund, *Understanding How Others Misunderstand You,* p. 70.

27. Voges, *Biblical Personal Profile,* p. 7.

28. Voges and Braund, *Understanding How Others Misunderstand You,* p. 70.

29. Voges, *Biblical Personal Profile,* p. 7.

30. Voges and Braund, *Understanding How Others Misunderstand You,* p. 70.

31. Kotter, "What Leaders Really Do," p. 103.

32. Ibid., p. 104.

33. My thinking in this area and the following material while different has been influenced by Bob Biehl and his work on the *Role Preference Inventory* (Laguna Niguel, Calif.: Masterplanning Group International, 1980).

34. "The 'Johnny Appleseeds' of Church Planting," *Leadership*, Spring 1984, p. 126.

35. Ibid.

36. Ibid., p. 127.

37. Ibid.

Chapter 7

1. George Barna, *The Frog in the Kettle* (Ventura, Calif.: Regal, 1990), pp. 142–43.

2. Walter L. Liefeld, *Luke*, vol. 8 of *The Expositor's Bible Commentary*, ed. Frank E. Gaebelein (Grand Rapids: Zondervan, 1984), p. 1008.

3. Ibid., p. 981.

4. Ibid.

5. Kennon L. Callahan, *Effective Church Leadership* (San Francisco: Harper & Row, 1990), p. 13.

6. Ibid., p. 8.

7. Ibid., p. 20.

8. George Gallup Jr., *The Unchurched American—10 Years Later* (Princeton, N.J.: Princeton Religion Research Center, 1988), p. 4.

9. Callahan, *Effective Church Leadership*, p. 26.

10. Barna, *Frog in the Kettle*, p. 135.

Chapter 8

1. Robert Clinton, *The Making of a Leader* (Colorado Springs: NavPress, 1988), pp. 9–10.

2. Bill Hybels, *Too Busy Not to Pray* (Downers Grove: InterVarsity, 1988).

3. Dallas Willard, *The Spirit of the Disciplines* (San Francisco: Harper & Row, 1988).

4. Charles R. Swindoll, *Leadership: Influence That Inspires* (Waco, Tex.: Word, 1985), pp. 19–20.

5. Ibid., p. 20.

6. In fact, as I was writing this section, I received a phone call from one of my former students pastoring in the Dallas area who is struggling with this very situation.

7. C. Peter Wagner, *Leading Your Church to Growth* (Ventura, Calif.: Regal, 1984), p. 74.

8. Lyle E. Schaller, *Effective Church Planting* (Nashville: Abingdon, 1979), p. 162, quoted in C. Peter Wagner, *Leading Your Church to Growth* (Ventura, Calif.: Regal, 1984), p. 75.

9. Larry Osborne, *The Unity Factor* (Carol Stream, Ill.: Word, 1989), p. 67.

10. Ibid., pp. 67–68.

11. Robert G. Gromacki, *Called to Be Saints: An Exposition of 1 Corinthians* (Grand Rapids: Baker, 1977), p. 134.

12. F. F. Bruce, *The Book of Acts* (Grand Rapids: Eerdmans, 1977), p. 43.

13. Ibid., p. 429.

14. Lyle Schaller estimates that one-fourth of all Protestant churches in America average fewer than thirty-five in the morning worship service and at least half average less than seventy-five. See Lyle Schaller, *Growing Plans* (Nashville: Abingdon, 1983), p. 18.

15. According to Acts 2:47, the church experienced significant growth after the 3,000 of Peter's first sermon were added and before the 5,000 of the second sermon. In verse 47 Luke chooses the imperfect indicative, which expresses continuous action in the past. Therefore, the passage could read, "And the Lord kept on adding to their number daily."

16. R C. H. Lenski, *The Interpretation of the Acts of the Apostles* (Minneapolis: Augsburg, 1934), p. 239.

17. *Leadership Journal*, Winter 1990, p. 26.

18. Wagner, *Leading Your Church to Growth*, p. 119.

19. Ibid., pp. 119–20.

20. Gene Getz, "Sharpening the Pastor's Focus," *Leadership,* Summer 1985, pp. 13–14.

Chapter 9

1. Bill Hybels, *Honest to God?* (Grand Rapids: Zondervan, 1990), pp. 107–8.

2. Peter F. Drucker, *Managing the Non-Profit Organization* (New York: HarperBusiness, 1990), p. 145.

3. Howard G. Hendricks, *Say It with Love* (Wheaton, Ill.: Victor, 1972), pp. 113–14.

4. Frank Tillapaugh, *Unleashing the Church* (Ventura, Calif.: Regal, 1982), p. 20.

5. Robert S. McGee, *The Search for Significance* (Houston, Tex.: Rapha, 1990), p. 15.

6. I first heard this term and the concept from my friend Bruce Bugbee, who was one of the pastors at Willow Creek Community Church in South Barrington, Illinois.

7. There aren't many assessment programs available. I would highly recommend the *Networking* program developed by Bruce Bugbee. It can be ordered from the Charles E. Fuller Institute. The address is in the appendix.

8. I've gotten several of my ideas for this process from Bruce Bugbee and the *Networking* program he's designed for Willow Creek Community Church.

9. The latter term, minister of involvement, is the title my friend Steve Stroope uses in his church, Lakepointe Baptist Church, located in the suburbs of Dallas, Texas.

10. This approach is illustrated in *Unleashing the Church* (Ventura, Calif.: Regal, 1982).

Chapter 10

1. Source unknown.

2. George Barna, *The Frog in the Kettle* (Ventura, Calif.: Regal, 1990), p. 49.

3. Donald C. Posterski, *Reinventing Evangelism* (Downers Grove: InterVarsity, 1989), p. 28.

4. Tom Peters, *Thriving on Chaos* (New York: Alfred A. Knopf, 1987), pp. 144, 150.

5. The exact source of this survey is unknown. Some credit Bill Hybels, pastor of Willow Creek Community Church near Chicago. Others credit Rick Warren, pastor of Saddleback Valley Community Church in Southern California.

6. Donald A. McGavran, *Understanding Church Growth* (Grand Rapids: Eerdmans, 1970), p. 223.

7. See Aubrey Malphurs, *The Pastor, Hermeneutics, and the Church* (Grand Rapids: Kregel Publications, 1999).

Chapter 11

1. Ronald Allen and Gordon Borror, *Worship* (Portland, Oreg.: Multnomah, 1982), pp. 67–68.

2. Ibid., p. 9.

3. Barry Liesch, *People in the Presence of God* (Grand Rapids: Zondervan, 1988), p. xi.

4. Allen and Borror, *Worship,* p. 16.

5. George Barna, "Leaving Your People Time to Minister," *Pastor's Update,* September 1991, p. 2.

6. A number of these worship tension points are taken from a cassette tape by Doug Murren entitled "Developing Dynamic Worship Services," a part of *The Pastor's Update Monthly Cassette Program* published by the

Charles E. Fuller Institute of Evangelism and Church Growth.

7. An excellent text on preaching is Haddon W. Robinson's *Biblical Preaching* (Grand Rapids: Baker, 1980). Another is *Scripture Sculpture* by Ramesh Richard (Grand Rapids: Baker 1995). Both books will be very helpful for anyone who's not had a course in homiletics, or who needs some review in the field.

8. This is the title of a sermon used by my friend Keith Stewart, who pastors Springcreek Community Church in Garland, Texas.

9. This is Dr. Bill Counts, who pastors Fellowship Bible Church of Park Cities, Dallas, Texas.

Chapter 12

1. Exact source unknown.

2. Floyd Bartel, *A New Look at Church Growth* (Newton, Kans.: Faith & Life, 1987), p. 59.

3. George Barna, *The Frog in the Kettle* (Ventura, Calif.: Regal, 1990), p. 115.

4. C. Peter Wagner, *Church Planting for a Greater Harvest* (Ventura, Calif.: Regal, 1990), p. 11.

5. C. Peter Wagner, *Your Church Can Grow* (Ventura, Calif.: Regal, 1976), p. 86.

6. W. Charles Arn, "How to Find Receptive People," in *The Pastor's Church Growth Handbook*, ed. Win Arn (Pasadena, Calif.: Church Growth, 1979), pp. 142–43.

7. Bill Hybels, *Honest to God?* (Grand Rapids: Zondervan, 1990), p. 126.

8. Ibid., pp. 126–32.

9. Tom Wolf, "The Biblical Pattern of Effective Evangelism," in *The Pastor's Church Growth Handbook*, ed.

Win Arn (Pasadena, Calif.: Church Growth, 1979), pp. 110–16.

10. Hans Walter Wolff, *Anthropology of the Old Testament* (Philadelphia: Fortress, 1974), pp. 214–15.

11. *Theological Dictionary of the New Testament,* ed. Gerhard Kittel and Gerhard Friedrich, trans. and ed. Geoffrey W. Bromiley, s.v. "oikos," by Otto Michel (1967), 5: 130.

12. Win Arn and Charles Arn, *The Master's Plan for Making Disciples* (Pasadena, Calif.: Church Growth, 1982), p. 43.

13. Steve Sjogren, *Conspiracy of Kindness* (Ann Arbor, Mich.: Servant Publications, 1993).

14. This list can be ordered from the Masterplanning Group International, Box 952499, Lake Mary, FL 32795.

Chapter 13

1. Paula Rinehart, "The Pivotal Generation," *Christianity Today,* October 6, 1989, p. 24.

2. Ibid.

3. Ibid.

4. Lyman Coleman and Marty Scales, *Serendipity Training Manual For Groups* (Littleton, Colo.: Serendipity House, 1989), p. 7.

5. Ibid., p. 9.

6. Ibid., p. 7.

7. Bob Logan has an excellent section that develops this concept in *Beyond Church Growth* (Old Tappan, N.J.: Fleming H. Revell, 1989), pp. 133–35.

Chapter 14

1. This analogy is not original with me. For example, Bob Logan and Jeff Rast use it in *Starting a Church That Keeps on Growing* (Pasadena, Calif.: Charles E. Fuller Institute of Evangelism

and Church Growth, 1986). In this work they give credit for this analogy to Don Stewart.

2. Actually these steps and those of the five other stages are crucial not only to church planting but to pastoring healthy churches and those in desperate need of renewal. Consequently, those ministering in these situations would profit by reading this book as well as church planters.

3. Peter Wagner has done some excellent work in this area. He includes a small section on prayer in *Church Planting for a Greater Harvest* (Ventura, Calif.: Regal, 1990), p. 49.

4. For an in-depth coverage of the values concept see Aubrey Malphurs, *Values-Driven Leadership* (Grand Rapids: Baker, 1997).

5. For an in-depth treatment of the missions concept, see my book *Developing a Dynamic Mission for Your Ministry* (Grand Rapids: Kregel Publications, 1998).

6. I provide a full treatment of the topic of vision in *Developing a Vision for Ministry in the Twenty-first Century* (Grand Rapids: Baker, 1992).

7. This section focuses on the organizational vision. Actually, church planters and anyone in ministry should have two kinds of vision. One is a personal ministry vision derived from their divine design. This concept was developed in chapter 5. The other is an organizational vision, which is the vision for the ministry or, in this case, the planted church. The same is true for values and mission.

8. I would like to give credit to my friend and former student, Mike Baer, for his thinking regarding this definition.

9. There is a further explanation of this and an example of what it will look like in chapter 4 of my book *Developing a Vision for Ministry in the Twenty-first Century.*

10. "Church Growth Fine Tunes Its Formulas," *Christianity Today,* June 24, 1991, p. 47.

11. Barna, *Frog in the Kettle,* p. 146.

12. Arnold Mitchell, *The Nine American Lifestyles* (New York: Warner, 1983).

13. Tex Sample, *U.S. Lifestyles and Mainline Churches* (Louisville, Ky.: Westminster/John Knox Press, 1990).

14. Percept. Their address is 151 Kalmus Drive, Suite A104, Costa Mesa, CA 92626 and their phone number is 714-957-1282.

15. C. Peter Wagner, *Your Church Can Grow* (Ventura, Calif.: Regal, 1976), p. 96.

16. Roger S. Greenway, *Apostles to the City* (Grand Rapids: Baker, 1978), p. 11.

17. Michael E. Gerber, *The E-Myth* (New York: Harper-Collins, 1986), p. 92.

18. James F. Engel and H. Wilbert Norton, *What's Gone Wrong with the Harvest?* (Grand Rapids: Zondervan, 1975), p. 45.

19. For more information on these times and on how to reach the community through mailers, advertising, and so on, read Robert C. Screen, "Effective Communication to Your Community," in *The Pastor's Church Growth Handbook,* ed. Win Arn (Pasadena, Calif.: Church Growth, 1979), pp. 206–20.

20. One person is Pastor Keith Stewart, who is planting Springcreek Community Church in Garland, Texas.

21. Ezra Earl Jones, *Strategies for New Churches* (San Francisco: Harper & Row, 1976), p. 92.

22. Lyle E. Schaller, "Southern Baptists Face Two Choices for Future," *Biblical Recorder*, April 27, 1991, p. 8.

23. Bob Biehl and Ted W. Engstrom, *Increasing Your Boardroom Confidence* (Sisters, Oreg.: Questar, 1988), p. 54.

24. *Performax 'DiSC' Profiles Trainer's Transparency Masters Manual* (Performax Systems International, 1987), #22.

25. Roy M. Oswald and Otto Kroeger, *Personality Type and Religious Leadership* (Washington, D.C.: Alban Institute, 1988), p. 122.

26. Schaller, "Southern Baptists," p. 8.

27. Keri Kent, "Adopting a Team Strategy," *Willow Creek Magazine*, September–October 1991, p. 9.

28. The steps that make up the conception stage are the steps leaders take when they do strategic planning. I plan to write a book within the next year on strategic planning that will include a much more in-depth treatment of these steps.

Chapter 15

1. I would like to give credit to Robert Salstrom for these general questions, not the details. He is a graduate of Dallas Seminary and the former director of Alumni Affairs who has encouraged a number of seminarians to pursue church planting.

Chapter 16

1. C. Peter Wagner, *Church Planting for a Greater Harvest* (Ventura, Calif.: Regal, 1990), pp. 97–98.

2. Donald J. MacNair, *The Birth, Care, and Feeding of a Local Church* (Grand Rapids: Baker, 1971).

3. Ibid., pp. x, 22.

4. Wagner, *Church Planting for a Greater Harvest,* pp. 119–20.

5. Ibid., p. 120.

6. Ibid.

7. Paul W. Powell, *Go-Givers in a Go-Getter World* (Nashville: Broadman, 1986), p. 59.

8. Ibid.

9. Ezra Earl Jones, *Strategies for New Churches* (New York: Harper & Row, 1976), p. 82.

10. Lyle E. Schaller, *44 Questions for Church Planters* (Nashville: Abingdon, 1991), p. 60.

11. Ibid.

12. Ibid., p. 62.

13. Lyle Schaller also recognizes this problem and refers to it as the "Second Sunday Syndrome" in *44 Questions for Church Planters,* pp. 92–94. I would strongly recommend that you look at his solutions to this problem as well as my own.

Chapter 17

1. In this chapter, I'll quote a lot of material from Peter Wagner, Lyle Schaller, and Win Arn. I consider these men to be experts in the field of church growth.

2. C. Peter Wagner, *Leading Your Church to Growth* (Ventura, Calif.: Regal, 1984), p. 89.

3. Lyle E. Schaller, *Growing Plans* (Nashville: Abingdon, 1983), p. 85.

4. C. Peter Wagner, *Your Church Can Grow* (Ventura, Calif.: Regal, 1976), chap. 3.

5. Wagner, *Leading Your Church to Growth,* p. 97.

6. You may want to turn back to chapters 5 and 6 and briefly review the section on the *Personal* and *Biblical Profiles.*

7. I have taken many of these characteristics from the interpretation section of Ken R. Voges, *Biblical Personal Profile* (Minneapolis: Performax Systems International, 1985), p. 7.

8. Again, you may want to review briefly the section on the *MBTI* in chapters 5 and 6.

9. Wagner, *Leading Your Church to Growth,* p. 59.

10. Lyle E. Schaller, *The Small Church Is Different* (New York: Abingdon, 1982), pp. 53–54.

11. Lyle E. Schaller, *Growing Plans* (Nashville: Abingdon, 1983), p. 115.

12. Ibid., p. 116.

13. Joel Arthur Barker, *Discovering the Future* (St. Paul, Minn.: IL, 1985), p. 32.

14. Wagner, *Leading Your Church to Growth,* p. 213.

15. Wagner, *Your Church Can Grow,* p. 77.

16. Ibid.

17. This program is available through the Charles E. Fuller Institute of Evangelism and Church Growth, P.O. Box 90910, Pasadena, CA 91109–0910.

18. Every church has three doors. The front door refers to the primary worship service which attracts most first time visitors. The side door refers to small group events which attract people who refuse to attend a worship service. The back door concerns those who eventually leave the church. Assimilation affects all three doors.

19. Ibid., p. 79.

20. Ibid.

21. Ibid., p. 7.

22. Surprisingly, an exception here is the recent seminary graduate. Most seminaries don't spend much time with practical ministry but focus more on theology and biblical studies. Many seem to think—incorrectly—that the practical aspects can be learned later. In these situations, seminarians should try to gain as much practical experience and knowledge as possible through their field education programs. If this doesn't work, then they should pursue an internship after they graduate before going into ministry.

Chapter 18

1. I've left out the second principle (a strong servant-leadership) because it will be covered in the next section of this chapter on the leadership of a maturing church.

2. Win Arn, "Have You Checked Your Ratios Recently?" *The Win Arn Growth Report,* vol. 1, no. 3.

3. Ibid.

4. In chapter 8, I develop this topic and discuss more fully the identity of the elders in the early church.

5. Lyle E. Schaller, *Growing Plans* (Nashville: Abingdon, 1983), p. 151.

6. Win Arn, "Average Driving Time to Church," *The Win Arn Growth Report,* vol. 1, no. 20.

Chapter 19

1. C. Peter Wagner, *Your Church Can Grow* (Ventura, Calif.: Regal, 1976), p. 96.

2. I have written *Pouring New Wine into Old Wineskins* (Grand Rapids: Baker Book House, 1993) to address why and how to revitalize churches.

3. Sherri Brown, "The Search for Saddleback Sam," *Mission USA,* July–August, 1988, p. 17.

4. Keri Kent, "Adopting a Team Strategy," *Willow Creek Magazine,* September–October, 1991, p. 9.

5. Ibid.

6. Ibid.

7. Dean Merrill, "Mothering a New Church," *Leadership*, Winter 1985, p. 103.

8. Ibid., p. 102.

9. Ibid., p. 103.

10. Ibid., p. 104.

11. Ibid., p. 103.

12. C. Peter Wagner, *Church Planting for a Greater Harvest* (Ventura, Calif.: Regal, 1990), pp. 119–20.

13. Merrill, "Mothering a New Church," p. 105.

14. Ibid.

15. Ibid., p. 100.

16. Ibid.

17. Ibid.

18. Ibid.

19. Ibid.

20. Ibid.

21. Ibid.

Index

Aubrey Malphurs, a veteran pastor and church planter, is professor and chairman of the Department of Field Education at Dallas Theological Seminary. He is also the president of Vision Ministries International, a training and consulting organization, and the pastor of Northwood Community Church in Dallas, Texas. He is the author of numerous books on topics relating to church planting, church revitalization, and leadership in general. You may contact him through

Vision Ministries International
3909 Swiss Avenue
Dallas, TX 75204
(214) 388-2389
(214) 841-3777